MEANING, KNOWLEDGE, AND REALITY

MEANING, KNOWLEDGE, AND REALITY

• • •

John McDowell

HARVARD UNIVERSITY PRESS
Cambridge, Massachusetts
London, England

Printed in the United States of America

Library of Congress Cataloging-in-Publication Data

McDowell, John Henry.
Meaning, knowledge, and reality / John McDowell.
p. cm.
Includes bibliographical references and index.
ISBN 0-674-00712-3
ISBN 0-674-55777-8 (alk. paper)
1. Meaning (Philosophy) 2. Knowledge, Theory of. 3. Realism.
I. Title.
B840.M43 1998
121—dc21 98-19801

CONTENTS

Preface

This volume, a companion to my *Mind, Value, and Reality* (Harvard University Press, 1998), collects some more of my previously scattered writings.

As in the earlier collection, I have resisted every temptation to make substantive improvements; I have limited myself to a few alterations of wording. I have allowed repetition from one essay to another to stand, with a view to leaving it possible in principle for the essays to be read singly.

I have divided the essays into four only loosely cohesive groups.

The first group contains papers that deal in a general way with questions about meaning. The inspiration here is Donald Davidson's proposal that one might codify an interpretation of a language by giving a theory of truth for it, in a sense derived from Alfred Tarski. I have put Essay 1 at the beginning because it starts with a comparatively full statement and justification of a version of this Davidsonian idea. (Apart from that, this essay might well be read with the papers in Part III of the volume; see below.) Essay 2 tries to disarm an objection to the Davidsonian way of thinking about meaning in general, grounded in the thought that it is more illuminating to analyse meaning in terms of communicative intentions, on lines proposed by H. P. Grice. Applying Tarski's techniques to natural languages is not routine, and Davidson's proposal requires detailed work on recalcitrant constructions in natural languages; Essay 3 discusses one of Davidson's own contributions at this level, his treatment of *oratio obliqua*. Essays 4 and 5 deal with Michael Dummett's objections against a certain unambitiousness, in respect of explaining concepts and indeed explaining the very idea of the conceptual, that comes naturally in spelling out the Davidsonian idea, though it is part of what is in question here whether the objections impinge on Davidson himself. Essay 6 considers what kind of account we might provide, within the general framework of the kind of Tarskian theory that Davidson envisages, for the semantical powers of expressions shorter than whole sentences, for instance names or predicates; this forms a transition to the second group of essays.

The second group centres on singular reference. The Davidsonian conception of meaning still occupies a framework position, which is spelled out particularly in Essay 8. That paper introduces the suggestion that, contrary to a widespread assumption, the Fregean notion of sense—the point of which is to enable us to individuate propositional contents finely enough for them to serve the purposes of a kind of understanding of subjects that is controlled by the concept of rationality—coheres perfectly well with a conception of singular propositional contents as dependent for their existence, their availability to be thought or expressed, on the existence of the objects they concern. Essay 7 finds a forerunner of blindness to the point of the Fregean notion of sense in a perhaps surprising place, an argument considered by Plato. Essays 9 through 12 deal with various aspects of the Fregean conception of object-dependent content, and its implications for the philosophy of mind as well as the philosophy of language. Essay 13 discusses parallel issues that are raised in the philosophy of mind by a conception of meaning in general, most conspicuously attractive for the meaning of natural-kind words, which has been propounded by Hilary Putnam.

The papers in the third group (which might well be read together with Essays 1, 4, and 5) consider Michael Dummett's objections against realism, in the sense of the idea that someone's understanding of a language might engage with the world by way of conditions that can transcend her ability to ascertain whether or not they obtain. On certain natural assumptions, this is exactly the nature of truth-conditions as they figure in Davidson's proposal, so we are still within the framework of the first group of essays; but whether Davidson's conception of meaning is realistic in Dummett's sense is part of what is in question in Essays 4 and 5. Essay 14 discusses Dummett's view of the positions that are open to a realist about the past, but with an eye to more general issues about realism. Essay 15 considers Dummett's argument that realism implies an unacceptable epistemology of understanding. Essay 16 tries to drive a wedge between an admitted unsatisfactoriness in mathematical platonism, which is a Dummettian starting-point, and the generalized anti-realism that he recommends; the later stages of this paper constitute a kind of transition to the papers in the final group.

The fourth group contains essays in the theory of knowledge. Essay 17 takes off from a protest against a common reading of how Wittgenstein uses the notion of criteria. I might have placed this paper with the readings of Wittgenstein in *Mind, Value, and Reality,* but it fits with the other papers in this group, as part of a campaign against a tendency to "interiorize" the basis on which knowledge of various sorts, around which philosophical problems readily arise, is acquired. Essay 18 is a general attack on the "interiorizing" tendency, and Essay 19 discusses a case with the potential for being especially puzzling, the epistemology of testimony.

I have cited works by author's name and title alone, reserving details of publication to the Bibliography at the end of the book.

PART I

MEANING, TRUTH, AND UNDERSTANDING

ESSAY 1

Truth-Conditions, Bivalence, and Verificationism[1]

1. If there can be such a thing as a theory of meaning for a language, meaning cannot be anything but what any such theory is a theory of. Hence a clear and convincing description of the shape that a theory of meaning for any language would take, not itself uncritically employing the notion of meaning, ought to remove all perplexity about the nature of meaning in general.

Frege held that the senses of sentences can be specified by giving truth-conditions, and that the sense of a sentence-constituent is its contribution to the senses of sentences in which it occurs.[2] ("Sense" may be paraphrased as "cognitive meaning".)[3] Those two ideas of Frege's are captured by the following conception of a theory of sense for a language: it assigns a suitable property to each simple sentence-constituent discerned in the language by an appropriate syntax, and states rules that determine suitable properties for complex expressions formed in each of the ways permitted by that syntax, given the relevant properties of their components; the property thus determined for a complete sentence is that of being true if and only if some specified condition holds. A theory of sense for a language, then, shows how to derive, for any indicative sentence, a theorem of the form "*s* is true if and only if *p*", where "*s*" is replaced by a suit-

1. This essay's debts to the work of others will be obvious. The forbearing comments of Michael Dummett, when he was confronted by an earlier version, helped me to understand his position better. I also had help from Gareth Evans, Samuel Guttenplan, Christopher Peacocke, and Mark Platts.

2. *Grundgesetze der Arithmetik*, vol. 1, §32.

3. See Dummett, *Frege: Philosophy of Language*, pp. 92–3.

able designation of the sentence and "*p*" by a sentence. Briefly, a theory of sense, on this conception, is a theory of truth.

Tarski's work shows how theories of truth, conforming to the above schematic description of a Fregean theory of sense, may be constructed for certain sorts of formalized languages;[4] and Donald Davidson has urged optimism about the possibility of doing the same sort of thing, one way or another, for natural languages.[5]

A promise to illuminate the notion of sense by way of the thesis that a theory of sense, for any language, is a theory of truth for that language involves an apparent obligation to say what, in general, a theory of truth for a language—any language—is. Discharging the obligation would be elucidating a general notion of truth, not relativized to some particular language or other. It would be suspect to rely on an assumed prior understanding of "true", as used in specifying the form that the theorems would take; and the promise of general illumination seems to block retreating to the position that what is at issue is a different predicate for each language, on the pattern "true-in-*L*", in which "true" is semantically inert.[6] An attractive strategy, now, would be to stipulate an appropriate general condition on the relation between replacements for "*s*" and replacements for "*p*", in theorems whose form is, initially, to be represented thus: "*s* is *F* if and only if *p*". The hope would be that a general condition that ensures that "*F*" may acceptably be replaced by "true" would constitute the apparently required answer to the question what, in general, a theory of truth is.

Frege, in whose terminology the sense of a sentence is a thought, says that when the sense of a sentence is specified by giving truth-conditions, the thought is determined as the thought that those conditions are fulfilled.[7] That implies the following general condition on the theorems: "*p*" must be replaced by a sentence that expresses the same thought as, that is, has the same sense as, the sentence designated by what replaces "*s*". Such a condition would ensure that "*F*" might acceptably be replaced by "true", but only by employing the notion of sameness of sentence-sense; which must presumably be

4. See "The Concept of Truth in Formalized Languages".

5. See, e.g., "Truth and Meaning".

6. Compare P. F. Strawson, "Meaning and Truth", at p. 180. See also Peacocke, "Truth Definitions and Actual Languages".

7. *Grundgesetze*, vol. 1, §32.

disallowed, in the context of a promise to illuminate the notion of sense.

Another formulation of the desired general condition might require conformity to Tarski's Convention T, thus: what replaces "*p*" must be the very sentence designated by what replaces "*s*", if the theory is stated in the language with which it deals; if not, a translation of it into the language in which the theory is stated.[8] But unless something can be said about when one sentence translates another, other than that they have the same sense, that is no improvement on the Fregean condition.

A better line is, at least apparently, a change of tack: spelling out the function of a theory of sense in a systematic description of what is involved in understanding a language. For this purpose, the form of the desired theorems can, initially, be represented still more schematically, thus: "*s . . . p*"; where, as before, "*s*" is to be replaced by suitable designations of object-language sentences, and "*p*" by sentences in the language in which the theory is stated.

A theory of sense must interact with a theory of force for the language in question.[9] A theory of force would do two things: first, license the identification of linguistic actions, given enough information about them, as performances of propositional acts of specified types (assertion, question, and so on); and, second, show how to recover, from a sufficiently full description of an utterance, which may be an utterance of an elliptical or non-indicative sentence, a suitable designation of a suitable indicative sentence. The idea is that a theory of sense and a theory of force, in combination, should enable one to move, from a sufficiently full description of a speaker's utterance, uninterpreted, to a description of his performance as a propositional act of a specified kind with a specified content, that is, a description on the pattern of "He is asserting that *p*", "He is asking whether *p*", and so on; where what replaces "*p*" is (waiving some syntactic complications) the sentence used on the right-hand side of the theorem that the theory of sense entails for the indicative sentence that is warranted by the theory of force as being suitably related to the utterance (possibly the sentence uttered).

8. "The Concept of Truth in Formalized Languages", pp. 187–8.
9. Compare Dummett, *Frege: Philosophy of Language*, p. 416.

Acceptability, in a bipartite theory of the sort constituted by combining a theory of sense with a theory of force, would require that the descriptions of propositional acts that it yields should fit coherently into a wider context, in which the speakers' behaviour in general, including both their linguistic behaviour, under those descriptions, and their non-linguistic behaviour, under suitable descriptions, can be made sufficiently intelligible in the light of propositional attitudes (centrally, beliefs and desires) whose ascription to them is sufficiently intelligible in the light of their behaviour, again, and of the facts that impinge on them. Actions are made intelligible by finding descriptions under which one can see how they might have seemed reasonable: on the conception sketched here, that applies, as it ought, to linguistic actions just as much as to others. Understanding linguistic behaviour, and hence understanding languages, involves no more than a special case of what understanding behaviour, in general, involves.

Understanding a language consists in the ability to know, when speakers produce utterances in it, what propositional acts, with what contents, they are performing: that is, the ability to know what would, with suitable input, be the output of a bipartite theory of the sort that I described above. Capacity to interact with a theory of force, in the appropriate way, would certify a theory as part of a systematic description of such understanding, and hence as part of a theory of meaning.[10] By way of Frege's doctrine that sense determines the content of propositional acts, it would certify such a theory as, precisely, a theory of sense.[11]

Certification of a theory as a theory of sense requires it to be capable of functioning in the ascription of propositional acts. That might suggest that the position I am outlining here promises elucidation of the notion of sense in terms of the notions of the propositional acts, assumed to be conceptually prior. But that would be a misrepresentation. Acceptable ascriptions of propositional acts must simultane-

10. See Dummett, *Frege: Philosophy of Language*, pp. 92–3.

11. See Frege, "On Sense and Reference". If the theory worked by determining conditions for the application of a predicate to sentences, it would conform to the Fregean condition and to Convention T; the requirement of interaction might be said to elucidate those formulations. Indexical elements in natural languages introduce complications about the claim of conformity; but the topic of this essay can be pursued at a level of abstraction at which we can ignore that.

ously meet two requirements: not only the requirement, from outside the envisaged bipartite theory, that the acts ascribed be intelligible, but also a requirement from within, evidently compulsory given even the dimmest insight into how language works, that it be possible to represent the content of propositional acts performed by uttering a sentence as dependent on the repeatable contribution of its components. The second requirement suggests that the notion of the content of a propositional act cannot be viewed as accessible in advance of, at least, an adumbration of the idea that the determination of such contents by the words used should be describable by a theory that works systematically across a language, generating a specification of the content of propositional acts potentially performed in the utterance of any sentence, by way of its structure and suitable properties assigned to its components.[12] That idea simply *is* the idea of a theory of sense. What I am proposing here, then, is not elucidation of the notion of sense in terms of other notions, still less any hope of reducing it to those others, but simply a description of its relation to those others; the hope being that a notion that is at first sight problematic may be rendered less so by an explicit account of its location, so to speak, in a conceptual space in which we normally find our way about without thinking.

An ordinary indicative sentence can be used to say something about the world. Quotation and similar devices yield expressions suitable for the construction of remarks about sentences, insulated, in general, from that normal concern with extra-linguistic reality. But appending a truth-predicate to a designation of a sentence produces a sentence apt, once more, for saying something about the world: the very thing, in fact, that could have been said by using the original sentence.[13] This guarantees the following: if a necessary and sufficient condition for the application of some predicate to any indicative sentence of a language is given by a sentence that can be used to specify the content of propositional acts potentially performed by uttering the former sentence, then the predicate applies to exactly the true sentences of the language. Thus if the lacuna, in "*s . . . p*", is filled, as before, by (schematically) "is *F* if and only if",

12. Unstructured sentences, if they are possible, could be viewed as a special case, with each as its own sole component.

13. See W. V. Quine, *Philosophy of Logic*, pp. 10–13.

the requirement of interaction with a theory of force ensures that an acceptable theory of sense will remain acceptable if "*F*" is replaced by "true".[14] So it might seem that the change of tack was only apparent: the requirement of interaction, on that assumption about the filling of the lacuna, serves the purpose for which the Fregean condition and Convention T were found wanting.

The concept of truth as such, however, need not figure in the certification of a theory as a theory of sense. A theory of force need not be sensitive even to the syntactic form of what fills the lacuna, let alone to its substance. Of course the lacuna must be filled somehow, if the theory of sense is to permit, as it must, the derivation of an acceptable theorem of the form "*s . . . p*" for every indicative sentence on the basis of its composition out of parts. We know, from Tarski, that "is *F* if and only if" will meet the bill, at least for languages with certain logical structures. And we know, from the considerations given above, that "*F*" may then be written "true". But this fact is not one that needs to be appreciated *en route* to acquiring, from the description of the requirement of interaction, a general conception of the nature of a theory of sense. So although the apparent obligation to elucidate a general notion of truth has indeed been discharged, the result is to show that there was, in fact, no need to undertake exactly that obligation in the first place. The thesis should be, not that sense is what a theory of truth is a theory of, but rather that truth is what a theory of sense is a theory of.[15]

It remains the case that, on that assumption about the lacuna, a theory of sense would conform to the original specification of a Fregean theory. And even if the lacuna were filled in some quite different way, the above considerations ensure that the theorems would continue to be acceptable if that unknown other filling were replaced by "is true if and only if". So either way a theory of sense would, as

14. Compare Davidson, "Truth and Meaning", pp. 22–3.

15. Given a theory that meets the requirement of interaction, we could construct a theory that matched it except, say, that some arbitrary true sentence was conjoined with what previously replaced "*p*" in each theorem. If the first was a correct theory of truth, the second would be, too. (See J. A. Foster, "Meaning and Truth Theory", and Brian Loar, "Two Theories of Meaning".) Such possibilities constitute a prima facie objection to Davidson's suggestion that a theory of truth for one language in another will characterize an acceptable translation scheme from the first to the second (constitute an acceptable theory of sense for the first in the second) if its theorems are true; see "In Defence of Convention T", pp. 73–4. The position I am recommending here is immune to such objections.

Frege thought, specify truth-conditions for sentences: either directly or by justifiable conversion.

2. Michael Dummett has suggested that there is an opposition between a truth-conditional conception of sense, on the one hand, and, on the other, verificationism: which, for present purposes, is the doctrine that ordinary mastery of a language, and hence of the application of the concepts of truth and falsehood to its sentences, is a state acquired solely by the acquisition of, and therefore consisting solely in, dispositions to suit one's linguistic behaviour to evidence for the truth and falsehood of sentences.[16]

In one version, the envisaged verificationist objection to a truth-conditional conception of sense turns on the thesis that such a conception presupposes the principle of bivalence (the principle that every significant indicative sentence is either true or false). If the truth-value of sentences in a language cannot always be settled, then purported knowledge, nevertheless, that every sentence is either true or false might be held to go beyond anything that can possibly be comprised, on the verificationist view, in competence with the concepts of truth and falsehood. It would follow that, in the presence of undecidable sentences, a verificationist is debarred from a truth-conditional conception of sense.

Adherence to the principle of bivalence, even in the presence of undecidable sentences, is, according to Dummett, characteristic of realism, a doctrine whose defining thesis I shall take to be that the truth-condition of a sentence may obtain, or not, independently of our capacity to tell that it obtains, or that it does not.[17] An appropriate alternative conception of sense for a verificationist who rejected a truth-conditional conception would, Dummett suggests, replace the notion of truth, as the fundamental notion of a theory of sense, with the notion of verification or warranted assertibility. A notion of truth would still be employed; but truth would be thought of only as a product of verification, not as something that may obtain indepen-

16. See *Frege: Philosophy of Language,* passim; and, for the opposition, also "Truth". (This essay was substantially completed before I had seen "What Is a Theory of Meaning? (II)".)

17. Dummett seems not to distinguish the defining thesis from adherence to the principle of bivalence; see, e.g., *Frege: Philosophy of Language,* p. 466, and "The Justification of Deduction", p. 315. I shall be arguing that they are distinct (§6).

dently of verification. This would be an abandonment of the defining thesis of realism. The alternative conception of sense would require a novel, anti-realist conception of the world: if truth is not independent of our discovering it, we must picture the world either as our own creation or, at least, as springing up in response to our investigations.[18] So verificationist objections to a truth-conditional conception of sense would have far-reaching metaphysical implications.

The verificationist attitude towards bivalence that I want to consider is a refusal to assert the principle, combined with a refusal to deny it. It might be thought that undecidable sentences, on which the refusal to assert the principle depends, would afford counterinstances and hence grounds for denying it. But a claim to know, in the absence of evidence, that a sentence is neither true nor false should be no less suspect than a claim to know, in the absence of evidence, that a sentence is either true or false. If an adherent of such a position decides, on the basis of arguments like the one I sketched above, that he may not think of truth as being independent of verification, he must not take himself to be thereby entitled to infer untruth from absence of verifying evidence. His proper course would be to withhold all pronouncements about the truth or falsehood of sentences whose truth-value is not determined by evidence.[19]

My main aim is to show that it is not because verificationism justifies such an attitude towards bivalence—if it does, a question that I shall not discuss—that it requires, if it does, an alternative conception of sense. I want to suggest that the real interest of verificationism, in its bearing on general issues about meaning, is to be sought elsewhere than at any rate one of the places where Dummett, on occasion, finds it, namely in the metatheory of intuitionistic logic.

3. At first sight, Dummett appears to argue on the following lines for the thesis that a truth-conditional conception of sense presupposes the principle of bivalence.[20] First, a theory that specifies truth-

18. Compare "Truth", p. 18.

19. If there can be such a thing as an identifiable, decidably undecidable sentence, there is perhaps room for a different position, in which the principle of bivalence is *denied* (on the ground that evidence that there *can* be no evidence that a sentence is true counts as evidence that it is not true, and similarly for falsehood). By what I concede, in §5, to the argument I consider in §3, such a position would be debarred from a truth-conditional conception of sense. But I shall not discuss it in this essay.

20. To find this argument in Dummett would be to misconstrue his intentions, as he makes clear in "What Is a Theory of Meaning? (II)". (His argument was not meant to

conditions for sentences can be taken to determine their senses only, if at all, in the context of a theory that gives an account of their actual use in the performance of speech acts of the various types that occur, including, centrally, assertion.[21] Second, in contrast with, say, betting, "the linguistic act of assertion makes, as it were, no intrinsic provision for the introduction of a gap between two kinds of consequence which the making of an assertion might be supposed to have".[22] The truth-value of an assertion is determined, by its content and the facts, in such a way that there are only the two possibilities, truth and falsehood. Hence the principle of bivalence must hold for sentences suited to be used in making assertions.[23] If we combine that with the first premise, it would follow that the principle of bivalence is a prerequisite for a truth-conditional conception of sense.

The above sketch ignores a concession of Dummett's that, even in the context of a truth-conditional conception of sense, the dictates of smoothness and generality, in an account of how sentences affect the truth-values of complex sentences in which they occur, may yield reasons for calling sentences of certain kinds "neither true nor false". Dummett reconciles the concession with the requirement derived from the nature of assertion like this: when one is concerned with the truth-value of a sentence of one of those kinds, used on its own with a view to making an assertion, one must regard the conceded status as a way of being true or a way of being false.[24] The concession is remote from my concerns in this essay; for what is yielded by the verificationist considerations that I sketched in §2 is, at most, a disinclination to assert the principle of bivalence, not an inclination, like the one that is partly indulged by Dummett's concession, to cite counter-instances.[25]

---

be for a stronger conclusion than the one I concede in §5 below.) In earlier versions of this essay I misconstrued Dummett in just this way. I retained discussion of this non-Dummettian argument as a convenient way to bring out the fact that there is no necessary connection between realism and accepting the principle of bivalence.

21. "Truth", pp. 2–4, 7–8; *Frege: Philosophy of Language*, pp. 295–7, 413–7. I have formulated the premise in a way that is reminiscent of §1, though Dummett's account of the need for a theory of force does not exactly match the account I gave there. (Compare §5.)

22. *Frege: Philosophy of Language*, p. 417.

23. Passages that at first sight might seem to argue on these lines for the second premise are "Truth", pp. 8–14; *Frege: Philosophy of Language*, pp. 344–8, 417–24.

24. Discussion of the concession pervades the passages cited in n. 23.

25. I discuss Dummett's views on truth-value gaps in Essay 9 below.

4. A theory of truth, serving as a theory of sense for a language, must show how to derive, for each indicative sentence of the language, a theorem of the form "*s* is true if and only if *p*", where what replaces "*p*" in each case is (to summarize the requirement of interaction with a theory of force) a sentence giving the content of propositional acts that speakers of the language can intelligibly be regarded as performing, or potentially performing, with utterances of the sentence designated by what replaces "*s*". In theories of truth of the sort that Tarski showed how to construct, derivation of such a theorem would start with a biconditional obtained by applying, to a suitable designation of a sentence, an outright definition of truth in terms of a subsidiary semantic concept, that of satisfaction; and would then eliminate semantic vocabulary from the right-hand side of that biconditional, by applying clauses from a recursive characterization of satisfaction and, possibly, clauses from recursive characterizations of other subsidiary semantic concepts, for instance that of denotation. So a theory of truth must incorporate a proof-theory adequate for any transformations that are needed in that systematic elimination of semantic vocabulary. Tarski's specimen truth-definition, for the language of the calculus of classes, incorporates a classical proof theory.[26] But that does not seem essential to the application of Tarski's methods. On the contrary, it seems obvious that a fundamentally Tarskian theory, for a suitable language, could be given in the context of a proof-theory that was, say, intuitionistic.[27]

Tarski's specimen truth-definition, unsurprisingly in view of its proof-theory, yields a proof that, whatever object-language sentence one takes, either it or its negation is true.[28] A corollary, given the principle that a sentence is false if its negation is true, would be the principle of bivalence for sentences of the object language. But a Tarskian theory with an intuitionistic proof-theory would not yield those conclusions. On the face of it, then, such a theory might seem apt to serve as a truth-conditional theory of sense, interacting in the standard way with a theory of force in which assertion is central, for a language for which, because of the verificationist scruples that I sketched in §2, we are disinclined to insist on the principle of bivalence.

26. See "The Concept of Truth in Formalized Languages", p. 175, n. 2.
27. See Gareth Evans, "Semantic Structure and Logical Form", p. 204.
28. "The Concept of Truth in Formalized Languages", p. 197.

5. If the argument I outlined in §3 were sound, that suggestion would be incoherent. For the suggestion involves appeal to interaction with a theory of force mentioning assertion, in order to justify the idea that a theory of the sort envisaged is a truth-conditional theory of sense; but that mention of assertion ought, according to the argument, to import the principle of bivalence, which a theory of the sort envisaged is designed, precisely, not to require.

Intuitionists do not accept the principle of bivalence. Hence, if intuitionists may consistently regard themselves as making assertions, it cannot be true that employment of the concept of assertion requires acceptance of that principle. And it is difficult to see how adoption of intuitionistic logic could preclude one from regarding oneself as making assertions.[29]

What about the argument I outlined in §3? Some form of its first premise seems unquestionable, but the second is open to objection.

In the first place, it should be pointed out that those passages in Dummett that look, at first sight, like a justification of the second premise are suspiciously redolent of the view that a truth-conditional conception of sense must, by way of something like the first premise, imply a conceptual priority of the notion of the content of an assertion over the notion of sense. We seem to be invited to extract a requirement that applies to assertions in any language whatever, from a purported grasp of the notion of the content of an assertion that is independent of exigencies deriving from the need to construct systematic theories of sense for particular languages. The idea that something like this can be done is especially clear in Dummett's handling of the concession I mentioned in §3. He allows, for instance, that the dictates of a systematic theory of sense may require atomic sentences containing bearerless names to be viewed as neither true nor false, but he insists, nevertheless, that an utterance of such a sentence with honest assertoric intent must, in deference to the requirement derived from the nature of assertion, be regarded as the assertion of a falsehood. That insistence could be warranted only by a conception of the content of an assertion that is independent of (since the content is not necessarily determined by) the sense of the sentence uttered, as specified by a systematic theory of sense.

29. If intuitionists were precluded from assertion, there would be an incoherence in Dummett's suggestion (see, e.g., "Truth", pp. 17–18) that a theory of sense suitable for intuitionists would centre on the notion of assertibility-conditions.

From the standpoint I set out in §1, the invitation to aim at comprehending such a prior notion of the content of an assertion may be simply declined. Assertion is not a casually observable phenomenon, correctly describable, wherever it occurs, independently of the construction of a systematic theory for the language in which it is occurring. Assertions are made only in languages, and what (if anything) is asserted by uttering a sentence cannot diverge from what would be said about the sentence by a systematic theory for the language that contains it.[30] Alleged general truths about assertion, announced in advance of systematic theories for particular languages, cannot survive if not preserved, for some language, by a systematic theory adequate on all other counts. And that, it might be said, is the situation with any alleged requirement that the principle of bivalence should be accepted; such a requirement is not preserved by an intuitionistic theory of truth.

However, although the protest against the implication about conceptual priority is justified, this line of attack is inconclusive. No doubt our grasp of the concept of assertion, as we apply it to ourselves, should be thought of as simultaneous with, not prior to, our acquiring mastery of our first language, that is, our coming to be correctly describable by a bipartite theory of the sort I sketched in §1; so that that grasp could not equip us with general truths about assertion, and its content, that would be independent of what an adequate theory of sense for our language would say about the appropriate sentences. Still, not just any type of speech act performed by others can be intelligibly viewed by us as assertion, the very speech act we sometimes ascribe to ourselves under that name. This suggests that we can reasonably require our grasp of the concept, as we apply it to ourselves, to yield general controls on intelligible application of the same concept to others; such controls being in some sense, after all, prior to the construction of systematic theories for the languages that others speak, even if not prior to what such a systematic theory would say about our own language. And now it may be suggested

30. Thus if a systematic theory does not allow atomic sentences containing names without bearers to be either true or false, and accordingly does not equip them with fulfillable truth-conditions, the right position will be that nothing can be asserted by the use of such sentences. The intention of making an assertion does not guarantee its own success. (Of course if nothing is asserted by the use of such sentences, *they* pose no threat to a link between assertion and bivalence.)

that bivalence does hold in our own language, and that that fact is essential to our grasp of the concept of assertion, as we apply it to ourselves; so that bivalence is, after all, a prerequisite for the extension of that concept to others. Certainly there is something plausible about the claim that assertion, as such, leaves no room for contemplating possibilities other than that one is saying something either true or (at worst, so to speak) false.

In the context of intuitionistic logic, however, there is a way of conceding this claim without accepting that assertion requires the principle of bivalence. For although the law of excluded middle is not a theorem of intuitionistic logic, its double negation is. Thus, although it would not be provable, in an intuitionistic theory of truth, that, whatever object-language sentence one takes, either it or its negation is true, nevertheless any purported counter-instance to that generalization would be provably inconsistent. Given that a sentence is false if and only if its negation is true, purported counter-instances to the principle of bivalence would be similarly inconsistent, even though the principle itself is not assertible. Hence an intuitionist who regards himself as making an assertion need not contemplate possibilities other than truth and falsehood for the sentence he uses, and indeed, granted the equivalence between falsehood and truth of the negation, he must not, on pain of contemplating the possibility of something that would be, by his own lights, inconsistent. In the context of classical logic, of course, such refusal to contemplate counter-instances amounts to acceptance of the principle of bivalence; but it would be peculiar to use that fact in arguing the insufficiency, for justifying the claim that the speech act in question is indeed assertion, of a refusal that does not amount to acceptance of the principle. If, as seems plausible, such refusal is sufficient, then there need be no incoherence, after all, in the suggestion that a Tarskian theory with an intuitionistic proof-theory might serve, for a suitable language, as a truth-conditional theory of sense, certified as such by interacting, in the standard way, with a theory of force mentioning assertion.[31]

The verificationist doubts about bivalence that I described in §2 yield, at most, disinclination to assert the principle, not an inclina-

31. I here concede the thesis that assertion requires bivalence, on one interpretation of it. What I do not concede is that it requires the *principle* of bivalence.

tion to cite counter-instances. This point is respected in the suggestion I have just defended.

6. Severing the connection, alleged by the argument I outlined in §3, between a truth-conditional conception of sense and insistence on the principle of bivalence leaves the realist conception of truth-conditions untouched.

Suppose that the understanding of sentences in some language is represented by a bipartite theory that incorporates, as its theory of sense, an intuitionistic theory of truth, and hence combines a truth-conditional conception of sense with avoiding the principle of bivalence. Strictly, the articulation of the bipartite theory—its division into the two sub-theories, and the deductive machinery of the sub-theories—need not articulate anything literally known by a competent speaker. The articulation answers, not to requirements of the speaker, but to requirements of the theorist who aims at a compendious description of the speaker's capacity to know, given suitable observations, an indefinite number of particular truths. Strictly, then, a speaker's understanding of a sentence is represented as consisting, not in actual knowledge of anything, but in the capacity to know, on suitable occasions of utterance of the sentence, something that a theoretical description of his capacity would generate by combining, with the deliverances, for those utterances, of the theory of force, the theorem of the theory of sense that specifies what it is for the sentence to be true. But it seems a harmless abbreviation to say, loosely, that a speaker's understanding of a sentence is represented as knowledge of what it is for it to be true. That goes, in particular, for sentences whose truth-value is not decidable by appropriate evidence. Absence of decisive evidence does not block understanding; and understanding is thought of, here too, as knowledge of a truth-condition. Thus speakers are credited (in a similar harmlessly abbreviated idiom) with a conception of truth-conditions as possibly obtaining, or not, quite independently of the availability of appropriate evidence.

This position is essentially realist, even though, by virtue of intuitionistic logic in the envisaged theory of sense, it concedes the verificationist doubts (§2) about the principle of bivalence. In the context of intuitionistic logic, to say, on the one hand, that the truth-condition of a sentence may obtain even if we cannot tell that it does, and may not obtain even if we cannot tell that it does not, is not to say, on the other, that the truth-condition of any sentence either does obtain or does not, even if we cannot tell either that it does or that it does not. For the position I have outlined combines, coherently if intuitionistic logic is coherent, refusing to say the latter with continuing to say the former.

7. Intuitionistic theories of truth would not necessarily be apt for imparting, *ab initio*, an understanding of their object languages. A theory that used sentences to state their own truth-conditions would be intelligible only if the sentences were already understood. A theory in a different metalanguage could in principle impart understanding of its object language; but it would do nothing for someone who professed not to understand speakers of its metalanguage: an adherent of classical logic, for instance, who professed general incomprehension of intuitionists' talk.

The point is not special to intuitionistic theories: an analogous point holds for classical theories of truth. And in itself the point is no objection to the adequacy of such theories as theories of sense. Any theory is intelligible only to someone who understands the language in which it is stated. A theory of sense can reasonably be required to play a part in a systematic description of what is involved in understanding the language of which it is a theory (§1); that is quite different from its being called upon to serve as a possible means to the acquisition of a command of its object language.

The possibility of general incomprehension of intuitionists, on the part of an adherent of classical logic, might seem to imply that there are special intuitionistic logical constants, differing in sense from the classical constants. On this view, the intuitionist could not be correctly regarded as refusing to accept some of the laws of classical logic. Certainly he refuses to assert some sentences that, in the mouth of an adherent of classical logic, would express, say, instances of the law of excluded middle; but in his mouth, since his logical constants differ in sense, they would not express instances of just that law.[32]

But the thesis that intuitionistic and classical logical constants diverge in sense is not entailed by the possibility of incomprehension. Understanding a linguistic action, like understanding any action, is a matter (executive failures aside) of finding a description under which

32. See Quine, *Philosophy of Logic*, pp. 80–91.

it can be seen how it might have struck the agent as a reasonable thing to do. Theories of sense would be parts of larger theories whose aim would be the systematic generation of such descriptions for linguistic behaviour (§1). Now in the case of intuitionists and adherents of classical logic, there is not only massive correspondence in linguistic behaviour, but also a possibility of explaining the residual divergence in terms of what seem to be arguments, on the intuitionists' part, against accepting the residue: notably the verificationist argument that, in the presence of undecidable sentences, we cannot know that every sentence is either true or false (§2). If we can understand the arguments as really being what they seem to be, that is, arguments against asserting the surplus classical laws, then it must be acceptable to translate the logical constants used in intuitionistic logic by their counterparts in classical logic; for it must, in that case, be acceptable to translate the intuitionists as refusing to assert precisely those classical laws. The translation would involve ascribing, to intuitionists, linguistic behaviour that, from a classical standpoint, is bizarre: for example, refusing to assert some instance of the law of excluded middle. But if we can see why they might suppose it is reasonable to refuse to assert that, we can agree that that is indeed what they refuse to assert. General incomprehension of intuitionists, on the part of an adherent of classical logic, might be explained, compatibly with the thesis that there is no divergence in the senses of the logical constants, in terms of a failure on his part to appreciate intuitionists' reasons for proceeding as they do.[33]

If intuitionism need not import novel senses for the logical constants, it could hardly require, on those grounds, at least, a novel general conception of sense. That it does not is a conclusion I have already argued above (§§4–5) by a different route.

8. The metatheory of intuitionism standardly contains systematic specifications of the conditions under which we have proofs of complex formulae, in terms of the conditions under which we have proofs of simpler formulae. If intuitionistic logic is to be applied to non-mathematical subject matter, the notion of proof, in such specifications, would need to be replaced with a notion, sufficiently general to suit all areas of discourse, of a sentence's having been verified. So a generalized version of something that intuitionists do in fact feel

33. See Adam Morton, "Denying the Doctrine and Changing the Subject".

called on to provide would conform to Dummett's description of the nature of a theory of sense appropriate for a verificationist who objects to a truth-conditional conception of sense. Of course that is no surprise; Dummett indeed holds that those systematic specifications of proof-conditions constitute explanations of the senses of special intuitionistic logical constants, and hence embody a conception of sense different from a truth-conditional conception.[34]

Those systematic specifications are intuitionistic substitutes for classical model theory. Suppose, for simplicity, that we have to deal with a language containing only unstructured sentences and truth-functional connectives. In specifying a particular classical interpretation we would assign, to each simple sentence, a truth-value (on the interpretation), truth or falsehood; common to the specification of all interpretations would be general clauses explaining how the truth-values (on an interpretation) of complex sentences depend on the truth-values (on the interpretation) of simpler sentences. Sentences true on all interpretations that share those general clauses would be the logical truths. Soundness in a proof-theory requires it to be able to prove nothing but logical truths, and completeness requires it to be able to prove all of them. Those properties of a proof-theory are of more than merely technical interest,[35] from a classical standpoint, since the common general clauses, if correct, capture that systematic dependence of the truth-values of complex sentences on the truth-values of simpler sentences that constitutes the contribution of the connectives to the senses of sentences in which they occur, that is, the senses of the connectives. Sentences true on all interpretations must owe their actual truth to what is invariant between the interpretations. Thus the model theory renders precise the conception of logical truths as owing their truth solely to the senses of the logical constants. Soundness in a proof-theory is a matter of its not being unfaithful to the senses of its logical constants; completeness is a matter of its capturing all that those senses require.

Each such interpretation would determine, for every sentence constructible out of the vocabulary of the language, one or the other of the two truth-values (on the interpretation), truth and falsehood. With orthodox general clauses, that would secure that the logical

34. See, e.g., *Frege: Philosophy of Language*, pp. 507, 611; "The Justification of Deduction", pp. 294–5, 305.

35. See "The Justification of Deduction", pp. 292–5.

truths included all instances of those laws of classical sentential logic at which the intuitionist jibs.

The intuitionist's inability to accept such a model theory need not reflect inability to accept its general clauses. Suppose the general clauses set out the information contained in the standard (two-valued) truth-tables. Although such general clauses determine the truth-values of complex sentences on the basis of assignments to simpler sentences of only the two truth-values, true and false, they do not themselves say that every sentence has one or the other of those two truth-values. The intuitionist does not deny the principle of bivalence, but simply refuses to assert it; and that refusal does not involve willingness to contemplate counter-instances (§5). Hence the intuitionist need not deny that general clauses corresponding to the standard truth-tables entirely capture the systematic dependence of truth-values on truth-values that, as before, constitutes the senses of the connectives. Whichever of the two truth-values the constituent sentences have, the clauses determine the truth-values of sentences composed out of them; and there is no further status that he is required to envisage the constituent sentences as possibly having, for which the clauses would leave the truth-values of complex sentences undetermined, thus being vulnerable to accusations of incompleteness. Sentences determined as true on all the classical interpretations owe that status, not just to the general clauses, but to the general clauses in conjunction with a built-in assumption of the principle of bivalence. The general clauses do not themselves assert the principle; on their own, they need not be unacceptable to the intuitionist. So far, then, the intuitionist's inability to accept classical model theory need not imply that his connectives differ in sense from the classical connectives, let alone that he requires a different general conception of sense.

It might now seem that defining soundness and completeness for intuitionistic proof-theory, in the context of preserving the thesis that the intuitionist's connectives do not differ in sense from the classical connectives, would require a model theory matching the classical model theory at all points except that the built-in assumption of the principle of bivalence is dropped. But this thought leads nowhere. The general clauses determine truth-values on the basis of truth-values; so something, in the envisaged intuitionistic model theory, would have to correspond to the assignment, in a classical interpretation, of a truth-value to each simple sentence. General clauses that say, at least, what the standard truth-tables say could be prevented from ensuring the truth, on all such interpretations, of the undesired theorems only if, in some interpretations, some simple sentences were assigned a status other than those of being true (on the interpretation) or false (on the interpretation). That would require, after all, additions to the general clauses, to deal with cases where constituents of sentences have that further status: hence an admission, contrary to the position I am trying to reflect, that the general clauses do not entirely capture the senses of the connectives.[36] Preserving the general clauses leaves no room for an intuitionistically acceptable conception of logical truth according to which, as before, it is owed solely to the senses of the logical constants.

The verificationism I described in §2 implies not that the principle of bivalence is false but, at most, that it is not known to be true. If such a verificationist accepts, as he has, so far, no reason not to, that the general clauses capture the senses of the connectives, then he can say, in the light of the classical model theory, that if the principle of bivalence is true (as it may be), then the classical theorems are true; indeed, if the principle of bivalence is true (as it may be), then the senses of the connectives guarantee the truth of the classical theorems. The trouble is that since he does not know that the antecedent is true, he cannot detach and assert the consequents of those conditionals. In his view, the classical logical truths are picked out, in the classical model theory, by a property amounting to no more than this: being such that, for all we know, the senses of the connectives guarantee their truth. Since that property does not ensure even the truth of sentences that have it, there is no particular point in a procedure that generates all and only the sentences that have it; that is what a sound and complete classical proof-theory would be.

The position I have just described requires a conception of the truths of logic, not as true solely in virtue of the senses of the logical constants—without assuming the principle of bivalence, there is no telling which sentences have that status—but as *knowable* solely in virtue of the senses of the logical constants. Such a conception could be made precise, in a way analogous to the way in which, on the assumption that the principle of bivalence holds, the other conception is made precise in classical model theory, by a systematic specifica-

36. If there are only two (or indeed any finite number of) values other than truth, the envisaged model theory will in any case not yield the right set of logical truths.

tion of the conditions under which we may claim to know the truth of complex sentences, in terms of the conditions under which we may claim to know the truth of simpler sentences. If we keep to the simplifying assumption that the only logical constants are the sentential connectives, such a specification may be thought of as constructed by considering how claims to know the truth of complex sentences could be justified by knowledge of the truth of simpler sentences, in the light of, first, that systematic dependence of truth-values on truth-values that, we continue to assume, constitutes the senses of the connectives; and, second, the verificationist insistence that we cannot claim to know that every sentence is either true or false. Any such systematic specification would certify sentences of some forms as knowable to be true whatever the epistemic status of their components, and, on the new conception, those would be the truths of logic. Soundness and completeness in a proof-theory are definable, as before, in terms of the notion thus rendered precise. Those properties have a more than merely technical interest, analogous to, but not the same as, the interest possessed, on the assumption of the principle of bivalence, by the classically defined notions. In particular, unsoundness no longer necessarily indicates unfaithfulness to the senses of the logical constants. Classical proof-theory is unsound not because it misrepresents the senses of the logical constants but because it purports to prove sentences that cannot be known to be true.

The metatheoretical utility of those systematic specifications of proof-conditions that I mentioned at the beginning of this section lies in the need, if interesting notions of soundness and completeness in an intuitionistic proof-theory are to be defined and investigated, for an interesting non-proof-theoretical specification of the intuitionistic truths of logic. I have accounted for that utility, here, without abandoning, and indeed on the basis of preserving, the thesis that intuitionism imports no novel senses for the logical constants, and therefore requires, on such grounds, at least, no novel general conception of sense.

A common generalization states that theses of soundness and completeness connect a syntactically (proof-theoretically) defined notion of logical truth (or logical consequence) with a semantically defined notion.[37] This might make the position I have adopted here seem im-

37. See "The Justification of Deduction", p. 290.

possible; for, surely, radical differences in the nature of definitions of semantic notions of logical truth would reflect radical differences in the underlying conception of meaning. But according to the position I have adopted here, the generalization is simply wrong. In the classical case, certainly, it is reasonable to regard the non-proof-theoretically defined notion of logical truth as a semantic notion; logical truth is viewed as owed solely to the senses of the logical constants. But the whole point of the argument I have given here is that no purely semantic notion of logical truth is available to a verificationist who adopts the attitude towards the principle of bivalence that I described in §2; an impurely semantic notion (so to speak) nevertheless serves analogous purposes. If the non-proof-theoretically defined notion that figures in the definitions of intuitionistic soundness and completeness need not be a semantic notion, its novel character cannot be used to argue that intuitionism requires a novel conception of meaning.[38]

9. If I am right, then, the verificationist attitude towards bivalence that I have considered requires a novel logic and a novel conception of how the senses of the logical constants enter into the marking out of the truths of logic. But it does not require a novel conception of sense, either directly (§§4–5) or by way of the required novel logic (§§7–8). There is no route, on these lines, from verificationism, through non-acceptance of the principle of bivalence, to abandoning our common-sense picture of reality.

10. A quite different verificationist argument for a novel conception of sense demands consideration at this point. The different argument would be a head-on attack, leaving bivalence aside, against the realist notion of truth-conditions, which, as we saw (§6), can survive non-acceptance of the principle of bivalence. The argument would be that the realist notion of truth-conditions involves viewing ordinary command of the concepts of truth and falsehood as something it cannot possibly be: something that cannot possibly have been acquired in the way in which ordinary command of those concepts

38. The considerations of this section undermine an objection that might be raised against the suggestion I made in §7, on these lines: the fact that the classical interdefinabilities of the connectives are not matched in intuitionistic logic shows that the connectives must diverge in sense. From the intuitionist viewpoint that I describe here, those classical interdefinabilities reflect not just the relations between the senses of the connectives, but those relations together with the assumption that the principle of bivalence holds.

must have been acquired, namely by acquiring habits of sensitivity to evidence (compare §2).

It is certainly the case that a theory of sense taking the form of a Tarskian theory of truth would not include an account of the evidence appropriate to the sentences with which it deals. It does not follow, however, that a bipartite theory containing such a theory of sense as a part (compare §1) would represent understanding as something independent of sensitivity to evidence. We would miss the point of the verificationist objection if we took it to be a complaint on those lines. Such a complaint (call it "the weak verificationist objection") would be too easy to meet.

If a bipartite theory is to be acceptable, its output—ascriptions of propositional acts with specified contents—must be intelligible in the light of intelligible ascriptions of propositional attitudes (§1). Now ascriptions of belief to a person are intelligible only if the beliefs ascribed can mostly be viewed as states partly formed by, or at least potentially sensitive to, evidence for their truth. Ascription of a whole set of beliefs to someone who has never been exposed to anything that one can count as evidence (even bad evidence) for their truth would be simply baffling. If a bipartite theory is to treat a speaker's (potential) utterances of sentences as assertion that p_1, . . . , assertion that p_n, such assertions being, standardly at least, made intelligible as manifestations of the belief that p_1, . . . , the belief that p_n, then it must be possible, in general, to regard the (potential) actions that are viewed as manifestations of those beliefs, like the beliefs themselves, as partly prompted by, or at least potentially sensitive to, evidence for those beliefs. The content of the belief appropriate to a given sentence would be given by the replacement for "*p*", in the relevant theorem entailed by the theory of sense. Hence assessment of a theory of sense for acceptability would essentially involve speakers' sensitivity to evidence, and the weak verificationist's point seems to have been met.

It would be a mistake to suppose that each theorem of the form "*s* . . . *p*" requires a theory-independent justification, involving observation of what actually prompts speakers' utterances of the sentence designated by what replaces "*s*". A representation of mastery of a language must be articulated primarily in terms of sentence-constituents and modes of combination, and only secondarily in terms of sentences. Thus warranting a theory of sense as meeting the weak verificationist's point could reasonably require, at most, that its representation of understanding be appropriately related to evidence in respect of each simple sentence-constituent and each mode of combination. That would be secured, ideally, by directly considering the evidential prompting of some sentences containing each. The systematic nature of the theory would involve its consequently representing the understanding of other sentences (in the abbreviated idiom that I explained in §6) as consisting—as with all sentences—in knowledge of truth-conditions, even though there might be no possibility, with those other sentences, of such direct consideration of evidential prompting. Even in the absence of such direct consideration, the theorist could claim, wholly on the basis of the acceptability, elsewhere, of his theory, that speakers' (potential) uses of those other sentences were potentially sensitive to appropriate evidence.

Opposition to this, it seems, would have to involve the idea that mastery of one sentence is a state independent of mastery of the next, as if sentences were always learned as disconnected units. But that idea, which leaves no room for the fact that a competent speaker can understand new sentences, is totally unacceptable.

The weak verificationist objection, then, seems to be untenable. But from the standpoint of a strong verificationism that is beside the point. The strong verificationist objection insists, not that mastery of a language should be represented as not independent of sensitivity to evidence, but that it should be represented as *consisting solely in* sensitivity to evidence. Perhaps we have seen how a truth-conditional conception of sense can meet the former insistence, but that is not to see how it can meet the latter.

11. In acquiring mastery of his language, the native speaker had nothing more to go on than encouragement and discouragement of his vocalizings in observable circumstances, together with the observable vocalizings of others in observable circumstances. He cannot have acquired anything more, thereby, than a set of dispositions to suit his vocalizings to observable circumstances. The radical translator, who sets out without benefit of tradition to give a systematic description of competence in some foreign language, has nothing more to go on than the infant learner. That summarizes a well-known doctrine of W. V. Quine.[39]

39. See *Word and Object*, chap. 2; and especially a remark at p. 26 of *Ontological Relativity and Other Essays*.

It captures, also, almost exactly, the position of the strong verificationist. The only difference is that the verificationist reference to evidence is replaced by a reference to observable circumstances, which presumably need not be restricted to (what is construed as) evidence for the truth and falsehood of sentences. Dropping the restriction will make no difference to the argument.

Suppose we believe that members of some community understand some of their own and one another's utterances as assertions: that is, we regard them as knowing, on suitable occasions of utterance of some sentence, something that we can specify by descriptions of actions on the pattern of "So-and-so is asserting that *p*". A systematic description of their capacity to know such things would represent them as knowing (in the abbreviated idiom that I explained in §6), concerning that sentence, that it is true if and only if . . . (here should follow the sentence that replaces "*p*" in that schematic description). Now suppose we regard the truth-value of assertions made by uttering the sentence as undetermined by what is observable; suppose, say, we regard it as expressing a theoretical statement belonging to an empirical theory that we construe realistically. In that case we credit our subjects (in the other abbreviated idiom that I explained in §6) with a conception of truth as being independent of what is observable. According to the strong verificationist, that is to credit them with something that they cannot have acquired, and so cannot possess.[40]

A scheme of translation would be a scheme for systematically generating, from suitable designations of uninterpreted sentences, appropriate replacements for "*p*" in (among other things) the schematic description "So and so is asserting that *p*".

It is thus possible to regard Quine's celebrated thesis of the indeterminacy of translation[41] as a version, not quite happily formulated, of the strong verificationist objection to realism in a theory of meaning; or, rather, of an objection that mirrors that objection,

40. See, e.g., Dummett, *Frege: Philosophy of Language,* p. 467. In "What Is a Theory of Meaning? (II)" the point is overlaid with other concerns, which I believe are both inessential to it and mistaken. But I cannot argue that in this essay.

41. *Word and Object,* chap. 2; and especially "On the Reasons for the Indeterminacy of Translation": note the argument called "pressing from above" (p. 183), which locates the indeterminacy precisely in sentences whose truth-value is not determined by observation.

but differs in that the starting point replaces the reference to evidence, as I noted above, by a reference to observable circumstances. The unhappiness of Quine's thesis, construed as making the verificationist point, lies in the fact that it is an indeterminacy thesis; its burden seems thus to be that the choice of a scheme of translation is underdetermined by the data on the basis of which it is undertaken, and that suggests that, in order to defend it, one is obliged to produce, or at least to show the possibility of, alternative schemes of translation in concrete cases. In the context of the strong verificationist objection to realism, availability of alternative schemes would be, at most, an inessential extra, and it would be a misrepresentation to describe the situation in terms of underdetermination by data. It does not matter, for the profound point that the verificationist is making and that, according to this suggestion, Quine was attempting to make, if there is only one way of making a scheme of translation fit people's dispositions to vocalize in observable circumstances. The point is that, even so, adoption of the scheme would involve going beyond the data; not because there are alternative schemes that would fit equally well, but because no scheme genuinely fits at all—adopting any scheme involves crediting its subjects with conceptions that they cannot have acquired.[42]

Obviously if the objection applies at all, it applies equally to our crediting ourselves, in similar circumstances, with similar conceptions.[43]

From the standpoint of a strong verificationist, then, the only hygienic concept of meaning would be something like Quine's concept of stimulus meaning,[44] which is tailored precisely to avoid going beyond what is accessible in dispositions to linguistic behaviour in observable circumstances. Any other conception of meaning, such as the conception we ascribe to ourselves and others when we describe ourselves and others as making, and knowing that we are making, assertions whose content goes beyond what is observable, must be

42. Critics of Quine, notably Noam Chomsky, have objected that indeterminacy of translation would be no more than the standard underdetermination of empirical theories by data; see Chomsky, "Quine's Empirical Assumptions". On the present construal of the point Quine was aiming at, such objections simply lapse.

43. As Quine says, "radical translation begins at home": *Ontological Relativity*, p. 46.

44. *Word and Object*, pp. 31 and ff.

simply mythical: a conception that we pretend we and they possess, when that cannot be the case.

An adherent of such a position is under an obligation to show how we might make linguistic behaviour, in general, intelligible to ourselves, satisfactorily answering the question "What are we all doing when we talk?", without employing the conceptual materials that he stigmatizes as merely mythical. It seems evident that, in any detailed attempt at discharging the obligation, the principle of bivalence would go by the board; but the line of argument would be, not through doubts about bivalence to rejection of realism (compare §9) but through rejection of realism to doubts about bivalence.

Anyone who is sceptical (as I am) about the prospects for a coherent and satisfactory anti-realism is under an equally stringent obligation to defuse the strong verificationist argument, or its generalized version. Even if we had a proof of the impossibility of anti-realism, the obligation would not lapse. What is required is to show how, in the face of the strong verificationist argument, a realistic account of the understanding of language is so much as possible. This seems to me to be a profoundly important task, but I am not at present sure how to begin on it.[45]

45. Quine has come close to posing the problem. But he thinks he can have things both ways: preserving a realism of first intention in genuine scientific theorizing, while relegating a realism of second intention (the mythical conceptual scheme) to everyday unscientific talk, where the standards can be relaxed (see *Word and Object,* pp. 216 and ff.: "The Double Standard"). The trouble is that the supposedly mythical scheme is needed, not just for the mundane purposes Quine recognizes, but for a coherent account of what we are doing when we engage in (realistically conceived) science. (See Dummett, *Frege: Philosophy of Language,* pp. 377–8.) Dummett has drawn attention to the problem, but he is less sceptical than I am about anti-realism.

ESSAY 2

Meaning, Communication, and Knowledge[1]

1. According to theorists of communication-intention, we should explain what meaning is in terms of the audience-directed intentions of speakers. According to theorists of formal semantics, the functioning of language can be illuminated by considering a certain sort of formal theory of a particular language: namely, a theory competent to specify truth-conditions for all of the language's indicative sentences. It seems likely that there is something to be gained from both these ways of thinking, but it is rare for much attention to be devoted to the question how they are related. However, a welcome exception is P. F. Strawson's provocative inaugural lecture,[2] from which the above characterizations are drawn.

Strawson's major thesis is this. The notion of truth-conditions is the fundamental notion of formal semantics, and the idea that meanings can be specified in terms of truth-conditions is all very well as far as it goes. But it does not go far enough. Further explanation of the notion of truth-conditions is called for; and this turns out to require an appeal to the characteristic conceptions of the communication-intention theorist. So while neither tradition is incorrect, the theorist of communication-intention can claim to be closer to the philosophical foundations.

In more detail, Strawson's central argument is as follows. The theorist of communication-intention can concede that "in almost all the things we should count as sentences there is a substantial cen-

1. I was helped in writing this essay by Brian Loar, Stephen Schiffer, and especially Gareth Evans.

2. "Meaning and Truth".

tral core of meaning which is explicable either in terms of truth-conditions or in terms of some related notion quite simply derivable from that of a truth-condition" (p. 178); and hence that theories of meaning for particular languages can hinge on the notion of truth. With its generality over languages, this concession constitutes, we might suppose, a potentially illuminating thesis about meaning in general; and it is one in which the explanatory weight rests on the notion of truth. But "we still cannot be satisfied that we have an adequate general account of the notion of meaning unless we are satisfied that we have an adequate general understanding of the notion of truth" (p. 180). Now when we look for accounts of truth in general—as opposed to the sort of account of truth in this or that particular language that semantic theories themselves provide—the best we can come up with seems to be such platitudes as this: "one who makes a statement or assertion makes a true statement or assertion if and only if things are as, in making that statement, he states them to be" (p. 180). If we combine this platitude with the concession that meanings can be specified in terms of truth-conditions, we arrive at the following conclusion: to specify the meaning of an indicative sentence is to specify how things are stated to be by someone who makes a statement by uttering it. (Presumably other sorts of sentence can have their meanings explained in some derivative way.) So we have arrived at the notion of the content of such centrally important speech acts as statement-making. Strawson goes on (p. 181):

> And here the theorist of communication-intention sees his chance. There is no hope, he says, of elucidating the notion of the content of such speech acts without paying some attention to the notions of those speech acts themselves . . . And we cannot, the theorist maintains, elucidate the notion of stating or asserting except in terms of audience-directed intention. For the fundamental case of stating or asserting, in terms of which all variants must be understood, is that of uttering a sentence with a certain intention . . . which can be incompletely described as that of letting an audience know, or getting it to think, that the speaker has a certain belief.[3]

3. This incompletely described intention is (at least in the version formulated in terms of getting the audience to think . . .) a component of H. P. Grice's analysis of utterer's meaning: see "Meaning", and the modifications proposed in "Utterer's Meaning and Intentions".

To determine the meaning of an indicative sentence is to determine what statement can be made by uttering it; and that is just to determine what belief the sentence can be used to get audiences to think the speaker has. Strawson concludes that the concession, "so far from being an alternative to a communication theory of meaning, leads us straight in to such a theory of meaning" (p. 182).

According to this argument, then, theories of meaning for particular languages might be essentially as theorists of formal semantics propose. But the work of explaining the concept of meaning is done, not by the central notion of such theories, the notion of truth, but by the conceptual apparatus required for the further elucidation of the notion of truth; and that is the favoured conceptual apparatus of the communication-intention theorist.

2. In Strawson's debate, the theorist of formal semantics is depicted as resisting pressure to appeal to the communicative nature of linguistic behaviour in order to underpin his interest in truth. But this misrepresents at least some of those who think about language within the tradition Strawson is considering. There is an attractive way to defend the philosophical interest of formal semantics, as applied to natural languages, that involves no such resistance.

Someone who understands a language can hear utterances in it, not just as productions of sound, but as significant speech acts. What he has is an information-processing capacity. His senses furnish him with information to the effect that people are uttering such-and-such sounds—information that is available equally to someone who does not understand the language. What is special about someone who does understand the language is that his sensory intake yields him, in addition, knowledge as to what speech acts, with what content, are being performed. The property that distinguishes him, then, would be captured by a theory with the following powers: given a suitable non-interpreting description of any possible utterance in the language—a formulation of information available equally, on hearing the utterance, to someone who understands the language and to someone who does not—the theory would enable anyone who knew it to derive that interpreting description under which someone who understands the language would be capable of recognizing the action performed.[4] Such a theory would compendiously describe the extra contribution, over and above the sharable sensory intake, that his competence with the language makes to his cognitive position on any of the relevant occasions. For any possible utterance in the language, it would yield a route from a non-interpreting description of it to an interpreting description. Thus it would reveal the relations between sound and—to speak intuitively—significance that, in a sense, constitute the language. It is hard to see what could have a better claim to count as a theory of meaning for a language.

If, for the moment, we ignore moods other than the indicative, we can restrict the scope of a theory of the envisaged sort to sayings. The theory would need, then, to make someone who knew it capable of specifying, for any indicative sentence in the language it dealt with, the content of the saying that an utterance of the sentence would be taken to be by someone who understood the language. This content-specification might be made possible by a theory that met the following description: for each object-language sentence, it entails a theorem whose form we can represent schematically as "*s . . . p*", where "*s*" is replaced by a suitable designation of the object-language sentence and "*p*" by a sentence, in the language in which the theory is stated, suitable for expressing what can be said by uttering "*s*". (We shall consider what goes in place of the dots shortly.)

We want to be able to see the content expressible by uttering a sentence as the upshot of contributions from repeatable parts or aspects of it. It seems inconceivable that a theory could yield specifications of content for all possible indicative sentences in a language whose complexity approached that of a natural language, unless the theory were organized in such a way as to meet something like that desideratum; the theorems would need to be deducible on the basis of the structure of the object-language sentences, in such a way that the premise that registers the contribution of, say, a word to a given sentence figures also in derivations that reveal its contribution to other sentences in which it occurs.

4. There is no implication that the theory is known by a possessor of the capacity it describes. Nor need he understand the language in which the interpreting descriptions are given; we can take a monoglot Frenchman to recognize another Frenchman as, e.g., saying that it is likely to snow. For the conception of a theory of a language that I set out here, compare Donald Davidson, "Radical Interpretation", and Essay 8 below.

Now suppose a theory for a given language can meet these requirements by taking this shape: what the replacements for "*p*" do, in the theorems, is to state necessary and sufficient conditions for the application of some predicate to the object-language sentences. One of the requirements is that replacements for "*p*" are to express what can be said by uttering the relevant object-language sentences. By way of something like Strawson's platitude (§1), this guarantees the weaker claim that the extension of the envisaged predicate is that of a truth-predicate. The envisaged theory would not be false if the predicate were written "true".[5]

Reintroducing non-indicative moods need not radically alter the picture. The task of generating sentences suitable for content-specifying can still be assigned to a component of the total theory that deals only with indicative sentences. If the object language has more than one mood, a theory competent to impose interpreting descriptions on all possible utterances in it will need to be able to classify utterances as performances of speech acts of this or that kind (assertion, question, command, or whatever). We can require the principles that effect this classification to be written in such a way that, in the case of a non-assertoric utterance, besides enabling us to identify the kind of speech act performed, they also equip us with an indicative sentence, related to the sentence uttered in such a way that the right-hand side of its theorem in the simple theory that I considered above—a sentence apt for expressing the content of sayings effected by uttering the indicative sentence—will equally serve (perhaps with minor syntactic modification) to express the content of the non-assertoric speech act performed by uttering a non-indicative counterpart. The relevant relations between sentences are quite systematic, and there is no reason to suppose they could not be codified in a theory.

The argument I have outlined does not purport to show that it is compulsory to formulate the central component of a theory of a language—the component that yields sentences suitable to specify the contents of utterances—as a characterization of a predicate. Nor does it guarantee that it is possible to do so; we know it is possible

5. Compare Davidson, "Truth and Meaning", especially at pp. 22–3. Indexicality introduces a complication, but one that is surmountable, as Strawson notes (pp. 179–80).

for languages with certain syntactic structures, but it is an open question whether we can wrench all of a natural language into syntactic forms that are amenable. But the policy of trying to do it this way, if possible, offers advantages. For it suggests a model of the kind of thing to aim at, in the truth-characterizations that Tarski showed how to construct for certain sorts of formalized language.[6] And Tarskian truth-characterizations have special attractions for those concerned with how languages relate to reality: they allow us to lay bare, in derivations of truth-conditions from semantic properties of sentence-constituents, how a sentence's bearing on the world is dependent on specific word-world relations involving its parts, and thus to meet a version of the desideratum that I mentioned three paragraphs back.

3. The appearance of the debate should now be somewhat altered. A theorist of formal semantics who defends his approach on the lines I have just sketched differs from his counterpart, in the dispute that Strawson stages, in this crucial respect: he evinces no reluctance to appeal to the notion of a communicative performance in what he offers in the way of general remarks about meaning—namely, a description of the shape that a theory of meaning for any particular language might take. On the contrary, the notion of the content of a saying is centrally important in his position. If one counts as a communication-intention theorist by virtue of thinking it unavoidable, in any adequate general account of meaning, to mention kinds of action that are standardly intentional and directed towards audiences, then Strawson's battle seems after all not to be joined. But this is not to say that the theorist of formal semantics I envisage concedes, in advance, the specific outcome of Strawson's debate.

Strawson's predominant picture involves the progressive extension of an analysis. At the first stage, the theorist of formal semantics offers an analysis of the notion of sentence-meaning in terms of the notion of truth-conditions. On behalf of the theorist of communication-intention, Strawson insists that the analysans stands in need of further analysis, and that the further analysis takes us to a second stage, at which the notion of sentence-meaning is analysed in terms of the notion of the content of an assertion. Given the aim of analy-

6. "The Concept of Truth in Formalized Languages".

sis, it looks suspect to stop at this point, with an analysis in terms of an overtly linguistic notion; an analysis should decompose a notion into conceptually prior components, and the notion of assertion seems to be on a level with the notion of sentence-meaning—too much so for analytic progress to have been achieved. As Strawson sets things out, such considerations may seem to render obligatory a third stage, in which the notion of assertion is itself analysed in non-linguistic terms—as in the account of assertoric communication, in terms of intention and belief, that Strawson recommends.[7]

Strawson's theorist of formal semantics sticks at the first stage of this progression. Anyone who had arrived at the second stage would be ill-placed to baulk at the third; and my theorist, as noted above, does not hesitate to appeal to the notion of the content of a saying. But it would be a mistake to suppose that this places him at the second stage of Strawson's debate. For he is not, like Strawson's disputant, driven to the notion of saying in order to underpin employment of the concept of truth in a first-stage analysis of the concept of sentence-meaning. Indeed, any such suggestion reverses the order of his reflections, in which the notion of truth enters only at the end. The predicate characterized, in its application to sentences of a given language, by a theory of the sort he envisages would be a truth-predicate; but this thesis appears, not as a purported analysis—even an interim analysis—of the notion of sentence-meaning, but as a subsequently-noticed consequence of what gives such theories their claim to count as components of theories of meaning.

It might be thought that my theorist is still not entitled to appeal to an unanalysed notion of saying, even if his doing so does not correspond to the second stage of Strawson's debate. But what seemed, in that context, to make it compulsory to attempt a reductive analysis of assertion—one that makes no use of notions essentially connected with language—was a thought about conceptual levels that is not so much as relevant if analysis is not the aim. Strawson himself remarks (though he relegates the remark to a footnote) that when

7. The full analysis would include more than the partial specification of intention that I quoted above. Not only would more need to be said about the intention (so far only "incompletely described"); the idea is that a fuller account would also introduce the notion of a conventional way of executing the intentions in question (see pp. 173–5). I am sceptical about the idea that linguistic behaviour is conventional in the way this suggests, but in this essay I shall not consider this element in the analysis Strawson recommends.

one sets out to give a philosophical account of something, conceptual analysis is not the only option (p. 172). Now nothing in the position that I sketched in §2 commits my theorist to analytic aspirations. And we lack an argument that meaning constitutes the sort of philosophical problem that requires analysis for its solution. The ability to understand a language is an ability to know what people are doing, in the way of performing significant speech acts, when they speak in it; if there is a problem about this, it is not unfamiliarity, or resistance to comprehension, on the part of the concepts employed in saying, occasion by occasion, what someone who understands a speech act knows, but rather an initial unclarity about how the general ability can be specifically described with a degree of systematic articulation sufficient to match the systematic way in which it evidently functions. What we need, on this view, is not conceptual analysis, but a perspicuous mapping of interrelations between concepts that, so far as this exercise goes, can be taken to be already perfectly well understood.

It is a striking fact that in the mapping offered by my theorist, the concept of meaning as such does not even appear. So far from analysing the notion of meaning, he suggests the radical thought that in describing the understanding of a language we can get along without it.

4. There is, however, a different line of argument available to Strawson: one that does not depend on the idea that what we need is analysis of the concept of meaning. It seems fair to claim that a satisfying general account of how language functions should make clear the peculiar importance language has in human lives; and it seems obvious that one could not achieve that goal without making it clear that language is essentially communicative—that speaking and understanding are primarily the issuing and the reception of communication. Now the position that I outlined in §2 does not involve denying the essentially communicative nature of language; it is not liable to the devastating objections that Strawson deploys against any such denial. But there would be justice in the complaint that more needs saying about what exactly communication is. (We might hope that this would have some bearing on the question when the application of an interpreting description to a speech act is acceptable—a question to which the position of §2 requires us to have some answer.) Strawson equates assertoric communication with the fulfilment of an

intention of the kind that figures in his favoured account of saying or asserting: that is, an intention that can be partly specified as that of getting an audience to believe that the communicator has a certain belief.[8] Here, then, we have a starting-point for an argument, quite distinct from one that appeals to the conditions for a satisfactory analysis, for accepting not just the innocuous concession to communication-intention theories implicit in §2, which I remarked on in the first paragraph of §3, but something more like the specific communication-intention theory that Strawson recommends.

But the proposed account of assertoric communication from which this line of argument starts is questionable.

5. According to the proposal, a partial account of what it is for a communicator (C) to communicate to an audience (A) that *p* by ϕ-ing is as follows: C fulfils an intention that A, through awareness of C's ϕ-ing, should come to believe that C believes that *p*.[9]

The form "communicate that *p*" is perhaps mildly barbarous. It may help to have in mind some plausible substitute for "communicate"; perhaps "get it across" will do. But if it will, the suggestion is in doubt, for this reason: it seems that one cannot get it across that *p* if it is not the case that *p*. Thus the analysandum requires the truth of what replaces "*p*", whereas the partial analysans obviously does not; and it does not seem that a more precise formulation of the analysans could repair the deficiency, so long as the operative notion remains the notion of inducing beliefs. (Simply adding "*p*" as a conjunct seems too ad hoc to be satisfactory.)

In the mildly barbarous idiom I am considering, then, "communicate" belongs to a class of verbs V whose defining property is that a sentence of the form "S V's that *p*" entails the truth of its embedded sentence. (Compare "disclose", "reveal", "convey".) Now Peter Unger has put forward the following attractive hypothesis: what makes a verb belong to this class is that it "yields us a decision as to the presence or absence of knowledge".[10] (Unger in fact restricts his hypothesis to lexically unstructured verbs, in order to avoid obvious

8. Strawson's formulation (p. 181) actually says "letting an audience know, or getting it to think, that the speaker has a certain belief". The former phrase introduces a quite different notion. See §5, and n. 12, below.

9. Only a partial account. The main omission here, in comparison with the account Strawson outlines, is a requirement of overtness in the intention. On this, see §6 below.

10. "Propositional Verbs and Knowledge"; the quotation is from p. 307.

counter-examples like "guess correctly"; but it seems reasonable to suppose that the structure of "get it across" is not of a disqualifying sort.) In the case of "communicate", understood as tantamount to "get it across", it is presumably the presence rather than the absence of knowledge that is determined by the true applicability of the verb. This suggests the suspicion: perhaps we should think of communication as the instilling not of beliefs but of knowledge.[11]

The suspicion is one that we might have wanted to entertain in any case, even without the detour through the dubious idiom. We can find it plausible, with Strawson, that the primary intention of a statement-maker, in "the fundamental case of stating or asserting" (p. 181), is to communicate something, to get something across. But we surely ought not to find it plausible that his primary intention is to induce someone else to form a belief about his belief. Consider what seems to be the corresponding thesis about questions: namely, that the intention of an inquirer, in the most fundamental case of inquiring, is to induce an audience to induce in the inquirer a belief about the audience's belief. Surely any such claim would be absurd. The primary point of asking questions is not to acquire beliefs about one's interlocutor's beliefs, but to find out how things are. Correspondingly, the primary point of making assertions is not to instil into others beliefs about one's own beliefs, but to inform others—to let them know—about the subject matter of one's assertions (which need not be, though of course it may be, the asserter's beliefs).[12]

Strawson's proposal represents a communicator as engaged in the manipulation of his audience's beliefs.[13] Whether the manipulation is in the audience's interest is simply left open. Of course a belief about another person's belief is sometimes a good thing to have; it might afford—if true—insight into the other person, and—if his belief is

11. "Suggests" only; Unger's hypothesis would require no more than that a communicator should have knowledge (on the assumption that it is the presence rather than the absence of knowledge that is at issue). But given that the concept of communication requires that a communicator should have knowledge, it seems irresistible to suppose that what he is doing when he communicates is sharing the knowledge.

12. On the importance of the notion of letting someone know something, in an account of communication, see Strawson, "Intention and Convention in Speech Acts", at p. 156. But here, as in "Meaning and Truth" (see n. 8 above), Strawson slides (p. 157) into a formulation in terms of getting someone to think something. (Even if we ignore "or getting it to think", the account in "Meaning and Truth" is still unsatisfactory from the standpoint I am suggesting, in that it restricts the content of the knowledge instilled to the communicator's beliefs.)

13. I owe this thought to Thomas Ricketts.

true as well—an argument to a truth about the world. But this view of communication yields no general presumption that communication, as such, is beneficial to its recipient. That depends on the good will, reliability, and so forth of the communicator. If communication is conceived, by contrast, as the sharing of knowledge, it will not seem an accidental fact about communication that it is potentially helpful to its recipient; communication, of its very nature, confers potential benefits, whose usefulness is grounded in that interest in how things are that no agent can lack.

6. Of course an assertoric linguistic repertoire can be exploited manipulatively—to mislead rather than to inform. Moreover, a statement-maker can be honestly mistaken even if his intention is informative. This, together with the existence of speech acts that are not assertoric at all, forces us to complicate the picture somewhat, if we are to combine the thesis that communication is the sharing of knowledge with the thesis that linguistic behaviour is essentially communicative in character.

A version of the latter thesis can still be defended on the following lines. We can say that a perceptual capacity is essentially a capacity to acquire knowledge, without committing ourselves to the false claim that knowledge is acquired in every exercise of a perceptual capacity; the concept of misperception is, precisely, the concept of a defective exercise of a capacity whose non-defective exercises issue in knowledge. In a similar way, we can say that the essential character of the assertoric use of language lies in its availability for communicating, in the sense of transmitting knowledge about the subject matter of assertions, without denying the possibility of using assertions to deceive. Communication, in the sense of the transmission of knowledge about the topic of discourse, need not actually take place in every exercise of the repertoire; nevertheless it can be essential to the repertoire that it is apt for communicating in that sense. (Indeed, we might say, it is precisely by purporting to communicate in that sense that a deceiver deceives.)

If we left it at that, however, we would be simply denying—highly implausibly—that communication takes place in deceptive or misguided uses of assertoric language. So far, moreover, we have no inkling how the concept of knowledge-sharing might be extended to non-assertoric uses of language. But the implication of our minimal concession to communication-intention theories (§§2, 3) was that, simply by virtue of being intentional and directed towards audiences, speech acts were quite generally communicative. So faithfulness to the concession requires us to find a further application for the concept of communication, one in which it is not restricted to actually informative assertions but true of speech acts in general. We shall see that we can preserve the idea that communication is the instilling of knowledge.

I shall approach the topic by way of the special overtness that is characteristic of linguistic communication.

A concept at least closely akin to the concept of knowledge-transmission applies to modes of behaviour that we can ascribe to creatures to which we would not think of ascribing intentional action. Absence of intentional action is no bar to possession of sensory capacities; that is, capacities for the acquisition of states of informedness about the environment, in the intuitively satisfactory sense of states, resulting from a systematic sensitivity to features of the environment, that enable behaviour to be suited, in the light of needs or goals, to the way the environment actually is. Such capacities obviously have survival value. Similar survival value would attach also to any behavioural disposition whose effect was to spread, among several individuals, the beneficial results of one individual's exercises of its perceptual capacities. A bird, say, might instinctively emit a characteristic sort of squawk on seeing a predator; other birds might acquire, on hearing such a squawk, a propensity towards behaviour appropriate to the proximity of a predator (flight, increased caution in feeding, or whatever). This propensity might match a propensity they would have acquired if they had seen the predator themselves. In such a case we can regard hearing the squawk as a further mode of sensitivity to the presence of predators, over and above more direct kinds of perception. The upshot of this further mode of sensitivity is no less appropriately thought of as possession of information (or misinformation if things have gone wrong) than is the state that standardly results from perceiving a predator. We might jib at the word "knowledge", but there is no risk of over-psychologizing our account of the birds—crediting them with an inner life—if we regard such behaviour as effecting the transmission of information, and hence as constituting a kind of communication.

Now a conspicuous difference between linguistic behaviour and this kind of information-transmission lies in the intentions that are overt in speech. In successful linguistic exchange speaker and hearer are mutually aware of the speaker's intentions, in a way that could have no counterpart in merely instinctive responses to stimuli.

Strawson indeed employs the notion of overtness, when he formulates a component of his favoured account of communicative intentions that I have so far passed over. In Strawson's sketch, the communicator's intention that the audience should form a certain belief about the communicator's belief is "wholly overt", in this sense: the communicator intends this very intention to be recognized by the audience (pp. 172–3).

It is open to question, however, whether this formulation successfully captures the special transparency of intention that is characteristic of linguistic communication. Such mutual awareness of intention as is involved in the overtness that Strawson describes could be fully achieved even though the intention that is alleged to be the communicative intention is not fulfilled; the audience might recognize the communicator's intention that he, the audience, should adopt a certain belief about the communicator's belief, but fail, or refuse, to oblige. Thus making the communicative intention overt—securing mutual awareness of it between speaker and hearer—is represented as independent of communicative success. What seems plausible, however, is this: the appropriate mutual awareness is actually what is aimed at by the speaker's primary communicative intention, so that securing the mutual awareness is not, as in Strawson's picture, a fallible means to communicative success, but rather constitutes it. This suggests the following position. The primary communicative intention is the intention, for instance, to say such-and-such to the audience. The appropriate mutual awareness is awareness that the speaker has indeed said such-and-such to the audience. Speech acts are publications of intentions; the primary aim of a speech act is to produce an object—the speech act itself—that is perceptible publicly, and in particular to the audience, embodying an intention whose content is precisely a recognizable performance of that very speech act. Recognition by an audience that such an intention has been made public in this way leaves nothing further needing to happen for the intention to be fulfilled.[14]

14. For the idea of speech acts as intentional acts such that the recognition of the intention *is* its fulfilment, see John R. Searle, *Speech Acts,* p. 47.

The notion of an intentional performance is more fundamental in this context than the notion of the intention to perform it. One can sometimes divine an intention to say such-and-such behind a bungled performance, but correctly executed speech acts carry their intentions on their surface; normal understanding of correct speech is not a matter of divination. And an account of the understanding of language must start with the understanding of correct speech.

Now intentions of this sort—intentions whose content is the publication of themselves—are communicative in a sense that involves no departure from the idea that communication is the instilling of knowledge. The intention to make such an intention public is the intention to let an audience know what speech act is being performed. Here, then, we have our required further application for the concept of communication. The concept applies, we can now say, at two levels. At the first level, communication takes place, as before, only when information is actually transmitted about the topic of discourse. But at the second level, the information whose sharing is relevant to the question whether communication is taking place concerns, not the topic of discourse, but the nature of the speaker's intentions; and when a properly executed speech act is understood, such information is always transmitted—not only in informative assertions but also in assertions by which information is not transmitted and in speech acts that are not assertoric at all.

If we take it that the content of the intention made public in a speech act—an intention that is communicative at the second level if not at the first—essentially involves the concept of the kind of speech act in question (it is the intention, for instance, to say such-and-such), then we cannot hope for a reductive account of kinds of speech act in terms of the intentions of their performers. But once we have turned our backs on analysis of the concept of meaning (§3), we have no obvious reason to regret this renunciation.

7. Strawson's debate has the centrality of assertoric speech acts as an undisputed background; the idea is that, if we can acceptably explain the notion of the content of these central speech acts, there should be no special difficulty about the content of other sorts of speech act. Now at the beginning of §6 I considered the thesis that availability for first-level communication—transmission of information about the topic of discourse—is of the essence of an assertoric

repertoire. I suggested that this thesis cannot be quickly ruled out on the score that assertions need not transmit information; but we lack, as yet, a positive reason for accepting the thesis. Perhaps finding one would be finding a way of domesticating, within a position in which reductive ambitions are renounced, Strawson's thought that "there is no hope . . . of elucidating the notion of the content of such speech acts without paying some attention to the notions of those speech acts themselves" (p. 181).

To specify the meaning of an indicative sentence, according to Strawson's concession to theorists of formal semantics (§1), is to specify conditions under which it could be used to assert the truth. Now Michael Dummett has argued that to connect meaning with truth-conditions in this way is merely superficial as long as the notion of truth is simply taken for granted. More specifically, such a connection is unilluminating if it is allowed to seem that truth and falsehood are simply a pair of coordinate properties, one or the other of which an indicative sentence will happen to have.[15] The implication is that such a connection might be illuminating if reinforced by an account of the special interest that attaches to the question whether a sentence is true or false: an account that makes clear a relation between the point of the classification of sentences into true and false, on the one hand, and the possession of content by sentences, on the other. In the pre-*Tractatus Notebooks,* Wittgenstein associates the fact that sentences represent states of affairs with their possession of a true-false polarity;[16] another way of putting what appears to be Dummett's suggestion is that if any such association is to be illuminating about how indicative sentences represent states of affairs, it must be reinforced by an explanation of the fact that the true-false polarity is not a matter of indifference.

Such considerations seem obviously akin to those that Strawson brings to bear against the theorist of formal semantics who figures in his debate—one who proposes an analysis of the concept of meaning in terms of the concept of truth-conditions. Their relevance to the different position that I outlined in §2, which claims no particular conceptual illumination from the notion of truth as such, is less obvious. However, that position seems vulnerable to an analogous accu-

15. See "Truth".

16. *Notebooks, 1914–16,* p. 94 (compare *Tractatus Logico-Philosophicus,* e.g. 4.022–4.024).

sation of superficiality. The Tractarian association has its attraction in the context of questions like this: "How can a sentence, which is after all a mere complex of lifeless sounds or marks, represent reality as constituted a certain way?" What Dummett stigmatizes as superficial is a purported answer to this question that appeals to the notion of truth-conditions but takes the notion of truth for granted. In the position of §2, what we find instead is an appeal to the notion of the content of an assertion or a saying, again—so far—without further explanation. But if the question puzzles us, the modification can hardly be an improvement. As long as we take the notion of content for granted, we are open to the accusation of simply refusing to feel the perplexity that the question aims to express: a perplexity about how mere objects can have content at all.

(If the point is generalized like this, it becomes, after all, doubtful whether it is congenial to the position that Strawson recommends. If we are not to take the notion of the content of an assertion for granted, because our perplexity is about the notion of content in general, then how do we make progress by moving to a position in which we take for granted, as Strawson seems to, the notion of the content of a belief? Here we may need to work at resisting an insidious temptation: the temptation to think of representing states of affairs as a quasi-magical feat, most easily comprehended, or at least accepted, as effected by mental states, conceived as configurations in an ethereal medium whose properties can be as mysterious as we like. But Strawson is surely not subject to this temptation.)

What Dummett suggests, as a way of beginning to cure the superficiality, is this: the point of the classification of sentences into true and false lies in the fact that we aim at making true statements. But it is not obvious that this suggestion is correct. Truth is not always our aim in statement-making. Nevertheless, the statements we make with deceptive intent still put themselves forward, so to speak, as representing things the way they are; content and truth-conditions seem no differently connected in their case. A modified version of the thesis about aims might at any rate be true; perhaps truth is the normal, or the proper, aim of a statement-maker. But the connection between content and truth-conditions seems to be exceptionless. It is natural to suspect that facts about the normal or proper aims of statement-makers are not themselves what we are looking for. (Perhaps they are consequences of it.)

A different possibility is suggested by the idea that communication is the instilling of information. Consider, first, instinctive communicative behaviour like that of the birds I described in §6. The function of such behaviour is to furnish information about the environment to birds that witness it; here "function" occurs in something like the sense in which it is the function of the heart, say, to circulate the blood. When what gets transmitted is misinformation, there has been a malfunction of a natural process. A malfunction is as such a defect (even if, on occasion, misinformation is better for its recipient than information would have been). In this case, then, the non-indifference of the distinction between truth and falsehood is simply the non-indifference of the distinction between proper functioning and malfunction. Aims pursued in communicating do not enter the story. There are no such aims, since the behaviour is instinctive. But in an account of the (no doubt rudimentary) notion of content that seems undeniably applicable in this case, the natural function of the behavioural repertoire can serve, as it were, instead; it can occupy a position analogous to the position that was supposed to be occupied, in an account of the notion of the content of an assertion, by the alleged fact that in making assertions we aim at truth.

When the communicative process functions properly, sensory confrontation with a piece of communicative behaviour has the same impact on the cognitive state of a perceiver as sensory confrontation with the state of affairs that the behaviour, as we may say, represents; elements of the communicative repertoire serve as epistemic surrogates for represented states of affairs. It is hard to see what perplexity there could be, about the application of the notion of content to pieces of behaviour of this kind, that would persist entirely unalleviated by this thought: elements of such a repertoire represent states of affairs by virtue of standing in for them in a creature's cognitive dealings with the world.

It is plausible that the assertoric core of linguistic behaviour is a descendant, now under intentional control, of the sort of instinctive communicative repertoire we have been considering. This would account for the plausibility of the suggestion that availability for transmission of knowledge is an essential characteristic of the assertoric component of a language (§6). Of course assertions can serve purposes other than the purpose of supplying information; once the behavioural repertoire is responsive to a variety of non-informative intentions, it no longer seems appropriate to think of the transmission of information as the natural function of its exercises. However, it remains a striking fact about assertions that knowledge can be acquired at second hand. If someone knows that *p* and says that *p*, then typically someone who hears and understands him is in a position to know that *p*. It seems unpromising to suppose that knowledge by hearsay owes its status as knowledge, quite generally, to the knower's possessing a cogent argument to the truth of what he knows from the supposed reliability of the speaker. A more attractive line of thought is that the linguistic repertoire retains, through the alteration of nature involved in the onset of self-consciousness, a form of the characteristic that was essential to its pre-linguistic ancestor: in suitable circumstances (to be spelled out in any fuller elaboration of this idea) its exercises are cognitive stand-ins for the states of affairs that they represent. An assertion will actually have that epistemological role only if the circumstances are right. But all standard assertions—excluding, that is, special cases like irony—purport to have it. Thus their possession of content—their capacity for representing states of affairs—is intelligible in terms of a suitable modification of the simple idea that seemed appropriate in the case of instinctive communication.

8. I have been ignoring the belief-expressing aspect of assertion on which Strawson concentrates. I have no wish to deny the central importance, in any account of what gives language its special place in our lives, of the way it enables us to reveal our states of mind to one another. Indeed, the belief-expressing aspect of assertion would be crucial in empirically assessing a theory of a language of the sort I envisaged in §2. A theory of that sort is acceptable if the interpreting descriptions of linguistic behaviour that it yields make the behaviour intelligible; the test of intelligibility is the question whether we can make sense of the behaviour, as described, in terms of propositional attitudes that the speakers' behaviour and circumstances permit us to attribute to them, and we typically make sense of assertions as expressive of beliefs. But to concede all this is not necessarily to conclude, with Strawson, that we must understand the possession of significance by indicative sentences in terms of their admitted availability for the expression of beliefs. In fact §7 suggests the possibility of a position in which things are the other way round.

The acquisition of linguistic competence by a contemporary human being may be expected to recapitulate, in some salient respects, the evolution of language from instinctive communicative behaviour that I found plausible in §7, with the learning of new dispositions taking the place of the evolution of increasingly complex instincts.[17] According to such a view, when an individual language-learner has become fully *au fait* with the practice of making assertions, the component in his competence that consists in his ability to treat assertions as representing states of affairs is a continuation of something that was already present in his behavioural dispositions at an earlier stage, before his operations with his repertoire were self-conscious. (This mirrors the evolutionary suggestion that I made at the end of §7.) What accounts for the possession of content—the capacity to represent states of affairs—on the part of pieces of behaviour of the kind that, in the fully-fledged competence, he recognizes as assertions is the part played by some such pieces of behaviour—for instance, utterances by his parents—in his acquisition of knowledge; a part that such pieces of behaviour were already playing before the competence was fully-fledged. Then this possession of content, on the part of pieces of behaviour of the relevant kind, can in turn account for the fact that they become capable of being taken as expressive of belief when the individual's dealings with the repertoire become self-conscious.

Exercises of instinctive communicative repertoires do not give expression to states of mind; there are no states of mind, in the relevant sense, to be expressed. Something similar is true if the repertoire is not instinctive but, as in the early stages of language-learning, a matter of something like conditioned reflex. A piece of communicative behaviour of a non-intentional kind simply represents reality, or misrepresents it if something goes wrong. But once communicative behaviour is under the intentional control of the communicator, so that deliberate misrepresentation of reality is possible, the communicat-

17. Here, as in the speculation about evolution in §7, I ignore that use of what, in due course, becomes a linguistic repertoire in which its effect is to get others to do things. No doubt this would be important in any treatment of these issues that was less sketchy and impressionistic than this one. But in concentrating on the assertoric, I am at any rate no worse off than Strawson. (And it might plausibly be argued that in the absence of anything assertoric, there would be no reason to regard the sort of behaviour I am ignoring as communicative, in any interesting sense, rather than as simply a particular way of making the environment more congenial.)

ing self joins external circumstances as a possible object of representation, or (now) purported representation. To go through the motions of supplying an audience with knowledge of some circumstance that one takes to be otherwise is potentially to mislead, not only about the circumstances, but also about the cast of one's thought—one's belief, in a sense that seems to apply only when questions arise in this way about the sincerity or insincerity of its expressions.[18] (I say "potentially" not just because an audience may see through one's deception, but also because an audience whose operations with the repertoire—responses as well as exercises—are still no more than conditioned reflex will not be capable of being misled about the second topic.) Now my suggestion is that it is because indicative sentences have the capacity of representing reality as constituted in certain ways—this being independently accounted for in terms of the pre-linguistic role of some of them in knowledge-acquisition—that they are available for representing their utterers as believing that reality is constituted in those ways, once dealings with the repertoire become self-conscious. It is not that their capacity for use as expressive of belief breathes into them the life that enables them to represent reality, but rather that their antecedent capacity to represent reality is what makes them capable of expressing beliefs.

Children start acquiring knowledge by being told things, long before they are capable of so much as raising questions about the sincerity and reliability of their informants.[19] Thus the utterances that they hear on the relevant occasions impinge on them with content, so to speak, in advance of being taken as expressive of belief, in the sense of "belief" that I mentioned in the last paragraph. There is a complication: if sentences contain terms that have their life in the context of some body of theory (a description that perhaps fits all sentences), then comprehension of their content is initially incomplete, and the knowledge is commensurately imperfect. What the child really has is a sentence that is confidently accepted though not properly understood. But what is needed for full exposure to the significance of the sentence is not thoughts about the mental state of the original informant, but acceptance of the further sentences that form the required theoretical context, and a capacity to employ them ap-

18. See Bernard Williams, "Deciding to Believe".
19. See Wittgenstein, *On Certainty* §§143, 160.

propriately in connected conversation.[20] Once the child has worked his way into a fair competence with an appreciable amount of a language, he will surely be engaged in, and sensitive to, assertion as expressive of belief. But it is not because belief-expression is by then in his picture of his dealings with language that content, gradually more fully understood, has for some time been an appropriate constituent of our picture of his dealings with language. Content is in our picture, rather, because the child's operations with sentences have fitted into his life in such a way as to permit us to suppose that the sentences have been serving as vehicles for the transmission of knowledge.

(Anyone who is inclined to suppose that this cannot be right, and that possession of content must be grounded in availability for belief-expression, needs to resist the temptation to rely on the dubious thought that I mentioned in §7: the thought that the possession of content is too mysterious to be understood except in terms of the peculiar properties of an ethereal medium, conceived as the stuff of which mental states are composed.)

9. The objects to which a formal semantic theory assigns semantic properties tend naturally to be rather formal objects: objects arrived at, then, by abstracting ruthlessly from the concrete detail of actual behaviour. In an access of mathematical enthusiasm about these formal objects and their formally assigned properties, it is possible to forget, or even deny, the anchoring of the discipline in the realities of speech or sufficiently speech-like behaviour. But semantics, formal or otherwise, is secondary to the theory of communication in at least this sense: if there were no subject matter for the theory of communication, there would be nothing for semantic theories to be about. Strawson goes further than this. He endorses a specific proposal about the nature of communication that I have found questionable. And in keeping with this view of communication, he takes the dependence of semantics on the theory of communication to involve a possibility of analysing, in purely psychological terms, the properties that fit words and sentences to be objects of semantic theories; whereas I have suggested that such reductive analysis is not compulsory, and that it misleads about what must be understood in terms of

20. "Light dawns gradually over the whole": *On Certainty* §141.

what. Strawson's main aim, however, in the lecture I have discussed, is to recall formal semantics from platonistic excess, and remind it that a semantic theory is nothing if not a component in an account of actual or possible communicative behaviour. That he is correct in this is the unquestioned foundation of the suggestions, divergent in detail from the position he recommends, that I have made in this essay.

ESSAY 3

Quotation and Saying That[1]

1. *Oratio obliqua* constructions pose well-known problems for a theory that systematically assigns truth-conditions to utterances in a language. In order to solve these problems, Donald Davidson, in "On Saying That", offers a paratactic representation of the logical form of sentences containing *oratio obliqua* constructions. Davidson's theory is beautiful and illuminating; perhaps there are difficulties in its further elaboration, but this essay will not criticize it on this or any other score. However, Davidson develops his approach by way of offering to correct "a subtle flaw" (p. 103) that he claims to find in a promising alternative, namely, an approach that employs quotation. In this essay I question the cogency of Davidson's objection to his quotational rival. In the course of doing so, I query the account of quotation that Davidson sketches in "On Saying That", and elaborate a promising competitor (§6). The competitor proves subject to difficulties, however (§7), which help to motivate a different later suggestion of Davidson's own (§8). If quotation is understood in this final, and I think satisfactory, way, then Davidson's argument against a quotational account of indirect discourse fails; but the quotational account still will not do (§10). I conclude (§11) with some remarks about what is achieved by Davidson's paratactic theory.

2. A convenient way to bring out the character of the quotational approach that Davidson discusses is to trace its emergence through the three stages of W. V. Quine's treatment in *Word and Object*.

1. I was helped in preparing this essay for its first publication by members of seminars in Oxford in 1972 and Birkbeck College, London, in 1974, especially Gareth Evans and Mark Platts.

At the first stage, the proposal is to regiment sentences like

(1) Galileo said that the earth moves

into sentences containing a two-place predicate, "_____ says-true _____", true of speakers and sentences. (For present purposes we can count proposals for regimentation as proposals about how to represent logical form.)[2] So (1) is represented by

(2) Galileo said-true "The earth moves".

The "said-true" of (2) is not to be confused with the "said" of direct quotation: (2) is to be true just in case (1) is, even though Galileo did not utter the words quoted in (2).

At the second stage, it is claimed that (2) is vulnerable to a possible indeterminacy of truth-value, over and above anything that affects (1). The claim (to which I shall return: §7) is that the singular term that fills the second argument-place of (2)'s predicate—the quotation "'The earth moves'"—refers to an item that, besides behaving in familiar ways in English, may conceivably also be a sentence of some other language, say Martian. Perhaps in Martian it means something different: something Galileo never said. If this is so, the relation that "said-true" is meant to express both holds and fails to hold between Galileo and "The earth moves". So the two-place predicate gives way to a three-place predicate, "_____ says-true _____ in _____", true of speakers, sentences, and languages; and (1) is now represented by

(3) Galileo said-true "The earth moves" in English.

Alonzo Church made trouble for this proposal by considering translations of sentences like (3) into other languages.[3] These considerations fail to impress Quine, since they turn on a notion of which Quine takes a dim view: the notion of sameness of meaning. But Quine dislikes the proposal anyway, because of its "dependence on the notion of *a* language" (p. 214). Questions about the identity of

2. See Quine, "Reply to Davidson".
3. See "On Carnap's Analysis of Statements of Assertion and Belief".

languages are at least as problematic as those questions about the identity of propositions whose intelligibility Quine doubts; and it was the hope of avoiding these latter questions that made a quotational approach to "propositional attitudes" attractive in the first place.[4] So Quine moves to a third version, in which the worry that prompted the second is met by having a third argument-place not for a language but for a speaker:

(4) Galileo said-true "The earth moves" in my sense.

Quine remarks, about this third version, that the third argument-place will "regularly" be occupied by the speaker of the whole, "since 'that' clauses are always given in our own language" (p. 214). This may prompt the suspicion that "in my sense", in (4), is redundant. I shall return to this later (§7).

3. As Davidson suggests (p. 104), (4) should be paraphrasable by

(5) Galileo uttered a sentence that meant in his mouth what "The earth moves" means now in mine.

His discussion of (5) runs as follows (p. 104):

> We should not think ill of this verbose version of "Galileo said that the earth moves" because of apparent reference to a meaning ("what 'The earth moves' means"); this expression is not treated as a singular term in the theory. We are indeed asked to make sense of a judgement of synonymy between utterances, but not as the foundation of a theory of language, merely as an unanalysed part of the content of the familiar idiom of indirect discourse. The idea that underlies our awkward paraphrase is that of *samesaying:* when I say that Galileo said that the earth moves, I represent Galileo and myself as samesayers.
>
> And now the flaw is this. If I merely *say* that we are samesayers, Galileo and I, I have yet to *make* us so; and how am I to do this? Obviously, by saying what he said; not by using his words (necessarily), but by using words the same in import here and now as his there and then. Yet this is just what, on the theory, I cannot do. For the theory brings the content-sentence into the act sealed in quotation marks, and on any

4. This sentence actually owes more to Davidson's purported exposition of Quine ("On Saying That", p. 164) than to *Word and Object.*

standard theory of quotation, this means the content-sentence is mentioned and not used. In uttering the words "The earth moves" I do not, according to this account, say anything remotely like what Galileo is claimed to have said; I do not, in fact, say anything.[5]

Davidson's own proposal is designed expressly to remedy this alleged flaw. The logical form of (1) is represented by

(6) Galileo said that. The earth moves.

To utter this is to make two utterances. In uttering the second sentence, one makes oneself a samesayer with Galileo; so the objection to the quotational account does not apply. The first utterance refers to the second (with the demonstrative "that"), refers also to Galileo, and predicates of them that the latter is related to the former by a relation expressed by "said".[6] This relation can be explained[7] in terms of samesaying, on these lines: the first utterance—which predicates the saying relation—would be true in the same circumstances as an utterance of "Some utterance of Galileo's, and this one, make us samesayers", with the demonstrative phrase, "this one", like "that" in (6), heralding and referring to the utterance of the content-sentence by the speaker of the whole.

In a typical self-standing utterance of "The earth moves", "the earth" would refer to the earth; that is, probably, the planet most referred to in discussions of Galileo. Given the identity, the truth of "The earth moves" guarantees the truth of "The planet most referred to in discussions of Galileo moves"; accepting such inferences is part of what it means to accept that "the earth", in "The earth moves", functions as a referring expression. If the sentence "The earth moves" is a semantic component of (1), and if "the earth" in this sentence—the content-sentence—has its ordinary semantic role, then a similar substitution in (1) should preserve truth. But Galileo did not say that the planet most referred to in discussions of Galileo moves.

5. These remarks are clearly meant to refute (5)'s claim to paraphrase (1). Contrast R. J. Haack, "On Davidson's Paratactic Theory of Oblique Contexts": at pp. 351–2 Haack takes (5) as Davidson's own offer of a paraphrase.

6. Predicates, not necessarily asserts. This disposes of one of Haack's difficulties (p. 356) about iterated *oratio obliqua* constructions.

7. Not analysed; see §11 below.

Frege's response is to abandon the assumption that the expressions of the content-sentence have their usual semantic role.[8] But according to Davidson's proposal, the expressions of the content-sentence function exactly as they would be said to function by a satisfactory semantic account of the content-sentence on its own.[9] This thesis is freed from unacceptable inferential implications by the fact that the content-sentence is not represented as a semantic component of the utterance whose truth-value is at issue when we assess the truth or falsehood of an *oratio obliqua* report. The truth of an utterance of "Galileo said that", with "that" taken as a demonstrative whose reference is fixed by pointing, as it were, in the direction of a certain item, could not entail (by virtue of the form of the sentence that expresses the truth in question) the truth of a different utterance of the same sentence, with the reference of the demonstrative fixed by pointing at a different item. But the items pointed at are utterances, by the utterer of the whole report, of sentences whose component expressions are functioning as they would function in ordinary utterances of those sentences; if I say "Galileo said that the earth moves", the phrase "the earth" normally refers, on my lips, to the earth.

An utterance of a content-sentence will not in general be an assertion. (In special circumstances it may be, for instance when prefaced by the explicitly performative "I hereby assert that".) But it would be a groundless prejudice to suppose that in uttering "The earth moves" one cannot be referring to the earth, and predicating of it that it moves, unless one's utterance is an assertion.[10]

4. Davidson's argument against the quotational approach can be summarized as follows. The primitive predicate that figures in a representation of logical form like (4) would need to be explained in terms of samesaying.[11] (How the explanation goes, for the particular case of (4), is sketched in the "awkward paraphrase" (5).) But the explanation introduces undesired possibilities of falsehood. An utterer of (4) says something that should be true just in case he and

8. See Frege, "On Sense and Reference".

9. If the content-sentence itself contains an *oratio obliqua* construction, the paratactic account (*ex hypothesi* a satisfactory semantic account) is applied to it in turn. As far as I can see, this answers the question that leads to the rather mysterious second difficulty Haack finds in iterated *oratio obliqua* constructions (pp. 357–8).

10. Against the prejudice, see P. T. Geach, "Assertion".

11. This would not be an analysis, any more than the similar explanation of the primitive that figures in (6). See n. 7 above, and §11 below.

Galileo are samesayers. If he omits to make them so—as he does if all he says is (4)—then his utterance of (4) should be false. But if he had said (1), he would have been uttering a truth. Under a rephrasing that ought simply to make the primitive clear, the regimentations may be false when what they regiment is true. So the account of logical form cannot be correct.

I shall question this argument on two counts. First, Davidson does not show that the explanation of the quotational primitive would need to appeal to samesaying in such a way as to introduce surplus possibilities of falsehood; another option is open, which he does not argue against. I shall elaborate this in §5. Second, the argument relies on the questionable thesis that to mention a sentence by quoting it is not to use it. I shall elaborate this in §§6–8.

5. The first criticism is independent of the second. So let us assume, for the moment, that to quote the sentence "The earth moves" is not to use it.

Does it follow that someone who only quotes the sentence cannot be a samesayer with Galileo? Obviously it depends on the nature of the samesaying relation. Davidson uses that term in forms like this: "*a*'s utterance *b*, and *c*'s utterance *d*, make *a* and *c* samesayers". So it seems that samesaying is a relation that utterances cause to hold between speakers. But the relation that really does the work, in the suggested explanations of primitives, would be the four-place relation between utterances and speakers, or perhaps the relation between utterances on which the samesaying relation is consequential.[12]

Now one reasonable way to think of utterances is as concrete particular events.[13] We might plausibly say that actual occurrence is to concrete particular events what actual existence is to material objects. So, just as we should be suspicious of the idea that there are possible but non-existent particular people,[14] we should equally be suspicious of the idea that there are possible but non-occurrent particular concrete events. If there are not, then unless one actually makes a suitable utterance—as the quotational approach, on our

12. See Ian McFetridge, "Propositions and Davidson's Account of Indirect Discourse", at pp. 138–9. In "True to the Facts" at p. 52, Davidson says that samesaying "holds between speech acts", i.e., presumably, utterances.

13. Davidson's way; see "Eternal vs. Ephemeral Events".

14. Compare Quine on the possible fat men in a doorway: "On What There Is", p. 4.

present assumption, fails to ensure that one does—one cannot be a samesayer with Galileo; there is nothing to fill one of the argument-places of the four-place relation formulated above.

But must samesaying be thought of this way?

Davidson proposes that we should try to construct Tarskian truth-characterizations for natural languages. At first sight, this project is vulnerable to objection on the ground that, if a language contains indexical elements, it cannot be sentences that are the bearers of truth-values. Davidson's standard response is to modify Tarski: the truth-predicate to be characterized is not, as in Tarski, a one-place predicate of sentences, but a three-place predicate of sentences, utterers, and times. An expression of the three-place truth-predicate takes this form: "*a* is true as potentially uttered by *b* at *c*".[15] This predicate, then, can hold of a sentence, a person, and a time even though the sentence is not then uttered by the person. The predicate gives a way of saying, in effect, that a certain potential utterance would have been true (this is a different use of "true", as a one-place predicate of utterances); but it does not require an ontology of non-actual concrete particulars.[16]

Why should samesaying not be reconstrued on similar lines? On this reconstrual, two speakers will be made samesayers not only by actual utterances of theirs that are, as Davidson puts it, "the same in import" (p. 104), but also by potential utterances that *would* match in import. As before, the appearance of quantifying over potential utterances is dispensable. We can capture the idea in a formulation like Davidson's formulation of his truth-predicate: if sentence *a*, as potentially uttered by person *b* at time *c*, is the same in import as sentence *d*, as potentially uttered by person *e* at time *f*, then *b* and *e* are samesayers in respect of those sentences and times. (As in the truth-predicate, "potentially" need not exclude "actually"; it simply signals that an actual utterance is not required.) On this account of samesaying, I need not utter a sentence in order to be a samesayer with Galileo, any more than I need utter a sentence in order to stand to it and the present moment in the relation expressed by Davidson's truth-predicate. When I claim to be a samesayer with Galileo, with respect to a certain sentence, I can specify the sentence in any way I

15. See Davidson, "Truth and Meaning", p. 34.

16. Talk of the truth-predicate as predicated of sentences may need a non-face-value construal, in view of §§7 and 8 below. Similarly with talk of words and sentences as subjects of predication elsewhere in this essay.

choose; I need not be embarrassed by the accusation that I have only mentioned the sentence and not used it. So if the quotational primitive is explained in terms of samesaying as reconstrued here, Davidson's "subtle flaw" disappears.

On occasion Davidson seems to suggest that there is no fundamental difference between truth-characterizations that deal with his three-place predicate, on the one hand, and truth-characterizations that deal with a one-place predicate of utterances, on the other.[17] We can certainly effect a simple connection between them if we construe utterances as ordered triples of sentences, persons, and times, so that what appears in one theory as a relation between three items becomes, in the other, a monadic property of a triple. But if utterances are construed in this way, there is no doubting the existence of utterances that do not get uttered; at any rate not on the sort of grounds considered above. Given the existence of the relevant sentence, person, and time, the existence of an utterance is guaranteed by part of set theory, whether the person utters the sentence at the time or not. Scepticism would have to be about the required part of set theory. On this construal, utterances are not concrete but abstract particulars. If utterances are thought of in this way, the six-place relation of my last paragraph can be seen as a spelling out of the original four-place relation; and if no suitable sentence gets uttered by me, it no longer follows that we have no occupant for one of the argument-places of the four-place relation.

What objection could there be to this reinterpretation of samesaying? Is the modified relation unintelligible? Surely not; we can explain it in terms of the relation that Davidson considers, as follows: if the relevant sentences are actually uttered by the relevant people at the relevant times, the relations coincide; if either or both of the sentences are not uttered, then the modified relation holds if and only if, had the sentences been uttered by the people at the times, they would have been producing utterances that would have occupied the appropriate argument-places in a true ascription of the four-place relation that Davidson considers.

This partly counterfactual explanation spells out the force of "potentially" in an earlier formulation. Is it objectionable? We have already seen that there is something similar in the theorems of a Davidsonian truth-characterization for a natural language. This is

17. See, e.g., "Truth and Meaning", p. 34; "On Saying That", p. 106, n. 16.

for good reasons. The point and interest of Davidson's truth-characterizations lies in this fact: they would show how the truth-conditions of utterances depend, first, on how the sentences uttered are constructed, by modes of construction exemplified in other sentences too, out of parts that occur in other sentences too; and, second, on the identity of the utterer and the time of utterance. No theory that had this sort of interest, and dealt with a language of even moderate complexity, could restrict itself to actual utterances; it would be bound to have implications about sentences that were constructed in ways it discussed out of parts it discussed, but that happened never to be spoken at all, and similarly implications about sentences as uttered by people who did not utter them, or as uttered at times at which they were not uttered, even if they were uttered by other people and at other times. This is analogous to the way in which, if a language is sufficiently complex, a systematic syntax for it is bound to certify as grammatical some strings that are never actually uttered.

On these lines it appears that, if a truth-theorist does aim to characterize truth as a monadic predicate of utterances, he will need to find a way of construing merely potential utterances as subjects of predication. But, as we saw above, this undermines Davidson's argument against the quotational approach.

We cannot, then, eliminate "potentially" from our formulation of the truth-predicate. Now this is not merely parallel to the partly counterfactual construal of samesaying whose intelligibility I am concerned with. The same considerations apply, in the end, to both cases.

Davidson's claim is that his truth-characterizations would be appropriate components of theories of meaning; that is, theories such that knowledge of what they say would suffice for interpreting utterances in the languages they deal with. The role of a truth-characterization in such a theory would be that the sentences used on the right-hand sides of its theorems—specifications of truth-conditions—could be employed to specify the content of speech acts effected by uttering the sentences mentioned on the left. If a truth-characterization of the appropriate kind tells us that a certain sentence *a*, as uttered by a person *b* at a time *c*, is true if and only if *p*, then it is to be acceptable to interpret *b*'s utterance of *a* at *c* as his saying that *p*. (The implicit limitation to the indicative is an eliminable simplification.)[18]

18. See, e.g., §1 of Essay 1 above.

Now we cannot dispense with the restriction "of the appropriate kind"; not all truth-characterizations that are correct, in that they specify conditions under which utterances really are true, will serve this interpretative purpose.[19] And we cannot explain the restriction without an appeal to the interpretative purpose itself. We cannot first construct a theory about the conditions under which utterances are true, and then draw conclusions about what speakers are saying; rather, we attempt to construct a truth-characterization precisely with a view to the acceptability of using its specifications of truth-conditions as specifications of what speakers are saying.[20]

Of course we can test this acceptability only by how well our interpretations make sense of actual utterances. But the system in the theory means that our theorizing will go beyond the actual. And this will be so not only in specifications of truth-conditions for merely potential utterances, as I have already noted, but also, and by the same token, in hypotheses about what speakers would be saying if they made those potential utterances. To try to construct a truth-characterization of the appropriate kind is inevitably to theorize about the acceptability of counterfactual *oratio obliqua* reports. If these reports must be understood in terms of samesaying, then no one who is prepared to theorize in this way can object to the counterfactual used above in the explanation of the modified samesaying relation.[21]

(It may be thought that we ought not to allow people to be actual samesayers by virtue of merely potential utterances. But if it is conceded that the counterfactual reports are intelligible, this point is only terminological. Say, if you like, no more than the following: if the people had made the utterances, they would have been samesayers—Davidson's samesaying, counterfactually employed. This still gives materials for an explanation of the quotational primitive, even if quoting a sentence is not using it. Thus: if I were now to

19. See the Introduction to Evans and McDowell, eds., *Truth and Meaning*, pp. xiii–xv.

20. It might seem that Davidson's account of radical interpretation in terms of the idea of holding-true (see "Radical Interpretation") bypasses the need to check the acceptability of hypotheses about what people say in testing a truth-characterization. But I believe any such appearance would be misleading.

21. The non-actuality introduced by these counterfactual *oratio obliqua* reports is at the other end of the samesaying relation, so to speak: in the reported utterance, rather than—as in the cases for which modified samesaying was introduced—the reporting utterance. But why should this matter?

utter the sentence "The earth moves", then that utterance and an utterance that Galileo made would have rendered Galileo and me samesayers. On this account, a more perspicuous "awkward paraphrase" than (5) would be

(7) Galileo uttered a sentence that meant in his mouth what "The earth moves" would mean now in mine.

And (7) is certainly less economical than (6). But this is not Davidson's point. Given the intelligibility of counterfactual *oratio obliqua* reports, (7) is immune to Davidson's argument against (5).)

There is a sense in which, on the view sketched above, the "judgements of synonymy" involved in ascriptions of samesaying are at the foundations of a theory of a particular language; this seems to contradict a remark of Davidson's that I quoted above ("On Saying That", p. 104).[22] The point Davidson should be making is not that judgements of samesaying are not fundamental in constructing a theory of a language, but rather that such judgements are not grounded in some deeper level, at which one recognizes that there is a single meaning, shared by the utterances that underlie a case of samesaying. (Compare §11 below.)

Dealing with formal languages, Tarski could take the notion of translation for granted, as determined by stipulation, and work from there to a characterization of truth. Davidson points out that when we say what it is to construct a semantic description of a natural language, we cannot simply recapitulate Tarski's procedure, since translation can no longer be taken for granted.[23] Now I am not suggesting that firm judgements of samesaying are made in advance of constructing a truth-characterization, when one interprets a foreign language from scratch; nor that the question what someone is saying—a question whose true answer is systematically determined by the words he utters and the context of utterance—is intelligible independently of the idea of something like a truth-characterization. So I am not making myself liable to Davidson's strictures.

22. Contrast "True to the Facts", p. 53, where Davidson speaks of "devising a theory of translation that does not depend upon, but rather founds, whatever there is to the concept of meaning"; this is nearer what I want.

23. Davidson, "In Defence of Convention T", pp. 73–4; "Radical Interpretation", p. 134.

But it seems wrong to suggest, as Davidson does, that we should reverse Tarski's direction.[24] I claimed above that we do not know independently what a truth-characterization of the appropriate kind is, and use the construction of such a truth-characterization as a route to judgements of samesaying (judgements about what people are saying). On the contrary, we have no notion of what the appropriate kind is except in terms of the acceptability of judgements about what people are saying. Constructing a truth-characterization of the appropriate kind, and putting oneself in a position systematically to interpret what people say, are a single activity; no worthwhile procedure moves in either direction. Nevertheless, there remains this sense in which we can say that the second description of the activity is nearer the foundations: it is by way of the question whether its implications about what people say are acceptable that a truth-characterization is confronted with the behavioural facts on which it rests.

6. The second objection to Davidson's argument is this: he does not show that there is no workable account of quotation according to which, if one quotes a sentence, one is thereby effecting an utterance of it. Armed with such an account of quotation, we could defend the quotational approach without needing to query whether actual utterances are required for the samesaying relation.

A workable account of quotation, for the purpose at hand, is one that shows how the occurrence of quotation in a stretch of discourse does not block the systematic assignment of truth-conditions.

It is natural to begin with the assumption that quotations are singular terms. (This was taken for granted in the development of the quotational approach that I outlined in §2.) Systematic assignment of truth-conditions requires that the singular terms be seen as structured combinations of components from a finite stock.[25]

Davidson (p. 97) sketches an account that exploits the structure articulated by spelling. A full-dress version might be as follows. There would be somewhat over thirty base clauses, each fixing what is denoted by the result of enclosing a letter (including spaces and punctuation marks) in quotation marks—namely, in each case, the letter itself; and a recursive clause dealing in the obvious way with

24. See the Introduction to Evans and McDowell, eds., *Truth and Meaning*, pp. xiii–xv.
25. See Davidson, "Theories of Meaning and Learnable Languages".

concatenation, treated perhaps as an iterable two-place functional expression that yields complex quotations when its argument-places are filled with quotations. The quotation "'the'" (say) is treated as abbreviating "('t' concatenated with 'h') concatenated with 'e'". The upshot is that any string consisting of left-hand quotes, a concatenation of letters, and right-hand quotes denotes the concatenation of letters: "'The earth moves'" denotes "The earth moves".

This account treats quotation as a variant notation for spelling out the quoted material. Reformulated in a way that makes explicit the semantic structure credited to it on this view, (4) becomes something like this:

(8) Galileo said-true, in my sense, the result of concatenating the following in this order: "t", "h", "e", " ", "e", "a", "r", "t", "h", " ", "m", "o", "v", "e", "s".

As Davidson says (p. 104), an utterance of "The earth moves" is not to be found in an utterance of (8). If this reformulation accurately reflects the semantic structure of (4), then any appearance that in uttering (4) one utters the sentence quoted is a mere accident of notation.

But this conclusion is rather hard to believe. (Try saying (4) aloud.) Davidson claims to find the spelling account of quotation "all but explicit in Quine" (p. 97), but Quine's discussion of spelling is offered not as a theory of the semantics of quotation but as an account of "an alternative device to the same purpose".[26] This seems the right description. Besides its desirable results (such as "'"The earth moves"' denotes 'The earth moves'"), the spelling account also serves up consequences like this: "'zxwt prt gjh'" denotes "zxwt prt gjh". Not that this is to be objected to on the ground that it assigns a semantic property to something we cannot say (let alone understand); we can *write* "'zxwt prt gjh'", and if it is written for an appropriate purpose—namely, to say something about that string of letters—we do understand it. But we are under no obligation to suppose that what we write and understand in such a case is a quotation.[27]

The structure articulated by spelling is not the only structure discernible in written quotation. There is also the superficial syntactic

26. *Word and Object,* p. 143.
27. Compare P. T. Geach, *Mental Acts,* pp. 85–6.

structure marked by spaces between words; and (with some complications) we can find the same structure in spoken language, marked by possibilities of alternative combinations. Exploiting this, we could construct an account that would be formally parallel to the spelling account. I shall sketch the idea, to begin with, in a version suited to quotations written according to standard modern English practice. Each base clause would assign a denotation to the result of enclosing a word in quotation marks, namely, the word itself. (The number of base clauses, in an account that deals with quotation of, say, English, would still be finite, though of course much larger.) The recursive clause would be as before. As before, "'The earth moves'" denotes "The earth moves". (Equally, "'Moves earth the'" denotes "Moves earth the". But "'zxwt prt gjh'" is not given a denotation by this theory.) There is an informal version of this account of quotation in P. T. Geach's *Mental Acts.*[28]

We can take the semantic treatment I have just described as formalizing the following view of quotation, in a way appropriate, so far, for the quotation-mark notation. All words are ambiguous in one extra dimension, over and above any we need to recognize apart from quotation: any word can occur as a name of itself. When uses of words that require this autonymous interpretation are concatenated, concatenation is not, as usual, a mere method of syntactic construction, but takes on the descriptive significance registered in our recursive clause. So the concatenation of the words "the", "earth" and "moves", in that order, with the words bearing their autonymous interpretation, denotes the concatenation of the words "the", "earth" and "moves", in that order.

Actual marks of quotation are treated here as a dispensable notational convention.[29] The purpose of the convention is to disambiguate; the notation allows us to indicate explicitly which interpretation of ambiguous expressions is intended. Apart from the greater generality of the convention, flanking words with quotation marks is on a par with writing "bank_1" when one means a financial institution and "bank_2" when one means a configuration of terrain. No one could suppose that embellishing an occurrence of "bank" with a subscript prevented it from being a use of a word. Similarly, then,

28. See especially pp. 81–3.
29. Nothing corresponds to quotation marks in standard *speech*.

with quotation marks: on the present account of quotation, there is nothing to prevent us from saying that words written within quotation marks are used, with the quotation marks serving the purpose of explicitly requiring the autonymous interpretation (and also of indicating, as noted above, that concatenation in the context acquires a descriptive significance).

On this view, it is after all misleading to state the semantic theory in terms of the quotation-mark notation. What we want is a general account of how words work in contexts of quotation. The effect of the previous base clauses can be achieved by a simple quantification over words: any word in such a context denotes itself.[30] (The domain of this quantification would be fixed by the syntax that is anyway a prerequisite to a semantic description of a language.) Otherwise the theory can be as before. Where we mention quotation marks is in a general account of the contexts in which this fragment of the semantics of the language applies. One such context is the kind indicated in writing by quotation marks. But we can recognize that there are other ways in which the intention to quote is signalled. (Sometimes we discern quotation simply because no other interpretation makes sense.)

Quotation marks, or—better now—inverted commas, serve not only to indicate quotation as here understood. We have already envisaged examples like

(9) The machine printed out "zxwt prt gjh".

And there is also transcription of vocal sounds, as in

(10) The song begins "a wop bop a loo bop a lop bam boom".

For (9), if we assume (as so far with quotations) that "'zxwt prt gjh'" is a singular term, we need something like Davidson's spelling account. We might parallel the suggested treatment of quotation marks in quoting: the spelling theory is labelled as applicable to con-

30. A simplification not previously available. We might have tried writing: the result of enclosing any word (letter) in quotation marks is an expression that denotes that word (letter). But "(w)('w' denotes w)" involves quantification into the scope of quotation marks; that this is intelligible, and how, is surely something to be demonstrated by an account of the semantics of quotation, not presupposed in it.

texts of copying, with inverted commas figuring, again, in a general gloss on the label, as a device for signalling such contexts. For (10), a spelling account would miss the point. Here we need an analogue to the spelling account, with phonemes substituted for letters. (There is a complication: a straightforward analogue would have concatenations of phonemes denoting themselves, but what is written between inverted commas in (10) is not a string of phonemes. The phoneme-spelling theory would apply to a spoken version of (10); we should think of (10), as it stands, as our written representation of what is primarily a spoken form. Similarly, (9) is primarily a written form.)

According to this picture, then, inverted commas signal one of at least three kinds of context: quotation, letter-by-letter copying, and vocal mimicry. This diversity is not a ground for disliking the theory, or set of theories, that I have described. The roles of inverted commas have a common feature that makes the diversity intelligible. In each case inverted commas signal autonymy: in the first case selecting the autonymous interpretation from among others to which the surrounding matter might be susceptible, in the other two indicating the only way in which the surrounded matter can in general be interpreted at all.

(The idea of autonymy helps to explain the sense in which (9) is primarily a written form and (10) primarily a spoken one. We have autonymy—letters denoting letters—only in the written form of (9). A spoken version might be transcribable thus:

(11) The machine printed out zed-ex-doubleyu-tee pee-ar-tee gee-jay-aitch;

where it is names of letters that denote letters, rather than the letters themselves. Analogously, we have autonymy—phonemes denoting phonemes—only in the spoken form of (10). As I noted above, the written version uses, to denote phonemes, something other than the phonemes themselves: namely, strings of letters such that to read them aloud as if they were words, according to standard principles of English spelling, is to utter the phonemes.)[31]

On the present view, the quotation fragment of a semantic description of English would deal with the autonymous use of English

31. Slightly untidily, it is the written form that has the inverted commas.

words only. (Recall that the domain of quantification, in what replaces the base clauses, is to be fixed by a syntax for our object language.) So such a theory would not handle sentences like

(12) He said "Sprechen Sie Deutsch?".

We might consider dealing with (12) in terms of spelling or mimicry; no doubt such an account would accurately reflect any understanding of (12) that is available to someone wholly ignorant of German. But we can also countenance another possible level of understanding, in which what follows "said" is understood as quotation in a sense that contrasts with spelling or mimicry. A semantic treatment that reflected this level of understanding would draw on the quotation fragment of a semantic description of German, and so represent (12) as a hybrid, not wholly in English.[32] (Notice that this level of understanding would not require comprehension of the standard meaning of the quoted words; the semantic treatment would draw on no more than a syntax for German and that fragment of the semantics that deals with the autonymous use of words.)

The account of quotation I have sketched in this section seems to protect the possibility of systematically assigning truth-conditions, by showing how denotations can be systematically assigned to quotations. But quoting the concatenation of words that constitutes a sentence is regarded as a (special) use of that concatenation of words. Certainly someone who utters (4) or (5) does not assert the sentence "The earth moves"; this matches Davidson's own (6), and is as it should be. But on the proposed view of quotation, such a person does utter the sentence. So if this account of quotation is acceptable, it undermines Davidson's complaint that an utterer of (4) or (5) has not made himself a samesayer with Galileo.

7. If quoting words is mentioning them by using them in a special, self-denoting way, then the denotation of a quotation depends on the identity of the words used in it. Now, what is a word? A view urged by Geach is that inscriptional or phonetic match does not suffice for word-identity; according to Geach, the German word "ja" (meaning

32. Compare Geach, *Mental Acts*, p. 90.

"yes") and the Polish word "ja" (meaning "I") are two different words.[33]

From the standpoint of this view of Geach's, there was something wrong with the development of the quotational approach that I outlined in §2. The ground for adding a third argument-place to the regimentations was that, in its intended interpretation, the original two-place relation of saying-true could both hold and fail to hold between a person and a sentence, since one and the same sentence might also belong to, say, Martian, and have a different sense in that language. But according to Geach's view of word-identity this ground was false. Whatever it is that conceivably belongs to Martian, it cannot be the very sentence we use in English, since it does not consist of the same words. If we do specify a language in a quotational regimentation, it must be as in

(13) Galileo said-true the English sentence "The earth moves"

where "English" must be taken as part of a complex singular term, designating the second argument of a two-place predicate. Its point is to make clear which sentence is used in the quotation, and hence which sentence is denoted by it.[34]

"In my sense", in (4), took over the purpose of "in English", in (3); and we are now seeing that purpose as being to make clear the identity of the second argument of a two-place predicate. Now it might seem that we could reason as follows. The reconstrued purpose of "in my sense" is presumably to indicate that the sentence designated is the one that the utterer of (4) would be using if, in uttering the quotation, he were using a sentence. But on the present view of quotation he *is* using a sentence when he utters the quotation. It would be pointless to preface everything one said with "This is in my sense". So must not "in my sense", in (4), be superfluous? (Recall the suspicion of redundancy that I mentioned at the end of §2.)

But this line of thought is superficial. It would be equally pointless to make a general practice of specifying the language in which one

33. *Mental Acts,* pp. 86–7.

34. See Geach, *Mental Acts,* pp. 86–7; and, for a corollary about the idea of language-relative truth-predicates, pp. 97–8.

was speaking. But one need not always speak one's own usual language or that of one's interlocutors. On the assumption that one speaks the words one quotes, sentences like (12) yield examples of slipping into another language, though of course such slipping is possible independently of quotation. Equiformities between languages can thus generate real possibilities of misunderstanding, which one can sensibly aim to avert by specifying the language to which a potentially confusing utterance is to be taken as belonging. Similarly, one can slip out of one's own usual idiom, while remaining, in any ordinary sense, in the same language—perhaps in a kind of play-acting, but equally in quoting words as they would be used by speakers of a different dialect; and here adding "in my sense" or "in your sense" might be the best way to avert similar possibilities of misunderstanding. So "in my sense" is not generally superfluous. If changing the dialect, like changing the language, gives a new word, "in my sense" must be thought of, like "in English", as part of a complex singular term, with the qualification helping to make it clear what is designated by a quotation.

Now there are at least two difficulties here for an account of quotation on Geach's lines.

First, how exactly do the qualifying phrases work? Geach says that the specifications of languages "logically attach not to the predicates . . . but to the subject".[35] But how does "English sentence" (for example) function in the putative complex singular term "the English sentence 'The earth moves'"?

We cannot assimilate its functioning to that of "whom we met yesterday" in "the Jones whom we met yesterday". For "Jones" in this phrase must be understood as a predicate univocally true of Joneses.[36] The Jones we met yesterday and the Jones we met the day before would each be a Jones in the same sense. The sense is, roughly, that they are named "Jones": "Jones"—one and the same name—is a name of each Jones. A parallel account of "the English sentence 'The earth moves'" and "the Martian sentence 'The earth moves'" would represent "'The earth moves'"—one and the same name, in an extended sense—as a name of each of the two sentences. But this contradicts Geach's account of the identity of quoted words.

35. *Mental Acts*, p. 87.
36. See Tyler Burge, "Reference and Proper Names".

Perhaps we could preserve that account by claiming that the qualifying phrases function like subscripts, in the disambiguating notation that I envisaged in §6. The subscripts signal that "bank" in "$bank_1$" (a word for a financial institution) and "bank" in "$bank_2$" (a word for a configuration of terrain) are not a single word;[37] just as, according to Geach, "'The earth moves'", in "the English sentence 'The earth moves'", and "'The earth moves'", in "the Martian sentence 'The earth moves'", are not a single expression. However, it would be pointless to look for semantic structure within "$bank_1$". The subscript is inscriptionally attached to "bank", but not semantically attached to anything. There is no semantic unit (for instance a word; in this notation "bank" is not a word) for it to be attached to. If this is a good parallel to what Geach's account requires, the account is hard to swallow. Geach's phrase "logically attach" suggests that he would not like the parallel; but if the phrase is meant to imply semantic attachment, then the manner of semantic attachment needs explaining.

Second, if the identity of words depends on the identity of languages (or, in the extension that I considered above in connection with "in my sense", on the identity of dialects), then words become problematic as objects of reference. Recall the motivation I ascribed to Quine, in §2 above, for preferring the third version of the quotational approach to the second. From a Quinean standpoint, languages as a kind of entity should be no more acceptable than meanings. Indeed, the ideas seem interdefinable: two speakers speak the same language when a sufficient number of their equiform utterances have the same meaning.[38] Words, conceived in Geach's way, would be in the same boat. When Geach puts forward a quotational account of indirect discourse, he discusses objections that presuppose a notion of synonymy sharp enough to warrant the thought that there is a meaning that two synonymous expressions both have. He re-

37. Note that any general thesis to the effect that ambiguity is plurality of words would need an exception for the proposed autonymous interpretation; otherwise autonymously used words could not name words that can also be used for other purposes.

38. Compare Davidson, "On Saying That", p. 99. We can distinguish dialects, within languages, by altering the conditions for equiformity, or our view of what counts as a sufficient number; this introduces extra indeterminacies, but for present purposes the essential point is the appearance of "have the same meaning". A variant of this gloss on "speak the same language", not designed to certify languages (or words) as proper objects of reference, will emerge in §11 below.

sponds like this: "I should demand of such a critic: 'What is your criterion of synonymy?'—with very little hope of getting a coherent answer".[39] But it appears that, in order to give the identity-conditions of the objects of reference required by his account of quotation, Geach needs the very sort of conceptual apparatus whose availability he here concurs with Quine in doubting.

Geach's view of word-identity is not a mere afterthought, readily detachable from an account of quotation like the one I outlined in §6. The only plausible alternative is a view of word-identity as determined by inscriptional or phonetic indistinguishability, or a combination of the two. But on such a view, given the conceivability of our speculation about Martian, there is no reason to say that, when one utters "'The earth moves'" in the course of uttering (4) or (5), one is designating (by making a special use of) English words in particular. Davidson's argument is thus reinstated: if I am not speaking English words when I utter sounds transcribable as "The earth moves", only an illusion could seem to justify confidence that I thereby make myself a samesayer with Galileo. On this view, the quotation is a self-sufficient singular term; what it designates is, once more, something found equally in English and in our hypothetical Martian, and we are back to the justification for a third argument-place originally envisaged in §2. In this context there no longer seems to be any reason to object to the idea that quotation functions by sheer reproduction of strings of letters or phonemes. But the point of the account of quotation in §6 was largely to insist on a distinction between quotation and mere reproduction.

8. The difficulties disappear if we change tack, and query the assumption, so far unchallenged, that quotations are structured singular terms.

In his John Locke lectures (given in Oxford in 1970), Davidson pointed out that the assumption is anyway untenable for sentences like

(14) Geach says that they "logically attach to the subject".[40]

39. *Mental Acts,* p. 90; in support Geach cites Quine, *From a Logical Point of View.*
40. See "Quotation".

This is a grammatical sentence, but it could not be (barring intolerably ad hoc modifications to syntactic theory) if what follows the first four words were a singular term. Such sentences cry out for a paratactic account of logical form. (14) is well regimented by

(15) Geach says that they logically attach to the subject,
in part by uttering this;

where the arrow and bracket indicate the reference of the demonstrative.

In (14) the material surrounded by quotation marks is part of the sentence in which the quotation marks appear.[41] But once we have a paratactic account of sentences such as (14), it is natural to extend it to sentences such as (2), yielding a representation of form like Davidson's (6) in that the quoted material is not part of the sentence asserted by one who asserts (2):

(16) Galileo said-true this. The earth moves.

What is referred to by the demonstrative in an utterance of (16)? It is not, at first sight, obvious that there is anything to prevent us from saying this: it is an item indistinguishable in all respects from that referred to by the demonstrative in an utterance of Davidson's own (6). In that case, if an utterer of (6) is immune to criticism on the ground that he has failed to make himself a samesayer with Galileo, an utterer of (16) should be likewise immune, and the quotational approach seems, once more, not liable to Davidson's objection. (The details of this argument will be modified in §10.)

Our question about the semantic role of expressions like "the English sentence", in "the English sentence 'The earth moves'", is answered by obvious applications of the paratactic machinery. (13), for instance, becomes something like this:

(17) The earth moves. That is an English sentence, and it was
said-true by Galileo.

We can now bypass the problem about the identity-conditions of words. The theory need not speak of reference to anything over and

41. Namely, "They 'logically attach to the subject'"; not (14). (See §3 above.)

above utterances: concrete particular events of writing or vocalizing. Many sentences seem, at first sight, to involve reference to words. But our theory can shirk the commitments that would be imposed by such an interpretation; we find reference only to utterances, and ensure acceptable construals of the sentences by means of an appropriate understanding of their predicates.[42]

The desirable distinction between quoting and mere reproduction is now located as a distinction between different sorts of predicate of utterances. Suppose someone makes inscriptions equiform with "The earth moves" and "zxwt prt gjh". In both cases he does what is, at a certain level of description, the same kind of thing, namely, effecting an utterance (in a broad sense). But there are properties that are not shared. In the first case the inscriber and his inscription may well stand in a certain complex relation to an equiform inscription by me: a relation that will serve to explain a two-place predicate, "____ writes the English words ____", which we can find in

(18) He wrote the English words "The earth moves".

In the second case the inscriber stands in no such relation to any inscription of mine. He stands in a different relation to an inscription I can produce: a relation that will serve to explain a different two-place predicate, discernible in

(19) He wrote the letters "zxwt prt gjh".

(This second relation holds in the first case also, but the first relation holds only there.) Predications explicable in terms of the first relation are typical cases of quoting; predications explicable in terms of the second are typical cases of reproduction.

The paratactic account of quotation has the advantage that concatenation no longer need be thought to play the dual role that I noted in §6. We might have wondered whether the utterance of "The earth moves" that we managed to find in, say, (4) could really be an utterance of the familiar sentence "The earth moves", as it

42. This manoeuvre is precisely analogous to the way Davidson's account of *oratio obliqua* obviates the need to find reference to propositions. Some find the claim to avoid problematic ontology fraudulent in the latter case, and will presumably find it fraudulent here too. I postpone discussing this until §11.

needed to be for the aim of defending the quotational approach against Davidson's objection. In the quotation, concatenation would be playing the role of a descriptive quasi-expression; but surely it plays no such role in the sentence. (I suppressed this doubt in §6 because I wanted to make the account of quotation as attractive as possible.)

Our current understanding of the quotational (2) is represented in (16). It is a question how, if at all, this differs from Davidson's (6).[43] I shall argue, in §10, that there is a difference, and that (6) is superior. But first I want to mention a consideration that has been thought favourable to quotational accounts of *oratio obliqua.*

9. Quine has made us familiar with a distinction, within a set of idioms that includes *oratio obliqua* reports, between forms that block the intersubstitution of co-referring singular terms and forms that do not.[44] As I noted in §3, from (1) and the identity of the earth with the planet most referred to in discussions of Galileo, we cannot standardly infer

(20) Galileo said that the planet most referred to in discussions of Galileo moves.

But we seem to be able to understand a different form of report, happily expressed by

(21) Galileo said of the earth that it moves,

in which we can, *salva veritate,* make such substitutions for "the earth". One reason why it seems that we must recognize the distinct form of (21) is that we appear to understand quantifications like

(22) There is something Galileo said to move.

And we cannot see this, or some such regimentation as

43. The difference is not that a form like (2) needs expansion on the lines of (3) or (4). If there is a need to avert potential misunderstanding of which language I am speaking, or in whose sense, when I utter words for purposes of quotation in uttering (2), construed as (16), then there is just the same need in the case of (6).

44. See, e.g., "Quantifiers and Propositional Attitudes".

(23) $(\exists x)$ (Galileo said that x moves),

as constructed by quantification from a complex predicate, "Galileo said that _____ moves", found also in (1), from which (23), on this view, would be seen as derivable by existential generalization. For we could make sense of such a derivation only if "the earth" occurred in (1) as a singular term, and one that referred there to the earth, since it would be the earth that made (23) true. But, as I noted in §3, the failure of substitution prevents us from supposing that this is so.[45] The upshot is that we seem to need two different primitive forms, exemplified in (1) and (21). A unification would be desirable.

Now consider the quotational regimentation (2). On an account of quotation like the one I outlined in §6, the quotation in (2) is a structural description. It consists of a concatenation of denoting expressions. There is no reason why the positions occupied by these expressions should not be accessible to variables bound by initial quantifiers. We can register this by constructing, from (2), the open sentence

(24) Galileo said-true α & "moves"

where the Greek letter is a variable to range over expressions,[46] and "&" is a sign of concatenation. (2) can be reconstituted from (24) by constructing, out of the putative singular term "'the earth'", what we might call "an individual quantifier", and using it to bind (24)'s variable, thus:

(25) "The earth" is an α such that Galileo said-true α & "moves".

The item denoted by the putative singular term (on an account of quotation like that of §6) stands in various relations to the earth: for instance, denoting it. A schematic representation of the form in which such relations are ascribed is

45. If "the earth" is a singular term referring to the earth, then it does not occur in (1), or, more exactly, it does not occur in the utterance that is assessed for truth when we determine the truth-value of an utterance of (1). The consequent of this is Davidson's position; see §3 above.

46. On the reason why a special style of variable is advisable, see David Kaplan, "Quantifying In", pp. 213–4.

(26) *R* ("'the earth'", the earth).

Here again, "the earth" occupies a position accessible to a variable; we can write

(27) "The earth" is an α such that *R* (α, the earth).

From (25) and (27) we have

(28) ($\exists\alpha$) (*R*(α, the earth) and Galileo said-true α & "moves").

And, since "the earth" occupies a referential position in (28), we can derive

(29) ($\exists x$) ($\exists\alpha$) (*R*(α,x) and Galileo said-true α & "moves").

Now it is attractive to suppose that, with a suitable interpretation of "*R*", (28) will serve as an analysis of (21), and (29) as a rendering of (22). And the only primitive relation of saying expressed in (28) and (29) is the relation expressed in (2), the quotational regimentation of (1). This unification of the conceptual apparatus of (1) and (21) might seem a reason in favour of a quotational approach.[47]

But unification of primitives is possible on the paratactic approach too. There is an independent argument for finding further structure, not hitherto needed, in Davidson's (6), thus:

(30) ($\exists x$) (Said (Galileo, x, this)). The earth moves.[48]

And now (21) can be represented thus:

(31) ($\exists x$) (Of (the earth, x) and Said (Galileo, x, this)). It moves.[49]

Once again, the same primitive saying relation is expressed in both.

47. For this proposal, and suggestions about "*R*" (including giving it an extra argument-place), see Kaplan, "Quantifying In". Compare Geach, *Mental Acts,* pp. 92–5.

48. See Davidson, "The Logical Form of Action Sentences".

49. For a more precise proposal on these lines, see Jennifer Hornsby, "Saying Of".

An inclination to prefer the former unification may be fuelled by the currency of such labels as "exportation",[50] for the inference from forms like (1) to forms like (21), or "quantifying in",[51] for the inference from forms like (1) to forms like (22). The quotational approach does not treat these inferences as formally valid, but it does treat them as proceeding, in the presence of an extra premise expressed in terms of "*R*", by formal manipulations of expressions that occur in the sentences from whose truth the inferences proceed ((1) in our case); and this conforms to what the labels suggest. Nothing similar could be said about an inference from (30), together with a further premise formulated in the terms used in an acceptable account of what it is for an utterance to be "of" something, to (31). But of course what the labels suggest is simply a denial of the paratactic theory's most striking claim, namely, that the expressions in question do not occur in the sentences in question. And the currency of the labels is not in itself an argument in favour of this denial.

In any case, the quotational unification depends essentially on an account of quotation like the one I outlined in §6; and the difficulties that I mentioned in §7 still threaten any such account.[52]

10. What is the difference between (6) and (16)?

Consider first what should be paradigm cases of quotation, namely, *oratio recta* reports like

(32) He said "The earth moves".

On a paratactic account of quotation this becomes

(33) He said this. The earth moves.

The primitive "said" of Davidson's (6) is explicable in terms of samesaying, which is intuitively expressible in terms of a match in content between a pair of utterances. Analogously, the different

50. Quine, "Quantifiers and Propositional Attitudes", p. 188.
51. Kaplan' s title.
52. There is a further difficulty over whether, in view of the cardinality of the set of expressions, the quotational account can be generally adequate for sentences like (22).

primitive "said" of (33) should be explicable in terms of a relation intuitively expressible by "is an utterance of the same sentence as".[53]

A pair of ordinary utterances by me of a sentence like "That cat is hungry" will not, in general, make me a samesayer with myself. Context may determine that the reference is to different cats. But the relation that underlies the *oratio recta* "said" (call it "the quoting relation") holds between such utterances.

Such a sentence may serve as content-sentence in an *oratio obliqua* report, thus:

(34) He says that that cat is hungry.

A quotational regimentation, parallel to (2), is

(35) He says-true "That cat is hungry".

And the paratactic account of quotation yields, parallel to (16), this:

(36) He says-true this. That cat is hungry.

Now obviously the *oratio obliqua* "says-true" of (36) cannot, like the *oratio recta* "said" of (33), be understood simply in terms of the quoting relation (compare §2 above). As Davidson urges (compare §3 above), something like samesaying must also enter into an account of it. But if there is to be any point in claiming that (36) exploits the apparatus of quotation in representing the logical form of (34)—that "says-true" is a quotational *oratio obliqua* primitive—then varying the identity of the utterance demonstrated in an utterance of (36) should not affect truth-value as long as the substitutively demonstrated utterance bears the quoting relation to the original.

But if this is right, the quotational approach to *oratio obliqua* is in trouble. If a given utterance of (36) by me does indeed lay bare the logical form of an utterance of (34), I should be able to achieve the same again with a subsequent utterance of (36), in circumstances in which, if I were saying "That cat is hungry" on my own behalf, I

53. This intuitive expression of the relation should not mislead us. We cannot simply assume that "x is an utterance of the same sentence as y" can be explained as "$(\exists z)(z$ is a sentence and x is an utterance of z and y is an utterance of $z)$". Compare §7 above and §11 below.

would be referring to a different cat. But if the first demonstrated utterance made me a samesayer with the person I aim to report when I utter (34), it will only be an accident if the second does so too. And if the context in which the second demonstrated utterance is made is somehow blocked from determining reference to the wrong cat, how could the context in which the first demonstrated utterance was made determine reference to the right one?

The utterance that, according to a paratactic account of quotation, is demonstratively referred to when one quotes "That cat is hungry"—call it "u_1"—may be indistinguishable, in respect of all properties other than those it acquires or loses by virtue of the fact that what one predicates of it is quotational, from the utterance demonstratively referred to in a version of (34) on the lines of Davidson's (6)—call it "u_2" (compare §8 above). Utterance u_1 may occur in a context in which, if it were not made for purposes of quotation, reference would be fixed, by interaction between the context and the sense of "that cat", to a certain cat. But given that what is said about u_1 is quotational, an utterance of the same sentence in a context in which, quotation aside, reference would not be fixed to the same cat should serve just as well as a subject of the predication in question; this is the claim I have made in the last two paragraphs. It follows that when an utterance is made in order to quote it, even if it occurs in a context that would otherwise determine references for expressions whose sense is insufficient to do so, like "that cat", the fact that what is said about it is quotational divests it of what would otherwise be a property consequential on occurrence in such a context, namely, that the expressions refer as so determined. Thus u_1 and u_2 do after all differ (compare §8), even if made in similar contexts, in that context enters into the interpretation of u_2 but is precluded from doing so with u_1 by the fact that what is predicated of it is quotational.

This generates a fatal tension in the putatively quotational *oratio obliqua* primitive "says-true". A samesaying component is evidently required in any explication of it that fits it to be an *oratio obliqua* primitive; and this demands that context operate to determine reference where the sense of a referring expression does not suffice on its own. But the quotational component thwarts this demand.[54]

54. Obviously modifying (35) on the lines of (3) or (4) will not meet the difficulty.

On a paratactic account of quotation, there is no reason to say that quoted words are not uttered. This is not why an utterer of (35) fails to make himself a samesayer with someone who says that a certain cat is hungry. So the modification, two paragraphs back, to the argument of §8 does not reinstate Davidson's objection to a quotational account of *oratio obliqua.* But the present objection suggests a different reading of his words "the theory brings the content-sentence into the act sealed in quotation marks" (p. 104): not that the words of the content-sentence are not used at all, but that the quotation marks seal them off from their context in such a way as to prevent interpretation of context-dependent referring expressions.[55]

It might seem possible to repair the quotational approach. Can we not construct predicates of utterances that are quotational but whose sense nevertheless cancels the usual sealing-off effect of quotation? Then we would be able to achieve the effect of an *oratio obliqua* report by making sure the demonstrated utterance is in a suitable context, and applying to it a suitable predicate, explicable in terms of samesaying and quoting together, that has the cancelling force. But why should we count a paratactic form that lacks the sealing-off effect as quotational? In particular, it would be a confusion to suppose that Davidson's three-place truth-predicate, with quotation paratactically construed, is just such a form. The truth-predicate does not in general cancel insulation from context. It makes room for explicit mention of relevant features of potential contexts. Certainly if the extra argument-places are occupied by the utterer of the demonstrated utterance and the time at which he utters it, the upshot is tantamount to a cancellation of the sealing-off effect. But the sealing-off effect of quotation is required for a proper understanding of such uses of the truth-predicate as

(37) "I am hot" is true as said by you now.

Intuitively speaking, quotation is a device for talking about words in abstraction from the circumstances in which the words happen to

55. The sealing-off effect does not work in examples like (14). If I say "Davidson finds the spelling account of quotation 'all but explicit in Quine'", it is important that I should be referring to the author of *Word and Object.* In such cases it is as if the words in question occurred twice, inside and outside quotation marks ((15) brings this out nicely); the occurrence outside quotation marks explains how context can affect interpretation. There is something similar in forms like (35).

be produced for purposes of such talk. The account of quotation that I sketched in §8 does not allow us to put it quite like that: in quotation, on this account, we talk not about words but about utterances. But the thesis that quotational predicates insulate quotationally demonstrated utterances from the usual interpretative impact of context is a suitable substitute, in the environment of this account, for the intuitive formulation.

There seems to be no point in calling a paratactic form "quotational" unless its predicate has the sealing-off effect. But in the end there is no need to insist on this terminological policy. What we can say is this: a quotational account of *oratio obliqua,* with quotation understood paratactically, is either unsatisfactory or indistinguishable from Davidson's account.

11. Failures of inferences involving substitution and quantification have seemed to some philosophers to justify the thesis that *oratio obliqua* reports relate speakers to propositions, construed as meanings of sentences. Words in "that"-clauses are taken to denote their own meanings—items that determine the meanings of sentences in which the words occur—and it becomes unsurprising that words whose normal denotation is the same should not be intersubstitutable in these contexts if their meanings differ. On this view, it is an application of a principle indispensable in the plainest extensional logic that pairs of words with the same meaning are intersubstitutable, *salva veritate,* in "that"-clauses of *oratio obliqua.*[56] However, pairs of synonyms that behave as expected fail to come to light (the Paradox of Analysis), and this might make us suspicious of the whole idea. Davidson's theory makes the idea superfluous: it yields accounts of logical form such that, without finding reference to meanings, we can see that there was no reason on grounds of form to expect the problematic inferences to go through (see §3).

This avoidance of reference to meanings may seem only a temporary subterfuge. Surely, it may be said, the idea of propositions, as entities that *oratio obliqua* reports are to be construed as referring to or quantifying over, will re-emerge when we look into the samesaying relation. What is it for a pair of utterances to make their utterers samesayers, if not that they are utterances of the same proposition?[57]

56. This is essentially Frege's position; see "On Sense and Reference".
57. See, e.g., Simon Blackburn, "The Identity of Propositions".

If this is to be damaging, however, the claim must be that there is no way to explain what samesaying is except in terms of a prior notion of meanings as objects of reference. Such a claim could not survive appreciation of Quine's writings on translation,[58] or—more to the point, since samesaying is not, in general, a relation exactly of translation—of Davidson's writings on interpretation.[59]

Given an equivalence relation between entities of a certain kind F, we can introduce entities of a new kind G, reconstruing the obtaining of the equivalence relation between two members of F in terms of the idea that both stand in a suitably expressed relation to one and the same member of G. For instance, a direction can be explained as what two parallel lines both have.[60] If samesaying—as explicated independently in behavioural and psychological terms, on the lines suggested by Davidson's work on radical interpretation—is an equivalence relation, it will similarly justify the introduction of things said (propositions) as possible objects of reference. This is not the place to discuss the Quinean considerations that cast doubt on the idea that we can make sense of such a samesaying relation. But one beauty of Davidson's account of *oratio obliqua* is that we do not need to raise the question. We can see that the problematic inferences need not have been expected to preserve truth, without being obliged to suppose that there is an intelligible samesaying relation of the kind that Quine doubts: one that would admit of reconstrual in terms of a common relation that utterances have to a single proposition. To understand the logical behaviour of *oratio obliqua* reports, we can make do with the rough and ready relation of samesaying that we actually use in reporting others, a relation whose describability and intelligibility nobody denies;[61] and, if we like, we can be agnostic about Quinean objections to propositions.

Quotation yields an instructive parallel. If we are to be faithful to the intuition that quoting differs from sheer reproduction, we cannot explicate the "quoting relation" (see §10) entirely in terms of equiformity. To capture what lies behind the intuition, and accounts for the plausibility of Geach's view about word-identity, we need to

58. See especially *Word and Object,* chap. 2.

59. See especially "Radical Interpretation".

60. Compare Frege, *The Foundations of Arithmetic,* pp. 74–5.

61. Contra Blackburn, p. 188, where he suggests that Quinean doubts about synonymy make, e.g., *oratio obliqua* reports unintelligible.

ensure that two utterances that bear the quoting relation to each other are made, as we may intuitively put it, in the same language. What this comes to, if we avoid the appearance of quantifying over languages, is something like this: each utterance issues from a practice or disposition of its utterer, such that some sufficient number of equiform utterances issuing from the two dispositions would be intertranslatable (compare §7). If Quine is right about the notion of translation, a quoting relation explained in terms of translation will not be the sort of relation from which we could generate words, conceived in Geach's way, as possible objects of reference. Geach finds reference to words, conceived his way, in quotations, and this puts him in conflict with Quine, much as finding reference to meanings in *oratio obliqua* reports would (see §8). But we can achieve an approximation to Geach's intuitions, without being vulnerable to Quinean attack, if we suppose, as in §8, that the only relevant reference is to utterances. We can make do with a quoting relation that is at least as rough and ready as the translation relation appealed to in its explication.

Confidence that there can be no substance to qualms about propositions may be reinforced by arguments designed to show that Davidson's account of *oratio obliqua* reports does not even get their truth-conditions right.[62] But the arguments I have in mind are inconclusive.

A preliminary clarification may help to blunt their edge. In "On Saying That" (p. 105), Davidson says that

(38) $(\exists x)$ (Galileo's utterance x and my last utterance make us samesayers)

becomes "Galileo said that"—the second part of a reversed version of (6)—by way of "definitional abbreviation". This is misleading. It suggests the idea of a concise way of expressing exactly what some longer form expresses. But there is no reason to say that an utterer of (6) refers, for instance, to himself; whereas an utterer of (38) does refer to himself. A formulation like (38) should be thought of, not as an expansion justified by analysis (definition) of the saying primitive

62. I cannot here discuss the source of such confidence, which I believe to be something profoundly suspect.

of (6), but as "an expository and heuristic device":[63] an aid in instructing novices in the use of the saying primitive. We instruct a novice by saying: when you could truly utter (38), then you may follow the utterance in question with an utterance of "Galileo said that", with the demonstrative referring to the utterance in question. This is a form of explanation of the primitive that need not confer on (6), the idiom explained, all the entailments of (38), in terms of which it is explained. Now an utterer of (6) not only does not refer to himself; he says nothing whatever about what he refers to with the demonstrative "that" (except that Galileo said it). "Galileo said that", uttered in the course of uttering (6) or its reversed version, no more entails

(39) $(\exists x)$ (x is an utterance of mine)

than "That's a red one", said of what is in fact a billiard ball, entails "$(\exists x)$ (x is a billiard ball)". Given a sufficiently careful account of the role of (38) in explaining (6)'s primitive, the fact that (38) entails (39) is irrelevant to this claim.[64]

Still, it may be said, Davidson directs us to understand (6) in such a way that an utterance of it cannot be true unless an utterance, by the same speaker, of (38) with "next" substituted for "last" would be true; this cannot be explained away by pedantry about entailment, and is sufficiently embarrassing for the account of *oratio obliqua*. But what exactly is the embarrassment supposed to be? Simon Blackburn's version of the argument comes to this:[65]

> There is no logical equivalence between [(1)] and [(6)]. For I cannot now make an utterance such that [(1)] entails that [Galileo said—an occurrence of the saying primitive of (6)—] that utterance.

Suppose we rewrite the second sentence of this as follows: "I cannot now make an utterance—call it 'u'—such that an utterance of (1) by me cannot be true unless Galileo said u". The point of the paratactic theory is that I cannot make an utterance of (1) without, in the course of doing so, making just such an utterance u. If the utterance

63. Davidson, "Reply to Foster", p. 177.
64. Compare William G. Lycan, "Davidson on Saying That".
65. "The Identity of Propositions", p. 185. (I have substituted the authentically Davidsonian form (6) for Blackburn's (D), which misformulates Davidson's proposal.)

of "The earth moves" that I make in the course of uttering (1) had meant something different, thereby falsifying the claim that that utterance and one of Galileo's make him and me samesayers, then (by the same token) the utterance of (1) would itself have been false. Modal considerations like this, which are what Blackburn appeals to, cannot make the truth-values of utterances of (1) diverge from the truth-values of utterances of (6) in the same circumstances.[66]

It may be replied that we should be concerned with the truth-conditions, not of utterances of (1), but of what (1) says—something that might have been sayable even if (1) had not been a way to say it. But to assume that this topic of concern is so much as available is to presuppose, at the outset, the acceptability of the contentious notion of a proposition. "Should" suggests that the notion must be acceptable, since we have a theoretical need for it. But it is really not at all clear why we should find it insufficiently ambitious to try to assign correct truth-conditions to all actual and possible utterances of our object language. And Blackburn's argument does not show that a paratactic account of *oratio obliqua* thwarts this aim.[67]

Davidson's account of *oratio obliqua* obviates the need for the full panoply of Frege's doctrine of sense. But there is still room for Frege's terminology, and in a theoretical context that makes employments of it echo Frege himself. We are bound to go on asking questions like this: if an utterance of a certain sentence makes me a samesayer with someone, why does an utterance of a sentence exactly like the first except that it substitutes for one name another name of the same thing not also make me a samesayer with him? Answers can be taken to spell out differences in the contributions made by the names to what is said in utterances of sentences containing them; that is—

66. Compare Peter Smith, "Blackburn on Saying That".

67. If we take formulations in terms of samesaying to be analyses of *oratio obliqua* constructions, there will seem to be a problem about a lack of parallelism between the following pair of forms of words. First: "Galileo made an utterance that, with my next utterance, puts him and me in the samesaying relation. The earth moves. What I have just said might have been so however the English language had evolved." Second: "Your car is the same colour as my car. What I have just said might have been so whatever had happened to my car in the paint shop." If we construe "What I have just said might have been so" in the first case in a way that is parallel to the most natural construal of it in the second, we shall not capture the thought that Galileo might have said the very thing he did say, even if my way of ascribing that saying to him had not been available. But we should not take the samesaying formulations as analyses. (This note is a partial response to pressure from Christopher Peacocke. The point needs much more elaboration.)

this equation is justifiable from Fregean texts[68]—differences in sense between the names. The crucial difference is that, although the terminology is thus preserved, *reference* to senses is nowhere needed. A follower of Quine need have no reason to object to this emasculated version of Frege. There is something very satisfying about this projected rapprochement.[69]

68. See Frege, *Grundgesetze der Arithmetik,* vol. 1, §32.

69. I offer more elaboration of the pared-down version of Frege, for the case of proper names, in Essay 8 below.

ESSAY 4

In Defence of Modesty[1]

1. A modest theory of meaning for a language—in the technical sense introduced by Michael Dummett—is one that gives no account of the concepts expressed by primitive terms of the language.[2] We should note that the use of "concepts" here is not Fregean, in two ways. First, Fregean concepts are associated only with predicative expressions, whereas Dummett's considerations are meant to apply to meaningful expressions in general. Second, Fregean concepts belong to the realm of reference, whereas the concepts Dummett is concerned with would belong to the realm of sense; they are determinants of content—determinants of the thoughts expressible by sentences containing the associated words.

Dummett's official exposition of the notion of modesty suggests that a theory gives an account of a concept just in case it is capable of conferring the concept on someone—just in case someone could acquire the concept by learning the facts that the theory states.[3] However, any

1. I read a paper with this title to Oxford discussion groups in 1974. In reformulating my thoughts on the topic, I benefited from responses by Michael Dummett to interim formulations of them, in Essays 8 and 15 below. I was also helped by years of discussions with Barry Lester; and by reading Sabina Lovibond's *Realism and Imagination in Ethics* (at first in its dissertation form). I delivered a longer version of this essay to an International Conference on Perspectives on Meaning held at Jadavpur University, Calcutta, in 1983, where I had the benefit of comments from Donald Davidson and W. V. Quine.

2. See "What Is a Theory of Meaning?", pp. 101–2, 107.

3. Dummett credits proponents of modesty with the view that "to demand of the theory of meaning that it should serve to explain new concepts to someone who does not already have them is to place too heavy a burden on it" ("What Is a Theory of Meaning?", pp. 101–2); and again, he suggests that what makes a theory modest is that, in the case of any concept expressed by a primitive predicate of its object language, "the theory would be intelligible only to someone who had already grasped the concept" (pp. 103–4).

theory (of anything) would need to employ *some* concepts, so that a formulation of it would presuppose prior possession of them on the part of any audience to whom it could sensibly be addressed; and it seems undeniable that any theory of meaning for a language would need to help itself to at least *some* of the concepts expressible in that language—and hence to resign itself to at least partial modesty in the sense determined by the official exposition. But Dummett nowhere suggests that the requirement of immodesty (in his terms, full-bloodedness) that he wishes to impose on theories of meaning is less than total, and indeed in places he suggests quite the opposite. I think this indicates that his official exposition is not quite right.[4]

It will help me to say what I think Dummett's real point is if I first outline a conception of meaning that would invite his objection as I understand it.

2. The basis of the truth-conditional conception of meaning, as I see it, is the following thought: to specify what would be asserted, in the assertoric utterance of a sentence apt for such use, is to specify a condition under which the sentence (as thus uttered) would be true. The truth-conditional conception of meaning embodies a conception of truth that makes that thought truistic. (I am inclined to think it is

4. Consider this passage ("What Is a Theory of Meaning?", pp. 103–4):

> . . . a translation manual presupposes a mastery of some one other language—that into which the translation is made—if we are to derive from it an understanding of the translated language; but a modest theory of meaning presupposes a mastery of *some,* though unspecified, language, if we are to derive from it an understanding of the object-language. The significant contrast would, however, appear to be not between a theory which (like a translation manual) makes a specific presupposition and one which (like a modest theory of meaning) makes as heavy a presupposition, though less specific; but between theories which (like both of these) rely on extraneous presuppositions and those which (like full-blooded theories of meaning) involve no such presupposition at all.

Suppose we interpret this talk of what a theory does or does not presuppose in terms of the question to what extent a theory might be capable of imparting *de novo* the concepts expressible in its object language. (This interpretation is certainly not discouraged by the suggestion that we should think in terms of what would be needed in order to *derive* from a theory an understanding of its object language.) In that case this passage presents us with the surely incoherent picture of a full-blooded theory as something that, while counting as a *theory,* employs (and so presupposes) no concepts at all; so that (presumably) it is not formulable in any language at all. (See Essay 8 below.) Something has to give, and I believe it is the official exposition.

the only philosophically hygienic conception of truth there is.) The truism captures what is right about the idea that ". . . is true", said of a sentence, functions as a device of disquotation, or, more generally, of cancellation of semantic ascent.[5]

Let us bracket, for the moment, the concerns of a theory of force for a language: that is, concerns with the different sorts of speech acts one can perform in speaking the language—the different modes in which thoughts can be propounded in it. Then we can say: our interest, as theorists of meaning, is in specifications of the *contents* of actual and possible speech acts—specifications of the thoughts propounded in them, in whatever mode (and we have singled out the assertoric for special attention).[6] Now the truism ensures that specifications of the contents of assertions will *be* specifications of truth-conditions for the sentences used to effect those assertions. (It does not matter whether we call them that or not; but since that is what they are, we may as well label them as such.) That is why a theorist of meaning cannot disclaim all interest in truth-conditions.

This sketch differs crucially from Dummett's understanding of the truth-conditional conception of meaning. According to my sketch, when a theorist comes to explain and justify the claim that the notion of truth might figure essentially in the "core" of a theory of meaning, he will do so by appeal to the notion of the content of an assertion.[7] In Dummett's view, by contrast, there is a requirement that one should be able to explain what one is about, in constructing the "core", *before* one goes on to bring its materials into relation with such notions, which belong to the theory of force.[8] This difference comes out most strikingly in Dummett's idea that, in a truth-conditional theory of meaning, the theory of force would have to li-

5. See W. V. Quine, *Philosophy of Logic,* pp. 10–13.

6. For the extension to other modes, see, e.g., Essay 1 above, §7. The sentences I have singled out for special attention should not be thought of as singled out on the basis of superficial syntax; we ought to leave room for not crediting sentences such as, say, "Vanilla ice cream is nice" with conditions of truth. David Wiggins, in "What Would Be a Substantial Theory of Truth?", gives considerations I would like to describe as showing why the bare idea of disquotation yields an insufficiently substantial notion of truth, if we apply it to a category of indicative sentences marked out by superficial syntax. The ingredients of Wiggins's more substantial treatment of truth (which, for present purposes, I would like to transpose into a more substantial specification of the appropriate category of sentences) are fully congenial to my main point in this essay; see especially his pp. 220–1.

7. For "core", see Dummett, "What Is a Theory of Meaning? (II)", at pp. 72–6.

8. This is implicit at p. 82 of "What Is a Theory of Meaning? (II)".

cense *derivations*—which Dummett evidently conceives as substantial—of contents of assertions from elements of the "core", namely, specifications of truth-conditions.[9] It is obvious that no such derivations would be called for in the position I have sketched.

3. My truism might be held to capture the intuition that finds expression in the redundancy theory of truth; and Dummett has consistently maintained that espousing a redundancy theory of truth debars one from a truth-conditional conception of meaning.[10] What is the basis for this view?

In some places Dummett argues for it on the basis of the assumption that one ought to be able to derive an understanding of a language from a theory of meaning for it.[11] This will not help us to explain the supposed global requirement of full-bloodedness; on the contrary, it takes us straight back to the difficulty I began with.

But we can extract a different idea from passages in which Dummett suggests that the redundancy theory gives a word for truth a role only *within* a language. That means that such a word "is of no use in giving an account of the language as from the outside", and he indicates that this is what excludes a truth-conditional conception of meaning.[12] The idea is, then, that a proper account of a language must be "as from the outside"; and I believe this is the key to a correct interpretation of the supposed global requirement of full-bloodedness.

How far outside are we required to go? We can envisage a theory of a language given in a distinct language, and hence, in one sense, given "as from outside" the first. But if part of the theory merely says, in the second language, what sentences of the first language can be used (for instance) to assert (compare §2), I think Dummett's view will be that the theory merely postpones discharging an obligation: that of giving an account, "as from the outside", of the background language. Such a theory would simply help itself to the contents expressible in its object language; whereas I think Dummett's

9. See "What Is a Theory of Meaning? (II)", p. 104.

10. See, e.g., *Truth and Other Enigmas,* p. 7.

11. As well as the passage cited in the previous note, see *Frege: Philosophy of Language,* pp. 458–9, and "What Is a Theory of Meaning? (II)", p. 77.

12. "Frege and Wittgenstein", p. 40.

idea is that a proper theory of meaning for a language would be formulated "as from outside" content altogether.

We can acquire some sense of what this might come to from the following passage:

> What is it to grasp the concept *square,* say? At the very least, it is to be able to discriminate between things that are square and those that are not. Such an ability can be ascribed only to one who will, on occasion, treat square things differently from things that are not square; one way, among many other possible ways, of doing this is to apply the word "square" to square things and not to others.[13]

This sketch of an account of (what it is to have) the concept *square* does not hesitate to employ that concept. So if we judged it according to whether it might serve to confer possession of the concept on someone, it would be exposed as hopeless. What makes it nevertheless pass muster in Dummett's eyes? The point is, I conjecture, that it uses the word "square" only in first intention—that is, never inside a content-specifying "that"-clause. Thus, although the concept is employed, it is not, so to speak, *displayed* in its role as a determinant of content; a grasp of that role is not taken for granted. It is in this sense, I believe, that the account is supposed to be apt for incorporation in a theory of meaning that explains (what it is to have) concepts "as from outside" content altogether.

Our difficulty was to see how full-bloodedness in respect of a given concept might be compatible with a theory's being constrained to employ that very concept. This conjecture yields an answer. On this view, a full-blooded theory of meaning is not, after all, one from which someone could derive possession of the concepts expressed by primitive terms of its object language. Rather, if a theory is full-blooded with respect to a given concept, that means that it describes a practical capacity such that to acquire it would be to acquire the concept—and it effects this description not necessarily without employing the concept, but, in the sense I have explained, "as from outside" its role as a determinant of content. If the description employs the concept, then certainly no one could acquire the concept by being taught the theory. But one *can* acquire the concept by being taught the practical capacity that the theory describes; and the the-

13. "What Do I Know When I Know a Language?", p. 98.

ory describes that practical capacity without helping itself to the notion of contents in which the concept figures.[14]

4. According to my conjecture, then, the supposed requirement of full-bloodedness is a requirement that a theory of meaning be constructed "as from outside" content and concepts. This may cast light on the way in which Dummett's understanding of the truth-conditional conception of meaning diverges (as I noted in §2) from the understanding of the conception that I sketched. If a truth-conditional "core" would need to be formulated "as from outside" content, it could not be the case, as in my sketch, that its specifications of truth-conditions were entitled to be regarded as such by virtue of their being—already—specifications of content for actual or potential assertions. In showing how to arrive at such specifications of content on the basis of material from the "core", a theory of force would be showing how to effect transitions from a standpoint "outside" content to a standpoint at which content has come into view, and such transitions would evidently be substantial. But two questions arise.

First: what would these specifications of truth-conditions, capable of being understood to be such without appealing to their being specifications of the contents of assertions, be like? There is a familiar philosophical temptation to suppose that the notion of a fact can be sharply separated from the notion of the content of a thought or assertion that would express it; and it seems that Dummett's assumptions saddle adherents of the truth-conditional conception of meaning with the idea that truth consists in correspondence to such items—items in the world whose nature is intelligible "as from outside" content.[15] This is plainly wrong about some prominent adherents of the truth-conditional conception; and that should cast doubt on the assumptions.[16]

14. Dummett himself suggests this idea of a theory of meaning as something not addressed to an aspiring speaker of a language but rather aiming to describe what such an aspirant would have to learn to do. See *Truth and Other Enigmas*, p. 6: "We can give an account of the meaning of 'and' by saying that we are in a position to assert ⌜P and Q⌝ when and only when we are in a position to assert P and in a position to assert Q. (This is not circular: one could train a dog to bark only when a bell rang *and* a light shone without presupposing that it possessed the concept of conjunction.)"

15. Against this conception of truth, see P. F. Strawson, "Truth", and Wiggins, "What Would Be a Substantial Theory of Truth?".

16. On the early Wittgenstein, who is sometimes saddled with a conception of truth on these lines, see Brian McGuinness, "The So-Called Realism of Wittgenstein's *Tractatus*".

Second: if a theory of force equips us to make transitions to content from a standpoint "outside" content, then the theory of meaning of which it is a part must, in effect, embody an explanation, "as from the outside", of the contents expressible in its object language. Dummett concedes frankly that we have virtually no idea what a theory of force that brought off the trick might be like.[17] But the serious question is this: do we have any reason to suppose that an explanation of content "as from the outside" is even in principle possible? It is easy to see how, if one took such explanation to be possible, one would think it obligatory for any theory of meaning worthy of the title. But there is a philosophical tradition, associated with the name of Brentano, whose key thesis is exactly that explanation of content "as from outside" is not possible.[18]

Has Dummett found a way to give the lie to the Brentano tradition? In order to address this question, we need more detail about Dummett's conception of meaning.

5. When one considers what gives utterances content, a natural first idea is that language functions as a *code* for the transmission of thoughts (whose possession of content is, one might suppose, not problematic). Now one strand in Dummett's objection to modesty is the view that modesty necessarily involves this conception of language as a code. A modest theory refuses to assign the task of explaining the contents expressible in its object language, "as from the outside", to the theory of meaning, and hence ultimately to the philosophy of *language;* and Dummett's idea is that this is intelligible

For the case of Frege, consider his arguments against the correspondence theory of truth in "Thoughts". For Davidson, see "True to the Facts".

17. See, e.g., "What Is a Theory of Meaning? (II)", p. 76. I think Dummett is disposed to hope for help, in addressing this question, from a supposed analogy with the way in which a theory of a game like chess would enable one to characterize the significance of a move in terms of the difference it makes to the state of the game—not the mere fact that such-and-such a piece is now here rather than there, but the change that the move effects in the prospects of the players. (See "What Do I Know When I Know a Language?", pp. 102–5, and *The Interpretation of Frege's Philosophy,* pp. 75–6.) But this analogy cannot help with the nature of the transition from "outside" content to "inside". For chess moves do not have contents; we do not hesitate to credit them with *significance,* but this is not a matter of their being expressive of *thoughts.* (Anyway, I doubt whether the significance of chess moves can be explained "as from outside games", as Dummett assumes; see Essay 15 below, §6.

18. See Roderick M. Chisholm, *Perceiving: A Philosophical Study,* chap. 2; compare §45 of Quine, *Word and Object.*

only on the supposition that adherents of modesty imagine the task—which they leave undone and which must be done somewhere—delegated to a prior and independent theory of *thought*.[19] But this conception of language as a code for thought, independently endowed with content, is objectionable, because it represents one person's judgement as to another person's understanding of a remark as "no more than a *hypothesis*";[20] whereas if communication is to be possible, that in which our understanding of the language we speak consists must "lie open to view, as Frege maintained that it does, in our use of the language, in our participation in a common practice".[21]

One may forgivably find it hard to accept the claim that what gives words meaning lies open to view in linguistic practice. It is easy to interpret the claim as a form of behaviourism, and accuse it of simply leaving out of account the involvement of mind in meaningful speech. According to Dummett, it is compulsory to suppose that the practice in which meaning resides is characterizable "as from outside" content; only by this rejection of modesty can we avoid the psychologistic conception of language as a code for thought. In this context, the suspicion of behaviourism can be understood as crystallizing my Brentano-inspired query about the possibility of full-bloodedness. The involvement of mind in meaningful speech is explicitly recognized only when we describe utterances in terms of content—in terms of thought expressed. How, then, can a description of the practice of speaking a language "as from outside" content succeed in registering the role of mind? How can it be more than a mere description of outward behaviour, with the mental (inner) aspect of language use left out of account?

Dummett has suggested a way to meet this objection: namely, by taking a characterization, "as from the outside", of the practical capacity that constitutes mastery of a language to specify something *known* by its speakers. The knowledge in question would be "*implicit* knowledge: knowledge which shows itself partly by manifestation of the practical ability, and partly by a willingness to acknowledge as correct a formulation of what is known when it is pre-

19. See "What Do I Know When I Know a Language?", pp. 97–100.
20. "What Do I Know When I Know a Language?", p. 102.
21. "What Do I Know When I Know a Language?", p. 102.

sented."[22] Our difficulty was to see how, when his recoil from the psychologism of the *hypothesis* idea induces Dummett to embrace full-bloodedness, he can make room for the involvement of mind in speech; and it is clear that this double-aspect conception of implicit knowledge is precisely designed to meet the difficulty. Psychologism is avoided because the implicit knowledge is (in, so to speak, its outward aspect) manifested in behaviour; nothing is hidden from view. But there is no lapsing into mere behaviourism, because the implicit knowledge is (in, so to speak, its inner aspect) capable of acknowledgement by speakers as what guides their practice.[23] Thus the characterization of the practice, "as from outside" content, that constitutes an object of possible acknowledgment by speakers is not a mere external description of behaviour but a set of principles by which speakers direct their use of the language. And this might seem to save the practice in which someone's understanding of a language is said to lie open to view—even though it is characterized "as from outside" content—from taking on the appearance of a mere outward husk or shell, not necessarily imbued with mentality at all.

6. But this attempt to steer between psychologism and behaviourism seems to me to fail. I shall mention two related difficulties.

First, there is a problem about the idea that linguistic practice might be guided by implicit knowledge of parts of a theory of meaning that employ concepts expressed by primitive terms of its object language. Consider Dummett's suggested explanation of the concept *square* (see §3). Perhaps a speaker of English might be induced to acknowledge it as correct. But the explanation contains uses of the word "square". So comprehension of this object of acknowledgment would be an exercise of the very capacity we were trying to see as guided by the implicit knowledge that the acknowledgement supposedly reveals. If we needed guidance in our overt practice, we would need it just as much in our understanding of the supposed guide.

There may be a temptation to respond that it is not the *words* of Dummett's suggested explanation by which one is guided in using the word "square", but *what they express*. But this risks lapsing, in

22. "What Do I Know When I Know a Language?", p. 96; compare p. 101.

23. It is much less obvious than Dummett suggests that a readiness to acknowledge a description of what one does as correct shows that one's practice is guided by implicit knowledge of what one acknowledges. But I shall not go into this.

connection with the propositions of the theory of meaning, into the idea that we can "strip off the linguistic clothing and penetrate to the pure naked thought beneath":[24] an idea that is of a piece with the conception of language as a code. Alternatively, it might be suggested that the idea of guidance by implicit knowledge does not apply in these basic regions of language. But since it was only that idea that made it seem possible for a theory of meaning "as from the outside" to recognize the involvement of mind in meaning, this suggestion would risk conceding the charge of mere behaviourism for the corresponding reaches of a full-blooded theory of meaning.[25]

The second difficulty concerns the outward aspect of the conception of implicit knowledge: the claim that the implicit knowledge can be manifested in linguistic behaviour, characterized "as from outside" content. Consider again Dummett's suggested explanation of the concept *square,* in terms of a practical capacity to treat square things in some distinctive way (for instance, to call them "square"). Can implicit knowledge that that is how *square* things are to be treated be manifested in behaviour, characterized "as from outside" content? It may seem that nothing could be simpler: the manifestation would be someone's treating a square thing in whatever way is in question. But any such performance would be an equally good manifestation of any of an indefinite number of different pieces of such implicit knowledge. (Consider implicit knowledge to the effect that that is the way to treat things that are either square or . . . .) If we assume a stable propensity, guided by an unchanging piece of implicit knowledge, we can use further behaviour to rule out some of these competing candidates. But no finite set of performances would eliminate them all; and finite sets of performances are all we get.

Of course no one, confronted with what is plainly a speaker of English calling a square thing "square", will so much as entertain any of the competing candidates. But with what right does one ignore them? It is illicit at this point to appeal to the idea of someone who is plainly a speaker of English; the issue is precisely whether someone could make it manifest (plain) in his behaviour that it is this rather than that language—as characterized, supposedly, by a

24. "What Do I Know When I Know a Language?", p. 99.

25. This difficulty perhaps partly accounts for Dummett's tendency to lapse into the idea that one ought to be able to derive an understanding of language from a theory of meaning for it.

full-blooded theory of meaning—that he is speaking. Obviously the other (inner) aspect of the suggested notion of implicit knowledge—its capacity to be acknowledged—cannot help; the acknowledgement would be acceptance of, say, Dummett's suggested explanation, and our right to take "square", as it figures in what the acknowledger accepts, to mean *square* rather than one of the competitors is exactly what is in question.[26] One may be tempted now to claim superior *simplicity* for the extrapolation, from a case of treating a square thing appropriately, to *square* things in general, rather than things that are square or . . . . But an appeal to simplicity is out of court: it would entail a concession that our attribution of implicit knowledge is a *hypothesis,* and the point of introducing the notion of manifestation was precisely to controvert that.[27]

7. Does this mean that the project of avoiding both behaviourism and psychologism is a failure?[28] There is another possible conclusion. The difficulty with Dummett's attempt on the project derives from his idea that the practice in which, to avoid psychologism, we must conceive someone's understanding of a language as lying open to view must be characterized "as from outside" content[29]—since the alternative, an acceptance of modesty, supposedly involves the conception of language as a code for thought, which is a lapse back into

26. See "What Do I Know When I Know a Language?", p. 101, for an indication that Dummett appreciates this point.

27. Disallowing appeals to simplicity may be reminiscent of an aspect of Quine's thesis of the indeterminacy of translation that has attracted complaints; see, e.g., Richard Rorty, *Philosophy and the Mirror of Nature,* pp. 203–4. The prohibition that is in question here can be understood only against the background of an aspiration to avoid both psychologism and behaviourism. This background is missing from Quine, who in effect equates mentalism (the rejection of behaviourism) with psychologism (the conception of the mental as hidden), and is thus left with nothing—apart from an apparently dogmatic physicalism—to justify refusing to allow ordinary scientific methods of resolving indeterminacies in theorizing about meaning and mind.

28. I take it for granted here that this would be a disappointment. In a different context, I would need to argue that it would not be satisfying simply to embrace psychologism.

29. It is this that is the source of the difficulty, rather than the appeal to implicit knowledge as such (something about which Dummett has never been more than tentative, except when—as in "What Is a Theory of Meaning? (II)"—talk of implicit knowledge was a mere *façon de parler,* replaceable without loss by talk of practical capacities). The difficulty would apply whatever device was adopted in order to try to reinstate the mind, in the face of the threat of behaviourism posed by insisting that linguistic practice must be characterized "as from outside" content.

psychologism. In fact, however, the argument that connects modesty with the psychologistic conception of language as a code *depends* on the assumption that contents must be capturable "as from outside", and hence cannot constitute any support for that assumption. *If* we assume that contents should (because they can) be explained "as from outside", we can find a refusal to attempt that task in a theory of meaning intelligible only on the supposition that it is pictured as executed in a theory of "the pure naked thought beneath". But if we understand acceptance of modesty to reflect a principled rejection of that assumption, the supposed connection of modesty with the conception of language as a code evaporates. And this makes room for a different way of avoiding both behaviourism and psychologism, according to which someone's understanding of a language lies open to view in a practice that is *not* characterizable, in such a way as to reveal the meaning that resides in it, "as from outside" content.

Dummett writes, of modest theories of meaning:

> If a theory of meaning of this type is taken literally, as relating to a theory of truth framed in actual sentences, it has no advantage over a translation manual, since it has to presuppose an understanding of the metalanguage.[30]

At first sight, this seems to involve a wilful neglect of the distinction between use and mention. One wants to protest that whereas a translation manual merely mentions sentences in a background language that it offers as translations of object-language sentences, the sentences on the right-hand sides of the theorems of a modest theory of meaning (actual sentences, by all means) are used rather than mentioned, and this makes a crucial difference.[31] But as long as the assumption is maintained that contents can be explained "as from outside", this protest, as a defence of modesty, can be heard only as directing attention away from the used metalanguage sentences to their contents, conceived as stripped of their linguistic clothing—as if we were to take the sentences to be serving as stand-ins for naked thoughts.

However, once we see that we can question the possibility of capturing contents "as from outside", and that this undermines the connection of modesty with the conception of language as a code, we

30. "What Is a Theory of Meaning?", p. 120.
31. See the Introduction to Evans and McDowell, eds., *Truth and Meaning*, pp. vii–xi.

can understand the protest differently: not as making the theorems into promissory notes for some pictured explanation of the contents in question, "as from outside", in a theory of thought, but as insisting that the theorems *give* those contents, *not* "as from outside", by uses of an intelligible language.[32] Our attention is indeed drawn to the contents of the used sentences, rather than the mere words (which are possible objects of attention even for someone who does not understand the language they are in): but not as something "beneath" the words, to which we are to penetrate by stripping off the linguistic clothing; rather, as something present in the words—something capable of being heard or seen in the words by those who understand the language.

On this different view, the possibility of avoiding both behaviourism and psychologism depends precisely on embracing modesty. This is exactly not what Dummett represents it as being, a lapse into psychologism. Rejecting psychologism is taking the view that the senses of utterances are not hidden behind them, but lie open to view: that is, that to be a speaker of language is to be capable of putting one's thoughts into one's words, where others can hear or see them. One great beauty of those modest theories of meaning that are "homophonic" is the distance they go towards making that idea unproblematic, by showing that we need not think of it as amounting to more than this: the thought (say) that some table-tops are square can be heard or seen in the words "Some table-tops are square", by people who would be able to put their own minds into those words if they had occasion to do so.

The essential move is a radical shift from Dummett's conception of language use—that practice in which understanding is to be conceived as manifested. For Dummett, language use—the outward aspect of linguistic practice—must be characterizable "as from outside" content. This means that particular episodes of language use must be recognizable for what they essentially are without benefit of understanding the language; and that is what makes Dummett's way

32. Not "as from outside": Charles Taylor's suggestion (in "Theories of Meaning") that truth-conditional theories of meaning would be constructed from the viewpoint of a pure detached observer outside language (and even—p. 255—"not cast in language") would be a travesty of the sort of theory of meaning I have in mind. (Note also that I do not assume that it will be always be possible to give the contents of object-language sentences in whatever background language a theorist has at his disposal; so I do not come into collision with Taylor's remarks—pp. 279–81—about the fusing of horizons.)

of trying to steer between psychologism and behaviourism problematic. We might suggest that the temptation to appeal to simplicity, and thereby implicitly to the notion of a hypothesis, in the face of the difficulty that confronts Dummett's claim about manifestation, brings out how, if one adopts an essentially behaviouristic conception of language use (as full-bloodedness requires), then one will find, however resolute one's anti-psychologistic intentions, that one cannot locate the mental aspect of speech anywhere except *behind* linguistic behaviour. To accept modesty, by contrast, is to insist that the outward aspect of linguistic behaviour is essentially content-involving, so that the mind's role in speech is, as it were, on the surface—part of what one presents to others, not something that is at best a hypothesis for them. What is crucial here is that we should not conceive the outward aspect that matters as something one presents to just anyone; one shows one's mind, in one's words, only to those who understand one's language.[33]

Dummett holds that the truth-condition of a sentence is not a feature of its use;[34] correctly enough, on his conception of use. But if we equate a sentence's truth-condition with the content it can be used to express, and conceive use in the way I have described, the claim is simply false. Unlike what Dummett prefers to truth-conditions in the explanation of meaning (properties of sentences that are in fact directly observable only on rather special occasions of use), the truth-condition of a sentence (its content) is audible or visible—to those who understand the language—whenever the sentence is meaningfully uttered. (This reconstrual of use transforms the look of the issue between "realism" and "anti-realism"; but I shall not elaborate this here.)[35]

8. We are now in a position to see that much of the detail in Dummett's attack on modesty is tendentious. I shall deal here with two aspects of this.

33. Of course the capacity to know someone else's meaning that partly constitutes command of a language is fallible. It is of the utmost importance to resist an epistemology that would conclude from this that even when the capacity does not trip up, the judgement about someone else's meaning it equips one with can be at best a hypothesis. (There are some remarks about such an epistemology in Essay 17 below.)

34. See, e.g., "What Is a Theory of Meaning? (II)", p. 75.

35. See Essay 15 below.

First, Dummett claims that a modest theory of meaning rejects the Fregean notion of sense. The sense of an expression is a determinant of the contents expressible by sentences in which it might occur; so one's conception of what it is to give an account of senses will coincide with one's conception of what it is to give an account of concepts (in the Dummettian sense: see §1) and contents. In Dummett's view, one can give an account of concepts only by characterizing, "as from outside", what it is to manifest thoughts involving them; and this, together with the coincidence, is institutionalized in his description of a theory of sense as something that does precisely that.[36] Of course it follows immediately that if a theory incorporates a denial that it is possible to explain concepts and contents, in general, "as from outside", it must be "a theory which repudiates the notion of sense altogether".[37] But Dummett's conception of a theory of sense depends on the thesis that it is possible to explain contents—if there are any—"as from outside". And I know no evidence that Frege would have accepted that thesis.

Second, holism. In Dummett's consideration of modesty, holism figures in the first instance as a corollary of an attempted response to the charge that a modest theory "merely exhibits what it is to arrive at an interpretation of one language via an understanding of another, which is just what a translation manual does".[38] The idea is that a modest theorist might answer this charge by saying that what matters is the theory, rather than some particular formulation of it in some specific background language.[39] Now the theory will no doubt have an internal articulation that might seem to capture the way the meanings of sentences depend on the meanings of their parts. But modesty is, by Dummett's lights, a refusal to give *any* account of practical abilities, on the part of a competent speaker of the language, that correspond to the particular propositions into which the theory is articulated; and, according to Dummett, this means that the appearance of structure is a fraud: "the articulation in the theory

36. "What Is a Theory of Meaning? (II)", p. 74; the ground for this identification is laid in the Appendix to "What Is a Theory of Meaning?".

37. "What Is a Theory of Meaning?", p. 128. (This would rule out the very possibility of the position I adopt in Essay 8 below.)

38. "What Is a Theory of Meaning?", p. 114.

39. See "What Is a Theory of Meaning?", p. 114; compare Davidson, "Reply to Foster", p. 175.

plays no genuine role in the account of what constitutes a speaker's mastery of his language".[40] Moreover, not only does such a theory not fulfil its promise to display the meanings of sentences as dependent on the meanings of their parts; by virtue of its modesty with respect to the theorems, it does not even warrant the idea that an individual sentence possesses a determinate content of its own.[41]

This attack, similarly, depends on the thesis that it is possible to explain whatever contents there are "as from outside". Given that thesis, a theorist who denies the possibility of explaining the content of an individual sentence "as from outside" is committed, like Dummett's holist, to denying that an individual sentence has a content of its own at all. But it is tendentious to equate denying that the content of a sentence is capturable "as from outside" with rejecting the very idea that a sentence has its own content.[42] Again, in order to claim that a modest theory effects *no* segmentation of the ability to speak a language into component abilities, Dummett must disallow as irrelevant a segmentation effected "as from *inside*" the contents expressible in the language, by specifications of practical abilities in such forms as "the ability to use 'NN' so as to be understood by speakers of the language to be expressing thoughts about NN". Here too, it is tendentious to equate the thesis that the capacity to speak a language should be articulated "from inside" content, on the one hand, with a picture of that capacity as wholly devoid of structure, on the other.

Holism makes a second appearance in Dummett's discussion of modesty. Here it is a feature of a truth-conditional conception of meaning that is supposedly not modest at all, but gives an account (in Dummett's sense) of a practical capacity correlated with each "core" proposition dealing with a primitive term of the object language. The account specifies a determinate totality of sentences that are held true, and describes a simultaneous determination of bearers for names and extensions for predicates figuring in those sentences,

40. "What Is a Theory of Meaning?", p. 116.

41. This is the burden of "What Is a Theory of Meaning?", pp. 116–20, where Dummett discusses the question whether a modest theory can avail itself of the notion of a mistake. Dummett's thought must be that the idea of a sentence's individual content could be rescued—the accusation of fraud rebutted—only on the basis of conceiving language as a code.

42. Although the equation does seem appropriate in the case of Quine; see *From a Logical Point of View,* p. 42.

aimed at making the largest possible number of them come out true.[43] Dummett argues, surely correctly, that it would be fantastic to credit a speaker with this conception of what it is for his words to mean what they do.[44] However, he ascribes this supposedly non-modest holism to Donald Davidson—a correction of his first impression that Davidsonian theories of meaning would be modest; and this seems a most implausible reading of Davidson.[45] As I understand the holism Davidson accepts, it is this thesis: attributions of content to sentences in a community's language, to their linguistic acts, and to their psychological states are systematically interlocked, in such a way that—to put it in our present terms—there is no explaining, "as from outside" the entire system, what it means to ascribe some specific content to an appropriate item.[46] Clearly this entails repudiating any aspiration to be anything but modest in theories of meaning. The notion of holding sentences true functions in Davidson's conception of radical interpretation (properly understood) as the key notion in certain judgements, already *within* the interlocking system, from which an interpreter would find it useful to begin in working his way into the whole. It is not, as in Dummett's picture, material for an account of content—what knits the interlocking system together—"as from the outside".

Davidson describes facts about the sentences that speakers hold true as *evidence* for a theory of meaning, and this is certainly misleading.[47] This practice of Davidson's results, I think, from the ancestry of his use of the notion of holding-true, in W. V. Quine's use of the notion of assent.[48] Quine wants assent to be capable of figuring in an account of the hard facts about linguistic dispositions. (We might say: he wants it to figure in an account of language "as from outside" content. For it is in the attribution of content that, in Quine's view, we move into the region where indeterminacy

43. See the Appendix to "What Is a Theory of Meaning?", at pp. 128–32.

44. See "What Is a Theory of Meaning?", pp. 132–8. It is worth asking why it is to the point to argue this, given the distinction (which Dummett draws at p. 121) between saying what a speaker knows and saying what it is for him to know it. Here an attempt at the latter seems to be criticized as if it were an attempt at the former. But I do not want to defend this version of holism.

45. See especially "Radical Interpretation".

46. See "Mental Events".

47. Compare a remark of Dummett's, in "What Is a Theory of Meaning?", p. 131.

48. See chap. 2 of *Word and Object*.

reigns.)[49] But if what Quine wants is available "outside"—not content-involving—then, whatever it is, it is not *assent.* This was already implicit in Quine's admission that the identification of assent behaviour is an "analytical hypothesis";[50] and it becomes explicit in Quine's lecture "Mind and Verbal Dispositions", in which he opts for a notion—that of "surface assent"—that is firmly "outside".[51] The analogue for holding-true ("surface holding-true") would not be congenial to Davidson.[52] But if, as this indicates, Davidson's holding-true is unambiguously part of the interlocking system, rather than, as Quine's assent long seemed to be, somehow both part of it and "outside", then Davidson ought not to describe facts about holding-true as *evidence* for another part of the interlocking system, the theory of meaning—as if such facts were definitely ascertainable independently of the theory of meaning, contrary to the thesis of holism about the interlocking system.[53] This is not what Dummett thinks is wrong with Davidson's talk of evidence. Dummett thinks Davidson ought to regard facts about holding-true not as distinct from a theory of meaning and so capable of being evidence for it, but as *part* of a *full-blooded* theory of meaning—one that gives an account of the contents expressible in a language "as from the outside". But to suppose that the idea of a speaker's holding a sentence true is so much as available "outside" content would be simply to fly in the face of the Davidsonian holism I have formulated.

9. Of course it would be wrong to suggest that once we abandon the aspiration to full-bloodedness, a middle course between behaviourism and psychologism becomes wholly unproblematic. Steering that middle course requires the difficult idea that competence in a language is an ability to embody one's mind—the cast of one's thoughts—in words that one speaks, and to hear others' thoughts in

49. See especially §45 of *Word and Object.*

50. *Word and Object,* p. 30; Davidson and Hintikka, eds., *Words and Objections,* p. 312.

51. See especially p. 91.

52. See "Reply to Foster", pp. 175–6.

53. Christopher Peacocke, in chap. 4 of *Holistic Explanation,* interprets Davidson's talk of evidence as evincing an aspiration for what Peacocke calls a "quasi-reduction" of, in effect, the content-involving scheme of concepts. It is not quite clear to me what the attraction of "quasi-reductions" is supposed to be. I am suggesting a simpler diagnosis of Davidson's practice: namely, the influence of a field of force emanating from Quine.

their words. If we envisaged the acquisition of this ability, with a first language, as a matter of suitably linking vocal propensities to an antecedent capacity to entertain the thoughts, we would be lapsing back into the conception of language as a code.[54] So we have to entitle ourselves to the idea that acquiring a first language is, not learning a behavioural outlet for antecedent states of mind, but becoming *minded* in ways that the language is anyway able to express.[55] We have to equip ourselves to see how our ability to have dealings with content can be, not a mere natural endowment (something we can take for granted), but an achievement, which an individual attains by acquiring membership in a linguistic community.

Now a modest theory of meaning, by design, starts in the midst of content; so it cannot contribute to this task of representing content as an achievement. This may make it seem that recognition of the task reinstates the obligation of full-bloodedness; but if I am right about full-bloodedness, that thought must be wrong. A better thought might be that it is precisely because full-bloodedness is impossible—because there is no explaining content in general "as from outside"—that the task of representing content as an achievement is as difficult as it is.[56] What is needed is an understanding of how content, explicitly conceived as inaccessible except "from inside", can be comprehended as a precipitate of simpler modes of activity and awareness than those in which it figures.[57]

Charles Taylor has urged us to see Herder's response to Condillac as a turning-point in the history of reflection about language.[58] Condillac explains the origin of language in terms of the linking of verbal propensities with thoughts; in doing so, he takes the content of thoughts for granted. This way of thinking exemplifies the Enlightenment's tendency to objectify not only nature but also the human subject.[59] An objectified view of linguistic behaviour cannot

54. Compare n. 28 above. One might seek to make the code conception innocuous by way of a functionalist account of the contents of mental states; see, e.g., Brian Loar, *Mind and Meaning*. I cannot discuss this here; I am confident, in view of "What Do I Know When I Know a Language?", pp. 98–9, that it would not convince Dummett.

55. I borrow this use of "minded" from Jonathan Lear, "Leaving the World Alone".

56. It should be clear that this is not a mere demarcation issue, such as Dummett discusses in "What Is a Theory of Meaning?", p. 118.

57. See Charles Taylor, *Hegel*, pp. 565–7.

58. *Hegel*, pp. 18–19; see also pp. 565–9.

59. *Hegel*, pp. 3–11.

see it as intrinsically imbued with content, any more than an objectified view of nature can see it as intrinsically purposive. So if linguistic behaviour, viewed in an objectified way, is to be credited with content, it can only be because the behaviour is taken to be an external effect of mental states, and mental states are taken to be the primary locus of content. With the outward surface of speech thus objectified, mindedness necessarily retreats behind the surface. When Herder protests that content as such cannot be taken for granted, as it is in this way of thinking, he strikes at the foundations of this whole Enlightenment picture. The "expressivism" he puts in its place rejects the objectification of speech, which would force us to see any content it carries as derivative from that of thoughts lying behind it. In this different view, there is no making sense of the idea of naked thought lying behind linguistic clothing; and what we might call "conceptual consciousness" is not a datum but an achievement, won by acquiring mastery of language, which is conceived as an intrinsically expressive (contentful) mode of activity.

Dummett's position seems to reflect a partial sharing of Herder's intuitions. There is a striking affinity between Herder's protest against Condillac and the motivation for Dummett's requirement of full-bloodedness. But we have seen reason to believe that Dummett's position comes adrift from its motivation. Full-bloodedness—the requirement that linguistic practice be completely characterized "as from outside" content—raises the threat of behaviourism; and, contrary to what Dummett supposes, the threat can be countered—the mind reinstated—only by relying on an essentially psychologistic appeal to simplicity (see §6). Now these historical considerations provide a suggestive diagnosis. The requirement of full-bloodedness—the idea that a language is fully characterizable "as from outside" content—looks like a typical piece of Enlightenment objectification. What has happened is that Dummett has tried to work out what is in fact an anti-Enlightenment insight in Enlightenment terms; and, perhaps unsurprisingly, the results are incoherent.

I can think of no better project for philosophy than to try to understand the place of content—of conceptual consciousness—in the world.[60] This is a task that is both more pressing and more difficult

60. If I understand Rorty correctly, he would regard a remark like this as expressive of a suspect desire to preserve for philosophy an ahistorical role as the foundation of culture. (See *Philosophy and the Mirror of Nature.*) But I think it would be a distortion to suggest that refusing to find content as such unproblematic requires as its background the concep-

in an age in which Enlightenment views of man and his relation to nature are in the ascendant. Suspicion of such views finds a natural home in the expressivist tradition, which yields a conception of the project as being—to put it in quasi-Hegelian terms—to understand how the mindedness of a community, embodied in its linguistic institutions, comes to realize itself in an individual consciousness. (Notice that this assigns the task squarely to the philosophy of language.) Of course constructing modest theories of meaning would be, in itself, no contribution to this task, and I believe it is a perception of this that underlies Dummett's insistence on full-bloodedness. But in fact full-bloodedness, so far from being a necessary means, is a positive obstacle to the fulfilment of the task; resignation to the idea that theories of meaning can be modest at best is an absolutely essential precondition.[61]

---

tion of philosophy whose development Rorty discusses. That is the Enlightenment's conception of philosophy; whereas—as the possibility of mentioning Herder indicates—the refusal is essentially a *reaction* to Enlightenment ideas. In fact Rorty's own refusal to find intentionality problematic smacks to me of an uncritical Enlightenment faith (especially perhaps in his suggestion—see pp. 26–7—that a functionalist account of thoughts could do for brain states the very thing that Wittgenstein does for utterances by situating meaning in human forms of life).

61. Taylor, in "Theories of Meaning", seems to me to have this completely wrong; see especially p. 279, n. 14. I am obviously in considerable sympathy with much of what Taylor says in his lecture. I cannot here deal with what I think goes wrong in his argument, but I shall make one remark. Taylor seems to me to be too willing to make his Enlightenment opponents a present of the notion of representation, and with it, of the notions of truth and the world; he then reads this Enlightenment view of what genuine representation would be, indiscriminately, into truth-conditional conceptions of meaning.

ESSAY 5

Another Plea for Modesty[1]

1. Modesty, in relation to meaning, is (in Dummett's words) the denial that we can "hope to give an account of the concepts expressible by the primitive vocabulary" of a language.[2]

The term first came into use, in this context, in connection with Donald Davidson's suggestion that a theory of truth for a language, in the style of Tarski, can be treated as if it were a meaning-theory for it.[3] Such a theory would deal with, say, a predicate belonging to the language in question by specifying a condition under which that predicate is true of objects. In one kind of case, the "homophonic", the theory would specify the condition by simply using the predicate itself, saying something on these lines: "is agile" is true of something if and only if it is agile. In another kind of case, the "heterophonic", in which the theory is given in a language that is not just an extension of the object language, it would use a predicate in the background language that, if the theory was doing its job, would be shown by that very fact to express the same concept as the predicate that was being dealt with. Either way, such a theory would not as-

1. This essay was written for a Festschrift for Michael Dummett. In one way I was sorry to persist, on such an occasion, with a topic Dummett thinks he has disposed of, and perhaps by now finds merely tiresome. But I do not think the matter is settled, and I know no better way to honour a philosopher than to continue to find his thoughts worth taking issue with. Dummett's attitude to modesty is not peripheral; it is intimately bound up with central themes in his work, as I hope parts of this essay will bear out.

2. *The Logical Basis of Metaphysics*, p. 108.

3. See "Truth and Meaning". (I formulate the suggestion in the terminology that Dummett explains at p. 22 of *The Logical Basis of Metaphysics*.) I used "modest" in an ancestor of Essay 8 below, and Dummett picked it up in "What Is a Theory of Meaning"?

pire to explain the concept. If the concept could be analysed, giving the analysis would in one sense serve to explain the concept, but the explanation would be off-stage, so far as the theory itself was concerned.[4] And if the concept was primitive, in the sense of being unanalysable, not even that option would be open. So on the face of it this kind of approach to the notion of meaning does not "give an account of concepts". Now to embrace modesty is to hold that this is not a matter of shirking a task that it would be sensible to undertake; rather, the lack of ambition is dictated by the nature of the case.

Dummett regards modesty as anti-intellectual and defeatist.[5] He has offered a putatively charitable reading of Davidson that sets aside his first impression that Davidson's approach to meaning is modest.[6] Whether this does Davidson a favour obviously depends on whether modesty is indeed deplorable. I shall return to Dummett's reading of Davidson, but first I shall begin questioning Dummett's impatience with modesty.

2. What exactly would it be to "give an account of concepts"? Perhaps the best way to come at this is to ask: what is "giving an account of concepts" supposed to be for?

Sometimes Dummett's formulations make it look as if the point is merely pedagogical: a meaning-theory for a language ought to be something that one could exploit in order to impart an understanding of the language—and not just, as in the "heterophonic" case of modesty, by trading on the audience's prior understanding of another language in which the same concepts can be expressed; rather, the theory ought to be capable of equipping an audience with the concepts.[7] But this thought will not support the idea that modesty is *everywhere* to be deplored. Surely no theory, about any reasonably rich language, could be used to impart all the concepts expressible in that language; at least some of them would be among the concepts

4. See Davidson's distinction between giving the logical form and analysing the primitives: "Truth and Meaning", pp. 30–2.

5. See in particular "What Is a Theory of Meaning?", and "Reply to John McDowell" (which is a response to Essay 4 above).

6. "What Is a Theory of Meaning?", Appendix; *The Logical Basis of Metaphysics*, pp. 108–10.

7. See, for instance, the talk of deriving an understanding of a language from a theory of it in "What Is a Theory of Meaning?", pp. 103–4.

that the theory itself employed, so that it would need to take for granted that anyone to whom it was addressed already had them.

But Dummett's real point is different, and much more interesting. Just by itself, saying that some predicate is satisfied by something if and only if it is agile does not even purport to tell us what the predicate *means*. (Consider saying that something satisfies "cordate" if and only if it has a kidney.) When Davidson suggests that a certain sort of truth-theory can be *treated as if it were* a meaning-theory, his point is that one could arrive at a truth-theory for a language by achieving a set of entitlements that are stronger than what the theory actually says. In the case of a theory that says something satisfies such-and-such a predicate if and only if it is agile, the relevant entitlement would be to suppose that predicating that predicate of something yields a form of words suitable for *expressing the thought*, of that thing, *that it is agile;* and similarly throughout the theory. I say "expressing the thought" and not, say, "asserting", because the entitlement relates in the first instance to forms of words that can figure as unasserted components of whole utterances, say as antecedents of conditionals; but ultimately the whole construction would need to be anchored in entitlement to suppositions about what complete speech acts, assertions in the case of indicative sentences, can be made by uttering forms of words in the language. What the truth-theory actually says can now recede into the background. What really interests us is the content of those entitlements, and a truth-theory established in the right way is no more than a manageable device for collecting the business parts of the entitlements, the connection between, on the one hand, words and combinations of words and, on the other, what one can express by using them, though the truth-theory does not itself specify anything as that.

Now what Dummett objects to is the way such an approach to meaning simply uses terms like (in the version I have given) "express the thought that . . .". This violates a condition he imposes on a proper meaning-theory (and hence indirectly on anything about which one could claim, as Davidson does about certain truth-theories, that it can be used as if it were a meaning-theory). Dummett's condition is that a proper meaning-theory must not "take as already given any notions a grasp of which is possible only for a language-speaker" (*The Logical Basis of Metaphysics,* p. 13). According to Dummett, a proper meaning-theory for a language must describe the practice of using words in it, which is what is mastered by someone who has a mastery of the language, without employing terms like "express the thought that . . .", or more specific terms that introduce different forces with which thoughts can be expressed, like "assert that . . ." or "ask whether . . ." (see *The Logical Basis of Metaphysics,* p. 53). So we may not help ourselves to ideas like that of expressing the thought, of something, that it is agile. A proper meaning-theory would yield an account of *what it is* to express such a thought in the language in question, in terms of using such-and-such an expression in such-and-such ways, where the ways are *not* captured only by saying something like "so as to be intelligibly taken to be expressing the thought, of something, that it is agile".

What drives the objection, taken this way, is not really a wish to have something non-trivial to say about this or that specific concept (from among the concepts that are expressible, like the concept of agility, in uses of language that are not themselves about language), or even about all such concepts.[8] The point of rejecting modesty relates rather to the very idea of content, as it might figure in an obvious gloss on phrases like "express the thought that . . .". Dummett's conviction is that a properly illuminating account of a language must describe what is in fact a practice of thought-expression, but in other terms; then we can say that the description spells out what it is in virtue of which the practice is the practice of thought-expression that it is. Philosophy demands an account of the practice of speaking a language that displays its character as linguistic, but is given from outside the idea of giving linguistic expression to thoughts.[9]

There is indeed a connection with the question how concepts might be imparted; but it is not that a subject ought to be able to acquire the concepts expressible in the language by being told what the theory states, but that, if the description of linguistic practice does what is required of it, a subject can acquire those concepts by achieving mastery of the practice that the theory describes.

What adherents of modesty deny, then, is the feasibility of this sort of account of the practice of speaking a language: an account

8. This is not to say that rejecting modesty has nothing to do with what is incumbent on philosophers when they come to say something about this or that concept. Rejecting modesty belongs with the requirement of non-circularity imposed on this activity by Christopher Peacocke in *A Study of Concepts.*

9. Compare Dummett's implication that a proper account of a language would be given "as from the outside": "Frege and Wittgenstein", p. 40. I gave this reading of the rejection of modesty in Essay 4 above, and Dummett tacitly accepted it in "Reply to John McDowell".

given from outside the thoughts expressible in the language, and indeed from outside the very idea of expressing thoughts, but nevertheless such as to display what makes the behavioural repertoire it deals with a case of speaking a language (compare *The Logical Basis of Metaphysics,* p. 13).

Dummett thinks there is no ground for claiming that this sort of account of the practice of speaking a language is "impossible, rather than merely difficult" (*The Logical Basis of Metaphysics,* p. 136). So of course he regards modesty as defeatist. But there is plenty of ground for doubting the feasibility of the sort of account that Dummett envisages. I shall mention two considerations.

3. First, the connection of language with rationality, on which Dummett rightly insists:

> I have many times remarked that a theory of meaning [i.e. a meaning-theory, in the terminology of *The Logical Basis of Metaphysics*] is not to be assessed as a scientific systematisation of regularities in complex phenomena; it is to be judged by whether it gives an intelligible description of a practice engaged in by rational agents. We are not looking for a theory with predictive power, but for a description that makes sense of the activity as one carried out by rational beings.[10]

This is hard to combine with insisting that the theory must not describe linguistic performances in such terms as "expressing the thought that . . .".

It is a familiar point that we make rational sense of the behaviour of ourselves and others only under appropriate descriptions. Not every true characterization of what someone is doing displays it so as to be intelligible as a bit of rational agency. Now on the face of it, our capacity for rational understanding gets its grip on linguistic behaviour precisely under descriptions of the sort Dummett disallows.

10. "Reply to John McDowell", p. 260. In this passage, which does indeed reiterate a frequent claim, Dummett is responding to an accusation of behaviourism that he takes me to have levelled against him in Essay 4 above. But I levelled no such accusation. On the contrary, I gave him full credit for the aim of steering between behaviourism and psychologism. My claim is that his way of trying to do that admirable thing does not work. (I did not accuse him of confusing use and mention either; compare "Reply to John McDowell", p. 265. I acknowledged that *given* Dummett's assumption that a proper meaning-theory is to be formulated as from outside the language, any such protest falls flat.)

We make rational sense of ourselves and others as saying that . . . , asking whether . . . , and so forth. Dummett envisages an account of the practice of speaking a language that avoids such terms, but somehow duplicates their potential for making sense of behaviour, presumably by displaying patterns within the activity, with their individual elements otherwise characterized. But what reason is there to suppose that the sense that we make of linguistic behaviour is still available to us, if when we contemplate the behaviour we are required to deny ourselves the very terms in which we ordinarily make sense of it? What reason is there to suppose that there are non-ordinary terms in which it will still make sense?

Dummett claims to be offering a schematic recipe for saying *what it is* for linguistic behaviour to be intelligible in the surface terms in which ordinary rational understanding engages with it. To me he seems rather to be telling us to describe linguistic behaviour in a way that would obliterate, not deepen, the rational intelligibility that we know it has. It is all very well to require that the envisaged account of a language must display the practice it describes as involving the exercise of rational agency. The sceptical thought is that when Dummett disallows the terms in which ordinary rational understanding engages with linguistic behaviour, so far from pointing the way to deeper understanding, he merely ensures that that requirement cannot be met. An account given from outside is an account that denies itself the only descriptions under which we know that linguistic actions make rational sense, and we have been given no reason to suppose we can still see the activity of a speaker as hanging together rationally if we are required to describe it in other terms.

Dummett suggests that when I express this kind of scepticism, I commit myself to the idea that a word's meaning what it does in a language (say) is "a mysterious non-natural property" of it, something that floats quite free of what mastery of the language permits speakers to do with the word; as if putatively linguistic behaviour, characterized in the terms that Dummett's restriction allows, could be just anyhow, without prejudice to its being intelligible in the way that competent speech in a language is.[11] But there is no such impli-

11. See pp. 259–60 of "Reply to John McDowell", where Dummett surmises that I take ascriptions of meaning to be "barely true"; the phrase I quote in the text is from p. 262, where Dummett is expressing a related thought.

cation. *Of course* it matters, for one's intelligibility as a speaker of a language, that one's utterances of its expressions should be appropriately related to one another, to utterances of others, to the environment, to one's own non-linguistic behaviour, and so forth. But that leaves it open that there is no way to give a complete characterization of the required patterning of linguistic behaviour—the sort of thing that might answer questions like "What does it *consist in* that people use such-and-such a word so as to predicate agility of things?"—without appealing to such ideas as the idea of acting in such a way that one can be intelligibly taken to be expressing the thought that something is agile.[12]

I suppose it could still seem that this scepticism is merely defeatist. Why not at least look and see if we can find a way to display linguistic behaviour as rationally intelligible without the disallowed conceptual materials? But I think much of the force of this thought depends on the illicit suggestion I have just rejected, the suggestion that we have to choose between holding that an account in the restricted terms must be possible, on the one hand, and holding (absurdly) that words carry their meanings in sheer independence of what people do with them, on the other. If we clear away that illusion of compulsoriness, I think we can see that there is really no plausibility in the idea that linguistic behaviour would still present itself to us as rationally intelligible, if we were restricted to viewing it in the terms that Dummett allows.

4. The second consideration is an idea from Wittgenstein's reflections on following a rule.

12. Dummett writes (p. 259 of "Reply to John McDowell"): "In my opinion, by contrast [to McDowell's], the words and sentences of a language mean what they do by virtue of their role in the enormously complex social practice in which the employment of the language consists." But I can accept that form of words. It is quite consistent with denying, not that "what renders [a correct ascription of meaning] true lies open to view", as Dummett says I do, but that there is anything, specifiable in the restricted terms Dummett allows, that renders such an ascription true. (In another sense, though, what renders a correct ascription of meaning true does lie open to view.) There is nothing here to rule out an interest in the detail of how competent linguistic behaviour is patterned, as described in terms of Dummett's restriction. (Something similar goes for Peacocke's non-circularity requirement.) My problem is just with the idea that there must be something to be said, in those terms, in the "consists in" or "what renders . . . true" style.

When we describe some linguistic performance as, say, asserting of something that it is agile, we make explicit a potential for rational intelligibility. In Dummett's conception, that potential can be duplicated by a description that does not presuppose the notion of giving expression to content, or any specific version of that notion. The second description can then be taken to say what it is for the first to be true of a performance. The duplicating description would have to work by placing the performance it describes in some pattern to which behaviour in the relevant language is required to conform. (The elements of the pattern must hang together rationally; that is the Dummettian requirement about whose feasibility, in conjunction with the restriction on conceptual material, I have been suggesting a doubt.)

Now the point from Wittgenstein is that for any pattern to which a stretch of linguistic behaviour can be made out to conform, as described in terms that function below the level of explicitly specifying meanings as such, there are always other patterns that the same stretch of behaviour can equally be made out to exemplify. Wittgenstein dramatizes this by considering cases in which someone is to extend a series of numbers. If we have to capture the pattern in someone's writing a series of numerals otherwise than in terms like "obeying the instruction to go on adding 2", there are always alternative patterns that fit any stretch of such behaviour; for instance, if the series-extender has not yet reached 1000, a pattern that goes ". . . , 998, 1000, 1002, 1004, . . ." and a pattern that goes ". . . , 998, 1000, 1004, 1008, . . . ".[13] But the point is really quite general; it extends outside the particular case of number series. And it is unaffected by Dummett's insistence that the patterns we are to look for must hang together rationally; indeed, in the representative case of the series "2, 4, 6, 8, . . . , 996, 998, . . .", the competing pattern is precisely an alternative candidate for making rational sense of the behaviour—if we are not allowed to make sense of it as obeying the instruction to add 2 (or executing the intention to add 2).

Dummett insists that, on pain of an intolerable psychologism, the meaning that speakers of a language attach to, say, a word must lie open to view in the use they make of it, rather than being a topic for

13. See *Philosophical Investigations* §185.

hypothesizing, something we would have to conceive as lying behind their linguistic behaviour.[14] This insistence strikes me as admirable. But I cannot see how it can be made to cohere with the Wittgensteinian point, in the context of Dummett's response to modesty. If I am watching someone writing down a series of numerals, and I am not allowed to conceptualize what she is manifestly doing in terms like "obeying the instruction to add 2", then what is open to my view at any time, including what has been open to my view up to that time, cannot make it more than a hypothesis for me that she is not putting into practice a pattern that goes, say, ". . . , 998, 1000, 1004, 1008, . . .". Obviously it makes no difference of principle if her series already includes ". . . , 1002, 1004, . . ."; there will still be points she has not passed, and we can rework the example accordingly. If it is true that the Wittgensteinian point is general, this seems devastating for Dummett's conception. The implication is this: if the fact that speakers mean this rather than that by, say, a word did consist in the sort of thing Dummett says it must consist in, it *could* not lie open to view in their linguistic behaviour. Described in the terms in which Dummett says we must describe what such facts consist in, the linguistic behaviour of any of our interlocutors always leaves open possibilities of futures that would be like the ". . . , 1000, 1004, 1008, . . ." continuation in the number-series case. It could be no better than a hypothesis that some such thing would not happen, and if it did, that would wreck our claim to have understood the interlocutor in question even before the noticeable peculiarity set in: even while it was still seeming that we could make sense of her by taking her speech at face value—that is, conceiving it in the disallowed terms. If her meaning what she does must not be a hypothesis, it cannot consist in the correctness of what would be a hypothesis if Dummett's restriction were in force: namely, that the pattern in her behaviour is not one that takes that sort of surprising turn at some point not yet reached.

We should not take the Wittgensteinian point to undermine Dummett's insistence that meaning is open to view in linguistic behaviour, or to reveal an unexpected fragility in our claims to understand one another. In real life, at least in some cases, it can be much better than a mere hypothesis for me that someone is not engaged on a pattern that

14. See especially "What Do I Know When I Know a Language".

goes on ". . . , 1000, 1004, 1008, . . .". I can know that she will not go on like that—barring mental aberration, a prank, or whatever. But that is because in such cases I know that what she is doing warrants a description at the level of "obeying the instruction to add 2". I have the knowledge I do of the pattern to which the behaviour conforms (and, failing aberration and so forth, will continue to conform), as described in terms that function below the level of that description, only derivatively from my knowledge that that description applies. If I suspend that knowledge, as I must if I am required to refrain from using the concepts that figure in it, the pattern takes on, as before, the aspect of a hypothesis, and we come into collision with Dummett's admirable insistence that mutual understanding does not involve going beyond what is open to view in linguistic behaviour.

In earlier essays I tried to summarize this point by claiming that we have perceptual access to the concepts expressed in performances in a familiar language.[15] Dummett can find nothing here but a phenomenological claim, of a sort one could equally make in a number of other cases. He can happily allow that one sees or hears its meaning in a familiar word, if that comes to the same sort of thing as the fact that one irresistibly associates a sound with a string of letters in a familiar script.[16] It seems evident that the phenomenological intimacy with which the thought of a sound is bound up with the sight of a letter-string is no bar to looking for accounts of what it consists in that such-and-such a string of letters is correctly read by uttering such-and-such phonemes. Such accounts are just what orthography (in a broad sense) provides. So the claim that we perceive meanings, taken in a parallel way, is no threat to Dummett's conception.

But I meant something more than this phenomenological claim. I meant to make an epistemological claim—one that I take to be warranted by the Wittgensteinian point. In the phonetic case, what corresponds, epistemologically, to the phenomenological point is a mere cognitive short-cut. Someone *could* arrive at judgements as to how a letter-string is to be pronounced by arguing explicitly from which letters occur in which order, against the background of an orthography

15. See Essay 4 above and Essay 15 below; and, for some background, "Wittgenstein on Following a Rule".

16. "Reply to John McDowell", pp. 257–8. See especially p. 258, where, having talked about familiarity with a script, Dummett says: "The phenomenon that obsesses McDowell, of hearing the meanings in the words, is surely similar."

for the script in which the string is written. In becoming familiar with the script, one acquires cognitive machinery that directly induces propensities to make judgements that could be reached in that way: "directly" in the sense that one does not need to judge on the basis of those considerations, although for someone else they might figure in explicit groundings for those judgements. But in the case of hearing meanings, it is not a question of a cognitive short-cut. The Wittgensteinian point implies that it *could* not be, on pain of violating Dummett's own principle that knowledge of meanings in a familiar language is not a hypothesis. Of course the features of utterances that would figure in a Dummettian description of linguistic practice do not drop out of conscious awareness; but we cannot reconstruct the epistemic entitlement constituted by knowledge of meanings in terms of awareness of such features, against the background of a theory that says in such terms what someone's meaning this or that consists in. The cognitive access to meanings possessed by someone who knows a language is perceptual in a richer sense than any that fits the cognitive access to sounds possessed by someone who is familiar with a script.[17]

5. One aspect of the question of modesty is an issue about the internal articulation within a meaning-theory, or equally within a truth-theory serving as a stand-in for a meaning-theory, as in Davidson's proposal. In Dummett's view, the appearance of articulation at a given level—at the level of what the theory says about sentences in the language if the theory is to be molecular, at the level of what it says about words if the theory is to be atomic—is revealed to be fraudulent (to give only an illusion of analysing mastery of the language into components), if the theory does not incorporate an account of *what it is* for a proposition at that level to belong in a characterization of mastery of the language. He understands this requirement of "giving an account" in terms of the restriction I have been discussing. It does not count as doing what is required, in connection with a proposition to the effect that something satisfies the predicate "agile" if and only if it is agile, to say that the fit of this to

17. Dummett suggests that on my account it ought to be mysterious what becoming accustomed to the practice of speaking a language has to do with acquiring the capacity to perceive meanings in its expressions: "Reply to John McDowell", p. 258. I think this reflects the false dilemma that I remarked on in the last section: the idea that, since I disbelieve in the sort of account of what, say, a word's having its meaning consists in that Dummett envisages, I must think a word's having its meaning floats quite free of how the practice of using it is shaped.

competence in the language consists in the fact that speakers of the language use "agile", in suitable conjunction with other expressions of the language, in such a way as to be intelligibly taken to be giving expression to thoughts to the effect that things are agile. So according to Dummett, if a theorist stops at that sort of thing, the appearance of atomicity that the theory presents, by virtue of containing clauses that deal with individual predicates, is shown up as bogus.[18]

This seems tendentious. It is one thing to hold that we ought to want mastery of a language to be articulated in terms that function beneath the level of content-specification. But, even independently of scepticism about that, which I have suggested is well-placed, it is surely quite another thing to hold that *no* articulation of mastery of a language is effected by saying things like, in effect: "agile" is used in this language to predicate agility of things. That exemplifies a kind of statement that is specifically about a single atom of the language, but could be exploited, together with suitable similar statements about other expressions, so as to display how what can be done with whole utterances containing the atom—as characterized, of course, in terms of what thought is expressed, perhaps in some specific mode—depends on the presence of that atom in the form of words uttered. It seems perverse to deny that something on these lines would effect *some* articulation of mastery of the language into components.[19] And this articulation would make contact with what speakers of the language actually do at—one might suppose—exactly the right points: namely, the descriptions under which they themselves make sense of their linguistic behaviour.

I described the task of fitting a structured theory to actual practice in terms of what it is for a proposition of the theory to belong in a characterization of mastery of the language. This formulation bypasses an issue that Dummett makes a great deal of. At corresponding points, Dummett speaks of what it is for a speaker of a language to *know* a proposition that figures in a meaning-theory for it. Dummett argues that such propositions cannot in general be the content of explicit knowledge, knowledge that speakers could state; and that that makes it incumbent on a meaning-theorist to do more than specify the content of such knowledge. A meaning-theorist must give an account of what

18. See especially "What Is a Theory of Meaning?".

19. Perhaps Dummett's thought is not that no articulation is effected here, but that what is articulated is not what mastery of the language consists in. That just takes us back to the issue of modesty in the form in which I have already discussed it.

it is for someone to have such knowledge, in terms of how it is *manifested* in linguistic practice, where (as usual) linguistic practice must be described without using terms like "express the thought that . . ." or "predicate of something that it is . . .".[20]

But it seems a bad idea for a meaning-theorist to identify mastery of a language with knowledge of any kind, explicit or not, of the propositions in a meaning-theory. The only point at which a meaning-theory need directly engage with linguistic practice is in the statements it yields about what can be done with whole utterances. Certainly it will aspire to display how what can be done with whole utterances depends on component expressions, but the theoretical apparatus it employs for this purpose need not be even implicitly at the disposal of just any competent speaker of the language—unless one counts as manifesting implicit knowledge that "agile" can be used to predicate agility if one can say things like "Michael Jordan is agile" so as to be intelligibly taken to be expressing the thought that Michael Jordan is agile, and can understand others similarly. If knowledge is generally in question only at the level of whole utterances, there is no threat to modesty in Dummett's principle about the intellectual obligations incurred by an appeal to non-explicit knowledge. The content of the relevant knowledge is given by the descriptions under which speakers make rational sense of their behaviour, and that knowledge is knowledge that ordinarily competent speakers *can* make explicit; they can say what, for instance, someone is saying.

No doubt a moderately reflective speaker will have quasi-explicit knowledge of such facts as that "agile" can be used to predicate agility. Even if learning a language were not typically bound up with explicitly learning, for instance, bits of its syntax, one would not need much reflection, about how one's ability to make sense of the relevant utterances relates to the manifestly perceptible features of those utterances, to acquire knowledge of that sort of theory-fragment.[21] But if such knowledge is at least quasi-explicitly possessed if at all, it does not come within the scope of Dummett's principle about attributions of non-explicit knowledge.

20. For an early version of this argument, see "What Is a Theory of Meaning?". A recent version is in chap. 4 of *The Logical Basis of Metaphysics*.

21. The manifestly perceptible features of utterances do not drop out of conscious awareness. Since I insist on that, I run no risk of falling into the "barely intelligible" picture of a putatively possible relationship to linguistic behaviour that Dummett considers at pp. 90–1 of *The Logical Basis of Metaphysics*.

If we decline to extend claims that speakers, in general, know things to the propositions that would make up the interior of a meaning-theory, we do not threaten our ability to display linguistic behaviour as rationally intelligible. That is secured by the way a modest meaning-theory would engage, at its periphery, with the descriptions under which speakers themselves make rational sense of their linguistic performances. Understanding a language is a capacity to see linguistic performances in it as intentional under such descriptions, and to make one's own linguistic performances intelligible in that way to others. A modest meaning-theory would articulate such a capacity at exactly the right joints to display the capacity as rational through and through: namely, at joints marked by articulation discernible in the descriptions under which the rational understanding of the participants makes sense of the behaviour, which mirrors articulation discernible in the manifestly perceptible features of the utterances that are intelligible under those descriptions. It seems harder to be confident that an immodest meaning-theory, articulating a capacity for linguistic behaviour in terms required to be other than those that figure in an ordinary speaker's understanding, can do justice to "the fact that the use of language is a conscious rational activity—we might say *the* rational activity—of intelligent agents" (*The Logical Basis of Metaphysics,* p. 91).[22]

22. At pp. 103–4 of *The Logical Basis of Metaphysics,* Dummett notes that Davidson (in the mature version of his proposal) does not credit speakers with knowledge of the propositions of a meaning-theory (or, better, of a truth-theory serving as if it were a meaning-theory). Davidson claims only that knowledge of the theory *would* enable a person to speak the language in question. Dummett says: "To this the natural response is to ask why we should adopt so roundabout a route to describing a practical competence: why not simply describe what it is that a competent speaker has the capacity to do? The right answer is that knowledge of a language is not merely a species of practical competence but is also genuine knowledge, and that the meaning-theory is intended as an organised and fully explicit representation of the content of that knowledge." I think this misses Davidson's point. A meaning-theory aims to capture a capacity for actual (explicit) knowledge, knowledge whose content is given by the descriptions under which speakers make sense of their behaviour; it seems clear that such a capacity would be compendiously described if we could formulate knowledge that, if explicitly applied in the relevant situations, *would* yield the knowledge that the capacity in fact yields. The point of that counterfactual formulation is that possessors of the capacity simply do not in general have such knowledge (not even a less systematic counterpart to it, which is what Dummett supposes Davidson must have in mind when he declines to attribute actual knowledge of the theory). As I have insisted, this denial fully respects the fact that linguistic behaviour on the part of possessors of such a capacity is an exercise of rational agency.

6. In this section, I shall briefly mention three further points on which Dummett's attitude to modesty leads him to claims that strike me as tendentious.

First, as I remarked at the beginning of this essay, Dummett disowns his initial impression that Davidson's approach to meaning is modest. He substitutes a reading that incorporates what Davidson calls "evidence" for a truth-theory (of a sort able to be treated as if it were a meaning-theory) into the content of the meaning-theory; on this reading, what it consists in for someone to know the propositions of the meaning-theory is that she knows the relevant stretches of the "evidence".[23] But as a reading of Davidson, this strikes me as fanciful. In speaking of evidence, Davidson expresses a certain conception of how facts about the circumstances in which speakers hold sentences true relate to an interpretation of a language, and Dummett admits that he has to discount that. This might be justified if, as Dummett thinks, taking Davidson at his word would leave him shirking intellectual obligations that everyone must acknowledge. But the supposed obligations are anything but unquestionable; we can understand Davidson's proposal *au pied de la lettre.*[24]

Second, in some places Dummett suggests that a meaning-theorist who declines to give an account, in the approved sense, of elements in mastery of a language is thereby disqualified from appealing to the Fregean notion of sense.[25] But the point of the Fregean notion of sense is just that we need a notion of content sufficiently fine-grained to allow our descriptions of content-possessing states to connect in

23. The shift takes place between the text and the Appendix of "What Is a Theory of Meaning?". See also pp. 108–10 of *The Logical Basis of Metaphysics.*

24. In suggesting that Davidson would have to acknowledge an obligation to answer the question what it consists in for someone to know the propositions of a meaning-theory, Dummett brushes aside Davidson's express refusal to equate mastery of a language with knowledge of such propositions. See n. 22 above.

25. See "What Is a Theory of Meaning?", p. 128. In "What Is a Theory of Meaning? (II)", Dummett equates a theory of sense with a theory that gives such accounts; the theory of sense is required to be in place, saying what it is for propositions from the theory of reference to be appropriately used in characterizing mastery of a language, before we embark on the theory of force, and that ensures that the theory of sense cannot avail itself of notions like that of thought-expression or its various modes. (See especially p. 74.) At p. 135 of *The Logical Basis of Metaphysics,* Dummett writes: "A good case can be made that a modest meaning-theory accords with Frege's ideas." I am not sure whether this is a repudiation of his earlier claim that modesty is incompatible with Frege's ideas, or whether the "good case" is supposed to be revealed as not good enough by what Dummett goes on to say (especially at p. 136).

the right way with our conception of rationality. If failing to distinguish senses would leave us liable to have to attribute to a rational and unconfused subject, at the same time, rationally opposed "propositional attitudes" (say, some pair of belief, disbelief, and suspended judgement) with the same content, then we must distinguish senses, so as to make possible a description of such a subject's stance that has different contents for the attitudes, and so does not raise a question about the rationality of the stance. To reject the notion of sense would be, for instance, to claim that a meaning-theory would never need to differentiate what it says about a pair of proper names for the same object. Now a modest approach to meaning can perfectly well make such a differentiation, if it matters—as it sometimes does—for achieving a fit to the linguistic activity of rational speakers. So it is quite unwarranted to suggest that the notion of sense is in play only within an account of mastery of a language that meets Dummett's restriction.[26] Indeed, the scepticism I expressed in §3 puts the boot on the other foot: Frege's notion of sense can be in play only if thoughts are in view (in the sense in which we can speak of "expressing (the thought) that . . ."), and at the conceptual level at which Dummett claims we must say what mastery of a language consists in, it is, as I have urged, open to doubt that thoughts or thought-expressions are in view at all.

Third, when Dummett imposes his restriction on the terms available for an account of what mastery of a language consists in, that amounts to stipulating a way of understanding the notion of use or linguistic practice (what meaning has to be manifest in). On this understanding, "features of use" (see, e.g., *The Logical Basis of Metaphysics,* p. 102) cannot include anything capturable only by, for instance, saying what someone who speaks in a certain way would be saying. By the same token, they cannot include the truth-condition of an utterance, on a conception fixed by the observation, which seems truistic, that if one specifies what someone who utters an assertoric

26. At pp. 263–4 of "Reply to John McDowell", there is a puzzling discussion of a previous attempt by me to make this point (Essay 4 above, §8). I would have thought it was clear that I quoted Dummett's phrase "a theory which repudiates the notion of sense altogether" (out of the specific context in which Dummett placed it) precisely in order to controvert the conditional about which Dummett nevertheless says "the passage from [its] antecedent [a theory refuses to give an account of senses, where 'give an account' is understood in terms of Dummett's restriction] to [its] consequent [the theory repudiates the notion of sense altogether] does not seem highly controversial".

sentence would be saying, one cannot but be specifying a condition under which the sentence, as then uttered, would express a truth. This is why Dummett can say that the central terms of a truth-conditional meaning-theory "do not directly relate to linguistic practice" (*The Logical Basis of Metaphysics,* p. 104). But if we take it that what we count as features of use or linguistic practice should be features credited to linguistic behaviour by the descriptions in terms of which the rational understanding of its participants engages with it, then this suggestion, that the notion of truth-conditions stands at some remove from what is manifest in linguistic practice, is the very reverse of the truth. (Things are precisely the other way round: what stands at a remove from linguistic practice is the features in terms of which an immodest meaning-theory describes it, denying itself the concepts under which participants make sense of it.) The suggestion is of course central to Dummett's campaign against truth-conditional approaches to meaning.[27]

7. What Dummett perhaps finds most scandalous about modest approaches to meaning is their insouciant attitude to the validation of logic.

A truth-theory of Davidson's sort would deal with the sentential logical connectives by saying things to this effect: "A and B" is true just in case "A" is true and "B" is true, "A or B" is true just in case "A" is true or "B" is true, "If A, then B" is true just in case, if "A" is true, then "B" is true, and "Not A" is true just in case "A" is not true.[28] But none of that is in dispute between an adherent of classical logic and an intuitionist. In Dummett's view, a proper meaning-theory "must have a semantic theory as its base" (*The Logical Basis of Metaphysics,* p. 138), in a sense of "semantic" according to which questions about soundness and completeness are about the relations between proof-theoretic and semantic characterizations of validity.

27. Dummett will no doubt say that a concept fixed solely on the basis of the truism is not yet the concept of truth-conditions that he attacks; that involves truth as understood by "classical two-valued semantics". I am sceptical that there is a special *notion* of truth in "classical semantics"; some of the considerations in the next section of this essay could be reworked to cast doubt on that. In any case, it would be illicit to use the disputable suggestion that the notion of truth as such is at a distance from practice to bolster the thought that if there is to be any point to conceiving meaning in terms of truth-conditions, that *must* involve giving some such extra theoretical weight to the notion of truth.

28. Strictly this should be put with corner-quotes, or some device to the same purpose. But I follow Dummett's example ("Reply to John McDowell", p. 253) in not bothering with this.

A soundness proof, on this conception, establishes that some set of rules for constructing inferences, of a broadly syntactical kind, yields nothing but inferences that are semantically valid, valid by virtue of the meanings of the logical expressions involved; a completeness proof establishes that it can be made to yield all such inferences. On this conception, a proper account of the meanings of the logical connectives would have to determine which inferences are valid in the "semantic" sense, valid by virtue of those meanings. So the question of the meanings of the logical connectives can scarcely have been so much as broached, if we content ourselves with something that leaves it open which inferences are logically valid, as a modest approach to the sentential connectives does.[29]

Those modest clauses for the sentential connectives amount to the standard truth-tables for them, and it is a way of putting the point I have just rehearsed to say that simply stipulating that the standard truth-tables are correct does not determine that classical sentential logic is valid, as against intuitionist sentential logic. The standard truth-tables yield the validity of the distinctive inferences of classical logic only given the principle of bivalence, which intuitionists do not accept, and which is not enshrined in the truth-tables themselves. This means that in Dummett's conception, giving those modest clauses (or, what comes to the same thing, giving the truth-tables) can be at best programmatic for a proper meaning-theoretical treatment of the sentential logical connectives. We can elaborate it into a fragment of a candidate meaning-theory that would validate classical logic, but only by making a substantial extra move: namely, placing the truth-tables in the context of "classical two-valued semantics", which reads the assignments of truth and falsity, in the lines of the truth-tables, in terms of the principle of bivalence. (Whether such a candidate meaning-theory could engage acceptably with the practice of speaking any except perhaps severely restricted languages is of course, for Dummett, another question.) There is no parallel way for the truth-tables to figure in a candidate meaning-theory that would validate intuitionistic sentential logic, so if that is what our meaning-theory ought to end up doing, the modest approach is not even programmatic for a meaning-theoretical treatment of the sentential connectives.

29. See "Reply to John McDowell", pp. 253–4, for a brief exposition of this thought, to which *The Logical Basis of Metaphysics* elaborates a large-scale background.

All this depends on the thought that the meanings of the logical connectives must be such as to determine which inferences, turning wholly on the presence of those connectives in premises and conclusion, are valid; so that from the disagreement over which inferences are valid, it follows that adherents of classical and intuitionistic sentential logic cannot use the connectives with the same meanings. This is something that Dummett evidently thinks beyond question.[30] However, I believe it can be questioned; most clearly, perhaps, in this very case, which Dummett evidently takes to be conclusive against modesty.

It is important that the intuitionistic view of the principle of bivalence is not that some sentences have another truth-value, or other truth-values, besides truth and falsity. That is reflected in the fact that intuitionistic logic does not deny the law of excluded middle, in the sense of negating it. The double negation of the law of excluded middle is an intuitionistic theorem, even though the law is not; so a putative counter-instance to the law of excluded middle would actually be inconsistent in intuitionistic logic. The status of the law of excluded middle, like that of the other "excess" classical laws, is not that it is denied but just that it is not affirmed.

This means that if we hold in abeyance for the moment the assumption I am questioning, that the meanings of the logical constants must determine the correct logic, we make it possible to understand an adherent of intuitionistic sentential logic whose position is as follows.

First, the meanings of the sentential connectives consist in how the truth-values of complex sentences formed by means of them depend on the truth-values of their component sentences, and that is completely captured by the standard truth-tables. The fact that the truth-tables determine truth-values for complex sentences on the basis of assignments to their components of only the two truth-values, truth and falsity, is no objection to this claim. Intuitionists agree that there are no other truth-values that a sentence can consistently be envisaged as having, so there are no possibilities for determination of truth-values by truth-values that the truth-tables fail to deal with; and the point of suspending the assumption is that it lets us envisage

30. He takes it for granted at the opening of "Reply to John McDowell", and almost throughout *The Logical Basis of Metaphysics*. (I shall consider later the one passage in *The Logical Basis of Metaphysics* where he seems to offer an argument for it.)

an intuitionist who thinks that fixing how truth-values are determined by truth-values is all that needs to be done in order to give the meanings of the sentential connectives. (When Dummett's intuitionist finds no "semantic" relevance in the truth-tables, it is not on the ground that they leave something out; rather, the thought is that they are framed in the wrong terms altogether.)

But, second, given only that a sentence is well-formed, this intuitionist insists that we are not thereby entitled to assume that the sentence is determinately either true or false. And, as is well known, the truth-tables underwrite classical logic only on the assumption of the principle of bivalence. So the question which inferences in sentential logic are valid cannot be wholly settled by the meanings of the connectives, since—the first element in the position—those meanings consist in how the connectives determine truth-values on the basis of truth-values. The question which inferences are valid requires that we consider what we *are* entitled to, at the points in our thinking where classical inferential practice, wrongly according to this thinker, exploits a supposed entitlement to the principle of bivalence. Reflection on these lines will yield a restriction on when, say, arguments by dilemma are acceptable: in fact, just the right restriction to separate intuitionistic sentential logic from the classical version. We may not, as in classical logic, conclude **B** from the fact that we can construct a proof of **B** from **A** and a proof of **B** from the negation of **A**, if all we know about **A** is that it is well-formed. Such arguments are cogent only if we know we could construct either a proof of **A** or a proof of its negation, because only then, as not in the general case, are we entitled to assume that one or the other of the starting-points of the two arguments for **B**, from **A** and from the negation of **A**, is true. This difference is quite characteristic of the difference between the two conceptions of logic. The resulting non-classical conception of which arguments are valid does not undermine the thesis that the meanings of the connectives consist in what the truth-tables say about them, because, as we recall, meanings of which that is true underwrite the distinctively classical inferences only given the principle of bivalence, and we have suspended the assumption that would allow us to infer, from the divergence in inferences endorsed, that the intuitionist's connectives must differ in meaning.

The point of suspending the assumption was to refuse to listen to Dummettian cries of incredulity, while we constructed a partial picture of what it might be like to do without the assumption, so that we can consider its status without prejudice. Of course the picture I have begun to give would need to be filled out.[31] But I think there is enough before us to make it worth asking this question: can we tell in advance that there will be something independently unacceptable about this understanding of the divergence over validity, however it is further spelled out? Is there any reason to insist on reinstating the assumption and ruling out this way of thinking? A hidden inconsistency, for instance, might serve; but is there any inconsistency in conceiving the divergence over validity on these lines?

One thing it would be illicit to exploit here is the label "classical two-valued semantics". If semantics says how expressions affect the bearing on reality of sentences in which they occur, the intuitionist I have envisaged embraces a two-valued semantics for the connectives: namely, the truth-tables. Certainly it is not "*classical* two-valued semantics", which includes the principle of bivalence. But given this understanding of the divergence, that does not make a difference to the meanings that are assigned to the connectives. Those are given in full by the truth-tables, whether or not we take ourselves to have the entitlement that the classical logician claims and the intuitionistic logician disavows. The label "classical semantics", with its implication that that divergence makes a semantical difference, in the sense of a difference in meanings, just begs the question against the position that I am proposing. From this standpoint, it is unclear why the principle of bivalence should be taken to characterize the *semantics* of the connectives as the classical logician understands them, in the intuitive sense of their effect on the way sentences containing them bear on reality; as opposed to being a thesis that is external to the agreed semantics of the connectives, and, in the view of the intuitionist, unwarranted.

There is one place in *The Logical Basis of Metaphysics* (pp. 302-3) where Dummett undertakes to argue for the assumption I have questioned:

> Our fundamental logical laws are those which it is an essential part of our practice in speaking the language to observe. The view that revision of them involves a change in the meanings of the logical constants is unshakable. This is so because it is impossible to deny either that the meanings of the logical constants determine the manner in which the

31. There is a primitive version, with slightly more detail, in §8 of Essay 1 above.

> truth of a complex sentence depends on its constituents, or that the validity of a form of argument depends on whether it is so constructed that the truth of the premisses guarantees the truth of the conclusion. Hence, if we come to view as invalid a form of argument we had formerly considered valid, although there was no mistake that could have been pointed out by appeal to existing linguistic practice, we must have changed the way in which we take the truth-values of the premisses and conclusions to be determined in accordance with their structure; and this entails that we have changed the meanings of the logical constants.

But as far as I can see, the understanding I have sketched of the divergence between classical and intuitionistic sentential logic gives the lie to this argument. I have denied neither of its premises, neither of the things that Dummett says it is impossible to deny. The adherent of intuitionistic logic I envisage holds that the meanings of the sentential connectives determine the manner in which the truth of a complex sentence depends on its constituents (specifically, on their truth-values). Since he thinks mere well-formedness does not guarantee the applicability of the principle of bivalence, this logician can combine that conception of the meanings of the connectives with refusing to grant, in the case of the "excess" classical inferences, that they are so constructed that the truth of the premises guarantees the truth of the conclusion. He might have reached this position by being converted from classical logic, without there being any question of altering the meanings of the sentential connectives.

Dummett insists that if a classical logician and an intuitionist are trying to come to mutual understanding, it is "entirely fruitless" ("Reply to John McDowell", p. 253) to take the truth-tables as common ground and the principle of bivalence as the point of divergence. This depends on assuming what I am questioning, which implies in this case that their problem is to get across to one another their divergent understandings of the connectives. But that is not a condition for making sense of the dispute. Certainly when they take the truth-tables as common ground, nothing has been done to locate a divergence in understanding; but there is still the disagreement, in principle intelligible to both sides, about the warrant for the principle of bivalence. So there is no implication that, say, a classical logician cannot comprehend a challenge from intuitionism. A modest meaning-theorist is indeed insouciant about which logic is correct, but only *qua* meaning-theorist; to suppose that that would ensure that one cannot take intuitionism seriously, if one has been brought up in a classical inferential practice, would be just one more version of the assumption that is under dispute.

If the position I am sketching is viable, it opens up (in application to this particular case) a gap between two conceptions of the semantic. According to the first, an interest in semantics is an interest in how expressions affect the bearing on reality of sentences in which they occur; I have claimed that someone pursuing this interest need not address such issues as the divergence between classical and intuitionist logic, even when the interest impinges on logical connectives. According to the second, an interest in the semantics of logical connectives is, just as such, an interest in the validation of logical inferences. Dummett's conception is the second; this shapes, for instance, his reading of Frege's notion of reference as a notion of "semantic value". If the two conceptions can come apart, the reading may be a distortion of Frege—who was not in a position to gloss his thinking about reference in terms of such ideas as those of soundness and completeness.[32]

Dummett is dismissive of philosophers who play down the significance of questions about soundness and completeness.[33] But I do not think I am engaging in intellectual Luddism, as he may be inclined to suggest. A proof of soundness can reassure us that a logical formalism does not violate some independently describable conception of validity, and a proof of completeness can assure us that the formalism captures the conception. The truth-tables will certainly not yield such a thing for a formal presentation of intuitionistic sentential logic, and there are other things that will. I am not questioning the intellectual utility of the exercise. What I am questioning is only the assumption that whatever serves the purpose *must* be a matter of semantics, in the sense of a divergent account of the meanings of the logical constants.

8. Dummett is impatient with modesty's refusal to address certain questions:

32. Though Dummett will surely find this shocking, I think the idea of "the semantic mechanism of the language" (*The Logical Basis of Metaphysics*, p. 38) is a superstition. We do Frege no favour if we read it into his thought.

33. See, for instance, "The Justification of Deduction".

> That the answers lie very deep is obvious; to maintain that they cannot be given at all is mystification. When the children ask for bread, will you give them a stone? ("Reply to John McDowell", p. 268)

No doubt not; but what are we to do if the children ask for the moon?

And that comparison is still not satisfactory, though it is an improvement. It is not simply that there is reason to doubt that Dummett's demands can be met. By itself, that would leave us liable to hanker after immodesty, if only it could be had.

The wish for immodesty reflects a familiar philosophical attitude to content. The attitude is one in which we wonder at the capacity of language to give expression to thought; we take that capacity to be something we must find mysterious unless we can reconstruct it in conceptually independent terms, and so see how we could integrate it into a picture of the world that does not already explicitly make room for it.[34] In Dummett's work, this attitude, together with his interest in the validation of logic, yields an original and deeply thought-out vision of what the philosophy of language ought to look like. By comparison, different visions tend to look ridiculously thin; alternatively, as with Davidson, Dummett strains to find more in them by reading them, with questionable charity, as if they shared his goals. I have suggested that, so far from showing how to display what makes linguistic behaviour linguistic, immodesty is a recipe for obliterating the intelligibility of linguistic behaviour, because it falsifies the way our understanding makes contact with our articulated linguistic practice. We should not unquestioningly inherit that attitude to content, and judge philosophies accordingly. Perhaps the task for philosophy of language is rather to exorcize the attitude.[35]

34. For a clear expression of this attitude on Dummett's part, see p. 210 of "Language and Communication".

35. I am not recommending a brusque dismissal. On the contrary, I think the roots of the attitude lie deep, and a satisfying exorcism would have to start with a sympathetic appreciation.

ESSAY 6

Physicalism and Primitive Denotation: Field on Tarski[1]

1. In this essay I want to discuss a contention made by Hartry Field, in his influential article "Tarski's Theory of Truth". Tarski claimed that his work on truth ("The Concept of Truth in Formalized Languages") made semantics respectable from a physicalist standpoint ("The Establishment of Scientific Semantics", p. 406). Field's contention is that Tarski thereby misrepresented what he had done, because of an erroneous belief that he had shown how truth (for formalized languages of finite order) can be interestingly defined without using prior semantic notions. What Tarski in fact did, according to Field, was to show how truth (for those languages) can be characterized in terms of a small number of primitive semantic notions. Physicalism requires something more, which Tarski did not offer: namely, explication of those primitive notions in physical terms.

I believe Field is right about Tarski's view of the relation between physicalism and his work on truth. I believe also that, given the physicalism he espouses (which is probably Tarski's doctrine too), Field is right to regard Tarski's claim as overblown. (This is not to suggest that Field depreciates the magnitude of Tarski's formal contribution; that is not affected if Tarski's somewhat incidental claims about physicalism are rejected.) What I want to dispute is a view about how semantics and physics are related, which Field aims to motivate by these considerations about Tarski.

1. It should be obvious that this essay's debts to Donald Davidson's writings far outrun those signalled in the notes. Gareth Evans and Colin McGinn helped me in revising the first draft, and I had aid and comfort from Hilary Putnam's 1976 John Locke Lectures (since published in *Meaning and the Moral Sciences*).

2. I shall begin by setting out the contrast, between what Tarski allegedly should have done and what he actually did, on which Field's argument turns.

We are to consider a simple first-order language L, with names (c_1, c_2, and so on to the appropriate last subscript; we use "c_k" as a variable to range over the names); one-place function symbols ($f_1, f_2, \ldots$; variable "f_k"); one-place predicates ($p_1, p_2, \ldots$; variable "p_k"); variables (x_1, x_2, and so on indefinitely; variable "x_k"); connectives $\sim$ and $\wedge$; and a quantifier $\forall$.[2] L's singular terms are: the names, the variables, and the result of writing any function symbol followed by any singular term. L's atomic well-formed formulae (wffs) are: the result of writing any predicate followed by any singular term. The wffs are: the atomic wffs, the negation of any wff, the conjunction of any two wffs, and the universal quantification of any wff with respect to any variable. Sentences are, as usual, closed wffs.

In the case of languages whose only complex sentences are formed by truth-functional compounding, it is straightforward to characterize truth for complex sentences in terms of truth for simple sentences. With quantification, the straightforward procedure is blocked, since the constituents of complex sentences are no longer necessarily sentences. Tarski saw that the obstacle can be circumvented with the concept of satisfaction. In the truth-functional case, the semantic impact of sentence-forming operations is captured in a recursive characterization of truth itself; when sentence-forming operations operate on open as well as closed sentences, their semantic impact is captured instead in a recursive characterization of satisfaction, in terms of which truth can then be directly defined. Satisfaction (of open or closed sentences, by sequences of objects) is, as the above might suggest, something of which truth can be regarded as a limiting case. For a closed sentence to be satisfied by any sequence whatever simply is for it to be true; for an open sentence to be satisfied by a sequence is for it to be true, so to speak, on the fiction that its free variables denote the corresponding members of the sequence. Field aptly describes the idea (p. 349) as being to treat free variables as "temporary names", and, in place of satisfaction by a sequence, he speaks of truth relative to a sequence.

2. I treat "c_1", etc., as names (in the metalanguage) of L's names, etc., which might be "Deutschland", etc.); this involves a notational divergence from Field. "$\forall$" is the name of L's quantifier, rather than a quantifier of the metalanguage; later in the essay I rewrite some of Field's formulae with the bracket notation for universal quantification.

In more detail: the construction has three components. Working backwards:

(i) Truth *tout court* is defined as satisfaction by, or truth relative to, any sequence whatever.

(ii) Truth relative to a sequence, for complex wffs, is recursively characterized in terms of the truth, relative to that sequence, of their simpler constituents. Obvious clauses handle the connectives:

(a) $\sim A$ is true$_s$ iff A is not true$_s$;[3]

(b) (A$\wedge$B) is true$_s$ iff A is true$_s$ and B is true$_s$;

and the clause for the quantifier is only slightly less obvious:

(c) $\forall x_k A$ is true$_s$ iff, for every sequence s' different from s in at most the k-th place, A is true$_{s'}$.

Using these clauses, we could, for any complex wff of L, determine conditions under which it would be true relative to a sequence, in terms of the truth or not, relative to that sequence, of its atomic wffs. What, then, are we to say about the base case: sequence-relative truth for atomic wffs? A *closed* atomic wff is true *(tout court)* just in case its predicate *applies* to what its name *denotes* (as "is wise" applies to what "Socrates" denotes, given that Socrates is wise); and we want it to be true relative to any sequence whatever in just those circumstances ((i) above). An *open* atomic wff is satisfied by a sequence just in case a corresponding closed wff, with the variable replaced by a name of the relevant member of the sequence, would be true (see above). Neatness recommends introducing the notion of sequence-relative denotation; then truth relative to a sequence, for atomic wffs open or closed, can be explained as a function of the predicate's application-conditions and the open or closed singular term's denotation relative to that sequence:

3. Concatenations of metalanguage names of object-language expressions denote corresponding concatenations of the named expressions. In such structural descriptions names may give way to variables. Open sentences are to be read as universally quantified (thus the present formula should be understood with quantifiers binding "*A*" and "*s*"). Brackets around designations of conjunctions (as in (b) below) are a scope-marking convention.

(d) $p_k t$ is true$_s$ iff there is something y that t denotes$_s$ and p_k applies to y.

(iii) Now we need an account of denotation relative to a sequence for singular terms. With closed singular terms, the relativity to a sequence is idle; thus, for names:

(a) c_k denotes$_s$ what c_k denotes.

What a variable denotes, relative to a sequence, has already been fixed:

(b) x_k denotes$_s$ the k-th member of s.

And obviously, with function symbols:

(c) $f_k t$ denotes$_s$ y iff there is something z which t denotes$_s$ and f_k is *fulfilled* by $\langle y, z\rangle$

(as "the capital of" is fulfilled by ⟨London, Great Britain⟩ in virtue of the fact that London is the capital of Great Britain).

That completes the truth-characterization, T1, that, according to Field, Tarski should have given for L.

Truth is defined in terms of the auxiliary semantic notion of truth relative to a sequence, or satisfaction. In the truth-characterization as it stands, the extension of the satisfaction relation is fixed only recursively; so we cannot simply write down, from the characterization, a formula coextensive with the truth-predicate from which the terminology of sequence-relative truth is absent. With sufficient set theory, we could convert the recursive characterization of the auxiliary notion into a "normal" or eliminative definition.[4] That would enable us to eliminate the terminology of sequence-relative truth from the definition of truth; but the resulting formula would still contain the subsidiary semantic terminology of sequence-relative denotation. The recursive characterization of sequence-relative denotation could similarly be converted into an eliminative definition, yielding an eliminative definition of truth free from the sequence-relative seman-

4. See "The Concept of Truth in Formalized Languages", p. 193, n. 1.

tic terminology. But the result would still contain, in a way that T1 yields no suggestions for eliminating, the evidently semantic terminology "applies to", "denotes", and "is fulfilled by".

T2, a truth-characterization that Tarski might actually have given for L, differs in just that respect. The difference is achieved by the following modifications:

(i) Instead of the general clause ((ii)(d) above) about sequence-relative truth of atomic wffs, each predicate has sequence-relative truth-conditions, for atomic wffs that contain it, spelled out individually. Thus, say:

(a) p_1t is true$_s$ iff there is something y that t denotes$_s$ and y is a country;
(b) p_2t is true$_s$ iff there is something y that t denotes$_s$ and y is a city;

and so on, one clause for each predicate; or they could all be collected in a disjunction.

(ii) Similarly, instead of the general clause about sequence-relative denotation of names ((iii)(a) above), the denotation of each name, relative to any sequence whatever, is specified individually. Thus, say:

(a) c_1 denotes$_s$ Germany;
(b) c_2 denotes$_s$ France;

and so on, one clause for each name, or a disjunction as before.

(iii) Correspondingly for function symbols; instead of the general clause ((iii)(c) above), T2 has, say:

(a) f_1t denotes$_s$ y iff there is something z that t denotes$_s$ and y is the capital of z;
(b) f_2t denotes$_s$ y iff there is something z that t denotes$_s$ and y is the president of z;

and so on, one clause for each function symbol, or a disjunction as before.

In T2, explicit employments of the semantic notions of application, denotation, and fulfilment disappear in favour of piecemeal specifications of (what are in fact) application-conditions, denotations, and fulfilment-conditions. The specifications are effected by using, for each simple object-language expression, a coextensive expression of the metalanguage. These metalanguage expressions are free from semantic terminology; obviously the trick would not be turned if they were expressions on the pattern of "is applied to by p_1", "what c_1 denotes", or "the first member of an ordered pair that fulfils f_1 and whose second member is". If we had a complete T2 for L, with a clause for every simple expression, and converted the recursive characterizations as before, the result would be a formula coextensive with the truth-predicate and, this time, entirely free from semantic terminology.

Notice that the masterstroke of approaching truth indirectly, using the notion of satisfaction to circumvent the problem posed by non-sentential sentence-components, is common to both T1 and T2. That is why Field's favouring of the only partially Tarskian T1 over the fully Tarskian T2 is compatible with a proper respect for Tarski's technical achievement.

3. There are three incidental points on which Field claims superiority for T1-style truth-characterizations over those in the style of T2.

(i) L may fail to conform to Tarski's condition that "the sense of every expression is unambiguously determined by its form".[5] For instance, a name may have more than one bearer. If the expressions mentioned are taken to be tokens, T1 is unaffected; whereas Field claims that "there is no remotely palatable way of extending" T2-style truth-characterizations to cope with such languages (p. 352).

(ii) If L is enriched, then provided only that the additions belong to semantic categories already represented, T1 needs no alteration; whereas T2 needs new clauses (pp. 353–4).

(iii) T2-style truth-characterizations can be given only in metalanguages with vocabularies that match, extension for extension, those of the object languages; whereas T1-style truth-characterizations are subject to no such restriction (p. 355).

How solid these points are, as advantages for T1, is open to question. Point (i) is vulnerable to the production of palatable treatments, in the style of T2, for, say, languages with promiscuous names.[6] That

5. "The Concept of Truth in Formalized Languages", p. 166.

6. I believe we can get such a thing out of an account of names on the lines of Tyler Burge, "Reference and Proper Names".

point (ii) tells in favour of T1 is a thesis that is not really independent of Field's central contention, which I shall discuss shortly (see the end of §4 and the end of §6). And from a certain perspective, which I shall sketch below, point (iii) simply disappears (see the end of §5). Field's main interest, however, is different, and I shall not devote further attention, except in passing, to the three points I have just listed.

4. Field's main concern is with the difference emphasized in my exposition of T1 and T2, namely, that T2 does, whereas T1 does not, permit construction of a formula coextensive with the truth-predicate and containing no semantic vocabulary.

The difference means that T1, Field's favoured candidate, is in violation of one of Tarski's ground rules. Tarski announced: "I shall not make use of any semantical concept if I am not able previously to reduce it to other concepts".[7]

Field argues plausibly (pp. 356–7, 368–9) that the motivation for that ground rule was the aspiration to make the notion of truth respectable from the standpoint of physicalism. Field's version of physicalism (probably close to Tarski's, in view of Tarski's interest in the unity of science) is this: "the doctrine that chemical facts, biological facts, psychological facts, and semantical facts, are all explicable (in principle) in terms of physical facts" (p. 357). If a physicalist found the notion of truth, and hence putative facts in whose formulation it figures, in some way suspect, he would hardly be content with other semantic notions: in particular those of denotation, fulfilment, and application, which Field collectively labels "primitive denotation" (p. 350). So T1 leaves the job of rehabilitating truth (for L) at best incompletely executed; whereas if one obeyed the ground rule that T1 violates, one might hope to perform the task all at once. In Field's view, however, T2, for all its obedience to the ground rule, does not fulfil the hope.

Obviously a lot depends on what it takes to make the notion of truth acceptable to a physicalist. Consider, for instance, a claim of Tarski's as to what is shown by the possibility of constructing T2-style theories for formalized languages of finite order: he says he has

7. "The Concept of Truth in Formalized Languages", pp. 152–3.

demonstrated that for each such language "a formally correct and materially adequate definition of true sentence can be constructed in the metalanguage, making use only of expressions of a general logical character, expressions of the language itself [he is speaking of the case in which metalanguage includes object language] as well as terms belonging to the morphology of language, i.e. names of linguistic expressions and of the structural relations existing between them".[8] If a T2-style theory for L, in a metalanguage that included L (so that the theory could use, in those of its clauses that effect T2's distinctive trick, the very expressions that the clauses deal with), had its recursive characterizations converted as before, and if we agreed for present purposes to count expressions of set theory as "expressions of a general logical character", the result would exactly conform to Tarski's description. Now suppose a physicalist is satisfied with the physical credentials of logic, set theory, and the morphology of language, and those of the non-logical vocabulary of L (which could not leave him unsatisfied, if we moved to the case in which metalanguage does not include object language, with the physical credentials of translations of that vocabulary in the metalanguage). Why could he not allay any doubts about "true" by reflecting on the availability of the long-winded substitute that Tarski showed he could construct?

Different languages would need different substitutes, even if the languages differed only in that, say, one contained a predicate that the other did not contain (compare §3, (ii)). But why should that matter? What Tarski promises is a set of physicalistically acceptable formulae containing a formula coextensive with "true" in its application to the sentences of each language of the relevant sort. To insist that what is needed, if a semantic predicate is to be respectable, is a physicalistically acceptable formula coextensive with it in all its applications, even across the boundaries between languages, could be justified on the basis of a physicalism that requires a single physical equivalent for every decent predicate; but that is something Field explicitly rejects (p. 357, n. 13).

Field's reason for being unimpressed by a defence of T2 on the above lines comes out very clearly in his use of an analogy from chemistry (pp. 362 and ff.).

8. "The Concept of Truth in Formalized Languages", p. 265.

We might have a theory that enabled us to determine the valences of chemical compounds on the basis of the valences of the elements out of which they are compounded. We could write it in this form:

(c)(n)(c has valence *n* iff *B(c, n))*;

where we fix the extension of the valence relation, as it holds between compounds and numbers, in terms of a formula "*B(c, n)*" that would contain the term "valence" as applied to elements. Then we could go on to specify the valence of each element, on these lines:

(e)(n)(e has valence *n* iff *e* is potassium and *n* is + 1, or . . . or *e* is sulphur and *n* is –2).

Substituting the right-hand side of this for occurrences of the predicate "ξ has valence ζ" in the formula "*B(c, n)*" would yield an open sentence, coextensive with the valence relation as it holds between compounds and numbers, in which "valence" did not appear. But such a construction would compare unfavourably with what we would have if we eliminated "valence" from "*B(c, n)*" by means of a *reduction* of the valence relation, as it holds between elements and numbers, to structural (physical) properties of atoms. The "valence"-free open sentence constructed in the first way would be revealed by the comparison as a pseudo-reduction of the concept of the valence of a compound.

What Field suggests is that T2's way of eliminating "denotes", "is fulfilled by", and "applies to" from the definition of truth parallels that pseudo-reduction. Parallel to what the pseudo-reduction is unfavourably compared with would be a theory like T1, but supplemented with genuine explications of the primitive-denotation relations in physical terms: something that does not merely, like T2, specify the extensions of those relations as far as L is concerned, but describes physical relations between expressions and things on which the semantic relations depend, and from whose description, together with suitable physical facts, the extensions of the semantic relations could be determined.[9]

9. Field, p. 367, cites Saul Kripke's work as a beginning on the task of giving the required explications. I prefer to take seriously Kripke's denial that he intended to produce a theory of denotation for names (see pp. 64, 93–4, of *Naming and Necessity*). Construed as correcting an alternative picture, rather than giving a substantive account of denotation,

The idea is, then, that T2 is merely T1 plus bogus reductions of the concepts of primitive denotation. By not purporting complete reduction, T1 advertises the fact that we do not yet have genuine explications of those concepts; T2 simply papers over that gap. Tarski's genuine achievement, reflected in T1, involves seeing how to specify the semantic properties of complex expressions in terms of those of simple expressions. T2 gives the appearance of going further, and eliminating the semantic properties of simple expressions. But the appearance is deceptive; we are told nothing interesting—in fact, nothing at all—by T2 about what it is for a simple expression to have one of the appropriate semantic properties, any more than we are told, by a list of the valences of elements, what it is for an element to have a particular valence.

Chemical concepts applied to compounds are reasonably conceived as relating indirectly to the physical facts on which their applicability depends, by way of the application of chemical concepts to elements; it is at the level of elements and their properties that we expect chemistry to be revealed as, so to speak, adhering to the physical facts. Field's picture of semantics is parallel: the semantic properties of complex expressions, in particular truth, relate to the physical facts about those expressions by way of the semantic properties of simple expressions, and it is at that level—the level of the *axioms* of a truth-characterization—that we must seek to reveal the adherence of semantics to the physical facts.

Given the chemical parallel, the vacuity of what is peculiar to T2, as against T1, seems undeniable. From that perspective, moreover, the differences between T2-style theories for different languages, even with the same semantic structure (see §3, (ii)), look like a symptom of how bogus the explication effected is. Differences between languages, in the extensions of the primitive-denotation relations, should be capable of being displayed as consequences of different instantiations of those general physical relations between expressions and things on which primitive denotation depends; not represented as brute differences, as at first glance they seem to be in T2-style theories, where the concepts of primitive denotation disappear in favour of, precisely, specifications of their extensions. (But see the end of §6 below.)

Kripke's work is quite compatible with the view of semantics, divergent from Field's, that I am going to give in §§6 and 7 below.

But a contrasting view, about the point of contact between semantical facts and the underlying physical facts, is possible. In order to sketch it, I shall begin (in §5) by rescuing Tarski's "Convention T" *(Kriterium W)* from the contumelious treatment to which Field subjects it.

5. According to Field, Tarski's "formal criterion of adequacy for theories of truth" was "roughly" this (pp. 360–1):

> (M) Any condition of the form
>
> (2)(*e*)(*e* is true iff *B*(*e*))
>
> should be accepted as an adequate definition of truth if and only if it is correct and "*B(e)*" is a well-formed formula containing no semantic terms.

Field remarks in a footnote (p. 361, n. 14) that "Tarski actually gives a different formulation, the famous Convention T, evidently because he does not think that the word 'correct' ought to be employed in stating a condition of adequacy".

Is there not something in that thought? In fact it is a travesty to represent Convention T as merely "a different formulation" of Convention M; for Convention M's "if and only if it is correct" begs the very question that Convention T is meant to settle. Convention T, as is well known, requires a truth-characterization to entail, for each object-language sentence, an instance of the schema "*s* is true iff *p*", where "*s*" is replaced by a designation of the object-language sentence and "*p*" by that very sentence, if the object language is included in the metalanguage; otherwise by a translation thereof.[10] Conformity with the requirement is a sufficient condition for the predicate characterized by a theory to have in its extension all and only the true sentences of the object language; that is, precisely, for the truth-characterization to be, in Field's term, correct.

Tarski has *two* prerequisites for acceptability in a truth-characterization: formal correctness and material adequacy.[11] Convention T is his condition of *material adequacy* (Field's "correct-

10. "The Concept of Truth in Formalized Languages", pp. 187–8.

11. See, e.g., "The Concept of Truth in Formalized Languages", p. 265 (which I quoted in §4 above).

ness"). Convention M does not address the question of material adequacy, but, with its insistence on an eliminative definition free of semantic terms, expresses a view of Tarski's about *formal correctness.* The second is detachable from the first: a truth-characterization could conform to Convention T while being, because of sparseness of set theory, incurably recursive in its account of satisfaction, and hence failing to conform to Convention M.

If we want a recipe for constructing truth-theories for languages in general (at least those amenable to Tarski's methods), we cannot evade the question when a truth-theory is correct (materially adequate). Nothing Field says supersedes Convention T (or some version of it: see §6 below) as a general test of correctness. But T1 as it stands yields no non-semantical truth-conditions for sentences, and so cannot be subjected to any such test. T1 yields assignments of truth-conditions like this (a simple case for illustration):

> p_1c_1 is true iff there is something y that c_1 denotes and p_1 applies to y.

One might suppose that that could not be false, so that Convention T is trivially met. But in a real case, we could not be confident of so much as the categorization of the expressions as a predicate and a name, in advance of checking assignments of truth-conditions that result from specific interpretations of them as such—that is, the sort of thing a T2-style truth-characterization would give.

Something in the spirit of Field's contrast can still be drawn, even between theories amenable for subjecting to Convention T. The modified contrast would be between:

(a) T2-style theories, which tell us nothing about the concepts of primitive denotation over and above fixing their extensions for the language dealt with; and

(b) a modified version of T1-style theories: theories that, unlike T1 as it stands, do fix the extensions of the primitive-denotation relations (so that they entail specific assignments of truth-conditions, which can be tested against Convention T); but that, unlike T2-style theories, represent the information as derived from the application, to physical facts about particular expressions, of those explications of the primitive-denotation concepts with which Field seeks to supplement T1.

Note, incidentally, that any truth-characterization, of either of these two sorts, will have to employ, in its specifications of primitive denotation, metalanguage expressions that aim at coextensiveness with the object-language expressions dealt with. (Conformity to Convention T would indicate success in the aim.) If the metalanguage does not, in advance of construction of the truth-characterization, contain expressions with suitable extensions, it must be enriched so as to do so (perhaps—the easiest way—by borrowing from the object language). So once we take seriously the assessment of truth-characterizations for correctness, there seems to be no substance to the idea that it is a merit of T1-style theories not to require object-language vocabulary to be suitably matched in the metalanguage. (Compare §3, (iii).)[12]

6. Once we appreciate the need for a test of material adequacy, we can see the possibility of inverting Field's conception of the point of contact between semantic theories and the physical facts.

Consider what would be involved in the interpretation, from scratch, of a foreign language. To simplify, suppose the language is used only to make assertions and that there is no indexicality.[13] Our interpretative needs would be met by a theory that entailed, for any sentence that might be uttered in the foreign language, a theorem of the (highly schematic) form "*s . . . p*"; where "*s*" is replaced by a suitable designation of the object-language sentence, and "*p*" by a sentence of ours such that, if a foreign speaker utters the object-language sentence, we can acceptably report what he says by using that sentence of ours. If we had a theory that met the requirement, replacements for "*p*" in its theorems would translate the sentences designated by the corresponding replacements for "*s*". So if our requirement-meeting theory worked by characterizing a predicate, "*F*", so that the gap between replacements for "*s*" and replacements for "*p*" was filled by "is *F* iff", then, by virtue of the theory's conforming to Convention T, the extension of "*F*" would be the extension of "true". A sufficient condition of correctness, then, in a truth-characterization for the language in question, would be the possibility of putting it to interpretative use in the way described

12. If truth-characterizations have to be got into a form in which they can be subjected to the test of Convention T (or some version of it), then it must be possible to circumvent problems posed by indexicality. (Compare §3, point (i).) I shall ignore the complications of doing so.

13. Not making these suppositions would complicate the exposition, but (I believe) introduce no new issues of principle.

above; that is, treating it as if its theorems were of the form "*s* can be used to say that *p*".[14]

We can picture ourselves equipped with all the physically formulable facts about language use in the community, and aiming to construct, via interpretation as above, a truth-characterization for their language. Two interlocking requirements would govern the fit between the truth-characterization and the physical facts.

(i) The first requirement is one of *system*. We want to see the content we attribute to foreign sayings as determined by the contributions of distinguishable parts or aspects of foreign utterances, each of which may occur, making the same contribution, in a multiplicity of utterances. This is secured by having the theorems deducible, as in T2-style truth-characterizations, from axioms that deal with simple expressions and figure as premises in the deduction of the appropriate theorems for any sentences in which their expressions occur. For the theorems to be so deducible, utterances must be identifiable in terms of structures and constituents assigned to them by a systematic syntax; and it must be possible to match up those structures (if necessary obliquely, through transformations) with configurations observable in physical utterance-events.

(ii) The second requirement is one of *psychological adequacy*. Used as an interpretative theory, the truth-characterization is to serve up, in the systematic way sketched under (i), specifications of the content of assertions that we can take speakers to be making. Not just any piece of physically described behaviour can be reasonably redescribed as a saying with a specific content. Whether such redescriptions are acceptable turns on whether the behaviour, as redescribed, is intelligible. That requires the possibility of locating it suitably against a background of propositional attitudes—centrally beliefs and desires—in terms of which the behaviour seems to make sense. Ascription of propositional attitudes, in turn, is constrained in complex ways by the physical facts about behaviour, the environment, and their interconnections; also (circling back) by the possibilities of interpreting linguistic behaviour in conformity with requirement (i). Interpretation can be pictured as the superimposition, on all that is available in physical terms about language use, of the content-specifying mode of discourse: ascriptions of sayings, beliefs, and desires. Partly because requirement (i) demands ramified interdepen-

14. Compare Davidson, "Truth and Meaning"; and §1 of Essay 1 above.

dencies between interpretations of different utterances, and partly for general reasons stemming from the character of intentional discourse, the superimposition has to be in principle holistic (which is not, of course, to deny that in practical theory-construction one would need to proceed by way of piecemeal hypotheses).

The hard physical facts, then, that constrain the construction of a truth-characterization for a language actually spoken are (i) the structural properties of physical utterance-events that permit the language to be given a syntactic description; and (ii) the complex relations between behaviour and the environment that permit (some of) the behaviour to be described and understood in intentional terms.

Now it is at the level of its *theorems* that a truth-characterization, on this account, makes contact with those hard physical facts. If the theorems are to be systematically deducible so that requirement (i) is met in the way I described above, then replacements for "*s*" must characterize utterances in terms of structures and constituents; so that the relation of match or transformational accessibility, which, according to requirement (i), must hold between the structures assigned to sentences by the syntax with which the theory operates, on the one hand, and configurations observable in physical utterance-events, on the other, is revealed or not at the theorem level. Moreover, interpretations of parts of utterances can be subjected to requirement (ii) only through interpretations of whole utterances; an assignment of denotation, for instance, is tested by whether assignments of truth-conditions derivable from it facilitate ascriptions of sayings that are for the most part intelligible; and of course it is the theorems that record interpretations of whole utterances. So requirement (i) makes itself felt, not only directly, in connection with the match between theoretical syntax and actual utterance-events, but in another way too: we can conceive the deductive shape that the theory assumes, in order to meet requirement (i), as setting up a complex of channels by which the impact of requirement (ii), bearing in the first instance on interpretations of whole utterances, is transmitted backwards, through the derivations of theorems licensed by the theory, to the premises of those derivations, in which the theory says what it does about sentence-components and modes of sentence-construction.

Describing, on the lines of requirements (i) and (ii), the nature of the fit between an acceptable truth-characterization's theorems and the physical facts can be regarded as spelling out what Convention T comes to, in a case in which what translates what cannot be taken (as it could in the cases Tarski considered) to be simply given or up for stipulation.

According to this picture, a truth-characterization fits the underlying physical facts from the theorems upward; not, as in Field's conception, from the axioms downward. The deductive apparatus used in deriving the theorems needs no anchoring in the physical facts, independently of the overall acceptability of the derived assignments of truth-conditions.[15] The relations between language and extra-linguistic reality that a truth-characterization describes hold in the first instance between simple expressions and things, and only mediately, via the laws of semantic combination set out in the truth-characterization, between complex expressions and the world.[16] But from its being at the level of primitive denotation that relations between words and the world are set up *within* a semantic theory, it does not follow—nor, according to the inverted picture, is it true—that it is at that level that the primary connection should be sought between the semantic theory *itself* and the physical facts on which its acceptability depends.

A T2-style truth-characterization specifies what are in fact denotations, fulfilment-conditions, and application-conditions. (It does not matter that the primitive-denotation concepts are not explicitly expressed in the T2-style theory sketched above: see below.) Now the axioms dealing with names, function symbols, and predicates play roles that are distinctively parallel within each of the three classes, and dissimilar between them, in the derivations of assignments of truth-conditions that the truth-characterization licenses. According to the view that inverts Field's picture, there is nothing to the specific primitive-denotation concepts over and above those distinctive deductive powers. To give an account of one of the modes of primitive denotation, what we should do is (a) spell out, on the lines of requirements (i) and (ii), what it is for a truth-characterization's assignments of truth-conditions to be acceptable; and (b) describe the relevant distinctive deductive capacity, so that the empirical content

15. Compare Davidson, "In Defence of Convention T", at p. 74.

16. This is a very important fact about Tarskian truth-characterizations. We are potentially liberated from much bad philosophy about truth by seeing that sentences need no special extra-linguistic items of their own (states of affairs, facts, or whatever) to be related to. (Talk of facts in this essay is, I hope, only a *façon de parler*.) See Davidson, "True to the Facts".

that (a) confers on the notion of truth can be channelled backwards through the licensed derivations into the relevant sort of premise. (Clearly the various modes of primitive denotation will not, on this view, be separately explicable; that is as it should be.)

If it is at the level of its theorems that a truth-characterization makes contact, obeying a version of Convention T glossed by requirements (i) and (ii), with the physical facts, then it does not matter a scrap whether the truth-characterization yields an eliminative truth-definition free of semantic vocabulary. What matters is the possibility of eliminating semantic terms from the right-hand sides of the theorems (unless the object language contains semantic vocabulary, so that semantic terms can properly occur in reports of what is, on occasion, said by its speakers). That elimination is possible even if we leave the characterization of satisfaction, in a T2-style theory, in its recursive form, so that the concept of satisfaction is still present in any equivalent that the theory yields for the truth-predicate. From this viewpoint, then, there is nothing to favour a direct truth-definition over an axiomatic truth-characterization, so long as the latter yields acceptable theorems.

Similarly, the absence for a T2-style theory of explicit expression of the primitive-denotation concepts is not in itself a virtue. We could construct a trivial variant of the T2-style truth-characterization that I partly sketched above, which would explicitly assign denotations, fulfilment-conditions, and application-conditions, labelled as such, so that the theory would lack that putative virtue; that would not matter, since the semantic terminology could still be made to disappear in deriving the final assignments of truth-conditions.

Eliminative "definitions" of the primitive-denotation concepts through specifications of their extensions, such as T2 yields, are not to be conceived as purporting to say what it is for one of those relations to hold; that task is discharged, rather, by the combination of (a) and (b) above. This should alleviate concern over how T2-style truth-characterizations would vary from language to language (§3 (ii)). What is said under (a) would be, details aside, common to anything recognizable as a language; and if there is any point in carrying over a specific batch of primitive-denotation concepts from one language to another, that would show up in similarities in what would be sayable about the deductive powers of the relevant sets of axioms, under (b). So the inter-language variations between T2-style theories would leave invariant that about them that contributes to the task of saying what it is for the relations to hold. If someone supposed that we were freed from obligations to look for further explications of the primitive-denotation concepts solely by virtue of the fact that the concepts were not explicitly expressed in eliminative definitions constructed from T2-style theories, then it would be reasonable to be perturbed by variation in the materials of those eliminative definitions (compare the end of §4). But the absence of explicit employment of the concepts is not rightly taken in that way. (Notice that it is not in a T2-style theory itself that, on this view, we find accounts of what it is for the primitive-denotation relations to hold; (a) and (b) would be metatheoretical remarks about T2-style theories.)

Tarski's own insistence on eliminative truth-definitions free of semantic terms, justified as it is by a mention of physicalism,[17] suggests that he himself conceived the virtues of T2-style theories, from a physicalist standpoint, in a way that is justly parodied by Field's chemical example. But we can accept Tarski's favoured style of truth-characterization without needing to agree with everything he thought about its merits.

7. Not only is there no need to look for physical underpinnings for the deductive apparatus of truth-theories, over and above their output. There is no reason to expect that the search would turn up anything interesting.

On the view sketched above, superimposing a semantic theory on the physical facts about a language-using community is a subtask in superimposing a way of describing and understanding their behaviour in content-specifying terms. For all its extensionality, the truth-characterization has its relation to the realm of the physical governed by the conditions that govern the relation of intentional to physical discourse. Now the nature of those conditions makes it quite implausible that the relation of semantics to physics should be anything like the relation of chemistry to physics.

When we shift from chemical to physical explanation, we shift to a style of explanation that, though at a deeper level, is still of the same general kind: a kind in which events are displayed as unsurpris-

17. "The Establishment of Scientific Semantics", p. 406.

ing because of the way the world works.[18] If we are physicalists, we hold that physics can in principle give a complete account of all events, so far as that mode of explanation is concerned. So if there is any substance in chemical explanations of compounding behaviour, then, since those explanations purport to reveal events as unsurprising *qua* instances of the world's workings, the laws that, in those explanations, state how the world is said to work should, law by law, have physical credentials. And that is how it turns out; the chemical laws that (roughly) determine the compounding behaviour of composite substances on the basis of that of elements are, by way of the (approximate) reduction of element valences to physical properties of atoms, (approximately) mirrored in physical laws that govern compounding transactions described in terms of atomic and molecular structure.

But the difference between physical explanation and the mode of explanation that is largely constitutive of the network of intentional concepts is not a difference within a broadly homogeneous kind. Intentional explanation makes an action unsurprising, not as an instance of the way the world works (though of course it does not follow that an action is *not* that), but as something that the agent can be understood to have seen some point in going in for.[19] An intentional explanation of an event does not, like a chemical explanation, offer, so to speak, to fill the same explanatory space as a physical explanation would. So we can go on claiming, as physicalists, that physics can completely fill that explanatory space, without requiring that, on pain of seeing intentional explanations as substanceless, we must be able to ground the details of those explanations, detail by detail, in physical counterparts.

Explanations of the semantic properties of complex expressions in terms of the semantic properties of simple expressions, appealing as they do to semantic laws whose formulation is part of the move from the physical to the intentional, should be of a piece with intentional explanations, in respect of their relation to the physical; because of the different explanatory pretensions of the intentional, there is no threat to the completeness of physics, as far as the appropriate kind

18. This is not meant to be more than a crude intuitive gesture in the direction of an account of the kind of explanation in question.

19. Again, this is intended only as a gesture.

of explanation is concerned, if those semantic laws and their special conceptual content cannot be physically mirrored in the way exemplified in the chemical case. Physicalism, construed as the doctrine that physics is in principle competent to yield an explanation of that kind for all that happens, affords no reason for insisting that such mirroring must be available if semantics is to be otherwise than empty; that is (given the assumption that semantics is not empty), for expecting that such mirroring will be found.

If intentional concepts are largely constituted by their role in a special kind of explanation, which does not compete with the kind that physics yields but offers a different species of comprehension, then we need not expect to be able, even approximately, to reduce those concepts to physical terms. The distinctive point of the intentional concepts makes it intelligible that there should be a kind of incommensurability between them and physical concepts.[20] And if the intentional concepts are not reducible to physical terms, then it is, if anything, still less to be expected that reductions should be available for the concepts of primitive denotation, whose conceptual identity, according to the position I sketched in §6, consists solely in their impact on a semantic property of complex expressions—truth-conditions—the concept of which we can explain only in terms of requirements for the applicability of intentional notions.

Field seeks to motivate the contrary thought that we must look for physicalistic explanations of the concepts of primitive denotation by arguing (p. 373) that "without such accounts our conceptual scheme [as physicalists] breaks down from the inside. On our theory of the world it would be extremely surprising if there were some nonphysical connection between words and things." This remark needs careful consideration.

I do not claim, on behalf of the position Field opposes, that there are no physical connections between words and things (which would certainly be surprising). Assignments of truth-conditions are partly controlled by, for instance, the possibilities of belief-ascription, and belief-ascription is governed in part by principles about how the content of beliefs is sensitive to the causal impact of their subject matter. That, together with similar features in a fuller account of acceptabil-

20. For the claim of irreducibility, see Quine, *Word and Object,* §45 (note his references to other authors there). On the ground of the irreducibility, see Davidson, "Mental Events".

ity in assignments of truth-conditions, requires the presence of causal, no doubt ultimately physical, connections between the world and words at the level of whole utterances, construed as (in our example) voicings of belief. Such causal connections presumably reflect, in ways corresponding to the derivability of assignments of truth-conditions from specifications of primitive denotation, causal connections between occurrences of simple expressions and physically describable circumstances. The position Field opposes is quite compatible with the thesis that whenever a name, say, occurs in an utterance-event, the event is suitably related, in physically describable ways, with events or circumstances involving the name's denotation.

What need not be true is a corresponding thesis with a quantifier shift: that there is some one physically describable relation that obtains between any occurrence of any name and its denotation. This denial is not just the reflection of a needlessly strict view of when we have a single relation. According to the thesis that I allowed at the end of the last paragraph, any instance of the denotation relation will have what we might call a physical realization. The physical realizations will differ from instance to instance, but that is not the issue; it is not necessarily Pickwickian to classify as a physical relation one that holds just in case some one of a set of physical relations holds. The question is about the principle on which the members of the set are collected. If the point of the grouping cannot be given in purely physical terms, but consists simply in the fact that those physical relations are the ones that obtain when the denotation relation, explicated on the lines that I suggested in §6, obtains, then there is no justification for claiming that a reduction has been effected.[21]

It seems right to conclude that denotation, on this view, is a non-physical relation; and similar considerations apply to the other primitive-denotation concepts. Now just how surprising is it that there should be such relations between words and things?

Semantic relations, on this view, are indeed not like chemical relations; if explicability in terms of physical facts, which is what Field's physicalism demands of all facts worthy of the name, requires the sort of grounding, in physical facts, of the facts into which genuine

21. This is relevant to Michael Friedman's remarks about weak reduction, in "Physicalism and the Indeterminacy of Translation".

relations enter that is exemplified in the chemical case, then the idea that semantic relations might be as I have here suggested is either offensive to physicalism or a condemnation of semantics. But perhaps we should look sceptically at Field's formulation of physicalism. Certainly his assimilation of the thesis of semantical irreducibility to such anti-materialistic theses as Cartesianism is unfair.

A doctrine with some claim to be called "physicalism" is this: (i) all events are physical events, that is, have physical descriptions; (ii) under their physical descriptions, all events are susceptible of total explanations, of the kind paradigmatically afforded by physics, in terms of physical laws and other physically described events. Field's version of physicalism excludes any thesis according to which there are facts irreducible to physical facts—"semanticalism" and Cartesianism alike. But the version I have just given discriminates; it allows some irreducibility theses but rejects others. Cartesianism, as standardly understood, is still excluded; for according to it, mental events have no physical descriptions, in violation of (i), and some physically describable events (for instance limb movements) have such events in their causal ancestry, in violation of (ii). However, "semanticalism"—the irreducibility thesis that I outlined above—is compatible with physicalism in the revised formulation. The events that comprise linguistic behaviour have physical descriptions, as required by (i). There is no reason to deny that under those descriptions they are explicable as instances of the way the world works, and if physics delivers on its claim to saturate the relevant explanatory space, it must be possible to put the explanations that reveal them as such, ultimately, into physical shape, as required by (ii). The irreducibility thesis turns on the idea that formulation of a truth-characterization subserves the compiling of a way of talking whose point lies in a kind of understanding, of those and other events, quite different from the kind that physics might afford; so, as I emphasized above, it poses no threat to the ambitions of physics to be complete in its own sphere. Cartesianism holds, by contrast, that there are questions of the sort physics purports to be able to handle, to which the answers are stubbornly non-physical.[22]

In a common usage of "science", the scope of science is taken to cover just such questions; if physicalism is good scientific methodo-

22. Similarly vitalism, which Field also cites (p. 358).

logy—which certainly seems plausible on that understanding of what science is—then doctrines like Cartesianism are unscientific. But it is a different matter to refuse to accept that *all* questions fall within the province of science so understood. We can agree that semantics, on the view I have taken here, is not in that sense scientific (though there is plenty to justify its claim to be scientific in some more relaxed sense), without thereby agreeing that it is *un*scientific. A discipline can be both rigorous and illuminating without being related to physics in the way Field wants semantics to be; the strong physicalism that denies that seems to me to be, as Field says (p. 357, n. 13) about a version he himself rejects, hard to take seriously.

PART II

REFERENCE, THOUGHT, AND WORLD

ESSAY 7

Identity Mistakes: Plato and the Logical Atomists

1. My main purpose in this essay is to offer one possible diagnosis of a puzzle of Plato's. At *Theaetetus* 188a–c, Socrates is made to sketch an argument that purports to prove that there can be no false judgements. Its outlines are as follows. With any given thing (e.g., Theaetetus) one either knows it or not. This applies, in particular, to things that figure in one's judgements. With two things (e.g., Theaetetus and Theodorus) there are four combinations:

(a) one knows both;
(b) one knows the first but not the second;
(c) one knows the second but not the first;
(d) one knows neither.

Now (1) it is impossible to judge that one thing is the other, whichever of these combinations obtains. Therefore (2) there can be no false judgements.

2. Even if (1) were granted, (2) would not follow. For (1) rules out judgements identifying two things, but leaves unchallenged the possibility of false judgements of at least the following kinds:

(i) false negative identity judgements (e.g., the judgement that Michael Innes is not J. I. M. Stewart);
(ii) false subject-predicate judgements involving one-place predicates, or many-place predicates other than "is identical with";
(iii) false judgements that are not about particular things at all.

It is perhaps not surprising, in view of, e.g., the *Sophist*'s account of statements, that the argument ignores the rag-bag category (iii). An explanation of its passing over category (i) will become available shortly (§7). It might be doubted that it ignores category (ii), on the ground that, in Greek at least, a form corresponding to "*x* judges that one thing is another" can be used to report singular subject-predicate judgements as well as identity judgements;[1] and the argument purports to show that no statement of that form can be true. But such a doubt would be mistaken. For if the form in question is taken in the sense in which it fits subject-predicate judgements as well as identity judgements, then it fits *true* subject-predicate judgements just as well as false ones. But it figures in our argument as a prima facie plausible form for reports of *false* judgements. The idea is that if one *could* judge that one thing is another, that would indeed be to make a false judgement. We can preserve the plausibility of that idea only by supposing that to judge that one thing is another, in the sense appropriate to our argument, is to make a judgement identifying two things; and hence, that category (ii) *is* passed over. I shall not here discuss why that should have been so.

From now on I shall ignore (2), and treat the argument as if it claimed no more than (1). Even so, we have a paradox on our hands. We need to look carefully at the mechanics of the move to (1).

3. Cases *(b), (c),* and *(d)* go together; in each case, one fails to know at least one of the two things. And Plato seems to be working with a principle that we can state like this: if something is to figure in one's judgements at all, then one must know it.[2] Obviously that principle would rule out the supposition that one might judge that one of two things to which one was related as in *(b), (c),* or *(d)* was the other.

We shall need to return to the principle. For the moment, I shall mention, and shelve for later discussion (§§9, 10), its similarity to a well-known doctrine of Russell's. Russell says: "Every proposition which we can understand must be composed wholly of constituents with which we are acquainted"; and, more specifically about judgements, "Whenever a relation of judging or supposing occurs, the

1. See, e.g., F. M. Cornford, *Plato's Theory of Knowledge,* p. 113.
2. See 188b8-c1, and compare 190d7-10.

terms to which the supposing or judging mind is related by the relation of supposing or judging must be terms with which the mind in question is acquainted."[3]

4. Now consider the remaining case. Suppose that someone judges that one thing is another, when his relation to the two things is as described in *(a)*. *Ex hypothesi,* then, he *knows* both. Indeed we now have, in the principle just mentioned, an argument that if someone is to judge that one thing is another, then he *must* know both, since both figure in his judgement; i.e., an argument that case *(a)* is, so to speak, the only real starter. However, Socrates suggests (188b3–5), the supposition that one judges that one of two things is another implies that one does *not* know the two things. Hence our putative description of a case of false judgement leads to a contradiction—the person both knows and does not know the two things—and the only real starter fails to stay the course.

5. I shall approach an account of what is going on here in a roundabout way. The first step is to derive a similar conclusion from Russell's doctrine that all true sentences of the form "*x* is *y*", where "*x*" and "*y*" hold places for names, are tautological.[4] Roughly speaking, if a sentence is tautological, then, taking syntax for granted, one need only understand its terms in order to be in a position to know that it is true. (This needs qualifying. But I think Russell would accept it for the sentences we are concerned with.) Hence if a sentence of the form "*x* is *y*" is true, then, according to Russell's doctrine, one would be in a position to know it to be true, if one so much as understood its terms. Now suppose some sentence of that form is false, and one understands its terms. Had the sentence been true, one could have known its truth straight off, simply by understanding its terms. Since its truth does not thus announce itself, one can conclude, with no further information, that it is false. So, quite generally, to understand the terms of a sentence of the relevant form is

3. "Knowledge by Acquaintance and Knowledge by Description", reprinted in Russell's *Mysticism and Logic,* pp. 219, 220–1 in the 1963 paperback edition. The principle survived Russell's rejection of the theory of judgement implied in the second quotation; see *Mysticism and Logic,* p. 220, n. 1, and *My Philosophical Development,* p. 169, and compare n. 20 below.
4. "The Philosophy of Logical Atomism", p. 245.

sufficient for one to be in a position to know whether it is true or false;[5] for either its truth announces itself or, by default, the sentence is revealed to be false. Now, given the assumptions (i) that one cannot judge what one is in a position to know to be false, and (ii) that one cannot correctly express a judgement with a sentence containing terms one does not understand, it follows that one cannot make a false judgement that one could correctly express with a sentence of the form "*x* is *y*". This is at least very similar to conclusion (1) of Plato's argument.[6]

6. Here is how Russell argues for his doctrine that true sentences of the form "*x* is *y*" are tautological. "You must observe that the name does not occur in that which you assert when you use the name. The name is merely that which is a means of expressing what it is that you are trying to assert, and when I say 'Scott wrote *Waverley*', the name 'Scott' does not occur in the thing I am asserting. The thing I am asserting is about the person, not about the name. So if I say 'Scott is Sir Walter', using these two names *as* names, neither 'Scott' nor 'Sir Walter' occurs in what I am asserting, but only the person who has these names, and then what I am asserting is a pure tautology."[7] That is: it is the *bearer* of a name that occurs in what I assert when I use the name. So what I assert in saying "Scott is Sir Walter" must be the same as what I assert in saying "Scott is Scott". Both contain the man, Sir Walter Scott—twice over, so to speak. But what I assert in saying the latter is a tautology. So what I assert in saying the former is a tautology too; indeed, the same tautology.

As it stands, this argument requires the difficult doctrine that when one says something about, say, a person, the person himself occurs in, or is a constituent of, what one asserts.[8] But we can capture what Russell is getting at without pressing a literal interpretation of that doctrine. We can take the argument to depend on this principle: what a sentence says (or, if you like, what is said by some-

5. Compare Wittgenstein, *Tractatus Logico-Philosophicus*, 4.243; and §10 below.

6. Russell would use the doctrine of logically proper names and the Theory of Descriptions in order to represent *his* conclusion as non-paradoxical. I am doubtful whether such a move should be accepted. I cannot go into that fully here; but see §11 below.

7. "The Philosophy of Logical Atomism", p. 246.

8. The difficulty becomes apparent as soon as one considers *false* assertions. What complex item, containing Scott as a constituent, could be what I assert if I say "Scott wrote *Bleak House*"?

one who uses a sentence to say something) depends not on its terms but on their *meanings*. Now the meaning of a proper name, according to Russell, is its bearer.[9] It follows that if two sentences differ only in that, where one has one name, the other has another name with the same bearer, then what they say is the same. In particular, any true sentence of the form "*x* is *y*" says the same as the corresponding sentence of the form "*x* is *x*". So what such a sentence says is a tautology. Such a sentence says that a thing is *itself*.

Now this position looks like the one into which, at the beginning of "On Sense and Reference",[10] Frege concedes that one may be tempted, if one treats identity as a relation of objects. But Frege wants *both* to maintain the legitimacy of treating identity as a relation of objects *and* to reject the view that a true sentence of the form "*x* is *y*" says the same as the corresponding sentence of the form "*x* is *x*". He is enabled to do so, of course, by the distinction between sense and reference. What a sentence says, according to Frege, depends not on the references of its terms but on their senses. And two names with the same reference may diverge in sense. When that happens, a true sentence of the form "*x* is *y*" will say something different from what is said by the corresponding sentence of the form "*x* is *x*".

We can perhaps describe the position like this. Frege might, with a caveat about ambiguity, accept the principle on which my reconstructed Russellian argument rests, viz., that what a sentence says depends on the meanings of its terms. But he would jib at Russell's interpretation of "meanings". For Russell, the relevant meanings, in the case of proper names, are bearers, i.e., *references;* and Frege would insist that the required interpretation of "meanings" is "*senses*".[11]

Now one thing that the theory of sense and reference is meant to do is to provide an account of the behaviour of terms in certain referentially opaque contexts: very roughly, contexts involving indirect quotation. If terms are held to have their ordinary references in such contexts, there is, notoriously, a breakdown of the compelling "Leibnizian" principle that reference-preserving substitutions in a sentence

9. See, for instance, *Introduction to Mathematical Philosophy*, p. 174.

10. "On Sense and Reference", p. 56.

11. Of course this is historically back to front. Russell thought he had disposed of Frege's position in "On Denoting" (reprinted in *Logic and Knowledge*). On his arguments there, see John R. Searle, "Russell's Objections to Frege's Theory of Sense and Reference".

preserve its truth-value. But the theory holds that in such contexts a term has as its reference what is in ordinary contexts its sense. Hence a reference-preserving substitution, in such a context, is a substitution of a term with the same ordinary sense; and if terms with the same reference can diverge in sense, the generality of the "Leibnizian" principle can be maintained.

Now I suggest that when we raise the question whether a true sentence of the form "*x* is *y*" says the same as the corresponding sentence of the form "*x* is *x*", we need to consider opaque contexts of the sort to which the Fregean theory is meant to apply. If a sentence is about some thing or things, it seems plausible that what it says depends on (1) what it is about, and (2) what it says about it or them. We can represent this as a slightly more precise version of the (perhaps ambiguous) principle that what such a sentence says depends on the meanings of its terms. My suggestion is that contexts like "Sentence S is about . . .", which we need to consider in order to determine (1), and hence in order to determine what such sentences say, are opaque in the relevant way. And whether or not a precisely Fregean account of such contexts is finally satisfactory, at least it recognizes their opacity; whereas Russell's argument does not.

To illustrate this, let "ϕ*a*" be a subject-predicate sentence, and suppose that *a* is in fact *b*. What is "ϕ*a*" about? My suggestion is that if this question is meant to determine (1), and hence to determine what "ϕ*a*" says, the answer is *"a"; not "b"*. So what "ϕ*a*" says is that ϕ*a;* not that ϕ*b*. Similarly with two-place predicates. Let "*a*R*b*" be a relational sentence, and again, suppose that *a* is *b*. What is "*a*R*B*" about? Here again the answer is not *"a"*, alone, or *"b"*, alone (one might add, echoing the Russellian argument with which I began this section, "twice over, so to speak"); but "*a* and *b*". The *x*-argument of the function *x*R*y* in the sentence "*a*R*b*" is *a*, not *b;* the *y*-argument is *b*, not *a*. The function has *two* arguments, namely, *a* and *b*.[12] In that case "*a*R*b*" does not say that *a* has R to *a*, i.e., that *a* has R to itself. A sentence says that something has R to itself only if it is of the form "*x*R*x*"; and "*a*R*b*" is not of that form, even though *a* is *b*. For in "*a*R*b*" we have *two* arguments; whereas a sentence is of the form "*x*R*x*" only if the two argument-places are both filled by

12. The opacity of the relevant contexts protects these claims from being represented, by way of Leibniz's Law, as incompatible with the hypothesis that *a* is identical with *b*. No *property* is here being ascribed to *a* but not *b*, or vice versa.

the *same* argument. In particular, with identity: the sentence "*a* is *b*", even if true, does not say that *a* is itself.[13] To suppose that that is what it says, as in effect Russell does, is to miss the point about opacity. What it says, on the contrary, is that *a* is *b*. On the other hand, the sentence "*a* is *a*" does say that *a* is itself. So "*a* is *b*" does not say the same as "*a* is *a*". And, generalizing: a true sentence of the form "*x* is *y*" does not say the same as the corresponding sentence of the form "*x* is *x*".[14]

7. Russell, then, adopts a position about identity statements from which a conclusion similar to Plato's paradox can be derived.[15] The position is, essentially, that a true sentence of the form "*x* is *y*" says that something is *itself*. And we can represent him as reaching that position like this. He holds that what a sentence says depends, in part, on what it is about ((1) above). But he reads the phrase "what it is about" transparently: what counts is which thing the relevant thing is, irrespective of how it is referred to in the sentence. Whereas if we read the phrase opaquely, his position collapses, and the paradox no longer threatens.

I suggest, now, that the line of thought about *judgements* towards which Plato is tempted is parallel to the line of thought about *statements* that Russell adopts. Parallel to the principle that what a sentence says depends, in part, on what it is about is the principle that what is judged in a judgement depends, in part, on what it is about. In this latter principle, it is tempting to do what Russell does in the former: that is, to read "what it is about" transparently. But if one yields to that temptation, as I suggest Plato is inclined to, then one has to suppose that all true positive identity judgements about something involve judging the same thing, viz., that the thing is itself. In that case all true positive identity judgements should be self-intimatingly true, in the sense that the determination of which judgement one is making leaves no further question about whether it is true. In that case, by an extension of the argument of §5, all false

13. Note the oddness of the suggestion that what the sentence says might depend on whether it is true or false.—The best argument against treating identity as a relation is undermined by the point made in the text.

14. Note a divergence from Frege here: this argument has "does not" where he would say "may not".

15. But see n. 6 above.

positive identity judgements should be self-intimatingly false. So how could anyone make them? Again, the paradox is avoided by reading the crucial phrase opaquely.

We now have an explanation of the fact that Plato's argument passes over cases like the judgement that Michael Innes is not J. I. M. Stewart (§2). My hypothesis is that Plato is tempted towards a view of *what is judged* parallel to Russell's view of *what is asserted.* And on that view, to judge that Michael Innes is not J. I. M. Stewart would be to judge that Michael Innes is not the same as himself; which seems inconceivable. On my hypothesis, it would be natural that such cases should simply not occur to Plato.

8. A principle on which Plato's argument seemed to depend (§§3, 4) was this: if something is to figure in one's judgements at all, then one must know it. Here what follows "know" is a pronoun functioning as a bound variable; so what follows "know" in an application of this principle would be a referring expression. This forces on "know" an interpretation corresponding to the French "*connaître*" (not "*savoir*"), and makes it natural to paraphrase in terms of acquaintance: compare Russell's versions of this principle, cited above (§3).

Now even apart from Russell's special views about acquaintance, this principle is not very plausible. There is no good sense in which I am acquainted with Bismarck, but that does not, on the face of it, stop me making judgements about him.[16] However, plausibility is immediately restored when we turn to Russell's *argument* for his principle. In favour of the first of his two versions cited above (§3), he says, "The chief reason for supposing the principle true is that it seems scarcely possible to believe that we can make a judgment or entertain a supposition without knowing *what it is* that we are judging or supposing about". And about the second, he says, "*This is merely to say* that we cannot make a judgment or supposition without knowing *what it is* that we are making our judgment or supposition about".[17] The principle stated in these quotations seems plausible enough. But it is not, as Russell claims, the same as his "acquaintance" principle. For the "acquaintance" principle involves

16. Russell manages with the fact that his principle prevents him from making judgements about Bismarck (see "Knowledge by Acquaintance and Knowledge by Description"); but only at the price of insisting that many judgements are not the judgements we thought they were.

17. "Knowledge by Acquaintance and Knowledge by Description", at pp. 219, 221; my emphasis.

"connaître"; whereas in the plausible principle stated in these quotations, "know" is followed by an indirect question, and the French would be *"savoir"*. It looks as though Russell mistakes phrases like "what it is that we are judging or supposing about", as they occur in the latter principle, for expressions designating the appropriate object. This would account for his taking the plausible *"savoir"* principle to be the same as his less plausible *"connaître"* principle.

The leading error in such a line of thought would be grammatical: a confusion between interrogative and relative-clause nominalizations, with (in this case) an associated confusion between interpretations of "know".[18] Compare:

(1) I know what you are smelling.
(2) What you are smelling is the dead cat under the floorboards.
So (3) I know the dead cat under the floorboards.

As these propositions would be ordinarily understood, such an argument would involve equivocation between the uses of "what you are smelling" in (1) and (2), and an associated equivocation between the uses of "know" in (1) and (3). In (2), "What you are smelling" is a relative-clause nominalization, related to, and tantamount to, "that which you are smelling". It can be taken as a referring expression, and (2) can be construed as an identity statement. But in (1), "what you are smelling" is an interrogative nominalization. It is not a referring expression. To regard (3) as licensed by substitution in (1) according to the identity statement (2) involves missing that point, and forcing on "know" in (1) the interpretation that it must have in (3), viz., *"connaître"*.[19]

In the line of thought that I attributed to Russell, there are parallel grammatical mistakes. And such mistakes would import, or strengthen, a tendency to be insensitive to the sort of point about opacity that I used (§7) to dissolve the paradox. For they result in the fact that particular applications of Russell's principle look like this: if I am to make a judgement about *a*, then I must be acquainted with (know) *a*. In the consequent of this, there is no reason to regard the position of *"a"* as anything but transparent. (We can have non-

18. Compare Dennis W. Stampe, "Towards a Grammar of Meaning", especially at pp. 149–54.

19. Compare J. L. Austin, *Philosophical Papers*, pp. 64–5; I have adapted an example of his.

transparency with "acquaintance" idioms, but only with forms of words like "acquainted with *a under that name*"; and there is no sign of that in Russell's principle.) Taking the formula as an application of the general principle, "*(x)*(if I am to make a judgement about *x*, then I must be acquainted with [know] *x*)", one would therefore regard the position of "*a*" in the antecedent as transparent too. In that case one would regard the position of "*a*" in "Judgement J is about *a*" as transparent.[20] Hence, in the principle that what is judged in a judgement depends in part on what it is about, one would be disposed to do what I called (§7) "reading 'what it is about' transparently". In Fregean terms, one would be disposed to limit oneself to *references;* whereas to dissolve the paradox one needs to admit opaque readings, or in Fregean terms to consider *senses.*

Note that with the "*connaître*" principle, if *a* is *b,* then to know what one needs to know in order to make judgements about *a* is *eo ipso* to know what one needs to know in order to make judgements about *b*. For the requirement in respect of *a* is that one know *a*. And if one knows *a* ("*a*" here occurring transparently), and *a* is *b,* then one *eo ipso* knows *b;* that is, satisfies the requirement in respect of *b*. With the "*savoir*" principle, on the other hand, the requirement for making a judgement about *a* is that one know that it is *a* that one's judgement is about; and the requirement for making a judgement about *b* is that one know that it is *b* that one's judgement is about. And even if *a* is *b,* the opacity of the context "It is . . . that my judgement is about" permits these to be two different bits of knowledge.

9. Plato's argument seemed to depend (§§3, 4) on something like Russell's principle in its implausible "*connaître*" version. I suggest now that, like Russell, Plato regards that version as interchangeable with the plausible "*savoir*" version. I shall offer, first, some evidence for this suggestion, and, second, a partial explanation.

The evidence is that in at least two places in the *Theaetetus* (147b2 with 4–5, 196d8 with 10), Plato makes it clear that he is pre-

20. It is in fact implicit in the theory of judgement that Russell was beginning to give up by 1917 (*Mysticism and Logic,* p. 220, n. 1) that the position of "*a*" in, say, "*n* judges that *a* has R to *b*" is transparent; and presumably, therefore, that its position in "*n* makes some judgement about *a*" is transparent. For the former is analysed as being of the relational form "J(*n, a,* R, *b*)". (See "On the Nature of Truth and Falsehood".) The retention of the acquaintance principle (see n. 3 above) means that this transparency survives the rejection of that theory of judgement.

pared to treat the forms (1) "know *x*" and (2) "know what *x* is" as interchangeable. And the two versions of the Russellian principle differ precisely in that where one has one of these forms, the other has the other.

The explanation is that Greek has an idiomatic form that is equivalent to (2) but can be literally represented by (3) "know *x* what it is". In occurrences of this form, what goes in place of "*x*" is the direct object of the verb, as in (1). And "what it is" looks like an adverbial clause, of a sort that one might expect to suffer ellipsis readily. Thus there would be an easy slide from (2), via its equivalent (3), to (1).

Now if Plato concentrated on (1), he would naturally think of knowing in terms of acquaintance *(connaître)*. Taking (2) to be equivalent, he would suppose that knowing there was a matter of acquaintance too. Hence, like Russell, he would be inclined to misparse phrases of the form "what *x* is", not as interrogative nominalizations suitable to follow "know" *(savoir)*, but as designations of suitable objects of acquaintance *(connaître)*.[21] As with Russell, this sort of grammatical mistake would import, or strengthen, an inclination towards transparent readings where opaque readings are required.

10. What still needs doing is to bring the line of thought that I have been discussing into closer relation with the details of Plato's argument; in particular, with the contradiction that he claims to derive from the supposition that someone judges that one thing is another (§4). By the Russellian principle (§3), such a person must know both, since both figure in his judgement. But his confusing them shows, allegedly, that he does *not* know both. So the fact that one *knows* two things is thought to imply that one cannot judge that one of them is the other. But why should such an implication have seemed plausible to Plato?

21. The supposed nature of these objects would vary according to what sort of expression is substituted for "*x*". *What Socrates is* would presumably be, simply, Socrates. But compare *what a bed is*. It is harmlessly true that what a bed is is a bed. But misparsed, that would yield a case of "Self-Predication". An ordinary bed is a bed, too. But an ordinary bed (being perishable, etc.) cannot be *what a bed is* ("Non-Identity"). So an ordinary bed is not *what a bed is,* but (since both are beds) like it (compare *Republic* 597a4-5). (For "Self-Predication" and "Non-Identity", see G. Vlastos, "The Third Man Argument in the *Parmenides*".)

One suggestion is that he is inclined to read "know" as "know all about".[22] That would indeed yield the required implication. But the drawback is that it would yield a lot more too. With "know" so interpreted, the Russellian principle (§3) would straightforwardly "prove" the impossibility of *any* false judgements about something, not merely those of the identity form. Perhaps, then, we should look for a less sweeping "justification" of Plato's implication.

One such "justification" could be extracted from the fact (§8) that with the *"connaître"* principle, if *a* is *b*, then to know what one needs to know in order to make judgements about *a* is *eo ipso* to know what one needs to know in order to make judgements about *b*. If *a* is *b*, and one satisfies the knowledge requirement in respect of *a* and *b*, then how (one might wonder) can one fail to notice that it is the *same* knowledge in each case? That is, how can one fail to know that *a* is *b*? And if it is obvious to one that the knowledge required in each case is the same, if *a* is *b* and one has the knowledge required in respect of *a* and *b*, then if *a* is not *b* and one has the knowledge required in respect of each, ought it not to be obvious, by default (compare §5), that the two bits of required knowledge are different? In that case, to satisfy the knowledge requirement in respect of *a* and *b*, i.e., according to this principle, to know *a* and *b*, is sufficient for one to be in a position to know that *a* is not *b*, if *a* is not *b*. And given the assumption that one cannot judge what one is in a position to know to be false, it follows that if one knows *a* and *b*, and *a* is not *b*, one cannot judge that *a* is *b*; which is Plato's implication.

Alternatively, a more logical (less psychological) "justification" can be constructed in terms of the sort of reasoning I attributed to Plato in §7. As before, I shall begin with a parallel argument from the theory of meaning. In the *Tractatus Logico-Philosophicus*, at 4.243, Wittgenstein asks, "Can we understand two names without knowing whether they signify the same thing or two different things? Can we understand a proposition in which two names occur without knowing whether their meaning is the same or different?" We are clearly meant to answer "No"; and an argument for the negative answer can be constructed on lines that are by now familiar. What a sentence says depends on the meanings of its terms, i.e., in the case of proper names, their bearers (3.203). So the true sentence "*a* is *b*" says the same as "*a* is *a*". But the latter sentence, and so the former

22. See Jürgen Sprute, "Über den Erkenntnisbegriff in Platons Theaitet".

too, is degenerate, in the sense that once one has settled what it says there is no further question about whether it is true (compare 5.5303). Thus, taking knowledge of the meaning of the identity-sign for granted: if one knows the meanings of "*a*" and "*b*", and "*a* is *b*" is true, then one has sufficient information to know that it is true. Now such a sentence is either self-intimatingly true in that sense, or not; and if not, it is revealed, by default, as false (compare §5). Thus, again taking knowledge of the meaning of the identity-sign for granted: if one knows the meanings of "*a*" and "*b*", one has sufficient information to know whether *a* is *b*. Some such principle is what is suggested by Wittgenstein's rhetorical questions.

Now (by 3.203) the meaning of "*a*" is *a*, and the meaning of "*b*" is *b*. Thus to know the meanings of "*a*" and "*b*" is simply to know *a* and *b*. If we substitute accordingly in the principle just elicited from 4.243, we get this: if one knows *a* and *b*, one has sufficient information to know whether *a* is *b*. And that is, near enough, what we need for Plato's implication. For it yields this: given that one cannot judge what one is in a position to know to be false, one cannot judge that *a* is *b* if it is not.

It would be inappropriate to explain Plato's line of thought in our passage by means of reasoning that explicitly involves talk of proper names and their meanings. But we are equipped to construct a parallel argument for Plato's implication that avoids such notions. What is judged in a judgement depends in part on what it is about (compare §7). If "what it is about" is read transparently, it will seem that the judgement that *a* is *b* is degenerate in the sense sketched above. It follows that if one knows what judgements about *a* are about and what judgements about *b* are about, one has sufficient information to know whether *a* is *b*. But to know what judgements about *a* are about, Plato might think, is just to know *a* (compare §9). Hence, by substitution, if one knows *a* and *b*, one has sufficient information to know whether *a* is *b*. So, as before, if one knows *a* and *b*, then, given that one cannot judge what one is in a position to know to be false, one cannot judge that *a* is *b* when it is not.

11. I have been concerned to bring out parallels between Russell's position about (some) identity *statements*, which is bound up with his doctrine about what is asserted by the use of a sentence, and involves a certain view about how genuine proper names must work; and on the other hand, a line of thought about identity *judgements*

towards which I suggest Plato was tempted, which is bound up with parallel views about what is judged in judgements, and about how things figure in judgements.[23]

I shall end with a remark about what might seem an obvious objection to this allegation of parallelism between Russell and Plato. Plato's paradox, it might be said, is about things in general. That is why it is paradoxical. Russell's position, on the other hand, is restricted to logical atoms—things that are named by logically proper names. Hence, according to this objection, it is unfair to represent Russell's position as parallel to Plato's.[24]

Now it would surely be implausible to suggest that Russell *starts* with the full-blown notion of a logically proper name. Rather, he begins from a certain conception of how any genuine referring device must work; that is, of what it must be for an asserted sentence to be genuinely *about* something. We see that conception operating in arguments like the one quoted in §6. And it is that conception that, I suggest, is parallel to Plato's conception of what it is for a *judgement* to be about something.

This claim of parallelism implies that if one takes ordinary so-called referring devices (e.g., ordinary proper names) to be genuine referring devices, according to such a conception of genuine referring devices, then one will find oneself involved in paradoxes like Plato's. It is partly for that reason that Russell denies that ordinary proper names are logically proper names. This denial is what prompts the objection of unfairness. But what I am claiming is that the denial itself is based, at least in part, on a conception of genuine referring devices that is wrong; and wrong in precisely the same way as the view about judgements that leads directly to the paradox.

23. For the parallel, compare J. L. Ackrill, "Plato on False Belief: *Theaetetus* 187–200", at p. 387: "Socrates . . . operates with ordinary proper names as though they were logically proper names applied to simple particulars."

24. Compare n. 6 above.

ESSAY 8

On the Sense and Reference of a Proper Name[1]

1. An interesting way to raise questions about the relation between language and reality is to ask: how could we state a theory knowledge of which would suffice for understanding a language? Donald Davidson has urged that a central component in such a theory would be theory of truth, in something like the style of Tarski, for the language in question.[2] A Tarskian truth-theory entails, for each indicative sentence of the language it deals with, a theorem specifying a necessary and sufficient condition for the sentence to be true. The theorems are derivable from axioms that assign semantic properties to sentence-constituents and determine the semantic upshot of modes of combination. Now Frege held that the senses of sentences can be determined by giving truth-conditions, and that the sense of a sentence-constituent is its contribution to the senses of sentences in which it may occur.[3] The parallel is striking. It suggests that we might construe Davidson's proposal as a proposal about the nature of a theory of (Fregean) sense for a language.

Tarskian truth-theories are extensional, and only minimally richer in ontology than their object languages (no need to mention possible worlds and the like). This attractive economy of resources has a consequence that is crucial to the proper understanding of the suggestion: namely, that not just any theory of truth, however true, could serve as a theory of sense.

The job of a theory of sense should be to fix the content of speech acts that a total theory of the language concerned would warrant as-

1. This essay has special debts to Gareth Evans and David Wiggins.
2. See Davidson, "Truth and Meaning" and "Radical Interpretation".
3. Frege, *Die Grundgesetze der Arithmetik*, vol. I, §32.

cribing to speakers.[4] Abstracting harmlessly from complications induced by indexicality and non-indicative utterances, we can put the point like this: in the case of any sentence whose utterance command of the language would make fully comprehensible as a saying—any indicative sentence—a theory of sense must fix the content of the saying that an intentional utterance of the sentence could be understood to be.

The adequacy of the total theory would turn on its acceptably imposing descriptions, reporting behaviour as performance of speech acts of specified kinds with specified contents, on a range of potential actions—those that would constitute speech in the language—describable, antecedently, only as so much patterned emission of noise. For that systematic imposing of descriptions to be acceptable, it would have to be the case that speakers' performances of the actions thus ascribed to them were, for the most part, intelligible under those descriptions, in the light of propositional attitudes; their possession of which, in turn, would have to be intelligible, in the light of their behaviour—including, of course, their linguistic behaviour—and their environment. The point of the notion of sense—what the content-specifying component of a total theory of that sort would be a theory of—is thus tied to our interest in understanding behaviour, and ultimately our interest in understanding—fathoming—people. We have not properly made sense of forms of words in a language if we have not, thereby, got some way towards making sense of its speakers. If there is a pun here, it is an illuminating one.

Now to specify the content of a saying we need a sentence. A theory might have the power to give us a sentence to meet the need, for any indicative sentence of its object language, by virtue of the fact that it entailed theorems in which the needed content-specifying sentences were used to state necessary and sufficient conditions for the application, to the relevant object-language sentences, of some predicate. The fact that the used sentences specified the content of sayings potentially effected by uttering the mentioned sentences would guarantee that the predicate could, if we liked, be written "true"; it would guarantee that the theory, with its theorems written that way,

4. See Frege, "On Sense and Reference". The sense of a sentence determines, or is, the thought expressed (p. 62); it would be specified in a "that"-clause (see the remark about reported speech, p. 59).

was a true theory of truth.[5] But it would be the guaranteeing fact, and not the guaranteed fact, that suited the theory to serve as a theory of sense. For, given a theory guaranteed to be a true theory of truth, by its serviceability in yielding content-specifications, we could exploit the extensionality of truth-theories to derive a new, equally true theory of truth that, in spite of its truth, would not be serviceable in yielding content-specifications, and so would not serve as a theory of sense.[6]

What emerges is that serving as a theory of sense is not the same as being one, on a certain strict view of what it is to be one. It was clear anyway that a truth-theory of the sort Davidson envisages does not, in saying what it does, *state* the senses of expressions. Why should we hanker after a theory that does that mysterious thing, if a theory that does some utterly unmysterious thing instead can be made to serve the purpose? Pending a good answer to that question, there is only the mildest perversity in shifting our conception of what a theory of sense must be, so that Davidsonian theories are at least not ruled out. As positive justification we still have the striking parallel noted at the outset between the Davidsonian *Ersatz* and Frege's own ideas about the genuine article.

2. I shall restrict attention throughout to occurrences of names in straightforwardly extensional contexts in which they function as singular terms; and I shall, in this essay, ignore names with more than one bearer.

For simplicity, I shall begin by considering theories that aim to deal with (fragments of) English in English (the restriction will be removed in §7). In a theory of truth of that kind, names might be handled by axioms of which the following is typical:[7]

"Hesperus" stands for (denotes) Hesperus.

The role played by some such clause, in the derivation of assignments of truth-conditions to sentences in which the name occurs,

5. See Davidson, "Truth and Meaning", p. 23.

6. See the Introduction to Evans and McDowell, eds., *Truth and Meaning*, pp. xv–xvii.

7. Smoothness in treatment of predicates (whose argument-places can be filled with variables as well as names) dictates, rather, the statement that each of a certain set of functions from singular terms (definite or indefinite) to objects assigns Hesperus to "Hesperus". But it comes to the same thing.

would display the contribution made by the name to those truth-conditions. Given the Fregean doctrine about sense that I mentioned at the beginning of this essay, this suggests that such a clause, considered as having what it says fixed by its location in a theory that yields acceptable content-specifications, gives—or, more strictly, in that context as good as gives—the sense of the name.

3. If there is to be any affinity between my use of "sense" and Frege's of "*Sinn*" I must keep room for a distinction between sense and reference. There must be contexts where "sense" is required and "reference" would not do. Now clauses of the sort that I have just exemplified specify, surely, *references (Bedeutungen)* of names, and it might be thought that the distinction has disappeared.

That thought would be wrong. Frege's notion of sense belongs with the notion of understanding, and we can get at what is involved in understanding a language by careful employment of the notion of knowledge. Recall my opening question about the nature of a theory knowledge of which would suffice for understanding a language. We can think of a theory of sense as a component of a total theory of that kind: a component that, in the context of principles adequate to determine the force (assertion, instruction, or whatever) with which particular utterances are issued, serves (as I suggested in §1) to determine the content of speech acts performed in issuing those utterances. Semantically simple expressions would be mentioned in axioms of such a theory, designed so that knowledge of the truths they express—in the context of knowledge of enough of the rest of the theory—would suffice for understanding utterances containing those expressions. The hypothetical knowledge involved here, then, is knowledge of truths (French "*savoir*", German "*wissen*"). The reference *(Bedeutung)* of a name, on the other hand, is, in Frege's usage, its bearer—an object.[8] To know the reference of a name would be, failing an unpardonable equivocation, to know that object: acquaintance, perhaps, but in any case not knowledge of truths but, what is grammatically distinct, knowledge of things (French "*connaître*", German "*kennen*"). It is not, then, the sort of knowledge that it

8. Notwithstanding Michael Dummett's assertion that Frege had two other uses of "*Bedeutung*" as well (*Frege: Philosophy of Language*, pp. 93–4). Casual occurrences of that ordinary German word should carry no weight against the intention that is plain in Frege's official exposition of the doctrine.

would make sense to *state* in clauses of a theory. The grammatical distinction between knowledge of things and knowledge of truths guarantees a difference of role for "sense" and "reference". Without putting that difference at risk, we can claim that a clause that does no more than state—in a suitable way—what the reference of an expression is may nevertheless give—or as good as give—that expression's sense.

This grammatical way of distinguishing sense and reference promises to free us from any need to worry about the ontological status of senses. As far as names are concerned, the ontology of a theory of sense, on the suggestion I am making, need not exceed the names and their bearers. To construe knowledge of the sense of an expression (knowledge of a truth) as, at some different level, knowledge of (perhaps acquaintance with) an entity (the sense of the expression) seems from this perspective, gratuitous.[9]

Verbal nouns like "reference" (and "*Bedeutung*") have a curious grammatical property that facilitates temptation to the equivocation I alluded to above. We would do well to immunize ourselves to the temptation by exposing its source. A phrase of the form "the reference of *x*" can be understood as equivalent to the corresponding phrase of the form "what *x* refers to", either (i) in the sense in which "what" amounts to "that which" (which yields the official Fregean use of "*Bedeutung*") or (ii) in the sense in which "what" is an interrogative pronoun. In this second sense, "what *x* refers to" gives the form of an indirect question, something suitable to follow "know" where knowledge of truths is what is meant. Knowledge of the *reference* of a name, in this second (non-Fregean) sense, could reasonably be held to be knowledge that, in the context of appropriate further knowledge not itself involving the name, would suffice for understanding utterances containing the name—that is, precisely, knowledge of its *sense*. It is presumably just this slipperiness of the word "reference" that motivates the introduction of the term of art "referent".

The possibility of equating a distinction between sense and (Fregean) reference with a distinction between (non-Fregean) reference and referent may, for those who are at home in the latter idiom, make it easier to see how crediting names with senses (to persist, with the plural, in an ontologically incautious formulation) is not

9. I am not suggesting that Frege attained this perspective himself.

necessarily crediting them with anything like connotation or descriptive meaning.

4. Frege's distinction was first put to use to solve a problem about identity sentences. Altered so as to involve undisputable instances of ordinary proper names, the question is this: how could someone possess knowledge sufficient to understand a sentence like "Hesperus is Phosphorus" without thereby knowing, already, that the sentence is true?[10] That question can be answered in the context of a theory that treats names in the austere way that I suggested above. The two names would be treated, in a theory of the sort I am envisaging, by clauses to this effect:

> "Hesperus" stands for Hesperus.
> "Phosphorus" stands for Phosphorus.

Since Hesperus *is* Phosphorus, the right-hand sides of these clauses can of course be interchanged *salva veritate*. But it does not follow, from the truth of the results, that they would be equally serviceable in a theory of sense (compare §1). The idea was that knowledge that "Hesperus" stands for Hesperus would suffice, in the context of suitable other knowledge not directly involving the name, for understanding utterances containing "Hesperus"; and similarly with knowledge that "Phosphorus" stands for Phosphorus and utterances containing "Phosphorus". Now if someone knows that "Hesperus" stands for Hesperus and that "Phosphorus" stands for Phosphorus, it does not follow that he knows either that "Hesperus" stands for Phosphorus or that "Phosphorus" stands for Hesperus. And for it to seem that knowledge sufficient for understanding the sentence would, of itself, suffice for knowing its truth, one or the other of those implications would have to be thought to hold.[11]

The point does not turn essentially on treating the *deductive apparatus* of the envisaged theory of sense (in particular, its axioms) as spelling out hypothetical knowledge (knowledge that would suffice for understanding). The inadequacy of a theory that used just one of

10. See "On Sense and Reference", pp. 56–7.

11. Michael Dummett alludes to an earlier version of this essay, in "What Is a Theory of Meaning?", at p. 122. This paragraph should make it clear that he has indeed misinterpreted me, as he conjectures (in his Appendix) at p. 126.

the two names on the right-hand sides of its clauses for both would show in its *consequences*, the theorems assigning truth-conditions to sentences. We would have to use those consequences in fixing the content of sayings, to be found intelligible in terms of propositional attitudes, our specification of whose content would need to be fixed partly by our interpretation of the sayings. And some utterances of "Hesperus is Phosphorus" would be unintelligible—we would not be able to see their point—if we were reduced to regarding them as expressing the belief that, say, Hesperus is Hesperus.[12] What we have here is a glimpse of the way in which, by requiring the theory's consequences to help us make sense of speakers of the language, we force ourselves to select among the multiplicity of true theories of truth. Bearing directly on the theorems, the requirement bears indirectly on the deductive apparatus that generates them. The failures of substitution that I exploited above, within contexts that specify hypothetical knowledge, simply make vivid how the indirect requirement operates.

5. According to Michael Dummett's reconstruction, Frege's own view was that the sense of a name is a criterion for, or way of, recognizing or identifying an object as its bearer.[13] I have so far left ways of recognizing objects entirely out of account. It is noteworthy how much of Frege it has nevertheless been possible to preserve. Frege's own examples undeniably manifest a richer conception of how sense might be represented; but the suspicion arises that that might be an unnecessary excrescence, rather than—what Dummett evidently takes it to be—something essential to any elaboration of Frege's basic ideas about sense.

What is the point of the notion of sense? According to Dummett's attractive suggestion, it is to capture (in part) a notion of meaning that makes it true that a theory of meaning is a theory of under-

12. What about a theory that used both names, but interchanged them? The inadequacy of this will emerge in §9.

13. Dummett, *Frege: Philosophy of Language,* p. 95 and ff. Whether the way of identifying is expressible in words or not seems unimportant, *pace* Dummett, who makes much of the claim that it need not be so expressible, as against those who attack Frege as a description theorist. It is profoundly unsatisfactory to treat the sense of a name as essentially descriptive (see §8 below), and this is not cured by allowing that there need be no explicitly descriptive *expression* that expresses that sense.

standing.[14] A theory of understanding is just what I have been thinking of a theory of a language as being. In my terms, then, the issue is this. Within the present restricting assumptions, would knowledge that "Hesperus" stands for Hesperus—in the context of suitable knowledge about other expressions, and suitable knowledge about the forces with which utterances may be issued—suffice for understanding utterances containing "Hesperus"? Or would one require, rather, knowledge to the effect that the bearer of the name may be recognized or identified thus and so? Now patently this second, stronger, requirement, interpreted in any ordinary way, insists on more than would suffice; for it insists on more than, in some cases, does suffice. One can have the ability to tell that a seen object is the bearer of a familiar name without having the slightest idea *how* one recognizes it. The presumed mechanism of recognition might be neural machinery—its operations quite unknown to its possessor.[15]

Understanding a language involves knowing, on occasion, what speakers of it are doing, under descriptions that report their behaviour as speech acts of specified kinds with specified contents. It helps to picture a possessor and a non-possessor of the state involved being subjected together to speech in the language. Assuming he is awake and attentive, the one will know truths expressible by the application of such descriptions; the other will not. Certain information is made available to both, in their shared sensory experience; certain further information is possessed only by one. Now in §1 I described a theory of a language as warranting systematic imposition of interpreting descriptions on the range of potential behaviour that would constitute speech in the language, thought of as describable, in advance of receiving the interpreting descriptions, only as emission of noise. Such a theory, then, would have the following deductive power: given a suitable formulation of the information made available to both the possessor and the non-possessor of the state of understanding on any of the relevant potential occasions, it would permit derivation of the information that the possessor of the state

14. Dummett, *Frege: Philosophy of Language*, pp. 92–3.

15. Neural, not psychological machinery; compare Dummett's revealing misconception, "What Is a Theory of Meaning?", p. 122. I mean to be denying what Dummett (*Frege: Philosophy of Language*, pp. 102–3) thinks uncontroversial, namely, that a speaker always has "a route that he uses" for getting from a name to its bearer.

would be distinguished by having. The ability to comprehend heard speech is an information-processing capacity, and the theory would describe it by articulating in detail the relation, which defines the capacity, between input information and output information.

In order to acquire an information-processing capacity with the right input-output relation, it would suffice to get to know the theory; then one could move from input information to output information, on any of the relevant occasions, by explicit deduction. It does not follow that to have such a capacity is to know any such theory. Nor, in any ordinary sense of "know", is it usually true. Comprehension of speech in a familiar language is a matter of unreflective perception, not bringing a theory to bear.

It is important not to be misled into a bad defence of the richer conception of the sense of a name. Certainly, it may be said, understanding a language does not consist in *explicit* knowledge of a theory. But we are not precluded, by that concession, from saying—as Dummett indeed does[16]—that understanding a language consists in *implicit* knowledge of a theory. And employment of the concept of implicit or tacit knowledge in the recent history of linguistics[17] might make one suppose that the point of this view of understanding lies in dissatisfaction with the unambitious aim of merely *describing* the state. The attraction of the notion of implicit knowledge, one might suppose, lies in its promise to permit us, more enterprisingly, to *explain* exercises of the capacity involved, in terms of a postulated inner mechanism. The workings of the mechanism are to be thought of as implicit counterparts to the explicit operations, with an explicitly known theory, whereby we might simulate the behaviour we view as the mechanism's external manifestations. Now a mechanism whose workings include an implicit counterpart to explicitly employing a method for recognizing or identifying the bearer of a name would seem to afford more explanation than an alternative mechanism constituted by implicit knowledge of an austere theory of sense. There is, with a rich theory, a specific operation of the mechanism to account for a person's getting on to the right object, and the austere conception yields nothing of the sort. And, on this view, it is beside

16. For a clear statement, see Dummett, "What Is a Theory of Meaning? (II)", p. 70.
17. See, e.g., Christina Graves and others, "Tacit Knowledge".

the point to appeal to those facts about what speakers explicitly know that I exploited, above, in the argument that the rich conception insists on more knowledge than would suffice.

But no such defence of the rich conception is available to Frege, as Dummett interprets him. Expounding Frege, Dummett connects the notion of sense, as I remarked above, with the notion of understanding. The notion of understanding is a psychological notion, and there is the threat of an objection to using it in this context, on the ground that it infects the notion of sense with the psychologism that Frege detested. Dummett meets the threat, on Frege's behalf, precisely by denying that the notion of sense is to be thought of as employed in the construction of a purportedly explanatory mechanism:

> A model of sense is not a description of some hypothesized psychological mechanism . . . A model for the sense of a word of some particular kind does not seek to explain *how* we are able to use the word as we do: it simply forms part of an extended description of what that use consists in.[18]

And the point is not just *ad hominem,* since a Fregean detestation of such psychologism is well placed. There is no merit in a conception of the mind that permits us to speculate about its states, conceived as states of a hypothesized mechanism, with a breezy lack of concern for facts about explicit awareness. Postulation of implicit knowledge for such allegedly explanatory purposes sheds not scientific light but philosophical darkness.[19]

It is certainly true that psychological explanations of behaviour are central in the conception of a theory of a language that I outlined above (§1). But their purpose is to confirm the descriptive adequacy of a theory, not to put an explanatory mechanism through its paces. The demand is that we should be able to see, in enough cases, why speakers might think fit to act in the ways in which, by application of the theory, they are described as intentionally acting—the point being to underpin our confidence that they are indeed acting intentionally in those ways. That is quite distinct from demanding explanations of how speakers arrive at knowledge of what others are doing, under those descriptions; or how they contrive to embody ac-

18. *Frege: Philosophy of Language,* p. 681.

19. The points made by Thomas Nagel, in "The Boundaries of Inner Space", and Stephen P. Stich, in "What Every Speaker Knows", have not been adequately answered.

tions that are intentional under those descriptions in their own verbal behaviour.

Hostility to psychologism, then, is not hostility to the psychological. It is of the utmost importance to distinguish rejection of psychologism, as characterized in the above quotation from Dummett, from anti-mentalism of the sort that issues from Skinnerian behaviourism. Indeed one of the chief objections to the psychologistic postulation of implicit knowledge stems from a concern that the notion of the inner life, the life of the mind, not be made unrecognizable.[20] Hypothesized mechanisms are not the way to save from behaviourist attack the indispensable thought that all is not dark within. We get no authentic and satisfying conception of the mind from either of these philistine extremes.

If Frege meant the notion of sense to figure in theories without the explanatory aspirations of psychologism, why did he hold the richer conception of the sense of a name? Partly, perhaps, because of the metaphorical form in which his treatment of the "Hesperus"–"Phosphorus" puzzle presented itself to him. The two names must not differ merely as objects—they must not be merely phonetic or orthographic variants for each other—if a genuine puzzle is to arise; they must differ also in their manner of presentation of the object that both present, and therein lies the solution.[21] Now, this metaphor of manners of presentation can be interpreted in the context of the austere conception. Difference in sense between "Hesperus" and "Phosphorus" lies in the fact that the clauses in the theory of sense that specify the object presented by the names are constrained to present it in the ways in which the respective names present it. They meet this constraint—surely infallibly—by actually using the respective names. But it takes subtlety to find the metaphor thus already applicable; it can easily seem to necessitate something more like a description theory of names. (Any tendency to find a richer interpretation of the metaphor natural would be reinforced by the view of thought that I shall discuss in §8 below.)[22]

20. Self-styled Cartesians in modern linguistics are in this respect notably unfaithful to Descartes himself.

21. "On Sense and Reference", p. 57.

22. There is also the wish (which is not satisfied in the austere conception) that differences in sense should not reflect but explain failures of substitution; see the last paragraph of §9 below.

6. Someone might be tempted to argue against the austere treatment of names in a theory of sense on the following lines. Knowledge that "Hesperus" stands for Hesperus is too easily acquired for it to suffice, even in the context of appropriate further knowledge, for understanding utterances that contain the name. To know that "Hesperus" stands for Hesperus, one needs no more than the merely syntactic knowledge that the expression is a name, together with mastery of a general trick of dropping quotation marks.

But this argument is worthless. Even adding the knowledge, hardly syntactic, that the name is not bearerless, what those easily acquired accomplishments suffice for is not knowledge that "Hesperus" stands for Hesperus, but knowledge that the sentence "'Hesperus' stands for Hesperus" expresses a truth. What we were interested in was the former state, knowledge of the truth that the sentence expresses, and not the latter.[23]

What exactly does the distinction amount to? Recall that we are concerned with these states of knowledge, not as actually possessed by all competent speakers, but as such that someone who possessed them would be able to use them in order to arrive by inference at the knowledge about particular speech acts that a fluent hearer acquires by unreflective perception. A clause like "'Hesperus' stands for Hesperus", on my account, would figure in a theory that, for speech acts in which the name was uttered, warranted specifying their content by means of sentences in which the name was used, that is, sentences that mentioned the planet. Such a clause would do no work in the description of a linguistic capacity actually possessed by a given speaker—knowledge of what it says would play no part in duplicating, by explicit employment of a theory, anything that he could do without reflection—unless he showed an ability to use the name, or respond intelligently (with understanding) to uses of the name on the part of others, in speech acts construable as being about the planet. Someone whose knowledge about "Hesperus" was limited to its being a name with a bearer would simply not be enabled thereby to behave in those ways.

If we are to find such an ability in a person, we must be able to find the relevant speech behaviour, and responses to speech behaviour, intelligible in terms of propositional attitudes possessed by him,

23. For the distinction, see Dummett, "What Is a Theory of Meaning?", pp. 106–7.

in the specification of whose content, again, the planet would presumably need to be mentioned. There is considerable plausibility in the idea that, if we are to be able to find in a person any propositional attitudes at all about an object, we must be able to find in him some *beliefs* about it. If that is right, these considerations capture what looks like a grain of truth in description theories of the sense of names; a person who knows the sense of a name must have some beliefs about its bearer. But that does not amount to a justification for a less austere treatment of the name in a theory of sense. The concession I am envisaging is that the person must have some *beliefs*—possibly sketchy, possibly false—about the object; not that he must *know* truths about it, sufficiently full to be true of it alone, and thus capable of generating a definite description that could replace the used name in the relevant clause of the theory of sense.

7. At this point I shall lift the restriction I imposed above (§2), and turn to theories that deal with one language in another. In fact, someone who constructed a theory that used English sentences to state their own truth-conditions might, anyway, think of his theory as using his own sentences to state truth-conditions for sentences that another person might use: and in that case the issues are the same. But it is easy to slip into viewing the sort of theory I have been considering from a solipsistic angle, with oneself as the only speaker who needs to be taken into account. That way, some issues are obscured, which become clearer when there is no mistaking the need for interpretation.

In the simplest case, someone interpreting a foreign language will himself already have a name for a suitable object (say a planet): that is, an object such that foreign utterances containing a certain expression can be interpreted as speech acts about that object, intelligible in terms of propositional attitudes about it, where generation of the content-specifications that represent the speech acts as being about the object employs clauses like this:

"Aleph" stands for Jupiter.

In a slightly less simple case, he will not antecedently have a name for a suitable object, having had no occasion to use one. But in the course of his attempt to interpret the foreign speakers, his attention might be drawn to some object in their environment, say a mountain (hitherto unknown to him). He would thereby acquire a batch of theory about the mountain. That theory (the facts about the mountain, as he sees them), together with plausible principles about the impact of the environment on propositional attitudes, might make it intelligible that his subjects should have certain propositional attitudes about the mountain, in terms of which he might be able to make sense of utterances by them containing some expression—say "Afla"—on the hypothesis that it is their name for that mountain.

As far as that goes, he might deal with "Afla" in his theory of their language by a clause to the following effect:

"Afla" stands for that mountain.

But the context drawn on by the demonstrative would be difficult to keep track of in using the theory. And it might be hard to come by a context-free unique specification to substitute for the demonstrative specification. A neat solution would be simply to adopt the subjects' name for his own use, both in stating the non-semantic facts he has discovered about the mountain and in expressing his theory about their name—thus:

"Afla" stands for Afla.

So far, then, things are much as before. Discussion of two complications should help to make the general picture clearer.

8. The first complication is the case of bearerless names, which brings us, I believe, to the deepest source of the richer conception of the sense of names. Suppose an interpreter finds an expression—say "Mumbo-Jumbo"—that functions, syntactically, like other expressions that he can construe as names, but for which he can find no bearer, and reasonably believes there is no bearer. Such an interpreter, then, can accept no clause of the form

"Mumbo-Jumbo" stands for *b*

where "*b*" is replaced by a name he could use (as above) to express a theory of his own about an object. Names that, in an interpreter's view, have no bearers cannot, by that interpreter, be handled in a theory of sense in the style I have considered so far. In his view they can have no sense, if a name's having a sense is its being able to be dealt with in that style.

Here we have a genuine divergence from Frege, and one that goes deep. Frege held that the sense of a name, if expressible otherwise than by the name itself, is expressible by a definite description. Definite descriptions are taken to have whatever sense they have independently of whether or not objects answer to them. Thus a name without a bearer could, in Frege's view, have a sense in exactly the same way as a name with a bearer.[24]

The non-Fregean view can be defended on these lines. An interpreter's ascription of propositional attitudes to his subject is in general constrained by the facts (as the interpreter sees them). This is partly because intelligibility, in ascriptions of belief at least, requires conformity to reasonable principles about how beliefs can be acquired under the impact of the environment; and partly because the point of ascribing propositional attitudes is to bring out the reasonableness, from a strategic standpoint constituted by possession of the attitudes, of the subject's dealings with the environment. Now, whether a name has a bearer or not (in an interpreter's view) makes a difference to the way in which the interpreter can use beliefs he can ascribe to the subject in making sense of the subject's behaviour. A sincere assertive utterance of a sentence containing a name with a bearer can be understood as expressing a belief correctly describable as a belief, concerning the bearer, that it satisfies some specified condition.[25] If the name has no bearer (in the interpreter's view), he cannot describe any suitably related belief in that transparent style. He

24. See "On Sense and Reference", pp. 62–3; especially (p. 63) the remark that the thought expressed by the sentence "Odysseus was set ashore at Ithaca while sound asleep" "remains the same whether 'Odysseus' has reference or not".

25. That is, describable by way of a transparent, or relational, attribution of belief; see, e.g., Quine, *Word and Object,* pp. 141–56. Of course that does not prevent it from being describable by way of an opaque belief-attribution too. Note that I do not withdraw here from the position I outlined in §4. From "He is expressing a belief that Hesperus is visible above the elm tree" (an opaque attribution) one can, according to the principle stated in the text, move to the transparent "He is expressing a belief, concerning Hesperus, that it is visible above the elm tree". From there, since Hesperus is Phosphorus, one can get to "He is expressing a belief, concerning Phosphorus, that it is visible above the elm tree". But there is no route back from there to the opaque "He is expressing a belief that Phosphorus is visible above the elm tree".

can indeed gather, from the utterance, that the subject believes himself to have a belief that could be thus described, and believes himself to be expressing such a belief by his words. That might make the subject's behaviour, in speaking as he does, perfectly intelligible; but in a way quite different from the way in which, in the first kind of case, the belief expressed makes the behaviour intelligible. In the second kind of case, the belief that makes the behaviour intelligible is a (false) second-order belief to the effect that the subject has, and is expressing, a first-order belief correctly describable in the transparent style. This second-order belief is manifested by the subject's action, not expressed by his words. No belief is expressed by his words; they purport to express a belief that could be described in the transparent style, but since no appropriate belief could be thus described, there is no such belief as the belief that they purport to express.[26]

Opposition to this, on behalf of Frege, involves, I believe, a suspect conception of how thought relates to reality, and ultimately a suspect conception of mind. The Fregean view would have to seek its support in the idea that thought relates to objects with an essential indirectness: by way of a blueprint or specification that, if formulated, would be expressed in purely general terms. Whether the object exists or not would then be incidental to the availability of the thought. Underlying that idea is the following line of argument. When we mention an object in describing a thought we are giving only an extrinsic characterization of the thought (since the mention of the object takes us outside the subject's mind); but there must be an intrinsic characterization available (one that does not take us outside the subject's mind), and that characterization would have succeeded in specifying the essential core of the thought even if extramental reality had not obliged by containing the object. From this standpoint, the argument for the non-Fregean view that I outlined above goes wrong in its principle that the thought expressed by a sentence containing a name, if there is any such thought, is correctly describable as a thought, concerning some specified object, that it satisfies some specified condition. That would be a merely extrinsic characterization of the thought expressed; it succeeds in fitting the thought only if reality obliges. If reality does not oblige, that does

26. Frege's difficulties over truth-value gaps (see chap. 12 of Dummett, *Frege: Philosophy of Language*) reflect the pressure that drives him towards accepting the view of this paragraph, in consequence of his wish to see denoting as a genuine relation between expressions and objects.

not show, as the argument suggested, that no thought was expressed after all. For the real content of the thought expressed would need to be given by an intrinsic characterization; and that would specify the content of the thought without mentioning extra-mental objects, and thus in purely general terms.[27]

The conception of mind that underlies this insistence on not mentioning objects, in specifying the essential core of a thought, is the conception beautifully captured in Wittgenstein's remark, "If God had looked into our minds, he would not have been able to see there whom we were speaking of".[28] It is profoundly attractive, and profoundly unsatisfactory. Rummaging through the repository of general thoughts that, when we find the remark plausible, we are picturing the mind as being, God would fail to find out, precisely, whom we have in mind. Evidently that (mythical) repository is not the right place to look. God (or anyone) might see whom we have in mind, rather, by—for instance—seeing whom we are looking at as we speak. That sort of thing—seeing relations between a person and bits of the world, not prying into a hidden place whose contents could be just as they are even if there were no world—is (in part) what seeing into a person's mind is.[29]

A proper respect for a person's authority on his own thoughts points, anyway, in a quite different direction. When one sincerely and assertively utters a sentence containing a proper name, one means to be expressing a belief that could be correctly described in the transparent style. One does not mean to be expressing a belief whose availability to be expressed is indifferent to the existence or non-existence of a bearer for the name. The availability of the second sort of belief would be no consolation if the first sort turned out to have been, after all, unavailable.

In practice, an interpreter might say things like "This man is saying that Mumbo-Jumbo brings thunder", and he might explain an utterance that he described that way as expressing the belief that Mumbo-Jumbo brings thunder. That is no real objection. Such an in-

27. I owe the formulation in terms of intrinsic and extrinsic characterizations to Brian Loar.

28. Wittgenstein, *Philosophical Investigations*, p. 217.

29. Ironically, Wittgenstein's dismantling of the conception of mind that I deplore here—the conception that underlies the Fregean idea that the sense of a name is indifferent to the existence of a bearer for it—can be seen as carrying Frege's hostility towards mechanistic psychologism to its extreme (and satisfactory) conclusion.

terpreter is simply playing along with his deluded subject—putting things his way. There is no serious reason here for assimilating what he has found out about "Mumbo-Jumbo" to what, in the case that I described above (§7), he has found out about "Afla".[30]

9. The second complication is the "Hesperus"–"Phosphorus" puzzle: we can get a clearer view of it by considering it in a context in which the need for interpretation is explicit.

Suppose a smoothly functioning hypothesis has it that the mountain that some of the interpreter's subjects call "Afla" (§7) is also called, by some of them, "Ateb".[31] Suppose competence with both names coexists, in at least some cases, with ignorance that there is only one mountain involved. Suppose, as before, that the mountain is new to the interpreter, and that he proposes to take over means for referring to it, in expressing his new theory about it, from his subjects. Since he knows (let us suppose) that there is only one mountain involved, his own needs in geographical description (and so forth) would be met by taking over just one of their names. But a theory of their language that said of both names that, say, they stand for Afla would, as before (§4), be incapable of making sense of some utterances. To leave room for the combination of competence and ignorance, an interpreter who follows the strategy of adopting names from his subjects needs, at least in his theory of their language, to use both their names: thus, as before (§4), "Afla" stands for Afla and "Ateb" for Ateb.

We should distinguish two sorts of case. In the first, the possibility of combining competence and ignorance is an idiosyncratic accident of an individual's language-learning history. Instances of this are provided by people's possession of both "official" names and nicknames, under which they may be introduced to the same person in situations different enough for him not to acquire knowledge of the truth of the appropriate identity sentence. In this sort of case, it seems plausible that for a speaker enlightened about the identity the two names are (aside from stylistic considerations) mere variants of each other (differ merely as objects). A theory of sense that aimed to cover only enlightened speakers, excluding even their dealings with

30. Names of fictional characters are another thing again. I do not discuss them in this essay.

31. This completes an example of Frege's (from a letter: *Philosophical and Mathematical Correspondence,* p. 80).

unenlightened audiences, could without trouble use the same name on the right-hand sides of clauses dealing with each of the two. Only an aim of comprehensive coverage—enlightened and unenlightened together—would require a theory to handle the two differently, thereby representing them as differing in sense.

In the second sort of case, exemplified by "Hesperus" and "Phosphorus", and, in the most probable filling out of Frege's fable, by "Afla" and "Ateb", the difference of sense is more deep-seated. Even if everyone knew that Hesperus is Phosphorus, that would not make the two names differ merely as objects; or, if it did, the names would have changed in sense. If someone used the two names indifferently in talking about Venus, so that we could find no interesting correlation between utterances containing "Hesperus" and (say) beliefs formed in response to evening appearances of the planet, and between utterances containing "Phosphorus" and beliefs formed in response to its morning appearances,[32] then he would not be displaying competence in our use of the names—or, rather the fictitious use, corresponding to our use of "the Evening Star" and "the Morning Star", that I am considering in order to be able to discuss Frege's problem without raising irrelevant issues about definite descriptions. Such connections, between the use of a name and the sort of situation that prompts the beliefs it helps to express, can be, not merely idiosyncratic facts about individuals, but partly constitutive of a shared language. (This suggests the possibility of a well-motivated translation of a pair of radically foreign names—not even culturally related to ours, like "Hespero" and "Fosforo"—by our "Hesperus" and "Phosphorus". The strategy of adopting the subjects' names is not essential to the sort of situation we are concerned with.)

The second sort of case can seem to support description theories of the sense of names—at least those that can figure in such examples. But it does no such thing. Recall what, in our terms, the issue would be between the austere conception and treatments of names more congenial to description theories. Would knowledge that "Afla" stands for Afla and "Ateb" for Ateb, in the context of suitable further knowledge not directly involving the names, suffice for understanding utterances containing them? Or would one need, rather, knowledge in whose spelling out the bearer of each name is specified in a more informative way? In the present case, the material

32. This is meant to be only the crudest sketch of the sort of consideration that counts.

from which a description theorist might hope to construct more substantial specifications is the obtaining of more or less systematic differences between the evidential situations that ultimately account for utterances containing the names. And here again it seems clear that to insist on knowledge of those differences is to insist on more than would suffice. A competent speaker need not be reflective about the evidential ancestry of his remarks. They have whatever evidential ancestry they do without his needing to know that they do. And it is their having it, not his knowing that they do, that counts.

It is certainly true that speakers are likely to have opinions about their own propensities to respond to different evidential situations with utterances containing different names. It is our possession of such opinions that confers initial plausibility on the idea that, for instance, the sense of "visible in the evening" is part of the sense of "Hesperus". But we should not let that initial plausibility deceive us. Those opinions are the result of an activity that comes naturally to the self-conscious and theory-seeking creatures we are: namely, theorizing, not necessarily with much explicitness, about our own verbal behaviour, as just one of the connected phenomena that constitute our world. In theorizing thus about the place of our speech in our world, we are no better placed than external observers of ourselves; indeed we may be worse placed, if we are less well-informed about the extra-linguistic facts (see §8). Speakers' opinions about their own diverging evidential susceptibilities with respect to names are products of self-observation from, so far as it is accessible, an external standpoint. They are not intimations, from within, of an implicitly known normative theory, a recipe for correct speech, which guides competent linguistic behaviour. It seems that something like the latter picture would have to underlie insistence that, for competence in the use of pairs of names that differ in sense in the deep-seated way, nothing less than knowledge (no doubt tacit or implicit) of the relevant differences in sensitivity to evidence would suffice. The picture is simply a version of the psychologism that Frege rightly rejected (see §5).[33]

Difference in sense between "Hesperus" and "Phosphorus" appeared, in the account I gave earlier (§4) of how the austere conception copes with Frege's puzzle, as a reflection of failures of substitu-

33. Dummett's discussion of this matter (at p. 123 of "What Is a Theory of Meaning?") seems to me to be vitiated by a non-explicit adherence to the essentially psychologistic idea that mastery of a language is possession of a recipe that guides linguistic behaviour.

tion in propositional-attitude contexts. That would not satisfy those who look to the notion of difference in sense (as Frege did) to *explain* the failures of substitution.[34] The present section yields the following amplification of the picture. The failures of substitution, together with the characteristics that those failures force into a theory of sense, are reflections of two different sorts of underlying situation: first, in the trivial cases, the accidental absence, from some speakers' linguistic repertoires, of propensities to behave in ways construable as evidencing assent to the relevant identity sentences; second, in the deeper-seated cases, the different roles of the names in speakers' more or less systematic propensities to respond to different sorts of situation with different sentences. We can picture the failures of substitution and the differences in sense as, jointly and inseparably, products of our attempts at principled imposition of descriptions in terms of speech acts, and explanations in terms of propositional attitudes, on to the hard behavioural facts about linguistic and other behaviour, with the point of the imposition being to see how sense can be made of speakers by way of sense being made of their speech. In this picture, the differences in sense are located no deeper than the failures of substitution. I entertain the suspicion that the ultimate source of the desire to see the differences in sense as underlying the failures of substitution, and hence as capable of affording genuine explanations of them, is the psychologism about sense that Frege (officially) renounced.

10. Dissatisfaction with theories that handle names in the way I have recommended is likely to focus on the modesty of any claims we could make on their behalf. The sense of a name is displayed, in these theories, by the deductive powers of a clause intelligible only to someone already competent in the use of the very name in question, or else another name with the same sense. This exemplifies, for the case of names, one strand of the quasi-technical notion of modesty, in a theory of meaning, discussed by Dummett in "What Is a Theory of Meaning?".[35] Dummett makes it appear that a theory that was ineradicably modest, in that sense, would amount to a repudiation of

34. Simon Blackburn made me see this.

35. Dummett's formulation in terms of concepts (p. 101) may suggest that only general terms are in question, but that is not his intention.

the concept of sense.[36] In this section I want to sketch the reason why I think his argument unconvincing.[37]

As I noted earlier (§5), Dummett talks of a theory of understanding as specifying (implicit) knowledge in whose possession understanding actually consists; but we can let his argument begin, at least, without jibbing at that. He insists that it is worthless to consider a practical capacity on the model of knowledge of the members of an articulated set of propositions, if one can give no account of what it would be to know the individual propositions. One thing such an account must do is to distinguish knowledge of one of the relevant propositions from mere knowledge that some sentence (which in fact expresses it) expresses a truth; the latter state would not be to the point. Now in §6 above some simple remarks seemed adequate to ensure, in the case of the knowledge that "Hesperus" stands for Hesperus that I claimed would suffice, in the context of other knowledge not directly involving the name, for understanding the name, that it did not crumble into mere knowledge that the sentence "'Hesperus' stands for Hesperus" expresses a truth. Why not say, then, that those remarks constitute (for that case) something meeting Dummett's demand that we specify not merely what would be known in the hypothetical state of knowledge, but also what knowing it would consist in? What is counted as constituting a manifestation in linguistic behaviour of the hypothetical state of knowledge (or, better, of the capacity with the name for which it is claimed that that knowledge, in its context, would suffice) is, according to that suggestion, something like this: whatever behaviour would manifest an ability to use the name, or respond intelligently to uses of it, in speech acts construable as being about the planet; more specifically, speech acts in stating whose content we can use the name that appears on the right-hand side of the relevant clause, in a way appropriately tied to the occurrence, in the utterance being interpreted, of the name mentioned on the left-hand side of the relevant clause.

If we give that sort of description, or purported description, of a component of the articulated practical capacity that, according to a

36. In the Appendix, which (among other things) relates the arguments of the lecture, which are not couched in Fregean terminology, to Frege; see especially pp. 126–8.

37. I regard what follows as a minimal defence of my continuing to attempt to locate myself in a place that Dummett thinks he has shown not to exist. His subtle and powerful argument needs much more discussion.

theory of a language, constitutes mastery of it, we make essential appeal to the interpretation of the language afforded by the theory itself. The manoeuvre preserves modesty, in the sense I outlined above; no one could employ the suggested account, in order to ascertain from someone's behaviour whether he had the relevant ability, without being able to understand sentences like "This man is engaging in behaviour construable as his saying that Hesperus is visible above the elm tree"—that is, without himself already being able to understand "Hesperus".

Now Dummett's exposition of the notion of modesty amalgamates two notions: first, the notion of a theory that, as above, refuses to make itself intelligible except to someone who already understands the expressions it deals with (or others with the same sense); second, the notion of a theory that refuses to say what would count as a manifestation of the individual component abilities into which it purports to segment the ability to speak the language—that is, refuses to say not only what would be known, in the knowledge of a structured theory that, it is claimed, would suffice for understanding the language, but also what the ability corresponding to each piece of this hypothetical knowledge would consist in.[38] Thus, on pain of the notion of modesty falling apart, those purported specifications of component abilities that I suggested above, since they preserve modesty in the sense of the first component notion, must not be allowed to count as anything but modest in the sense of the second. They are debarred, then, from being accepted as effecting a genuine segmentation of the ability to speak a language. Dummett equates refusing to say what the knowledge in question would consist in, as well as what would be known—modesty in the sense of the second component notion—with repudiating the concept of sense.[39] Thus the amalgamation reflects the position that I mentioned at the beginning of this section: that is, that a theory that is ineradicably modest in the sense of the first component notion cannot but repudiate the concept of sense.

Why are those theory-presupposing specifications not allowed to count? Since Dummett does not even contemplate them, his lecture contains no explicit answer. It is easy to guess, however, that they do

38. Note, in "What Is a Theory of Meaning?" on p. 101, the way Dummett oscillates between explaining concepts and explaining what it is to have concepts.

39. See the Appendix to "What Is a Theory of Meaning?"

not occur to him, even as candidates to be ruled out, because he assumes that the acceptability of the demand to say what the knowledge would consist in is the acceptability of a demand for a reduction. The idea is that a genuine segmentation of the ability to speak a language would segment it into component abilities describable, as nearly as possible, in purely behavioural terms. And the theory-presupposing specifications refuse to attempt any such reduction.[40]

Why, though, should reduction be either necessary or desirable? It is extraordinary that he should take a reductive construal of the demand that one say what the states of knowledge in question would consist in to be so obvious as not to need explicit acknowledgement, let alone defence.

Dummett's lecture is shot through with intimations of an idea that would make that intelligible: namely, the idea that a theory of a language ought to be such that we could picture implicit knowledge of it as guiding competent linguistic behaviour.[41] Obviously a theory could not perform that service if understanding the theory required an exercise of the very ability it was to guide. If a theory is to guide speech it must generate instructions for doing things with sentences, intelligible independently of understanding those sentences. That would make congenial the search for a theory that—to illustrate with a simple case—might, in the case of a sentence combining a name with an unstructured predicate, generate instructions on this pattern: "First find the object (if any) that is thus and so. Then apply such-and-such tests to it. If the outcome is thus and so, adopt a preparedness to volunteer the sentence or utter 'Yes' on hearing it."[42] A theory that systematically generated such instructions, on the basis of structure within sentences, would presumably be compelled to

40. That this is how he understands the demand for segmentation emerges, I believe, from Dummett's employment of the demand in order to make difficulties for realist (truth-conditional) theories of meaning; see "What Is a Theory of Meaning? (II)", and compare *Frege: Philosophy of Language*, p. 467. "As nearly as possible" is meant to allow, as Dummett does, for the employment of concepts like that of assent (see "What Is a Theory of Meaning? (II)", p. 80).

41. He speaks throughout of theories of meaning being *used to obtain* understanding of a language (e.g., p. 114). Note also his talk of "the undoubted fact that a process of derivation of some kind is involved in the understanding of a sentence" (p. 112).

42. Another part of the theory of a language (the theory of force) is needed to get one from this sort of thing to an ability to engage in conversation; see "What Is a Theory of Meaning? (II)", e.g., pp. 72–4. It is clear that on this conception such a theory will have a great deal of work to do.

handle names by means of clauses that specified ways of identifying or recognizing objects; thus richness (in the sense of §5), as opposed to austerity, is the shape that immodesty takes in the case of names.

If pressed to its extreme, the idea from which that line of thought begins—the idea that a theory of a language ought to be such that we could picture implicit knowledge of it as guiding competent linguistic behaviour—leads to the incoherent notion of a theory that cannot be stated in any language.[43] Coherence might be preserved by demanding no more than an approximation, as close as may be, to the impossible ideal of a theory we could state to a person in order to teach him to talk. But in any case the idea that underlies these aspirations—the idea that linguistic behaviour is guided by implicit knowledge—is nothing but a version of the psychologism that Frege denounced and Dummett officially disclaims.

If we try to preserve everything Frege said about sense, we characterize a position with an internal tension. On the one hand, there is Frege's anti-psychologism, which in Wittgenstein's hands transforms itself into a coherent and satisfying view of the mind's place in reality, stably intermediate between the crass extremes of behaviourism and a psychologism that is objectionable not because it is mentalistic but because it is pseudo-scientific. On the other hand, there is the idea that a theory of sense would be rich or immodest. My claim is that the latter idea can only be justified on the basis of vestiges of the psychologism rejected in the first part of the position. If I am right, something has to be repudiated. It is a terminological issue whether "sense" belongs with the second part of the position; but fairness to Frege seems to justify trying to find a place for his terminology in a position purged of those elements that can only be grounded in hidden psychologism. Modesty in our demands on a theory of meaning is, in this view, not a repudiation of Frege's notion but an insistence on the feature that makes it an effort at something truly great; immodesty is not a vindication of Frege but a betrayal.[44]

43. See "What Is a Theory of Meaning?", pp. 103–4, where Dummett comes close to imposing the incoherent requirement on the full-blooded theories of meaning that he recommends.

44. I hope it is clear that I want no truck with the theory devised by Dummett in his Appendix under the title of "holism". That theory is an attempt (wholly unconvincing, as Dummett rightly says) to meet the reductionist demand that I reject. The topic of holism is too difficult (and confused) to be dealt with *ambulando* in this essay.

11. An adherent of a causal theory of names need not, in the interests of his theory, be unsympathetic to what I have said so far. His concern would be, not to enrich the right-hand sides of the specifications of denotation that I have been considering, but to say something substantial about the relation.[45]

Deduction within a truth-theory moves from axioms that assign semantic properties to sentence-constituents (for instance, denoting some specified thing), by way of clauses dealing with modes of combination, to theorems that assign truth-conditions to sentences. That is what warrants the claim that such a theory displays the sense of a sentence-constituent as, in Frege's metaphor, its contribution to the truth-conditions of sentences in which it occurs. The deductive direction can make it seem that the whole structure floats unsupported unless the nature of the semantic properties and relations from which the derivations start is independently explained. Thus it can seem that we need a general account of what it is for a name to denote something, conceptually prior to the truth-theory itself, from which the truth-theory's assignments of denotation to names can be seen as derivable, and in terms of which, consequently, they can be seen as explained. A causal analysis of the relation between a name and its bearer might seem well suited to meet that apparent need.[46]

But the need is only apparent. It is not true that we condemn a truth-theory to floating in a void, if we reject the alleged obligation to fasten it directly to the causal realities of language use by way of its axioms. On my account, those truth-theories that can serve as theories of sense are already anchored to the facts of language use at the level of their theorems; the anchoring is effected by the requirement that assignments of truth-conditions are to be usable in specifications of content of intelligible speech acts. Since the theorems must be derivable within the theory, the requirement bears indirectly on the theory's deductive apparatus, including assignments of denotation; and the deductive apparatus needs no attachment to the extra-theoretical facts over and above what that affords. Thus we can acquire such understanding as we need of the deductive apparatus (in particular, of the denoting relation) by reversing the theory's deductive direction, starting from our understanding of the requirement of

45. *Pace,* apparently, Dummett, "What Is a Theory of Meaning?", p. 125.
46. Compare Hartry Field, "Tarski's Theory of Truth".

serviceability in interpretation imposed on its consequences. We grasp what it is for a name to denote something by grasping the role played by the statement that it does in derivations of acceptable assignments of truth-conditions to sentences—assignments, that is, that would pull their weight in making sense of speakers of the language we are concerned with.[47]

According to Frege, it is only in the context of a sentence that a word has meaning.[48] What he meant was that we should not look for accounts of the meaning of particular words except in terms of their contributions to the meanings of sentences. But it seems in the spirit of his slogan to suggest also, as I did above, that we should not look for accounts of the sorts of meaning possessed by words of general kinds—for instance, an account of denotation, as possessed by names—except in terms of the contributions made by words of those kinds to the meanings of sentences.

To reject the search for a causal analysis of denotation, conceived as prior to interpreting a language by constructing a truth-theory, is not to deny the relevance of causal relations in determining what a name denotes. In fact causal relations will be involved in any adequate elaboration of the requirement imposed on a theory's consequences. To illustrate: suppose a candidate theory of a language would have us describe a certain speaker as saying that *p*, where we imagine "*p*" replaced by a sentence that mentions a particular concrete object. Can we make sense of his saying that *p*? Standardly, we make sense of sayings as expressing the corresponding belief. And ascription of the belief that *p* to our speaker is constrained by a principle on the following lines: one cannot intelligibly regard a person as having a belief about a particular concrete object if one cannot see him as having been exposed to the causal influence of that object, in ways suitable for the acquisition of information (or misinformation) about it.[49] Such principles, operating in the ascription of propositional attitudes that we need to go in for in order to make sense of linguistic behaviour, make causation crucial in the determination of what at least some names denote.

There is, however, not the slightest reason to expect that one could construct, out of such materials, a general relational formula

47. Compare Davidson, "In Defence of Convention T".

48. *The Foundations of Arithmetic,* p. 73.

49. See Gareth Evans, "The Causal Theory of Names", at pp. 197–200.

true of every name and its bearer. And even if a formula with the right extension could be constructed out of these materials, it would not constitute the prior fixed point of suspension for a truth-theory that was dreamed of in the argument I sketched at the beginning of this section. The ultimate justification for an assignment of denotation would be, not some causal relation between an object and utterances of the name, accessible independently of interpreting the language, but—as ever—the acceptability of interpretations that the assignment helps to confer on whole sentences.

Saul Kripke, who is often described as a proponent of a causal theory of denotation for names, in fact expressed the suspicion that any substantial theory of names—like any philosophical theory—is most likely to be wrong.[50] I think Kripke's suspicion was well placed. In this essay I hope to have indicated how we might find that situation possible to live with.

50. See *Naming and Necessity,* at pp. 64, 93–7.

Truth-Value Gaps[1]

Frege and others have held that if one utters an atomic sentence containing a singular term that lacks a denotation, then one expresses neither a truth nor a falsehood.[2] I want to contrast two justifications for that thesis.

1. According to Dummett,[3] the only justification lies in the smoothness that the thesis permits, in an account of how atomic sentences function as constituents of complex sentences.

The background is a distinction between two ways of approaching the notion of truth-value, in the context of the idea that a theory of meaning for a language might centre on the notion of truth.[4] In the first approach, the notion of truth-value constitutes the point of connection between, on the one hand, an account of what it is to make an assertion, and, on the other, the general form of statement whereby the theory determines the content of assertions that can be effected by uttering sentences, simple or complex, in the language. In the second approach, truth-values are ascribed to sentential constituents of complex sentences, in such a way as to facilitate a systematic account of their impact on the truth-values of the sentences of which they are constituents.

1. This essay owes a great deal to conversations over many years with Gareth Evans.

2. For Frege, see, e.g., "On Sense and Reference". See also, e.g., Strawson, "On Referring".

3. See "Truth"; "Presupposition"; *Frege: Philosophy of Language,* chap. 12; *Truth and Other Enigmas,* pp. xiv–xviii.

4. See *Frege: Philosophy of Language,* p. 417.

Of course, these two approaches cannot be wholly disconnected. For the systematic account of sentential compounding that the second approach would yield could have no point other than to subserve the needs of a systematic determination of the content of assertions effected by uttering whole (complex) sentences. So its assignments of truth-values to whole (complex) sentences would have to conform to whatever requirements the first approach imposes. In particular, they would have to respect the thought that the notion of truth that the first approach needs is anchored in the grasp we acquire, in learning to speak, of what it is for an assertoric utterance to be correct. However, there is no *a priori* assurance that the way in which the notion of truth-value is employed in the second approach, in connection with a sentence considered as a potential component of complex sentences, will correspond neatly with the way in which it is employed, in connection with the very same sentence as used on its own to make an assertion, in the first approach.

Dummett's justification, now, appeals to considerations from the second approach. Specifically: it is natural to take a sentence of the form "*a* is not *F*" as the negation of the corresponding sentence of the form "*a* is *F*"; and it is natural to connect negation and falsehood, by way of the principle that a sentence is false if and only if its negation is true. If we were to count a sentence of the form "*a* is *F*" false when the singular term lacks a denotation, then the two natural thoughts would commit us to counting the corresponding sentence of the form "*a* is not *F*" true; but that would not cohere with the indispensable connection between the notions of truth and correctness in assertion. (Here the second approach is, as I noted, constrained by the first.) Obviously, counting the original sentence true would directly flout the indispensable connection. So if we find it desirable to preserve the two natural thoughts, that constitutes a justification for counting such sentences neither true nor false.

These considerations do not preclude Dummett from insisting, as he does, that employment of the notion of truth-value in the first approach must conform to the principle *tertium non datur,* on the ground that (vagueness and ambiguity aside) our understanding of what it is to make an assertion leaves no room for a gap between the conditions under which an assertion is correct and the conditions under which it is incorrect. This argument applies in particular to the utterance, with assertoric intent, of a sentence of the form "*a* is *F*". According to Dummett's argument, the sense of such an utterance is determined, like that of any assertoric utterance, by the distinction between the condition under which it would be correct and all other conditions. The content of an assertion effected by such an utterance is such as to rule out any condition whose obtaining would render it incorrect. Conditions thus ruled out include both that in which our considerations from the second approach permit us to count the sentence false, and that in which those considerations recommend counting the sentence neither true nor false. Thus if we use the word "false" in the way that seems most natural from the standpoint of the first approach, the states that the second approach led us to distinguish, as being false on the one hand and being neither true nor false on the other, appear rather as two different ways of being false.

A terminological manoeuvre will remove the confusing appearance that the two approaches conflict. The simplest proposal is probably this: to concede the word "false" to the second approach, but to defer to the requirement of *tertium non datur* in the first, by collecting the states described as "being false" and "being neither true nor false" together as possession of undesignated truth-values, as opposed to the designated truth-value, truth. The principle *tertium non datur* now takes this form: vagueness and ambiguity aside, no assertion has neither a designated nor an undesignated truth-value.

On this view, then, the line of thought that justifies Frege's "neither true nor false" thesis would culminate in the following idea: if singular terms without denotations can occur in a language, then the impact of negation on the truth-values of negative sentences is best captured, not by the usual two-valued truth-table, but by a three-valued table, with the additional stipulation that negating a sentence that has the undesignated truth-value called "being neither true nor false" yields a sentence with that same truth-value. A full elaboration of the idea would require, also, that we specify the impact of a constituent with this third truth-value on the truth-values of other sorts of complex sentence, by providing three-valued truth-tables for the other sentential connectives as well.

Note that the third truth-value is just that, a truth-value. Strictly speaking, on this view, there is no question of a truth-value *gap*. This means that, about Frege himself, we can suppose at most that he took only the first step along the path that Dummett describes; for what Frege held was that the sentences in question lacked truth-values altogether. According to Dummett, what this stemmed from—the obstacle that debarred Frege from the natural culmination of his intuition—was the doctrine that sentences stand to their *Bedeutungen*, truth-values, in a relation that is not just analogous to, but is a case of, the name-bearer relation.[5] For it is a compelling principle that if a complex name has a constituent that lacks a *Bedeutung*, then the complex name lacks a *Bedeutung* too. If Frege had allowed himself to suppose that the relation between a sentence and its truth-value was only analogous to the relation between a complex name and its bearer, then it need not have seemed obvious that the principle must apply to the case at hand, and Frege would not have been precluded from the three-valued theorizing that lies at the end of the path on which, according to Dummett, he started. Taking the principle to apply, however, Frege thought natural language confronted him with the possibility that a sentence might have a sense but (since it lacked a *Bedeutung*) lack a semantic role; and, given that view of the situation, it was reasonable for him to suppose natural language beyond the reach of coherent theory.

In the three-valued treatment, the conditions for the truth and the falsity of a sentence of the form "*a* is *F*" overlap; both include the absence of the condition under which the sentence is said to be neither true nor false. We might introduce a label, say "presupposition", for the relation between the sentence, or an utterance of it, and this overlapping condition.[6]

Thus introduced, the notion of presupposition is clearly not fundamental in the way that the notion of assertion is. That a certain utterance presupposes that a certain condition obtains is not conceived as a hypothesis that casual observation of the practice of speaking a language might recommend to us, independently of theorizing about the internal structure of sentences, in the same sort of way as it might recommend the hypothesis that a certain utterance is an assertion that a certain condition obtains; as if it might be independently attractive to preserve hypotheses of both sorts, if possible, in the subsequent task of theorizing about how the structure of utterances bears on their correct interpretation. On the contrary: this notion of presupposition emerges only in the course of theorizing about structure. The aim of the theorizing is to secure the neatest possible fit between the theory's deliverances about the correctness and incorrect-

5. See *Frege: Philosophy of Language*, pp. 185–6, 427–9. I suppress, for simplicity's sake, the ambiguity that Dummett finds in the notion of *Bedeutung*.

6. See Dummett, *Truth and Other Enigmas*, p. xiv.

ness of assertions, on the one hand, and the observable practice of speaking the language, on the other; and whereas the concept of assertion occupies a point of direct contact between an acceptable theory of a language and what its speakers observably do, the concept of presupposition has its utility, if any, only inside the theory.

Dummett contrasts this view of presupposition with a view according to which presupposition is as fundamental as assertion; so that the use of the notion is intelligible, and potentially informative about the meanings of utterances, without benefit of information or theory about structure. Suppose we have a pair of sentences, *A* and *B*, each of which can be correctly asserted if and only if both of a pair of conditions, C and C′, obtain. Then this different view of presupposition would involve the idea that, independently of any account of structure, we can be told something intelligible about a difference in meaning by being told that in the case of *A*, but not *B*, the obtaining of C is only a presupposition. As Dummett insists, this idea is utterly implausible.[7]

Frege himself remarks that the assertoric use of a sentence containing a singular term presupposes that the term designates something; and he does not embark on the three-valued theory that alone, according to Dummett, gives the notion of presupposition its proper theoretical context. But this does not license accusing Frege of treating presupposition as independently fundamental. Frege's remark about presupposition expresses the same intuition about natural language as the "neither true nor false" thesis: an intuition that seems to Frege to preclude systematic theory about natural language as it stands. The remark about presupposition is not a fragment of a serious theory; rather, that it is needed would strike Frege as a reflection of the very fact about natural language that makes serious theory impossible.

Strawson puts the notion of presupposition to a similar use, equally without a backing of three-valued truth-tables.[8] And Strawson lacks Frege's reason for supposing that natural language is not amenable to serious theory; indeed, he evidently takes the notion of presupposition to be an essential ingredient in any serious account of referring in natural languages. Since Dummett thinks it is only in the

7. *Truth and Other Enigmas*, pp. xv–xviii.

8. See "On Referring" (with different terminology); *Introduction to Logical Theory;* "Identifying Reference and Truth-Values".

context of three-valued truth-tables that the notion of presupposition, if regarded as theoretically important at all, has its properly secondary role, he can thus interpret Strawson's failure to concern himself with three-valued truth-tables only as an indication that Strawson holds the implausible view that I distinguished above: namely, that the notion of presupposition is on a level with the notion of assertion.[9]

2. A different justification, which Dummett refuses to countenance, turns on the following idea. The syntax of sentences of the relevant sort fits them to express singular thoughts if any; where a singular thought is a thought that would not be available to be thought or expressed if the relevant object, or objects, did not exist. It follows that if one utters a sentence of the relevant sort, containing a singular term that, in that utterance, lacks a denotation, then one expresses no thought at all; consequently, neither a truth nor a falsehood.

This conception of singular thoughts, which is in essence Russell's,[10] must be separated from two accretions that would preclude using it for the present purpose.

First, Russell held that, if members of a syntactic category of apparent singular terms can lack denotations, then even those members of the category that have denotations are not genuine singular terms. For Russell, lack of denotation on the part of a putative singular term shows, not that utterances of sentences in which it occurs express no thoughts, but that utterances of all sentences in the relevant syntactic category express non-singular thoughts. This is the line of argument that convinces Russell that the only genuine singular terms are logically proper names. The conception of singular thoughts that I characterized above promises to open truth-value gaps, but this line of argument would ensure that the promise is not fulfilled.

Second, Russell found it natural to describe singular thoughts (or propositions) as propositions in which objects themselves occur.[11] It may seem an obvious gloss on this to say that a Russellian singular

9. See *Truth and Other Enigmas*, p. xviii.

10. See "On Denoting", pp. 45–6; though this passage also contains the argument for the first accretion, applied to definite descriptions.

11. See "On Denoting", p. 45, where Russell says that the view of "denoting phrases" that he is arguing against represents them "as standing for genuine constituents of the propositions in whose verbal expressions they occur".

thought, of a sort expressible by using a one-place predicate, is well represented as an ordered couple whose members are the appropriate object and (perhaps) the appropriate property.[12] In that case there cannot be two different singular thoughts that ascribe the same property to the same thing. It follows that a genuine singular term—one fitted for the expression of singular thoughts—is one that allows no room for a distinction between sense and reference. If this were a necessary corollary of the Russellian conception of singular thoughts, then that conception could not figure in an account of a possibly Fregean ground for the "neither true nor false" thesis.

Both these accretions are detachable.

As for the first: Russell achieves his radical restriction of genuine singular terms by applying, to any category of apparent singular terms whose members can lack denotations, an argument that runs in effect as follows.[13]

(1) If such terms are genuine singular terms, then one expresses no thought by uttering an atomic sentence containing a denotationless member of the category.[14]
(2) One does express thoughts by such utterances.[15]

Therefore

(3) Such terms are not genuine singular terms.

12. This obviously generalizes to relational thoughts. For the ordered-couple conception of monadic singular thoughts, see, e.g., Donnellan, "Speaking of Nothing", pp. 11–12.

13. I reconstruct the argument from "On Denoting", pp. 45–7 (the application to definite descriptions)

14. Russell says ("On Denoting", p. 45) that the sentence "ought to be nonsense". As against Frege (on the standard interpretation; but see below)—the target of Russell's argument—this is inept; for Frege is at pains to equip such terms, and hence sentences containing them, with sense. But what Russell is expressing is an inability (with which we can sympathize: see below, on the intuition I seek to liberate from the second accretion) to see how a term can both be a genuinely singular term and have a sense indifferent to the nonexistence of anything for it to refer to. (It is not clear, *pace* the standard interpretation, that Frege thought these could be combined either; see the end of this essay.)

15. Russell says that such a sentence "is plainly false". I take this to express the conviction that the sentence expresses a thought, together with a resolve to use the word "false" in the way that would be appropriate in the first of the two approaches to the notion of truth-value that I distinguished in §1.

(1) formulates the conception of singular thoughts from which I aim to detach the accretion. But the accretion requires (2) as well, for any category of atomic sentences utterances of members of which one can take oneself to understand even if one is mistaken in supposing that a suitable object exists. The upshot is, in effect, that one can understand an utterance as expressing a singular thought only if one's conviction that there is an object for the thought to be about is proof against Cartesian doubt. If, where that is not so, we continue to suppose that we understand some of the utterances as expressing singular thoughts, then we are committed to the idea that the impression of understanding, in the other cases, is an illusion: one takes oneself to understand an utterance as expressing a singular thought, but the singular thought that one thinks one understands the utterance to express does not exist. (2) disallows this; it registers insistence that the impression of understanding cannot be an illusion. But what grounds are there for this insistence?

One might think one could support Russell's argument on the following lines. If an utterance expresses a singular thought, it must be by virtue of its logical form that it does so. Thus, when we contemplate resisting the argument, as applied to some category of utterances, by exploiting the idea of an illusion of understanding, we are contemplating treating the category as having some members that have the appropriate logical form, and others that do not. The difference between the two sub-categories would turn on facts about what does and what does not exist. Ignorance of such facts is not the sort of thing we usually take to impugn someone's competence in a language. But should it not impugn someone's competence in a language if he takes an utterance to have a logical form that it does not have?[16]

The basis of this defence is the following idea. Granting that logical form may diverge from superficial syntactic form, nevertheless superficial syntactic form is all that is presented to a hearer of an utterance. Hence if understanding an utterance—which involves sensitivity to its logical form—is an exercise of competence in a language, then logical form should be recoverable from superficial syntactic form by "pure" linguistic knowledge, without one's needing to draw also on "extra-linguistic" knowledge, such as would be constituted by knowledge of what does and what does not exist.

16. See Dummett, *Frege: Philosophy of Language,* p. 163.

But this is inconclusive. I am not contemplating a possibility in which logical form is cut completely adrift from syntactic form. That would indeed make a mystery of the connection between syntax and the capacity to understand utterances in a language. But resistance to Russell's argument, on the lines I am contemplating, allows that syntactic form determines logical form, to this extent: it is recoverable from the syntactic form of an utterance of one of the relevant kinds, without knowledge of what does and what does not exist, that the utterance has subject-predicate logical form *if any;* that is, that it expresses a singular thought *if any.* Here "if any" leaves a question open, to be resolved by knowledge of whether or not an appropriate object exists. If one thinks one can object to this suggestion by claiming that this knowledge is extra-linguistic, one must suppose that "pure" linguistic competence, conceived as untainted by knowledge of what does and what does not exist, ought to carry its possessor all the way to the thought expressed by any utterance he understands. But that supposition is not an independently obvious truth, something one could properly appeal to in order to eliminate resistance to Russell's argument. On the contrary, it is at least as compelling to contrapose; if a language can encompass the expression of singular thoughts about the sorts of items our knowledge of whose existence is a substantial and precarious achievement, then understanding some utterances must involve bringing to bear knowledge of just that kind—with the attendant risk that the appearance of understanding may be illusory.[17] If the knowledge is extra-linguistic, then so much the worse for the idea that "pure" linguistic competence suffices for understanding absolutely any utterance in a language.

(Whether knowledge of existence is plausibly thought of as extra-linguistic may, anyway, vary from case to case. Falsely supposing that there is a denotation for some utterance of "that lime-tree" need not impugn one's linguistic competence; whereas the belief that "Vulcan" had a bearer was arguably a defect in command of the language.)[18]

17. Compare Frege, "Thoughts", p. 23: "By the step with which I win an environment for myself I expose myself to the risk of error." By "error" Frege here means "lapsing into fiction"; on this, see the last paragraph of this essay.

18. The envisaged illusion of understanding, in the case of, e.g., an utterance of a sentence such as "That lime-tree is covered with leaves", need not be an illusion of understanding the sentence. Russell's argument would work, for cases of this kind, if it followed from the meaningfulness of a sentence that any utterance of it would express a thought. But it does not follow. This seems to me to be the best way to understand Strawson's point in "On Referring".

As for the second accretion: it is true that the ordered-couple conception of singular thoughts would yield the thesis that singular thoughts depend for their existence on the existence of the objects they are about. But it is not true that one can embrace the thesis only by endorsing the ordered-couple conception. On the contrary, there is a plausible way of formulating the thesis without commitment to that conception. This alternative exploits the idea that in order to specify a thought-content, which one does typically in a "that"-clause, one must express the thought oneself.[19] In this context, a singular thought is a thought that one cannot ascribe to someone, or assign as the content of an assertion, without oneself making a reference to the appropriate object. Now if one knows that the existence of an appropriate object is an illusion, then one cannot specify a thought-content in the appropriate form. There is, one knows, no thought that one could ascribe in that form. This is the Russellian thesis—formulated here in terms of reflections about "that"-clauses that are compatible with denying what the ordered-couple conception implies, namely that co-referring singular terms are interchangeable *salva veritate* in "that"-clauses of the relevant sort.[20]

As standardly interpreted, Frege's distinction between sense and reference of singular terms has two characteristic elements: first, that such terms can possess the sort of sense appropriate to them whether or not they refer to anything; and, second, that two such terms can differ in sense (hence, fail to be interchangeable *salva veritate* in thought-ascribing "that"-clauses) while referring to the same thing. If we construe Russell's thesis that objects occur in singular propositions as an expression of the ordered-couple conception, then we are taking it as a blanket rejection, on Russell's part, of *both* elements of that standard interpretation. Now Russell certainly found no merit in the doctrine of sense and reference. But it is possible, and arguably charitable, to detach the thesis from the main body of Russell's attacks on the doctrine, and construe it as expressing a laudable recoil from the first element of the standard interpretation, without in itself involving commitment as to the second.

On this view, the thesis expresses an intuition on the following lines. If a term has a sense that is indifferent to the non-existence of

19. This idea is well captured by, though it does not require, the view of "that"-clauses suggested by Davidson, "On Saying That".

20. For more on this, see Essay 8 above.

any suitably related object, then it is not recognizable as a singular term—one whose sense fits utterances containing it to express thoughts that are about an object, on a certain attractive conception of what that amounts to. If an object's non-existence would not matter for the existence of certain thoughts, then the object's relation to those thoughts falls short of an intimacy that, Russell insists, sometimes characterizes the relation of things to thoughts, namely, that the thoughts would not exist if the things did not. The difference between thoughts that have this intimate relation to objects and thoughts that do not is sufficiently striking to deserve to be marked by the stipulation that only the former should count as being in the strictest sense about objects.

This intuition has no necessary connection with the ordered-couple conception. The intuition recognizes a relation between objects and thoughts so intimate that it is natural to say that the objects figure in the thoughts; but it has no tendency to recommend the idea that, for a given object that can thus figure in our thoughts, there is only one way in which it can figure—only one mode of presentation.[21]

It seems appropriate to credit this intuition to a robust sense of reality. If we insist that we think some thoughts of Russell's singular kind, then we conceive objects as sometimes present to our thoughts, in a way that contrasts with the most that is available on a picture according to which we could have all the thoughts we are entitled to think we have even if no objects besides ourselves existed. It is a pity that Russell allowed the first accretion to override his robust sense of reality, and convince him that the second picture was the best that could be had, in all cases in which Cartesian epistemology would represent the conviction that an appropriate object exists as uncertain. And if we let the second accretion persuade us to abandon our robust sense of reality wherever the ordered-couple conception is inappropriate (because it matters how one refers to an object in the specification of a thought), then we arrive at a similar, and similarly deplorable, upshot: like Russell in consequence of the first accretion, we almost lose hold of the best of Russell's insights into the relation between thought and things.

21. For more on this, see Essay 8 above; Evans, "Understanding Demonstratives"; and Evans, *The Varieties of Reference*, chap. 1.

If the first element is anyway a misinterpretation of Frege, then the intuition is even less anti-Fregean than I have so far suggested. I shall return to this at the end.

Three-valued truth-tables seem necessary only on the assumption that an utterance of one of the problematic sentences, with assertoric intent, constitutes a "move in the language-game"; so that the sentence must be credited with a semantic role—hence, a *Bedeutung*. But according to the second justification, an utterance of the problematic kind, though it may masquerade as a "move in the language-game" of the kind constituted by the assertoric expression of a singular thought, in fact simply fails to be what it purports to be. So on this view there are genuine truth-value gaps.

The notion of presupposition has a natural use in this position, for the relation that a singular sentence, or an utterance of it, bears to the condition, or conditions, that must be satisfied if the utterance is to express a thought. This use of the notion of presupposition emerges from, and is intelligible only in the context of, reflections about how the structure of singular sentences suits them to express the kind of thought they are capable of expressing. It is thus unfair to claim, as Dummett does, that anyone who makes serious use of the notion without a backing of three-valued truth-tables must take the notion to be "given naturally and in advance of the analysis of any particular forms of sentence".[22] What Dummett overlooks is the possibility of locating the use of the notion in the context of considerations about the structure, not of complex sentences, but of atomic sentences themselves. (Dummett appeals to facts about how it is natural to use the word "false" in theorizing about sentential compounding, specifically negation; within the second position, these facts will seem pointers to the correctness of what the position claims about the structure of the atomic sentences that figure in such compounding.)

22. *Truth and Other Enigmas,* p. xviii. Dummett complains (*Frege: Philosophy of Language,* p. 423) that "in the absence of a distinction between designated and undesignated truth-values, the mere proposal to regard a certain kind of sentence as being, in certain kinds of case, neither true nor false does not tell us whether the state of being neither true nor false is to be regarded as a sub-case of correct assertibility or of incorrect assertibility, and hence does not determine the assertoric content of the sentence". But in the present case the proposal does not purport to effect such a determination. Rather, it *flows from* such a determination (namely, that, in the relevant circumstances, the sentence has no assertoric content), independently effected on the ground of the sentence's internal structure.

Dummett himself sees no merit in the idea that underlies this second justification for the "neither true nor false" thesis. He refuses to allow that there can be the sort of illusion of understanding that I have discussed above.[23] Thus he endorses, in effect, the leading idea of the first accretion; and, since he has no truck with Russell's conception of the logically proper name, this means that he makes nothing of the intuition that I credited to a robust sense of reality. But this refusal to allow illusions of understanding, so far from being, as Dummett suggests, the only alternative to an obvious absurdity, requires a view that, from the standpoint of the robust sense of reality, looks quite unattractive: a view according to which knowing one's way about in a language—being able to recognize the thoughts expressed in it—is prior to and independent of knowing one's way about in the world.[24]

It may seem that Dummett is on stronger ground when he refuses to read the second justification into Frege. The first element of the standard interpretation would certainly preclude this. But it is not obvious that that element is correct. The question is too complex to discuss properly here; but I shall mention two difficulties for the standard interpretation.

First: Dummett's view certainly entitles us to introduce a notion of presupposition. But it does not entitle us to distinguish what an utterance presupposes from the content of an assertion effected by it.[25] Precisely not: on Dummett's view the content of an assertion is fixed by the line between the condition under which the assertoric utterance of a sentence is correct and all other conditions; the content is such as to rule out all these other conditions—including a presupposition's failing. There is thus no explanation here for a view accord-

23. See *Frege: Philosophy of Language*, p. 404. Dummett says that the idea that one of the problematic utterances expresses no thought "would be absurd, since we can understand such an utterance, and if we wrongly suppose the name to have a bearer, we can also believe it". But that we really understand the problematic utterances is not an argument against the second justification, but exactly what such an argument would need to make out. And, of course, it does not follow, from the fact that we may believe that such an utterance expresses a truth (which is the most that is uncontroversial), that we may believe some proposition expressed by such an utterance.

24. Dummett also adduces, as a reason against truth-value gaps, the implausibility of the presumed consequence that some truth-functional compounds would lack truth-value (*Frege: Philosophy of Language,* pp. 425–6). But see Geach, "Critical Notice of Dummett, *Frege: Philosophy of Language*", p. 441.

25. Though Dummett unaccountably claims this, at *Truth and Other Enigmas,* p. xiv.

ing to which the fulfilment of presuppositions is not part of what is asserted when a sentence is assertorically uttered. But this view is perfectly intelligible in the context of the second justification for the "neither true nor false" thesis. And it is evidently this view, according to which presuppositions are distinguished from content, rather than a distinguished component within content, to which Frege is attracted.[26]

Second: in those passages that constitute the evidence for the first element of the standard interpretation, there is typically an appeal to the notion of fiction.[27] Frege's use of the notion of fiction is peculiar; he cites examples of fictionally *intended* utterances, but he also uses the notion in such a way that it is possible to lapse into fiction without knowing it—this is what happens, in his view, whenever one utters, with serious assertoric intent, a sentence containing a denotationless singular term. Now the idea that one can unknowingly lapse into fiction is so wrong-headed about fiction that we urgently need an account of why it should have attracted so penetrating a thinker.[28] A satisfying explanation is suggested by a revealing passage in the posthumously published *Logic* of 1897,[29] in which Frege writes that in fiction we are concerned with apparent thoughts and apparent assertions, as opposed to genuine thoughts, which are always either true or false. This coheres neatly with the idea that Frege's ground for the "neither true nor false" thesis was on the lines of the second justification. It suggests that what attracted Frege to his peculiar use of the notion of fiction was that it seemed to soften the blow of the implication that there is an illusion of understanding. By the appeal to fiction, Frege equips himself to say that it is not a complete illusion that one understands one of the problematic utter-

26. In "On Sense and Reference", p. 40, Frege implicitly denies "that the sense of the sentence 'Kepler died in misery' contains the thought [its presupposition] that the name 'Kepler' designates something". The context makes it difficult to argue that the topic is ingredient sense, as opposed to content.

27. See, e.g., "On Sense and Reference", pp. 32–3. I owe to Gareth Evans my appreciation of the peculiarity of Frege's use of the notion of fiction, and of how important this is for understanding his views about reference.

28. Compare Dummett, *Frege: Philosophy of Language,* p. 160: "We should not, as Frege often does, cite as examples of names having sense but no reference personal names used in fiction . . . We need names used with a serious, though unsuccessful, intention to refer." What Dummett misses here is that for Frege any case of a name used with a serious, though unsuccessful, intention to refer *is* a case of fiction.

29. *Posthumous Writings,* p. 130.

ances, any more than it is an illusion that one understands an overtly fictional utterance. But the 1897 passage shows that in Frege's view the understanding of the problematic utterances that he entitles himself to recognize is separated by a great gulf from understanding of informative speech. It would be in the spirit of his talk of apparent thoughts to talk of apparent understanding; certainly the belief that one understands one of the problematic utterances as expressing a genuine thought would be an illusion, just as the second justification for the "neither true nor false" thesis requires. If this is the point of Frege's appeal to fiction, then the standard passages do not undermine the attribution to him of the second justification, or support the ascription to him of the thesis with which he is usually saddled: that a genuine singular term—one suited for use in the expression of genuine thoughts, as opposed to a *Scheineigenname*—has a sense (an impact on the thoughts expressible by sentences containing it) that it could have whether or not it referred to anything.[30]

30. Although Evans, in "Understanding Demonstratives", does not saddle Frege with the thesis as a general claim about singular terms, he does ascribe to Frege the thesis that there is a category of genuine singular terms (called "Fregean" in Evans, "Reference and Contingency") whose sense is existence-indifferent. Russell would have seen no naturalness in a classification that grouped these together with "Russellian" singular terms, but Evans aims (in "Reference and Contingency"; see also chap. 2 of *The Varieties of Reference,* which appeared after the first publication of this essay) to show that there is a semantic natural kind that includes both. I do not want to express a view on the success of this endeavour. But I believe the considerations in the text disarm the passages Evans might cite to justify counting Frege himself as an ally. I know no clear evidence that Frege believed in genuine singular terms—as opposed to *Scheineigennamen*—that were "Fregean" in Evans's sense. I think we can credit Frege with a view of the natural boundaries that matches the core of Russell's view, and has the enormous advantage of avoiding the two accretions.

ESSAY 10

De Re Senses

1. It is commonly believed that a Fregean philosophy of language and thought can represent an utterance, or a propositional attitude, as being about an object only by crediting it with a content that determines the object by specification, or at least in such a way that the content is available to be thought or expressed whether the object exists or not.[1] To resist this restriction would be to hold out for the idea that utterances and thoughts can be essentially *de re;* and that idea is supposed to be incapable of being made to fit within the framework provided by the theory of sense and *Bedeutung.*

I believe that this picture of the possibilities for Fregean theory is quite wrong. Gareth Evans has argued that Frege himself is positively committed to *de re* senses for singular terms, and at least to some extent recognizes the commitment; and Evans has given the outlines of a perfectly Fregean account of some sorts of *de re* sense.[2] My purpose in this essay is not to repeat or embellish Evans's positive considerations, but to criticize a theoretical structure within which they are bound to seem incomprehensible.

2. What supposedly rules out accommodating the essentially *de re* within Fregean theory is a certain conception of the contrast between

1. This latter formulation cannot be right where the object's existence is necessary absolutely, or necessary relative to the fact that the thought in question is being expressed or entertained at all (e.g., the *Bedeutung* on an occasion of "now", and perhaps of "I"; but see Evans, *The Varieties of Reference,* pp. 249–55). But having noted this, I shall ignore it; the issue I want to consider is whether Fregean theory can accommodate *de re* thoughts outside that area.

2. Evans, *The Varieties of Reference,* chaps. 1, 6, and 7.

de re and *de dicto*. I shall follow Tyler Burge's exposition, which is the most explicit and thoughtful that I know.[3]

At the level of logical form, the contrast is between *de dicto* attributions of, say, belief, which relate the believer to a "complete" (p. 343) or "completely expressed" (p. 345) proposition, and *de re* attributions, which relate the believer to a *res* and something less than a "complete" proposition. Underlying this semantic distinction is an "epistemic" distinction (pp. 345–6): this is between beliefs that are "fully conceptualized" (p. 345: *de dicto*), and beliefs "whose correct ascription places the believer in an appropriate nonconceptual, contextual relation to objects the belief is about" (p. 346: *de re*).

It would be a merely terminological question whether one should say that there are no propositions but "complete" ones, so that *de re* attributions involve no propositions; or whether in connection with *de re* attributions one should recognize propositions of a different kind: "Russellian propositions", which are not "completely expressed" but contain objects as constituents along with "expressed" items that are less than "complete" propositions.[4] The second choice brings out neatly why Fregean theory cannot countenance the essentially *de re*, conceived on these lines. In Fregean theory, utterances and propositional attitudes have thoughts as their contents, and thoughts are senses with nothing but senses as constituents: "we can't say that an object is part of a thought as a proper name is part of the corresponding sentence."[5]

3. Burge's fundamental intuition is this: if a propositional attitude (or utterance) is essentially *de re*, that is in virtue of the fact that a context involving the *res* itself enters into determining how the attitude (or utterance) can be correctly ascribed.[6]

3. See Burge, "Belief *De Re*": page references in the text are to this article.

4. "Russellian propositions" in view of, e.g., p. 246 of "The Philosophy of Logical Atomism". Burge remarks (p. 343): "In Russellian propositions, the relevant *res* are not expressed but shown." His own formalizations of *de re* attributions do not group their relata, aside from the believer, into Russellian propositions, but a trivial notational change would make them do so.

5. *Posthumous Writings*, p. 187.

6. Burge does not discuss utterances, but the extrapolation is natural. My formulation avoids another merely terminological issue, about the word "content". One might count Russellian propositions (if one believed in them) as a species of content; alternatively, one might tie content to "complete" propositionality, so that an attitude's *de re* character

But why should the essentially *de re*, conceived in conformity with this intuition, be deemed inaccessible to Frege? Frege writes:

> If a time indication is conveyed by the present tense one must know when the sentence was uttered in order to grasp the thought correctly. Therefore the time of utterance is part of the expression of the thought.[7]

Again, in connection with "yesterday" and "today", and "here" and "there", he writes:

> In all such cases the mere wording, as it can be preserved in writing, is not the complete expression of the thought; the knowledge of certain conditions accompanying the utterance, which are used as means of expressing the thought, is needed for us to grasp the thought correctly.[8]

He is writing of thoughts that are not completely expressed by words abstracted from contexts of utterance, but he is precisely *not* conceding that the thoughts are not completely expressed, *simpliciter.* So where Burge speaks of a *res*-involving context partly determining the shape of a correct *de re* attribution, it is not clear why this cannot be transposed, in the light of this passage from Frege, into a conception of how such a context contributes to the expression of a fully expressible but nevertheless *de re* thought.

It is sometimes supposed that the "thoughts" of this passage cannot be classically Fregean thoughts. This idea is a response to Frege's allowing that if one utters a sentence containing "yesterday" one can express the same thought as one could have expressed on the day before by uttering a sentence containing "today"; the idea is that this same thought would be, not a Fregean thought, but a Russellian proposition, containing the day in question as a constituent.[9]

However, if Frege had intended to alter his use of "*Gedanke*" so radically as to encompass these Russellian propositions, he would

---

would come out in the fact that its content falls short of a complete proposition. Burge's preference is for the second of these; see n. 2 (p. 119) of "Other Bodies".

7. *Logical Investigations,* p. 10.

8. *Logical Investigations,* p. 10; see also pp. 27–8.

9. David Kaplan takes this view in "Demonstratives"; so also, by implication, John R. Searle, *Intentionality,* p. 229. On this reading, Frege's remarks would amount to suggesting that if we give due weight to the expressing role of "accompanying conditions", we can allow that even Russellian propositions can be completely expressed. If accepted, this would disrupt Burge's apparatus; but it would not vindicate the possibility of a genuinely *Fregean* approach to the *de re.*

surely have remarked on it. (That is putting it mildly, since the alteration would undermine the fundamental point of his notion of sense, which includes thought: namely, to capture differences in cognitive value. One can take opposing "cognitive" attitudes simultaneously to one of these Russellian propositions.)[10] If there were no alternative explanation of what Frege is driving at, we might be forced to suppose that he has slipped inadvertently into a non-Fregean use of "*Gedanke*". But there is an alternative explanation. Evans has suggested that Frege's idea is this: if one "keeps track of" a day as it recedes into the past, thinking of it successively as *today, yesterday, the day before yesterday,* and so on, that enables one to hold on to thoughts about it—thoughts that preserve their identity through the necessary changes in how they might be expressed.[11] These "dynamic thoughts" are not Russellian propositions; not just any mode of presentation of the day in question would demand the appropriate capacity to keep track of it, so a dynamic thought is not determined by the sheer identity of its object.[12]

4. If we had only the linguistic expression of thoughts to consider, it would be somewhat mysterious why Burge assumes—contrary to the apparently reasonable line that Frege himself, as we have seen, seems to take—that contextual factors must be extraneous to the expressive capacities of context-sensitive utterances. An explanation emerges from Burge's treatment of the "epistemic basis" for his semantic distinction between *de re* and *de dicto*.

He writes (pp. 345–6):

> The rough epistemic analogue of the linguistic notion of what is expressed by a semantically significant expression is the notion of a concept. Traditionally speaking, concepts are a person's means of representing objects in thought. For present purposes, we may include as

10. See John Perry, "Frege on Demonstratives", pp. 482–5.

11. See Evans, "Understanding Demonstratives", pp. 291–5. One can take opposing "cognitive" attitudes to one of these "dynamic thoughts", but not simultaneously, and there is a perfectly Fregean explanation of how it happens; by losing track of the object, one loses track of the thought.

12. Note how Evans's reading of the passage answers Colin McGinn's query, *The Subjective View*, pp. 61–3: if, as Frege allows, a "yesterday"-utterance and a "today"-utterance, or a "here"-utterance and a "there"-utterance, can express the same thought, why not an "I"-utterance and a "you"-utterance? The answer is that an "I"-utterance and a "you"-utterance could not be connected by expressing a single dynamic thought. This pre-empts McGinn's speculatively Cartesian answer to his query, pp. 63–4.

> concepts other alleged mental entities that the empiricist tradition did not clearly distinguish from them—for example, perceptions or images—so long as these are viewed as types of representations of objects. From a semantical viewpoint, a *de dicto* belief is a belief in which the believer is related only to a completely expressed proposition *(dictum). The epistemic analogue is a belief that is fully conceptualized.* That is, a correct ascription of the *de dicto* belief identifies it purely by reference to a "content" all of whose semantically relevant components characterize elements in the believer's conceptual repertoire.

Given that conceptual content is made up of *means* of representation in thought, a belief's being fully conceptualized can mean only that it has a fully propositional content exhausted by some collection of thought *symbols;* and it would follow that there is no room for contextual factors to contribute to determining how such a belief may be correctly ascribed. This makes Burge's picture of the relation between conceptual content and context obligatory; and, applied to the linguistic expression of thought, with a plausible equation between conceptual content and what can be completely expressed, it generates Burge's curious deafness to what Frege seems to be trying to say in the passage that I have quoted.

But Burge makes this look inexorable only by a patent slide; from concepts as parts or aspects of the *content* of a representational state, such as a belief, to concepts as *means* of representation. In the former sense (which is non-Fregean, but for present purposes only harmlessly so), concepts would indeed be analogous to *what is expressed* by words, as Burge says. In the latter sense, they would be analogous to *what does the expressing:* to the words themselves.

Once we discern this conflation, the direction of argument can reverse. It is not that an independently compulsory division between content and context undermines Frege's wish to make a different use of the concept of expression, but rather that the evident coherence of Frege's remarks, with the same plausible equation between "conceptual content" and what can be "completely expressed", shows that Burge's picture of the relation between context and content is unwarranted. There is no more reason to accept that contextual factors are extraneous to the content-determining powers of a conceptual repertoire than there is to accept, in the face of what Frege says, that what is expressed by a context-sensitive utterance cannot be partly determined by the context in which it is made. So for all that Burge shows, a conceptual repertoire can include the ability to think of objects under modes of presentation whose functioning depends essentially on (say) the perceived presence of the objects. Such *de re* modes of presentation would be *parts* or *aspects* of content, not *vehicles* for it; no means of mental representation could determine the content in question by itself, without benefit of context, but that does not establish any good sense in which the content is not fully conceptualized.

It would be illuminating to consider why it is so tempting to conflate mental content with means of representation, but for my purposes here it is enough to point out that it is a conflation. Writers on Frege typically assume without much argument that a Fregean sense, of the sort suitable to be the sense of a singular term, must be available to be expressed whether or not it determines an object.[13] Burge supplies an explicit argument, whose premises are, first, the plausible thesis that we can make room for existence-dependence in, say, beliefs only by giving contextual factors an essential role in determining their correct attribution; and, second, the separation of content from context. Failing an alternative, it seems fair to suppose that something like Burge's argument lies behind the usual assumption about the possibilities for Fregean theory; indeed something on the lines of Burge's division of content from context is a near orthodoxy in writers on these matters, usually without Burge's self-consciousness about it. But this division of content from context is recommended only by a conflation.[14]

5. A *de re* sense would be specific to its *res;* perhaps Frege is simply drawing out the implications of this, as applied to a sort of *de re*

13. There are passages where Frege seems to say this. But given the plausible connection of the concept of *Bedeutung* with the concept of semantic value, the idea of a sense that determines no *Bedeutung* is very difficult (see Evans, *The Varieties of Reference,* pp. 22–8); and the passages can be neutralized by adverting to peculiarities in Frege's use of the notion of fiction (see Evans, pp. 28–30). Contrary to something implied at p. 197 of Christopher Peacocke, "Demonstrative Thought and Psychological Explanation", Frege's apparent attribution of sense to empty singular terms is quite distinct from his doctrine that senses have only senses, not *Bedeutungen,* as constituents (and much more peripheral to his thinking).

14. Evans's rebuttal, in "Understanding Demonstratives", of Perry's "Frege on Demonstratives" turns on the lack of any basis for Perry's assumption that Fregean senses for singular terms must be "descriptive". This objection is quite correct; but it risks being met with incomprehension, as long as the framework that holds the assumption in place is not challenged.

sense whose instances present a thinker as himself, when he writes that "everyone is presented to himself in a special and primitive way, in which he is presented to no-one else".[15] Commentators have made heavy weather over two issues about this: first, whether it is consistent with the constant "linguistic meaning" of a context-sensitive expression; and second, whether it is consistent with Frege's doctrine that thoughts are objective.

On the first issue, some philosophers have written as if accommodating the constancy of linguistic meaning would require crediting a context-sensitive expression with a mode of presentation constant across all univocal uses of it.[16] Such a mode of presentation would not be a Fregean sense, since it would not determine the appropriate sort of *Bedeutung* except in conjunction with a context. What would serve would be something on the lines of David Kaplan's notion of *character*. Characters are functions from contexts to "Russellian propositions" or their constituents.[17]

This may seem to yield independent support for Burge's picture of the relation between content and context. But that is an illusion, since constancy of linguistic meaning can be accommodated in terms of *de re* senses. Particular *de re* senses, each specific to its *res*, can be grouped into sorts. Different *de re* senses (modes of presentation) can present their different *res* in the same sort of way: for instance, by exploiting their perceptual presence. And the univocity of a context-sensitive expression can be registered by associating it with a single sort of *de re* sense.[18]

These two ways of accommodating constancy—in terms of character and in terms of sort of *de re* sense—are very different. Given a context, a suitable sub-sentential character will determine an object, or else—if no object is suitably involved in the context—nothing. Even

15. *Logical Investigations*, p. 12.

16. See, e.g., McGinn, *The Subjective View*, pp. 64–5.

17. See Kaplan, "On the Logic of Demonstratives"; compare the concept of *role* introduced by Perry, "Frege on Demonstratives", p. 479.

18. See Evans, "Understanding Demonstratives", p. 298. This point removes the motivation for Michael Dummett's idea (*The Interpretation of Frege's Philosophy*, chap. 6) that indexical expressions force on Frege a distinction (which he however fails to draw) between sense as linguistic significance and sense as mode of presentation. A corollary is that there is no need to play down Frege's interest in linguistic meaning in order to defend his thinking about sense; compare Burge, "Belief *De Re*", p. 357, and, with more elaboration, "Sinning against Frege", pp. 399–407.

in the latter sort of case, the character is still, according to this way of thinking, available to be expressed: a constituent of a sub-propositional conceptual content. Contrast *de re* senses. Given a context, a sort of *de re* sense may determine a *de re* sense (if one cares to put it like that), or else it too may determine nothing. And in the latter sort of case, according to this way of thinking, there can only be a gap—an absence—at, so to speak, the relevant place in the mind—the place where, given that the sort of *de re* sense in question appears to be instantiated, there appears to be a specific *de re* sense.[19]

It may seem, contrary to what I have just said, that one could capture the effect of a Fregean conception of *de re* thoughts in terms of a special kind of Russellian proposition: Russellian propositions with both *res* and characters as constituents. On this view, an ordered pair of *res* and character might represent a *de re* sense; such an item certainly depends on the *res* for its existence, and it determines, but is not determined by, a *Bedeutung* of the appropriate sort, namely the *res*.[20] However, although this suggestion does thus mimic aspects of a genuinely Fregean position, the resemblance is only superficial. This suggestion secures a *de re* nature for these "thoughts" only by violating Frege's doctrine that thoughts are senses with senses, not *Bedeutungen*, as constituents. It is another way of making the same point to say that at best this suggestion shows the possibility of grafting a version of the Fregean terminology on to a picture of the *de re* that would be quite congenial to Burge; this can raise at best a verbal question about Burge's conception of the relation between content and context.[21]

19. Perhaps there is a thought symbol (a means of representation) at a place corresponding to the gap. But to accept this would not be to accept that there is, at that place, an *aspect* or *ingredient* of content. What there is at that place, if we accept this suggestion, is a putative *bearer* or *vehicle* of content.

20. See Peacocke, "Demonstrative Thought and Psychological Explanation", p. 197. At p. 195, Peacocke denies that what he calls "type modes of presentation" are characters, but on the doubtful ground that "character is essentially linguistic"; I cannot see that he says anything that excludes interpreting his "type modes of presentation" as functions from contexts to objects. The fact that such functions are available to be expressed even when they determine no objects makes the "type"-"token" terminology very odd, but in a way that Peacocke seems not to mind; see his *Sense and Content*, p. 9, n. 6.

21. See McGinn, *The Subjective View*, p. 68, n. 17. I think McGinn's point tells against Peacocke, and also against Evans's "notational variant" argument against Perry ("Understanding Demonstratives", pp. 298–300), which seems to me to be a slip on Evans's part. It does not apply to the position I am defending.

6. The second issue is about the consistency of *de re* senses, and in particular Frege's remarks about the pronoun "I", with Frege's doctrine that thoughts are objective.[22]

It is true that Frege sometimes connects the objectivity of thoughts with their being communicable. And it is true that he cannot see how thoughts involving the "special and primitive way" in which each person is presented to himself can figure in communication. What he suggests is that for purposes of communication a person "must use 'I' in a sense which can be grasped by others, perhaps in the sense of 'he who is speaking to you at this moment'".[23] In fact this is quite unsatisfactory, as becomes clear if we try to construct a parallel account of the role of "I"-thoughts in receiving communication as opposed to issuing it. Suppose someone says to me, "You have mud on your face". If I am to understand him, I must entertain an "I"-thought, thinking something to this effect: "I have mud on my face: that is what he is saying." Frege's strategy for keeping the special and primitive way in which I am presented to myself out of communication suggests nothing better than the following: the "I"-sense involved here is the sense of "he who is being addressed". But this would not do. I can entertain the thought that he who is being addressed has mud on his face, as what is being said, and not understand the remark; I may not know that *I* am he who is being addressed.[24]

Frege's troubles about "I" cannot be blamed simply on the idea of special and primitive senses; they result, rather, from the assumption—which is what denies the special and primitive senses any role in communication—that communication must involve a sharing of thoughts between communicator and audience.[25] That assumption is quite natural, and Frege seems to take it for granted. But there is no obvious reason why he could not have held, instead, that in linguistic interchange of the appropriate kind, mutual understanding—which is what successful communication achieves—requires not shared thoughts but different thoughts that, however, stand and are mutually known to stand in a suitable relation of correspondence. (Notice that the correspondence in question is not the one that Frege recognizes in this passage:

22. For commentators' worries about this, see especially Perry, "Frege on Demonstratives", and McGinn, *The Subjective View*, chap. 5.

23. *Logical Investigations*, p. 13.

24. See Evans, *The Varieties of Reference*, p. 314.

25. Evans questions the assumption: *The Varieties of Reference*, pp. 40, 315–6.

> . . . with a proper name, it is a matter of the way the object so designated is presented. This may happen in different ways, and to every such way there corresponds a special sense of a sentence containing the proper name. The different thoughts thus obtained from the same sentences correspond in truth-value, of course; that is to say, if one is true then all are true, and if one is false then all are false. Nevertheless the difference must be recognized.[26]

Here we have thoughts related by mere co-reference in modes of presentation that they contain; whereas in view of the point about "he who is being addressed", that would not suffice for the communication-allowing correspondence that I am envisaging.)[27]

When he insists that thoughts are objective, Frege's main purpose is to deny that the being of a thought is dependent on its being entertained (or grasped), as the being of an idea is dependent on its having a bearer. This purpose is in no way obstructed by countenancing *de re* senses for "I", one for each person. This gives me (for instance) "I"-thoughts that only I can entertain; but it does not follow that they are not available to be entertained independently of my actually entertaining them. Sustaining the idea that even special and primitive "I"-thoughts are mind-independent in this sense would perhaps be facilitated by showing that such thoughts can figure in mutual understanding, as I have claimed that Frege could have done. Publicity in any stronger sense is not needed; Frege is led to suggest otherwise by his connecting communication with the sharing of thought, but the connection is not compulsory. The notion of *de re* "I"-senses need not be in tension with anything that is essential to a Fregean conception of thought.[28]

26. *Logical Investigations*, p. 12.

27. This paragraph suggests a possible alternative to Evans's treatment of certain phenomena of "cognitive dynamics" (Kaplan's phrase) in terms of "dynamic thoughts", which I sketched in §3 above. I shall not pursue this here.

28. These considerations undermine the motivation for Peacocke's insistence ("Demonstrative Thought and Psychological Explanation", pp. 191–3) that we must everywhere distinguish between expressing ("employing") modes of presentation and referring to them. Certainly on a Fregean view senses are referred to by words in content-specifying "that"-clauses; but the best construal of Fregean theory has them expressed there as well. This fits Dummett's dissolution (*Frege: Philosophy of Language*, chap. 9) of the supposed problem of an infinite hierarchy of oblique senses. Peacocke mentions Dummett's discussion approvingly, but he makes an exception for demonstrative modes of presentation. But there is no need for the exception. (Of course not just any mention of a mode of presentation will count as expressing it.)

7. I have argued that Burge's theoretical framework is not cogently supported; I shall end with two considerations that tell against it.

On a Fregean account of the *de re,* Burge's supposedly unitary distinction between *de re* and *de dicto* would divide into two distinctions, which it would be open to us to regard as largely independent: first, a distinction between *de re* and *de dicto attributions* of, say, belief, marked by whether or not designations of the relevant *res* can be replaced *salva veritate* by other designations of them or by variables bound by initial existential quantifiers; and, second, a distinction between *contents* that are *de re,* in the sense that they depend on the existence of the relevant *res,* and contents that are not *de re* in that sense.[29] A belief with a *de re* content may be attributed in the *de re* way, but it need not. And it is not obvious that any belief that is attributable in the *de re* way has a *de re* content.[30] In any case, even if *de re* attributability does imply *de re* content, *de re* attributions do not display the logical form of states with *de re* content; on the Fregean view, a *de re* attribution—one in which the relevant *res* is mentioned outside the specification of content—is true, if it is, in virtue of the truth of an attribution involving a "complete" propositional content.[31] (If, as may happen, we cannot place ourselves in a context such as we would need to exploit in order to give "complete expression" to the content, we may retain the capacity for a *de re* attribution, true in virtue of the truth of a *de dicto* attribution whose expression is beyond us.)

Now consider the logical form of a *de re* attribution of, say, a belief. Roughly speaking, it is a relational expression with argument-places occupied by designations of the believer, the *res,* and a propositional fragment.[32] How does the relational expression relate

29. "*De dicto*" is clearly inappropriate to mark this contrast.

30. Uncontaminated by philosophy, we are quite casual about "exportation" in cases of the "shortest spy" sort. (For the terminology there, see W. V. Quine, "Quantifiers and Propositional Attitudes"; and David Kaplan, "Quantifying In".) Burge's insistence ("Belief *De Re*", p. 346) that the logical form is different in such cases (involving a complete *dictum,* unlike canonical cases of *de re* attribution) seems strained; his excellent motivation for this claim (to preserve a robust conception of *de re* propositional attitudes) can be gratified in a different way.

31. "True in virtue of" rather than—as suggested by, e.g., Kaplan, "Quantifying In"—"analysable in terms of". I doubt whether there is much system in our practice with *de re* attributions.

32. We can ignore such niceties as that the second argument should really be a sequence (so that we can vary the number of *res* without needing new relations). We can also ignore divergences over the nature and internal structure of the propositional fragment.

the *res* to the propositional fragment?[33] In the state of affairs that the attribution represents, the propositional fragment should figure as somehow tied to the *res* by a predicational tie; can this intuitive requirement be met? If, as in the Fregean position, the *de re* attribution is conceived as true in virtue of the truth of a *de dicto* attribution, this question holds no terrors; in the underlying *de dicto* attribution, the required predicational tie will be explicitly expressed. But if, as in Burge's framework, the *de re* attribution is conceived as "barely true",[34] the belief relation has to secure the presence of the predicational tie all on its own; and it is quite unclear that it can be explained so as to carry the weight. This difficulty for any position like Burge's is due to Russell (following Wittgenstein);[35] so far as I know it has never been dealt with by adherents of this sort of position.

8. The second consideration is that Burge's framework forces us to choose between a pair of positions each of which is compellingly motivated by the deficiencies of the other.

With the framework in place, the only Fregean treatment of context-sensitive singular terms is to credit particular uses of them with senses that determine objects in such a way that the senses are expressible whether the objects exist or not. At best this generates a falsification of, for instance, demonstrative thought, akin to the falsification of perceptual experience that is induced by representative realism. Representative realism postulates items that are "before the mind" in experience whether objects are perceived or not, with the effect that even when an object *is* perceived, it is conceived as "present to the mind" only by proxy. Analogously, if an object thought of demonstratively is present to the mind only by way of something that could have been deployed in thought even if the object had not existed, the object is before

33. Having fixed the logical form, we go on to look for elucidation of the semantical primitive: see Donald Davidson, "Truth and Meaning".

34. In Dummett's sense; see "What Is a Theory of Meaning? (II)", p. 89.

35. For Russell's exposition, see "The Philosophy of Logical Atomism", pp. 224–7. If we understood how Russellian propositions could be a kind of proposition, we would certainly have no problems in saying what it would be for one of them to be true. But the point Russell takes from Wittgenstein is that a precondition for so much as supposing that we are dealing with a bearer of truth-value is not satisfied. (That is not how Russell puts the point.)

the mind only by proxy.[36] Without some seemingly inescapable compulsion, it is hard to believe anyone would tolerate this indirectness in an account of how demonstrative thinking relates us to objects.

The felt compulsion comes from a perception of how genuinely unattractive is the only alternative the framework allows.[37] Consider, for instance, how strange it is to suggest that what a belief is about can be partly determined by something that is "not part of the cognitive world of the believer"[38]—by something "external to what cognitively transpires in the mind of the thinker".[39] The resistance that this suggestion naturally elicits cannot be disarmed by introducing a use of "mind" according to which a *de re* "content", jointly determined by aspects of a thinker's "cognitive world" and by matters external to it, can count as "in the mind".[40] Once the subject's cognitive world has been segregated from his involvement with real objects,[41] this merely terminological move cannot restore genuine sense to the idea that we can get our minds around what we believe—even when the belief is *de re*.[42] Here again, it seems implausible that any-

36. This description fits the theory of indexically expressible thought expounded by Searle, *Intentionality*, pp. 218–30; note Searle's insistence that such thoughts could be entertained by a brain in a vat. On Searle's account, the object of a perceptually demonstrative thought is specified in terms of a causal relation to a current perceptual experience; *qua* object of thought, the object is present to the mind only by proxy, and this virtually necessitates a construal of the current perceptual experience on representative lines (which spoils the insight Searle expresses at p. 46 by saying the perceptual experiences are presentations rather than representations). At p. 350, n. 12 of "Belief *De Re*", Burge mentions a connection between rejecting his view of the *de re* and representative realism, but he does not elaborate; this may be partly because he does not consider a position like Searle's at all. Certainly his objection of obscurantism (p. 353; compare "Sinning against Frege", pp. 427–30) seems not to apply to Searle; it fits a mere postulation of Fregean senses, not the highly detailed specifications Searle offers.

37. This motivation is very clear in Searle, *Intentionality*.

38. Burge, "Belief *De Re*", p. 359.

39. McGinn, *The Subjective View*, p. 68.

40. See McGinn, "The Structure of Content", especially p. 257, n. 31.

41. It is worth noting how bizarre the segregation makes this use of "cognitive".

42. There is supposed to be an argument from the nature of explanation of behaviour for separating off this supposed aspect of the mental (whatever one calls it); but this is well answered by Evans, *The Varieties of Reference*, pp. 203–4. Dissatisfaction with the terminological move is not alleviated, but if anything reinforced, when one notes how adherents of this bipartite conception of mind typically single out the supposed cognitive aspect of the mental by means of distorted forms of features that are intuitively attributable to the mental as such. Examples are, first, interiority, which in fact fits the mental as such (*de re* beliefs are just as internal as any other mental states in the appropriate sense, which is a metaphorical one), but which is literalized ("in the head") and used to characterize the

one could fail to see how unattractive this position is, except under a felt compulsion to suppose that this must be how things are; and a felt compulsion towards that conclusion can derive in turn from the deficiencies of the supposedly unique alternative.

This sort of oscillation, which is familiar in philosophy, should lead one to look for a suspect common assumption. Countenancing *de re* Fregean senses gratifies both the natural motivations that Burge's framework represents as incompatible; it yields thoughts that are both *de re* and part of the thinker's cognitive world. The justification for the framework is quite unconvincing, as I have pointed out. A combination of strongly held belief and uncompelling argument often betrays something philosophically deep; I believe that reflecting on the possibilities for a Fregean account of the *de re* is an excellent way to undermine pervasive and damaging prejudices in the philosophy of mind.[43]

---

supposed cognitive aspect of the mental; and, second, availability to introspection, which is oddly glossed in this position as requiring infallibility (see McGinn, "The Structure of Content", pp. 253–5)—whereas in the only good sense we can give to the notion of introspection, *de re* beliefs are (fallibly, of course) available to it, no less than other mental states. Simon Blackburn's phenomenological argument for a version of the position I am attacking (see chap. 9 of *Spreading the Word*) is answerable by an application of the ideas I outline in Essay 17 below; or, to put the point another way, it involves a misuse of the relation between appearance and reality entirely analogous to that which vitiates the Argument from Illusion.

43. A useful label is "psychologism". In "The Basis of Reference", Stephen Schiffer tries to rebut the charge that occupying the first horn of this supposed dilemma is psychologistic. The attempt leaves me unconvinced; but it may somewhat allay Schiffer's sense of injustice if I make it clear that I think the charge applies to occupying the other horn too. It is psychologism, in the end, that makes the dilemma seem inescapable.

ESSAY 11

Singular Thought and the Extent of Inner Space

1. In defending the Theory of Descriptions, Russell presupposes an interlocking conception of genuinely referring expressions ("logically proper names") and singular propositions; logically proper names combine with predicates to express propositions that would not be available to be expressed at all if the objects referred to did not exist. Thus Russell objects to the idea that a sentence in which a definite description is combined with a predicate should be counted as sharing a form with a sentence in which a logically proper name is combined with a predicate, on the ground that if the description fits nothing, as it may, this assignment of logical form implies that the description-containing sentence is "nonsense";[1] and it is plain that he might have said "expresses no proposition". The point of the alternative logical form proposed by the Theory of Descriptions is to ensure that the proposition that such a sentence is held to express is one available to be expressed in any case, whether or not there is something answering to the description.

It seems clear that Russell's conception of singular (object-dependent) propositions is intended in part as a contribution to psychology: propositional attitudes whose contents are singular propositions are meant to be recognized as a distinctive kind of configuration in psychological reality. But Russell takes this psychological application of the idea to be possible only under a severe restriction on its scope. And more recent philosophers have tended to follow him in this; those who have taken the Russellian idea of a sin-

1. "On Denoting", p. 46.

gular proposition seriously at all have acquiesced in something like Russell's restriction,[2] or else, if they wanted to recognize object-dependent propositions outside Russell's limits, they have located them within the purview of a discipline of "semantics" further removed than Russell's semantics was meant to be from aiming to delineate the contours of thought.[3] I believe a version of Russell's idea can help with some venerable philosophical difficulties about the relation between thought and reality; but first we must see how its directly psychological application can be detached from Russell's restriction.

2. Russell's restriction results, in effect, from refusing to accept that there can be an illusion of understanding an apparently singular sentence (or utterance), involving the illusion of entertaining a singular proposition expressed by it, when, since there is no suitably related object, there is no such proposition available to be entertained. Whenever a strictly singular parsing of a range of sentences (or utterances) would involve postulating such illusions, the apparatus of the Theory of Descriptions is brought to bear, in order to equip sentences (or utterances) of the range with non-singular propositions that they can be understood to express whether or not there is a suitably related object. This generalizes the original argument against counting definite descriptions as genuinely referring expressions. The generalized argument applies also to ordinary proper names, and indeed to nearly all expressions one might intuitively regard as devices of singular reference. The upshot, in Russell's hands, is that we can entertain and express singular propositions only where there cannot be illusions as to the existence of an object of the appropriate kind: only about features of sense-data or items present to us with similar immediacy in memory, and (when Russell recognized them as objects) our selves.

Why should we find it intolerable to postulate the sort of illusion that Russell disallows? Why not say that some sentences (or utterances) of a given range express singular propositions, whereas others present the illusory appearance of doing so (to those not in the know)—rather than, with Russell, devising a kind of non-singular proposition to be associated with all alike? If we suggest that the

2. See, e.g., Stephen Schiffer, "The Basis of Reference".

3. This is true of David Kaplan's "Demonstratives", and of a great deal of work inspired by it.

idea of this sort of illusion is harmless, we risk undermining the Theory of Descriptions itself, not just its extension beyond the case of definite descriptions. But we can recover a special plausibility for the original Theory of Descriptions by introducing another piece of Russellian apparatus, the notion of acquaintance.[4]

When the Russellian conception of singular propositions is given its directly psychological application, it implies that which configurations a mind can get itself into is partly determined by which objects exist in the world. One might have expected the topology of psychological space, so to speak, to be independent of the contingencies of wordly existence; Russell's thought is that we can intelligibly set that expectation aside, but only when the mind and the objects are related by what he calls "acquaintance". The real point about definite descriptions can then be this: although someone who understands a sentence (or utterance) in which a definite description occurs *may* be acquainted with the appropriate object, the way in which the description is constructed out of independently intelligible vocabulary makes it absurd to require acquaintance with an object, on top of familiarity with the words and construction, as a condition for entertaining a proposition as what the sentence (or utterance) expresses. (This is less plausible for some uses of definite descriptions than others; but I am not concerned with evaluating the argument.)

This opens the possibility that we might equip Russell with a defence of some form of the Theory of Descriptions, strictly so called, on the ground that an appeal to acquaintance would be out of place in an account of how at least some definite descriptions (or utterances of them) are understood; while at the same time we might consistently resist Russell's own extension of the Theory of Descriptions to other cases, with the idea that acquaintance makes it possible to entertain singular propositions, and illusions of acquaintance generate illusions of entertaining singular propositions, so that there is no need to look for non-singular propositions to suit both sorts of case. But we cannot make anything of this abstract possibility until we give more substance to the notion of acquaintance.

When Russell defends the claim that one can entertain a singular proposition about an object only if one is acquainted with the object, he equates that claim with the claim that one can entertain such a

4. See "Knowledge by Acquaintance and Knowledge by Description".

proposition only if one knows which object it is that the proposition concerns.[5] The equation betrays insensitivity to the grammatical difference between the use of "know" implicit in "is acquainted with" and the use in "knows which . . . ,"[6] but the grammatical conflation is theoretically suggestive. The underlying idea is that to entertain a proposition one must know how one's thinking represents things as being. If the proposition is singular, one can satisfy that requirement only by knowing which object is represented, and how it is represented as being; and half of this condition is Russell's requirement in the "know which . . ." version. The notion of acquaintance with an object, now, is the notion of an immediate presence of object to mind such as would make it intelligible that the mind in question can entertain singular propositions, targeted on the object in the special way in which singular propositions are, in conformity with that requirement. I shall illustrate this idea in a not strictly Russellian application, and then comment on the divergence from Russell.

A Russellian paradigm of acquaintance is perception. As I mentioned, Russell allows as objects of perceptual acquaintance only features of sense-data. But we can extract the notion of acquaintance from that epistemological framework, and apply it to at least some perceptual relations between minds and ordinary objects. A typical visual experience of, say, a cat situates its object for the perceiver; in the first instance egocentrically, but, granting the perceiver a general capacity to locate himself, and the objects he can locate egocentrically, in a non-egocentrically conceived world, we can see how the experience's placing of the cat equips the perceiver with knowledge of where in the world it is (even if the only answer he can give to the question where it is is "There"). In view of the kind of object a cat is, there is nothing epistemologically problematic in suggesting that this locating perceptual knowledge of it suffices for knowledge of which object it is (again, even if the only answer the perceiver can give to the question is "That one"). So those visual experiences of objects that situate their objects can be made out to fit the account I suggested of the notion of acquaintance; abandoning Russell's sense-datum epistemology, we can say that such objects are immediately present to the mind in a way that, given the connection between lo-

5. See *The Problems of Philosophy*, p. 58.
6. See Essay 7 above.

cation and identity for objects of the appropriate kind, makes possible the targeting of singular thoughts on the objects in conformity with the Russellian requirement in its "know which . . ." version. Anyone who knows Gareth Evans's seminal work will recognize that what I have done here is to read Russell's notion of acquaintance into a simplified form of Evans's account of perceptual demonstrative modes of presentation.[7]

The most striking divergence from Russell is this: the position I have just sketched leaves it an evident possibility that one can be under the illusion of standing in a relation to an object that would count as acquaintance, the impression being illusory because there is no such object. There would be an independent justification for Russell's disallowing this possibility if some such principle as this were acceptable: a capacity or procedure can issue, on a specific occasion, in a position that deserves some epistemically honorific title (for instance "acquaintance with an object") only if it *never* issues in impostors. But it is not acceptable—indeed, it is epistemologically disastrous—to suppose that fallibility in a capacity or procedure impugns the epistemic status of any of its deliverances. There is no independent justification, from general epistemology, for refusing to allow that there can be illusions of entertaining singular propositions.[8]

3. Russell envisages singular propositions having as constituents, besides what is predicated of their objects, simply the objects them-

7. See *The Varieties of Reference,* chap. 6. I have tried to formulate the position in such a way as to suggest the lines of an answer to Christopher Peacocke's complaint of "a curiously unmotivated asymmetry" in Evans's proposal: *Sense and Content,* p. 171. But this is not the place to elaborate.

8. In a fuller treatment, it would be necessary at this point to consider in detail the possibility of liberalizing the notion of acquaintance outside the case of perceptually presented objects. Topics for discussion here would include the non-compulsoriness of Russell's assumption that acquaintance with a self could only be acquaintance with a Cartesian ego (see Evans, *The Varieties of Reference,* chap. 7, for material for an argument against that assumption); a liberalization of the notion's application to memory, parallel to the liberalization I have suggested for its application to perception (hinted at perhaps in the Appendix to chap. 8 of *The Varieties of Reference,* but not achieved in the body of that work because of what is arguably an excessive concern with recognition); and the idea of an autonomous variety of acquaintance constituted, even in the absence of other cognitive relations to an object, by mastery of a communal name-using practice (rejected by Evans at pp. 403–4 of *The Varieties of Reference,* but perhaps on the basis of an excessive individualism). But in this essay I am concerned with the general structure of a possible position rather than the details of its elaboration, and the perceptual case should suffice as an illustration.

selves.[9] This has the effect that there cannot be two different singular propositions in which the same thing is predicated of the same object. The upshot is that we cannot make singular propositions beyond Russell's restriction figure in the direct delineation of the contours of thought without flouting a principle we can associate with Frege: that if some notion like that of representational content is to serve in an illuminatingly organized account of our psychological economy, it must be such as not to allow one without irrationality to hold rationally conflicting attitudes to one and the same content. As long as Russell's restriction is in force, it seems unlikely that Russellian singular propositions will generate violations of this principle; a feature of a sense-datum, say, will not be liable to figure in one's thinking twice without one's knowing that it is the same one—which would protect one, assuming rationality, from the risk of conflicting attitudes about it. But singular propositions about, say, ordinary material objects, on Russell's account of their constituents, would be too coarsely individuated to conform to the Fregean principle. Is this a justification of Russell's restriction?[10]

No. Russell's idea of the constituents of propositions reflects a failure to understand Frege's distinction between sense and reference; it is not essential to the real insight that his notion of singular propositions embodies. The insight is that there are propositions, or (as we can now put it) thoughts in Frege's sense, that are object-dependent. Frege's doctrine that thoughts contain senses as constituents is a way of insisting on the theoretical role of thoughts (or contents) in characterizing a rationally organized psychological structure; and Russell's insight can perfectly well be formulated within this framework, by claiming that there are Fregean thought-constituents (singular senses) that are object-dependent, generating an object-dependence in the thoughts in which they figure. Two or more singular senses can present the same object; so Fregean singular thoughts can be both object-dependent and just as finely individuated as perspicuous psychological description requires. So the Fregean principle does not justify Russell's restriction on object-dependent propositions.

The possibility of Fregean singular senses that are object-dependent typically goes unconsidered. As if mesmerized by the The-

9. See, e.g., "The Philosophy of Logical Atomism", at p. 245.

10. An affirmative answer is implicit in Simon Blackburn's remark, at p. 328 of *Spreading the Word,* that the considerations to which Frege is sensitive are "the primary source of argument" against the existence of thoughts that are intrinsically object-dependent.

ory of Descriptions, philosophers typically assume that Frege's application of the distinction between sense and reference to singular terms is an anticipation of the Theory of Descriptions in its extended form, without even Russell's exception in favour of logically proper names—so that there is no such thing as an object-dependent Fregean thought.[11] But as far as one can tell from the mysterious passage in "On Denoting" where Russell discusses the distinction between sense and reference,[12] this does not seem to have been Russell's own view of Frege's intention.[13] And it is notoriously difficult to make this reading of Frege cohere with at least one seemingly central strand in Frege's thinking, namely, the idea that reference-failure generates truth-value gaps; this seems most smoothly understood on the view that thoughts of the appropriate kind are, precisely, object-dependent, so that where there is reference-failure there cannot be a thought of the appropriate kind to bear a truth-value.[14]

Admittedly, Frege occasionally offers, as specifying the sense of, say, an ordinary proper name, an expression to which Russell would certainly want to apply the Theory of Descriptions. But we can see this as manifesting, not an anticipation of the extended Theory of Descriptions as applied to, say, ordinary proper names, but a converse assimilation: a willingness to attribute object-dependent senses

11. Even Blackburn, who does not have the excuse of being ignorant of Evans's work, strangely proceeds as if the object-independence of Fregean senses were uncontentious. See n. 10 above; and note how on p. 317 he represents "the singular thought theorist" as holding that the identity of a singular thought "is given by the object referred to", which suggests a Russellian rather than Fregean conception of the constituents of singular thoughts. Whatever explains this, it may in turn partly explain why Blackburn does not see that he would need to demolish (among other things) the neo-Fregean account of object-dependent perceptually demonstrative thoughts given in chap. 6 of *The Varieties of Reference* before he could be entitled to conclude, as he does at p. 322 on the basis of a discussion of the arguments about communication in chap. 9 of that work, that the question whether we should count someone who uses an empty singular term as expressing a thought can only turn on "some semantic issue concerning *expression*" and is "a boring issue". (I find Blackburn's discussion of the arguments about communication unsatisfactory also, but I cannot go into this here.)

12. *Logic and Knowledge,* pp. 48–51.

13. At pp. 330–1 of *Spreading the Word,* Blackburn represents Russell as complaining that a Fregean thought could not be closely enough related to the right object. But the complaint in Russell's text seems to be the reverse: a Fregean singular thought is so closely related to its object that Russell cannot see how it maintains its distinctness from a Russellian singular proposition, with the object rather than a sense as a constituent.

14. See Essay 9 above; and, for a convincing account of Frege's general semantical framework, Evans, *The Varieties of Reference,* chap. 1.

to all members of Frege's wide category of singular terms *(Eigennamen)*, including even definite descriptions. It is characteristic of Frege's lofty attitude to psychological detail that he should think in terms of singular (that is, object-dependent) thoughts without devoting attention to the nature of any necessary epistemological background, and hence without arriving at the thought, which I formulated above in terms of acquaintance, that makes this assimilation unattractive.

Admittedly again, Frege often writes of singular terms having sense but lacking reference. This may seem to show that the attribution of sense to singular terms reflects something parallel to the motivation of the extended Theory of Descriptions: a desire to ensure that "singular" utterances are assigned thoughts that they can be credited with expressing whether or not appropriately related objects exist. But this appearance can be at least partly undermined by noting, first, that Frege is prepared to count the serious utterance of a sentence containing an empty singular term as a lapse into fiction; and, second, that in at least one passage he treats fictional utterances as expressing "mock thoughts". Mock thoughts should have only mock senses as constituents. If the purpose of Frege's saying that empty singular terms have senses would be better served by saying that they have mock senses, then what is in question here is not going along with the motivation for the extended Theory of Descriptions, but rather disarming it—registering that it will *seem* to a deluded user of an empty singular term that he is entertaining and expressing thoughts, and (so to speak) supplying merely apparent singular thoughts for these to be, rather than real non-singular thoughts.[15]

Of course this does not straightforwardly fit what Frege says; at best this may be what he is driving at, in an anyway unhappy region of his thinking. But in any case the question should not be whether Frege himself clearly embraced the idea of object-dependent singular senses, but whether the idea is available, so that we can recognize object-dependent thoughts outside Russell's restriction without flouting the Fregean principle about the topology of psychological space. And the dazzling effect of the Theory of Descriptions should not be

15. For an elaboration of this reading, with citations, see Evans, *The Varieties of Reference*, pp. 28–30.

allowed to obscure the fact that there is nothing in the notion of sense itself to preclude this. But something deeper, whose nature will emerge in due course, tends to sustain the usual reading of Frege.

4. It is not plausible that Russell sees his restriction as dictated extraneously, by the result of applying some independently compulsory general epistemological principle, such as the one I canvassed in §2 above, to the notion of acquaintance. Rather, Russell finds it evident in its own right that the illusions that the restriction disallows must be disallowed, and the epistemology of acquaintance shapes itself accordingly into a rejection of fallibility. (General epistemological preconceptions would make this come more naturally to Russell than it does to us.)[16] If we lift Russell's restriction, we open the possibility that a subject may be in error about the contents of his own mind: he may think there is a singular thought at, so to speak, a certain position in his internal organization, although there is really nothing precisely there.[17] It seems that Russell would reject this possibility out of hand; that will be why he finds it clearly absurd to say that sentences that people think they understand are "nonsense". This makes it plausible that the ultimate basis for Russell's restriction is a conception of the inner life, and the subject's knowledge of it, that it seems fair to label "Cartesian".[18]

One reason, then, to pursue a less restricted conception of object-dependent propositions is the interest of its radically anti-Cartesian implications. In a fully Cartesian picture, the inner life takes place in an autonomous realm, transparent to the introspective awareness of its subject; the access of subjectivity to the rest of the world becomes

16. In a post-Russellian epistemological climate, there seems to be something bizarre about Daniel C. Dennett's suggestion that "Russell's Principle" (the "know which . . ." requirement) leads inevitably to Russell's restriction; see pp. 87–8 of "Beyond Belief". Dennett's conception of the epistemology of acquaintance is shaped to suit an independently accepted restriction on the scope for object-dependent thought, not something that could serve as a ground for the restriction.

17. Nothing precisely there; of course there may be all sorts of things in the vicinity. See Evans, *The Varieties of Reference,* pp. 45–6. This gives the lie to Blackburn's implication, at pp. 318–22, that Evans (and I) would "deny that there is thinking going on in the empty world". Anyone who believes in singular thoughts in the sense of this paper will (by definition) hold that they are "not available" in the absence of an object. At p. 318 Blackburn implies misleadingly that this position is characteristic only of "strong singular thought theorists", who represent the mind as simply void when a seeming singular thought lacks an object. It is not clear to me that there are any strong singular thought theorists in Blackburn's sense.

18. See Evans, *The Varieties of Reference,* pp. 44–6.

correspondingly problematic, in a way that has familiar manifestations in the mainstream of post-Cartesian epistemology. If we let there be quasi-Russellian singular propositions about, say, ordinary perceptible objects among the contents of inner space, we can no longer be regarding inner space as a locus of configurations that are self-standing, not beholden to external conditions; and there is now no question of a gulf, which it might be the task of philosophy to try to bridge, or to declare unbridgeable, between the realm of subjectivity and the world of ordinary objects. We can make this vivid by saying, in a Russellian vein, that objects themselves can *figure in* thoughts that are among the contents of the mind; in Russell himself, formulations like this attach themselves to the idea that singular propositions are individuated according to the identity of their objects rather than modes of presentation of them, but a Fregean approach to singular thoughts can accommodate such locutions—firmly distinguishing "figure in" from "be a constituent of"—as a natural way of insisting on object-dependence.

Russell credits Descartes with "showing that subjective things are the most certain";[19] presumably he would not think it impugned the acceptability of his restriction to suggest that it has a Cartesian basis. But the climate has changed; contemporary sympathizers with Russell will usually disclaim a Cartesian motivation.[20] I want to maintain nevertheless that, independently of Russell's own unashamedly Cartesian stance, the point of recognizing object-dependent thoughts outside Russell's restriction, with the Fregean fineness of grain needed for them to serve in perspicuous accounts of how minds are laid out, lies in the way it liberates us from Cartesian problems. To make this plausible, I need to digress into a general discussion of the nature of Cartesian philosophy.

5. The feature of the classically Cartesian picture to focus on is the effect I have already mentioned, of putting subjectivity's very possession of an objective environment in question. It is hard for us now to find Descartes's purported regaining of the world, in the later stages of his reflections, as gripping as we can easily find his apparent loss of it in the opening stages.

19. *The Problems of Philosophy*, p. 18.

20. See, e.g., Schiffer, "The Basis of Reference"; and Blackburn, *Spreading the Word*, pp. 324–5 (on which see §7 below).

What generates this threat of loss? We cannot answer this question simply by appealing to a generally sceptical tendency in Descartes's epistemological preoccupations. Not that they have no such tendency, of course. But ancient scepticism did not call our possession of a world into question; its upshot was, less dramatically, to drive a wedge between living in the world and (what is meant to seem dispensable) knowing about it.[21] What, then, was distinctive about the scepticism that Descartes ushered on to the philosophical scene, to make this comfortable distinction no longer available?

I doubt that we can construct an adequate answer out of the detail of Cartesian epistemology. Barry Stroud, for instance, plausibly traces the Cartesian threat of losing the world to this principle: one can acquire worldly knowledge by using one's senses only if one can know, at the time of the supposed acquisition of knowledge, that one is not dreaming.[22] This sets a requirement that Stroud argues cannot be met; no proposed test or procedure for establishing that one is not dreaming would do the trick, since by a parallel principle one would need to know that one was not dreaming that one was applying the test or procedure and obtaining a satisfactory result. So Stroud suggests that if we accept the requirement we cannot escape losing the world.

Now one drawback about this for my purposes is that it does not address the question that I raised above: why does the threatened conclusion that the senses yield no knowledge of the world seem, in Descartes, to threaten loss of the world, given the ancient sceptics' alternative that it is not by way of knowing about the world that we are in possession of it? But it is more to my immediate purpose that if losing the world is to seem inescapable on these lines, we need to be persuaded not to claim conformity to the requirement on the following ground: one's knowledge that one is not dreaming, in the relevant sort of situation, owes its credentials as knowledge to the fact that one's senses are yielding one knowledge of the environment—something that does not happen when one is dreaming. Of course this does not meet the requirement as Descartes understands it; the Cartesian requirement is that the epistemic status of the thought that one is not dreaming must be established *independently* of the episte-

21. On the contrast between ancient and Cartesian scepticism, see M. F. Burnyeat's very illuminating paper, "Idealism and Greek Philosophy: What Descartes Saw and Berkeley Missed".

22. See chap. 1 of *The Significance of Philosophical Scepticism.*

mic status of whatever putative perceptual knowledge of the environment is in question, serving as a test case for the possibility of acquiring such knowledge at all. But why must the direction of epistemic support be like that? We are not allowed to depend on our possession of the world for knowledge that we are not dreaming at the relevant times; so our grip on the world must have been loosened already for the Cartesian epistemological reflections to take the course they do.

I have followed M. F. Burnyeat on the newly radical character of Cartesian scepticism. In a perceptive discussion, Burnyeat identifies one Cartesian innovation that certainly helps account for this: in ancient scepticism, the notion of truth is restricted to how things are (unknowably, it is claimed) in the world about us, so that how things seem to us is not envisaged as something there might be truth about, and the question whether we know it simply does not arise (although appearances are said not to be open to question); whereas Descartes extends the range of truth and knowability to the appearances on the basis of which we naively think we know about the ordinary world. In effect Descartes recognizes how things seem to a subject as a case of how things are; and the ancient sceptics' concession that appearances are not open to question is transmuted into the idea of a range of facts infallibly knowable by the subject involved in them. This permits a novel response to arguments that conclude that we know nothing from the fact that we are fallible about the external world. Whatever such arguments show about knowledge of external reality, we can retreat to the newly recognized inner reality, and refute the claim that we know nothing, on the ground that at least we know these newly recognized facts about subjective appearances. Notice that the epistemological context in which, on this account, the inner realm is first recognized makes it natural that the first of its inhabitants to attract our attention should be perceptual experiences, with other inner items at first relegated to the background. I shall stay with this focus for some time.

To the extent that this response to scepticism leaves the old arguments unchallenged, it may seem to suffice already for the characteristically Cartesian willingness to face up to losing the external world, with the inner for consolation.[23] But, although the introduction of

23. Descartes himself thinks he can do better than this, but, as I remarked, it is difficult to find this part of his thinking convincing.

subjectivity as a realm of fact is an essential part of the story, we still do not have a complete account of what is special to Descartes. We are still faced with a version of the question that ancient scepticism makes pressing: even if the inward step to a region of reality where we can call a halt to scepticism involves conceding that we have no knowledge of outer reality, why should that threaten us with the conclusion that we have no access to outer reality at all? Why should the availability of infallible knowledge about the newly recognized inner region of reality encourage us to such defeatism—as opposed to either the ancient option of deeming knowledge inessential to our hold on the world, or an even less concessive approach whose suppression needs explaining: namely, trying to construct a conception of fallibly acquired outer knowledge, which could peacefully coexist with a conception of infallibly acquired inner knowledge?[24]

Simply accommodating subjectivity within the scope of truth and knowability seems, in any case, too innocent to account for the view of philosophy's problems that Descartes initiates. We need something more contentious: a picture of subjectivity as a region of reality whose layout is transparent—accessible through and through—to the capacity for knowledge that is newly recognized when appearances are brought within the range of truth and knowability.[25]

Short of that picture, the newly countenanced facts can be simply the facts about what it is like to enjoy our access, or apparent access, to external reality. Access or apparent access: infallible knowledge of how things seem to one falls short of infallible knowledge as to which disjunct is in question. One is as fallible about that as one is about the associated question how things are in the external world. So, supposing we picture subjectivity as a region of reality, we need

24. Besides the extending of truth and knowability to what thereby comes to be conceivable as the *realm* of subjectivity, Burnyeat mentions as a Cartesian innovation the preparedness to count one's own body as part of the external world. So long as scepticism does not seem to threaten loss of the world, one's own body will not naturally come within the purview of one's sceptical doubts (after all, one needs a body in order to engage with the world). This suggests that the externalizing of the body is not something independently intelligible, which could help to explain why Cartesian sceptism induces the threat of losing the world. The direction of explanation should be the reverse: if we can understand how the threat of losing the world comes about, we should be equipped to see why Descartes's conception of the external world is so revolutionary.

25. Burnyeat's phrase "a new realm for substantial knowledge" (p. 49, n. 53) does not distinguish the specifically Cartesian conception of the new realm from the innocent alternative.

not yet be thinking of the newly recognized infallibly knowable facts as constituting the whole truth about that region. Of facts to the effect that things seem thus and so to one, we might say, some are cases of things being thus and so within the reach of one's subjective access to the external world, whereas others are mere appearances.[26] In a given case the answer to the question "Which?" would state a further fact about the disposition of things in the inner realm (a disposition less specifically mapped by saying merely that things seem to one to be thus and so); since this further fact is not independent of the outer realm, we are compelled to picture the inner and outer realms as interpenetrating, not separated from one another by the characteristically Cartesian divide. Arguments designed to force the admission that one cannot know that it is the first disjunct that is in question would be powerless, in the face of this position, to induce the threat of losing the world. Even if we make the admission, it does not go beyond the ancient sceptics' renunciation of knowledge of external reality. There is nothing here to exclude the ancient option of living comfortably in the world without aspiring to know it. And it should seem a good project, in this position, to try to resist the admission by breaking the link between knowledge and infallibility.

We arrive at the fully Cartesian picture with the idea that there are no facts about the inner realm besides what is infallibly accessible to the newly recognized capacity to acquire knowledge. What figures in the innocent position I have just outlined as the difference between the two disjuncts cannot now be a difference between two ways things might be in the inner realm, with knowledge of which is the case available, if at all, only with the fallibility that attends our ability to achieve knowledge of the associated outer circumstance. Such differences must now be wholly located in the outer realm; they must reside in facts external to a state of affairs that is common to the two disjuncts and exhausts the relevant region of the inner realm. We cannot now see the inner and outer realms as interpenetrating; the correlate of this picture of our access to the inner is that subjectivity is confined to a tract of reality whose layout would be exactly as it is however things stood outside it, and the common-sense notion of a vantage point on the external world is now fundamentally problematic. The ancient option of giving up the claim that knowl-

26. See Essay 17 below; and J. M. Hinton, *Experiences*.

edge is among the ties that relate us to the world no longer seems to the point, since the very idea of subjectivity as a mode of being in the world is as much in question as the idea of knowing the world. And it no longer seems hopeful to construct an epistemology that would countenance not only infallible knowledge, of how things seem to one, but also knowledge acquired by fallible means, of how things are. Once we are gripped by the idea of a self-contained subjective realm, in which things are as they are independently of external reality (if any), it is too late for such a move (worthy as it is in itself) to help—our problem is not now that our contact with the external world seems too *shaky* to count as knowledgeable, but that our picture seems to represent us as out of touch with the world altogether.[27]

I approached this fully Cartesian picture of subjectivity by way of the thought, innocent in itself, that how things seem to one can be a fact, and is knowable in a way that is immune to familiar sceptical challenges. Short of the fully Cartesian picture, the infallibly knowable fact—its seeming to one that things are thus and so—can be taken disjunctively, as constituted either by the fact that things are manifestly thus and so or by the fact that that merely seems to be the case. On this account, the idea of things being thus and so figures straightforwardly in our understanding of the infallibly knowable appearance; there is no problem about how experience can be understood to have a representational directedness towards external reality.

Now the fully Cartesian picture should not be allowed to trade on these innocuous thoughts. According to the fully Cartesian picture, it cannot be ultimately obligatory to understand the infallibly knowable fact disjunctively. That fact is a self-standing configuration in the inner realm, whose intrinsic nature should be knowable through and through without adverting to what is registered, in the innocuous position, by the difference between the disjuncts—let alone giving the veridical case the primacy that the innocuous position confers on it. This makes it quite unclear that the fully Cartesian picture is

27. It is superficial to chide Descartes for not contemplating the possibility of a fallibilist epistemology, as if Cartesian scepticism was merely the result of judging all putative knowledge by the standards of introspection. The course of Cartesian epistemology gives a dramatic but ultimately inessential expression to Descartes's fundamental contribution to philosophy, namely, his picture of the subjective realm.

entitled to characterize its inner facts in content-involving terms—in terms of its seeming to one that things are thus and so—at all. Ironically, when reverence for the authority of phenomenology is carried to the length of making the fact that internal configurations are indistinguishable from the subject's point of view suffice to establish that those configurations are through and through the same, the upshot is to put at risk the most conspicuous phenomenological fact there is. The threat that the Cartesian picture poses to our hold on the world comes out dramatically in this: that within the Cartesian picture there is a serious question about how it can be that experience, conceived from its own point of view, is not blank or blind, but purports to be revelatory of the world we live in.

6. I have stressed that there is a less than Cartesian way of recognizing subjectivity as a realm of knowable truth. This makes it necessary to ask why the distinctively Cartesian way is as gripping as it is. The realm of subjectivity comes to our notice initially by way of our noting a range of infallibly knowable facts. But however seriously we take the picture of a region or tract of reality, that seems insufficient to explain why it should be tempting to suppose that the whole truth about the tract in question should be knowable in the same way.

We can approach an explanation by bracketing the directly epistemological character of the Cartesian picture, and focusing initially on the idea of the inner realm as self-standing, with everything within it arranged as it is independently of external circumstances. Why might Descartes have found this idea tempting? And why should the temptation have first become pressing around Descartes's time? Both these questions can be answered in terms of a plausible aspiration to accommodate psychology within a pattern of explanation characteristic of the natural sciences. (Of course the aspiration need not have struck Descartes in just those terms.) It seems scarcely more than common sense that a science of the way organisms relate to their environment should look for states of the organisms whose intrinsic nature can be described independently of the environment; this would allow explanations of the presence of such states in terms of the environment's impact, and explanations of interventions in the environment in terms of the causal influence of such states, to fit into a kind of explanation whose enormous power to make the world intelligible was becoming clear with the rise of modern science, and is even clearer to us than it would have been to Descartes. It is plausible that Descartes's self-standing inner realm is meant to be the locus of just such explanatory states.

Now this intellectual impulse is gratified also in a modern way of purportedly bringing the mind within the scope of theory, in which the interiority of the inner realm is literally spatial; the autonomous explanatory states are in ultimate fact states of the nervous system, although, in order to protect the claim that the explanations they figure in are psychological, they are envisaged as conceptualized by theories of mind in something like functionalist terms.[28] This conception of mind shares what I have suggested we should regard as the fundamental motivation of the classically Cartesian conception; and I think this is much more significant than the difference between them.

The most striking divergence is that the modern position avoids Cartesian immaterialism. But how important a difference is this? In one way, it is obviously very important; the modern position simply escapes a metaphysical and scientific embarrassment that the classically Cartesian picture generates. But in another way it need not be very important, because we can understand Cartesian immaterialism as derivative rather than fundamental: the natural upshot of trying to satisfy the common impulse at a certain juncture in the history of science.

One submerged source of immaterialism may be a sense of the problem that I canvassed at the end of §5: that once we picture subjectivity as self-contained, it is hard to see how its states and episodes can be anything but blind. Magic might seem to help, and magical powers require an occult medium.[29]

Another explanation of immaterialism reintroduces the bracketed epistemological concerns. It is helpful to revert to the contrast between the fully Cartesian picture and the less than Cartesian picture that I described in §5. By itself, there is nothing dangerous about the

28. See, e.g., Brian Loar, *Mind and Meaning*.

29. I intend this to echo some thoughts of Hilary Putnam's; see his *Reason, Truth, and History*, pp. 3–5. However, I believe Putnam misses the full force of his insight. Rather than rethinking the conception of what is in the mind that leads to the temptation to appeal to magic, as I urge in this essay, he retains that conception (see, e.g., p. 18), avoiding the need to appeal to magic by making what is in the mind only a partial determinant of content. I argue below (§§8 and 9) that positions with this sort of structure cannot avoid the problem about inner darkness that makes the appeal to magic seductive. (In a fuller discussion, I would want to connect the temptation to appeal to magic with elements in Wittgenstein's approach to meaning; but I cannot elaborate this now.)

idea that how things seem to one is a fact, knowable in a way that is immune to the sources of error attending one's capacity to find out about the world around one. We can think of this "introspective" knowledge as a by-product of our perceptual capacities, available on the basis of a minimal self-consciousness in their exercise. There is no particular incentive to think of the facts that the newly countenanced knowledge-acquiring capacity finds out as configurations in an immaterial medium. (Not that it is natural to conceive them specifically as material. There is simply no reason to find the question "Material or not?" pressing.) It is a related point that, short of the fully Cartesian picture, there is nothing ontologically or epistemologically dramatic about the authority that it is natural to accord to a person about how things seem to him. This authority is consistent with the interpenetration of the inner and the outer, which makes it possible for you to know the layout of my subjectivity better than I do in a certain respect, if you know which of those two disjuncts obtains and I do not. In this framework, the authority that my capacity for "introspective" knowledge secures for me cannot seem to threaten the very possibility of access on your part to the facts within its scope.

In the fully Cartesian picture, by contrast, with the inner realm autonomous, the idea of the subject's authority becomes problematic. When we deny interpenetration between inner and outer, that puts in question the possibility of access to the external world from within subjectivity; correspondingly, it puts in question the possibility of access to the inner realm from outside. "Introspective" knowledge can no longer be a by-product of outwardly directed cognitive activities, with nothing to prevent its objects from being accessible to others too. The idea of introspection becomes the idea of an inner vision, scanning a region of reality that is wholly available to its gaze—since there is no longer any room for facts about the subjective realm that the subject may not know because of ignorance of outer circumstances—and that is at best problematically open to being known about in other ways at all. It is difficult now not to be struck by the question how such a tract of reality could possibly be a region of the familiar material world; immaterialism seems unavoidable.[30]

30. Note that these considerations simply bypass the standard objection to Descartes's argument for the Real Distinction.

We can understand Cartesian immaterialism, then, as the result of trying to accommodate features that seem essential to subjectivity—representational bearing on the world and availability to introspection—within a conception of the inner realm as autonomous; if we think of the temptation to appeal to magic as sufficiently submerged, we can say "within a conception of the inner realm as a suitable subject for science". It seems clear that Descartes intended his conception of the inner to figure in a scientific account of the world; this emerges from his willingness to worry about the physics, as it were, of the interaction between mind and matter. At the time it would not have been contrary to reason to hope for an integrated psychophysics that would incorporate immaterial substances into a fully scientific view of the world. Now, with physical conservation laws well entrenched, that looks simply out of the question. But of course that need not cast suspicion on those intuitive marks of subjectivity: Cartesian immaterialism, and the closely associated picture of the inner realm as knowable through and through by introspection, reflect a distortion that those marks undergo when forced to combine with the scientifically motivated conception of the inner realm as autonomous.

This makes it worth wondering whether it is the insistence on autonomy that is the real disease of thought, with the superficially striking peculiarities of Descartes's own picture of mind no more than a symptom that something is amiss. In the modern version of the insistence on autonomy, something on the lines of functionalism in effect takes over the purpose served by what, in conjunction with the insistence on autonomy, generates Cartesian immaterialism: namely, to make it plausible that the envisaged conception of an autonomous inner realm is at least a partial conception of the mind.[31] As I have granted, this frees the insistence on autonomy from the immediately uncomfortable postures of a fully Cartesian metaphysic.

31. The qualification "at least a partial conception" is meant to accommodate positions like that of Colin McGinn, "The Structure of Content". I do not mean to suggest that the Cartesian marks of subjectivity (introspectability and the presence of representational content) are simply missing from the modern version of the insistence on autonomy. But there are complications about their status and position, some of which will emerge below (§§7 and 9); they can no longer do exactly the work they are credited with in my reconstruction of the Cartesian picture.

But it is a serious question whether the improvement—which is undeniable—is more than the suppression of a symptom.

7. It has been easiest to expound the classically Cartesian picture by concentrating initially on perceptual experience. But the picture will not look like a picture of the mind unless it is enriched to include at least propositional attitudes.

Now it is clear that object-dependent propositional content, at least outside Russell's restriction, cannot be an intrinsic feature of states or episodes in a self-standing inner realm. Self-standingness disallows this, independently of the specifically Cartesian conception of inner knowledge that seems to be operative in Russell's own imposition of the restriction. However, it is worth examining a particular way of pressing the insistence on self-standingness against intrinsic object-dependence in thoughts, which exploits considerations closely parallel to the fully Cartesian conception of experience.

I distinguished an innocuous disjunctive conception of subjective appearances from the fully Cartesian picture, in which a difference corresponding to the difference between the disjuncts is external to the inner realm, with the only relevant occupant of that realm something wholly present whether things are as they seem or not. There is a parallel contrast between two ways of conceiving singular thought: first, the idea that if one seems to be thinking about an ordinary external object in a way that depends on, say, its appearing to be perceptually present to one, the situation in one's inner world is either that one is entertaining an object-dependent proposition or that it merely appears that that is so; and, second, the idea that a difference corresponding to the difference between those disjuncts is external to the layout of one's inner world, which is for these purposes exhausted by something common to the two cases.[32]

Simon Blackburn has tried to pinpoint the motivation for the view that, at least outside Russell's restriction, thoughts that one might want to ascribe in an object-involving way are not object-dependent in their intrinsic nature. Blackburn's argumentative strategy is what

32. We can continue to think of the inner world as the realm of appearance, but with the introduction of propositional attitudes the notion of appearance loses the connection it has had up to this point with perceptual experience in particular.

he calls "spinning the possible worlds".[33] In the sort of circumstances in which it is plausible to speak of singular thought and singular communication, a situation in which one object figures can be indistinguishable, from the subject's point of view, from a situation in which a different object figures or one in which no object figures in the right way at all, though there is an illusion of, say, perceptual presence. According to Blackburn, this constitutes an argument for saying that the intrinsic character of the thoughts in question is something that can be constant across such variations; so that object-dependence is not an intrinsic feature of thoughts, but reflects a style of ascription of thoughts that takes account not only of their intrinsic nature but also of their external relations.[34]

Blackburn anticipates the charge that this argument is Cartesian. He rejects the charge on the following grounds:

> The *doppelganger* and empty possibilities are drawn, as I have remarked, so that everything is the same from the subject's point of view. This is a legitimate thought-experiment. Hence there is a legitimate category of things that are the same in these cases; notably experience and awareness. Since this category is legitimate, it is also legitimate to ask whether thoughts all belong to it.[35]

But in the context of my pair of parallel contrasts, these remarks seem to miss the point. The uncontentiously legitimate category of things that are the same across the different cases is the category of how things seem to the subject. In the case of experience, the less than Cartesian position I described, exploiting the idea that the notion of appearance is essentially disjunctive, establishes that although that category is certainly legitimate, that does nothing to show that worldly circumstances are only externally related to experiences; to think otherwise is to fall into a fully Cartesian conception of the category. Analogously with the parallel contrast: the legitimacy of the category of how things seem is consistent with an essentially disjunctive conception of the state of seemingly entertaining a singular thought, and is hence powerless to recommend the conclusion that thoughts are only extrinsically connected with objects. Extracting

33. *Spreading the Word,* p. 312.

34. As Blackburn notes, the argument belongs to the genre of Twin-Earth thought experiments introduced into philosophy by Putnam; see "The Meaning of 'Meaning'".

35. *Spreading the Word,* p. 324.

such a recommendation from the phenomenological facts to which Blackburn appeals betrays a conception of the realm of appearance more philosophically contentious than anything that sheer phenomenology could deliver.

Notice how, instead of "Everything seems the same to the subject", Blackburn uses locutions like "Everything is the same from the subject's point of view". This insinuates the idea—going far beyond the fact that there is a legitimate category of how things seem to the subject—of a realm of reality in which samenesses and differences are exhaustively determined by how things seem to the subject, and hence which is knowable through and through by exercising one's capacity to know how things seem to one. That idea seems fully Cartesian. (It should be clear by now that immaterialism is beside the point of this charge.)[36]

8. In disconnecting experience from the external world, the fully Cartesian picture makes it problematic how the items it pictures can be anything but dark (see §5 above). Independently of any general empiricism about the materials for concept-formation, it seems plausible that if we conceive propositional attitudes on the same principles, as occupants of the same autonomous inner realm, we make it no less problematic how it can be that they have a representational bearing on the world.

36. At pp. 32–5 of *Spreading the Word*, Blackburn offers a different way of responding to the charge of Cartesianism, in terms of the idea that we should "see the facts about a subject's thoughts as facts about his relation to the environment", but insist that "the relevant features of an environment are themselves universal". But with this idea (which Blackburn does not himself endorse), the empty case is no longer supposed to be one in which the intrinsic nature of the subject's psychological state is the same. And that makes it hard to see any intelligible motivation for the position's "universalism". To put the point in terms of experience: if the actual presence of some cat or other (say) is necessary for an experience as of a cat of a certain character, what can there be against saying that such a "universalistic" description applies in virtue of the experience's being an experience of that particular cat? In another case the same "universalistic" description may apply in virtue of a relation to a different cat; but if the "universalistic" description cannot apply in the empty case, there is no threat here to a position according to which the "universalistic" description supervenes on non-"universalistic" descriptions of the intrinsic nature of experiences. (Discussing experience at p. 311, Blackburn omits the empty case; the argument for "universalism" seems seriously incomplete until the empty case is introduced.) Perhaps the gap in this argument can be filled somehow; but it would still be quite mysterious how this could constitute a defence of the orginal phenomenological argument—which trades essentially on the empty case—against the charge of Cartesianism.

In the physicalistic modern version of the insistence on autonomy, the self-standingness of the inner realm suffices to exclude intrinsic involvement with the world, without any need for an appeal to phenomenology. And in the most clear-sighted form of the position, the darkness of the interior is institutionalized. The intrinsic nature of inner states and events, on this view, is a matter of their position in an internal network of causal potentialities, in principle within the reach of an explanatory theory that would not need to advert to relations between the individual and the external world. Representational bearing on the external world figures in a mode of description of those states and events that takes into account not only their intrinsic nature but also their relations to the outside world.[37] Light enters into the picture, so to speak, only when we widen our field of view so as to take in more than simply the layout of the interior.[38]

Since there is light in the full composite picture, it may seem absurd to suggest, on the basis of the darkness in the interior, that this position leaves us squarely in the Cartesian predicament without resources to deal with it. The composite picture is offered as, precisely, a picture of the mind in full and intelligible possession of its perspective on the external world. If we want to consider the mind's relation to the world, according to this position, we ought not to worry about the nature of the internal component of the picture taken by itself.

What makes this unsatisfying, however, is the way in which the internal component of the composite picture, and not the compositely conceived whole, irresistibly attracts the attributes that intuitively characterize the domain of subjectivity. Consider, for instance, the idea of what is accessible to introspection. If introspection is to be distinguishable from knowledge at large, it cannot be allowed access to the external circumstances that, according to this position, partly determine the full composite truth about the mind; so its scope must be restricted to the internal component (remarkably enough, in view of the darkness within).[39] Again, consider the topological constraint

37. The clearest formulation I know of a position like this is McGinn, "The Structure of Content".

38. Here one of those intuitive marks of subjectivity (see §6, and in particular n. 31, above) shifts its location in our picture of mind.

39. See McGinn, "The Structure of Content", pp. 253–4. Here the other of those intuitive marks of subjectivity undergoes a sea change.

derived from Frege (see §3 above). It is in the internal component that we have to locate the difference Frege's constraint requires us to mark between pairs of (say) beliefs that in the full composite story would be described as involving the attribution of the same property to the same object, but that have to be distinguished because someone may without irrationality have one and not the other. There is nowhere else to locate the difference, once the picture of the mind is structured in this way. So Frege's notion of a mode of presentation is supposed to have its use in characterizing the configurations of the interior (remarkably enough, in view of the fact that they are in themselves blind).[40] But a mode of presentation should be the way something is presented to a subject of thought. The same point emerges more generally in the way it is natural, in this two-component picture of mind, to speak of an item's role in the strictly internal aspect of the composite truth about the mind as its *cognitive* role;[41] something's cognitive role should be its role in the cognitive life of (surely) a subject of thought. It is impossible not to be concerned about the boundary around the internal component of the two-component picture, and the darkness within it, if one is concerned at all about the relation between subjectivity and the objective world.

Quite generally, nothing could be recognizable as a characterization of the domain of subjectivity if it did not accord a special status to the perspective of the subject. But we create the appearance of introducing light into the composite picture precisely by allowing that picture to take in all kinds of facts that are *not* conceived in terms of the subject's point of view. So if the composite picture contains anything corresponding to the intuitive notion of the domain of subjectivity, it is the dark interior. The difficulty is palpable: how can we be expected to acknowledge that our subjective way of being in the world is properly captured by this picture, when it portrays the domain of our subjectivity—our cognitive world—in such a way that, considered from its own point of view, that world has to be conceived as letting in no light from outside? The representational content apparently present in the composite story comes too late to meet the point. The difficulty has an obviously Cartesian flavour, and it

40. See, e.g., McGinn, "The Structure of Content", p. 230 (sense as "intra-individual role"; compare pp. 220–1, 223–4).

41. See McGinn, "The Structure of Content", p. 219 (cognitive role as "an entirely intra-individual property").

seems fair to suggest that the answer to the question I raised and left open at the end of §6 is "No". It is possible to embrace the modern position with a clear scientific conscience, something that is no longer true of the full-blown Cartesian picture of mind. But if the result is merely a materialized version of the Cartesian picture, complete with characteristically Cartesian problems about our relation to external reality, the philosophical advance is unimpressive.[42]

It may not be to everyone's taste to accept an invitation to reflect philosophically about the position of subjectivity in the objective world, with Cartesian pitfalls as a real danger, calling for vigilance if we are to avoid them.[43] Modern analytic philosophy has to some extent lost the sense of the Cartesian divide as a genuine risk for our conception of ourselves. But I suspect the reasons for this are at least partly superficial. It is true that we have epistemologies whose drift is not towards scepticism. But these can seem to yield a stable picture of our cognitive grasp on reality only if the Cartesian divide is genuinely overcome; and modern fallibilist epistemologies typically do not embody any clear account of how that is to be done, but rather reflect a (perfectly intelligible) refusal to persist in a task that has become too plainly hopeless to bother with. In any case, it should be clear by now that the Cartesian danger is not specifically a threat to our knowledge of the external world; the problems of traditional epistemology are just one form in which the Cartesian divide can show itself.

9. Modern philosophical thinking about the relations of thoughts to objects was for a long time captivated by the extended Theory of De-

42. McGinn's anti-Cartesian remarks, at pp. 254–5, betray an insensitivity (by my lights) to the genuineness of the concerns about subjectivity that generate the Cartesian anxiety. (Contrast McGinn's "third person viewpoint".) McGinn's soundly anti-Cartesian intentions cannot save him from the Cartesian anxiety because he does not see the point at which it impinges on his position.

43. McGinn's remarks about "the third person viewpoint" suggest a refusal to acknowledge a problem characterizable in these terms. See also Jerry A. Fodor, *The Language of Thought,* p. 52, for a refusal to allow that the distinction between the personal and the sub-personal matters for "the purposes of cognitive psychology". Fodor seems to me to be right (and more clear-sighted than others here) in supposing that cognitive science should not seek to involve itself in issues of this sort; but by the same token quite wrong to suppose that cognitive science can take over the function of philosophy of mind. Freud, whom Fodor cites, cannot be appealed to in support of the idea that psychology (in the sense of discourse, with a theoreticity suitable to its subject matter, about the mind) can simply disown an interest in subjectivity (or the personal); Freud's point is rather that there are aspects of one's subjectivity that are not transparent to one.

scriptions. Saul Kripke's *Naming and Necessity* and Keith Donnellan's "Proper Names and Identifying Descriptions" inaugurated a revolt, the tenor of which was this: in accommodating almost all cases of singular thought under the descriptive model (according to which the object, if any, on whose doings or characteristics the truth or falsity of a thought depends is determined by conformity to an object-independent specification that figures in the content of the thought), philosophers had given insufficient attention to the possibility of a different kind of case, where what matters is not the object's fitting a specification in the content of the thought but its standing in some suitable contextual relation to the episode of thinking.[44]

Richard Rorty has suggested that when this recoil from the descriptive model is accorded deep philosophical significance, we are confronted with a piece of broadly Cartesian philosophy—that is, philosophy whose problems are set by the Cartesian divide—in what we ought to hope is its terminal phase: fearing that the descriptive model leaves thought out of touch with reality, proponents of the alternative model want reference to constitute an extra-intentional relation between language or thought and objects. Rorty can plausibly stigmatize this as a matter of succumbing to a hopeless "demand . . . for some transcendental standpoint outside our present set of representations from which we can inspect the relations between those representations and their object".[45] Apart from the imputation of hopelessness, this view of the philosophical significance of the anti-descriptivist revolution is shared by many of its adherents. But it is not compulsory.

What generates the appearance of a hopeless transcendentalism is an assumption to this effect: the intentional nature of a thought could determine, as a factual matter, that it was about a certain object only in the manner codified in the descriptive model.[46] The revolt against descriptivism is largely fuelled by counter-examples—

44. I exploit "tenor" to permit myself to adapt what Kripke and Donnellan actually say to my purposes, in particular to formulate their intuitions in terms of thought rather than language. For an opposed reading of Kripke, see Evans, *The Varieties of Reference*, chap. 3.

45. *Philosophy and the Mirror of Nature*, p. 293.

46. At *Philosophy and the Mirror of Nature*, pp. 288–9, Rorty (*in propria persona*) implicitly disallows the possibility of something both intentional and (in the manner of a genuine relation) object-dependent. I transpose Rorty's reading into a concern with thought rather than, in the first instance, language, in parallel with my sketch of Kripke and Donnellan.

cases in which we know more than someone else, and a routine application of that assumption yields unilluminating accounts of him: we want to say, for instance, that he has and expresses false thoughts about something that could not be determined as the object of his thoughts in that way, since the materials available for such determination would take us to a quite different object if they took us to anything at all. In Rorty's account, there is nothing wrong with this impulse towards redescription; although "it does not mark an invocation of our intuitions concerning a matter of fact",[47] so the "intentionalist" assumption, formulated as above, can be sacrosanct. What is problematic, according to Rorty, is this thought: the superiority of the redescriptions shows that what is wrong with, say, the extended Theory of Descriptions is an implication to the effect that "the more false beliefs we have the less 'in touch with the world' we are".[48] What happens here is that descriptivism is allowed to induce a quasi-Cartesian fear of loss of contact with objects, which "the new theory of reference" seeks to assuage by picturing thought and objects as connected by a substantial extra-intentional relation.

This reading is shaped by the initial assumption, which is admittedly prevalent among anti-descriptivist revolutionaries and descriptivist counter-revolutionaries alike. What makes the assumption seem compulsory is the way of thinking that underlies the usual reading of Frege (see §3 above). That should suggest the general character of a radical alternative to Rorty's reading. According to the alternative, the intuitive disquiet that led to the revolt against descriptivism reflected an insight—not at first available for sharp formulation—to the effect that the assumption should be dismantled; the revolt should culminate in a conception of object-dependent thought extended outside Russell's restriction, and enriched with Fregean fineness of grain, like the one I outlined at the start of this essay.[49] The trouble with descriptivism, on this view, is indeed a quasi-Cartesian loss of connection between thought and objects; but

47. *Philosophy and the Mirror of Nature,* p. 291.

48. *Philosophy and the Mirror of Nature,* p. 288.

49. A fuller treatment would need to incorporate also a critique of the conception of truth implicit in Blackburn's distinction, at *Spreading the Word,* p. 341, between "thoughts, identified as the truths and falsehoods about the world" and "thoughts identified as the objects of propositional attitudes".

the response is not, in Cartesian style, to try to bridge an acknowledged gap, but to undermine the way of thinking that opens it.

It is worth noting a couple of detailed divergences from Rorty that this permits. In Rorty's reading, "the new theory of reference" conceives itself as fulfilling the task that Cartesian epistemology attempted with familiar discouraging results.[50] But in the different reading, there can be no question of trying to bridge an epistemological gulf between mental states whose nature is independently determined and a reality that threatens to be beyond their grasp; the upshot of the revolution is that scepticism about the existence of the objects of seeming singular thoughts is equally scepticism about the layout of the mental realm. Second, the counter-examples can now be integrated with the complaint that descriptivism leaves thought out of touch with objects. The counter-examples are a natural, if oblique, way of recommending the intuition that object-dependence, understood in terms of relations of acquaintance, can be a feature of the intentional nature of a thought, on the ground that the materials otherwise available for intentional determination of the object of a thought seem incapable of generally getting the answer right. There is no need to deny that getting the answer right here is establishing a matter of fact, as Rorty does—with a view to insulating the counter-examples from the idea that descriptivism threatens the connection between thought and objects—on the basis of a curiously old-fashioned restriction of the factual to, in effect, the value-free.[51]

Predictably, the anti-descriptivist revolt has led to a descriptivist counter-revolution. A sympathetic consideration of this movement can bring out the character of the way of thinking that underlies the usual reading of Frege, and suggest the liberating potential of the alternative.

Consider a case in which, according to the anti-descriptivist revolution, it is the contextual presence of an object itself that determines it as the object of a thought. As long as it is assumed that this fact cannot enter into the thought's intentional nature, it follows that the thought's intentional nature is insufficient to determine which object

50. *Philosophy and the Mirror of Nature,* pp. 293–4.

51. I believe that Rorty's view of "the Cartesian problematic" is in general spoiled by an over-concentration on epistemology; and that his view of the possibilities for epistemology and philosophy of mind is debilitated by his restricted conception of what can be a matter of fact.

it is that makes the subject's thinking true or false, and consequently insufficient to determine what it is that the subject thinks. But now this complaint seems natural: if we try to see intentionality as at most partly determining what it is that a subject thinks, we leave ourselves without anything genuinely recognizable as a notion of intentionality at all. The two-component picture of mind that I discussed in §8 aims to codify the thesis that in these cases intentionality is only a partial determinant of what the subject thinks; and the complaint can be focused by noting that the internal component is the only place in the two-component picture for the ideas associated with the aspect of intentionality that concerns the directedness of thought to specific objects: the Fregean idea of modes of presentation, and the idea of (as it were) cognitive space that regulates the application of the idea of modes of presentation. Directedness towards external objects enters the picture only when we widen our field of view to take in more than the internal component. So on this conception there is no object-directed intentionality in cognitive space.[52] (Note that there is no object-directed intentionality, conceived as at most partly determining what it is that the subject thinks, anywhere else in the two-component picture either. If we allow ourselves the whole composite story, we have all the determinants of content in view.)

52. This is clear in McGinn. Less clear-sighted versions of the two-component picture obscure the point (holding back from a wholesale form of the relocation that I mentioned in n. 38 above) by purporting to locate "narrow contents" in the interior considered by itself. These "contents" could not yield answers to the question what it is that someone thinks; there is really no reason to recognize them as *contents* at all. Importing that notion serves merely to mask the distance we have come from an intuitive notion of mental phenomena. (See Evans, pp. 200–4.) These remarks apply to what Dennett calls "hetero-phenomenology"; "Beyond Belief", p. 39. Hetero-phenomenology brackets the involvement of mental states with specific objects, stuffs, and so forth (a version of the insistence on autonomy); it arrives at specifications of "notional attitudes" by asking questions like "In what sort of environment would this cognitive system thrive?" (It does not take a "brain's eye view" [p. 26]; this is why it is *hetero*-phenomenology.) This generates the appearance that we can find (narrow) content-bearing states in the interior considered by itself. But the idea looks self-deceptive. If we are not concerned with the point of view of the cognitive system itself (if, indeed, we conceive it in such a way that it has no point of view), there is no justification for regarding the enterprise as any kind of phenomenology at all; the label serves only to obscure the fact that, according to this picture, all is dark within. To put the point another way: Dennett fails to accommodate his philosophy of mind to his own insight that "brains are *syntactic engines*", not "*semantic engines*" (p. 26).

It is a version of the point I made in §8 to say that this seems unrecognizable as a picture of the mind's directedness towards external objects; and, with the assumption in place, that can seem to necessitate staying with the descriptivist view of how thought relates to objects.[53] So we can understand the counter-revolution as motivated by a partial form of an insight: that, because of essentially Cartesian difficulties, the two-component conception of mind fails to supply a satisfying account of the mind's directedness towards the external world.[54]

But any seeming stability in the descriptivist upshot depends on not taking this insight far enough. The descriptivist counter-revolutionaries do not entertain the possibility that object-dependence might be a feature of a thought's intentional nature, and this shows their adherence to a conception of cognitive space that matches that of the two-component theorists in this respect: it is a conception of a realm whose layout is independent of external reality. The counter-revolutionaries take this to be undamaging so long as content is restricted to the purely descriptive; as if the two-component picture succeeded in allowing light into the mind by way of the *predicative* element in a singular thought, so that what is called for might be simply enriching cognitive space with more of the same sort of thing. But the fact is that the principles of the shared conception keep light out of cognitive space altogether. Content in general, not just the focusing of thoughts on objects, requires directedness towards reality. We achieve a representation of something not wholly unlike that directedness when we situate this narrowly circumscribed cognitive space in the world around it. But when we consider the in-

53. "Descriptivist" need not imply that the specification by conformity to which the object of a thought is supposed to be determined must be linguistically expressible. It should be clear by now that my objection to the view is not—what that concession preempts—that we sometimes lack linguistic resources to express the "descriptive" modes of presentation it envisages. The point of the label "descriptivist" is to stress (by way of allusion to the Theory of Descriptions) the crucial point that these modes of presentation are not object-dependent. (Compare Blackburn, pp. 316, 323.) Rather than "descriptivist" I would use Blackburn's term "universalist", except that I am not sure whether his "universalist thoughts" are meant to be the bearers of truth-values in their own right envisaged by the position that I am describing here or the bogus "narrow contents" envisaged in some versions of the two-component picture (see n. 52); the differences must not be blurred.

54. A counter-revolutionary who makes essentially this motivation very clear is John R. Searle; see chap. 8 of *Intentionality*.

habitants of cognitive space from their own point of view—a stance that it is irresistible to contemplate, since the narrowly circumscribed cognitive space is as near as these pictures come to giving us the idea of the domain of subjectivity—we cannot find them anything but blank. (We must guard against a temptation to avoid this by an appeal to magic.)[55] Pushed to its logical conclusion, then, the insight that motivates the descriptivist counter-revolution undermines it, revealing the counter-revolution as mired in the same essentially Cartesian problems.[56] We should reject the shared picture of cognitive space, which is what disallows object-dependence as a feature of intentionality and holds the usual reading of Frege in place.[57]

Notice that, although countenancing object-dependence as a feature of intentionality is a direct response to a threatened loss of contact with objects on the part of singular thoughts in particular, it promises a more general exorcism of Cartesian problems. The idea of cognitive space—the space whose topology is regulated by the Fregean principle—is clearly metaphorical. Allowing intrinsic object-dependence, we have to set whatever literally spatial boundaries are in question outside the subject's skin or skull. Cognitive space incorporates the relevant portions of the "external" world. So its relations

55. Cognitive science manages to find content in the interior as it conceives that; but it does so by situating cognitive space (on its conception) in the world, not by considering things from the point of view of the cognitive system conceived as a self-contained mechanism. So it is beside the point here to say (quite correctly) that cognitive science is not an appeal to magic. I confess myself baffled to understand McGinn's suggestion (p. 215) that "purely 'qualitative'" content could be strictly internal; is it perhaps a trace of the seductive power of a magical conception of content?

56. This is why I am unconvinced by Schiffer's protestations that there is nothing Cartesian about the counter-revolution. Schiffer does not consider the conception of object-dependent modes of presentation that I am recommending in this essay, but one can infer how he would argue against it from his argument against causal chains as modes of presentation (not an idea I want to defend). The argument assumes that modes of presentation would have to be a matter of intra-individual "cognitive role", and so rests on a version of the insistence on the autonomy of the inner, which I have been suggesting we should regard as the essence of a Cartesian picture of mind.

57. The nemesis of the counter-revolution is almost explicit in Searle's remarkable claim (p. 230) that we are brains in vats. As Dennett says, the brain is only a syntactic engine. If we were brains inside our own skulls we would have no inkling of the outside world, in a particularly strong sense: there would be no content available to us. It is an insight on Searle's part that intentionality is a biological phenomenon (see *Intentionality*, chap. 10). But intentionality needs to be understood in the context of an organism's life in the world. We cannot understand it, or even keep it in view, if we try to think of it in the context of the brain's "life" inside the head.

to that world should not pose philosophical difficulties in the Cartesian style.

So long as we make the assumption that shapes Rorty's reading of the anti-descriptivist revolution, we are stuck with the conception of what thought is like, considered in intentional terms, that generates the fear of being out of touch with objects; and only the transcendental move that Rorty describes could so much as seem to assuage the fear. If we succumb to the move, we are embarking on a piece of philosophy in a recognizably Cartesian mode. Rorty brings out very clearly how discouraging the prospects are. But with the assumption in place, however well we appreciate the hopelessness of our predicament once we allow ourselves to feel the Cartesian fear, that does not seem enough to confer intellectual respectability on suppressing it. We have to be shown how to make ourselves immune to the fear of losing the world; but with the assumption about intentionality maintained, the best we can do seems to be to avert our gaze from a difficulty that we choose (intelligibly, by all means) not to bother with. The point of the conception of singular thought that I have been recommending is that it treats the Cartesian fear of loss in a different, and fully satisfying way: not by trying to bridge a gulf between intentionality and objects, nor by a cavalier refusal to worry about the problem, while leaving what poses it undisturbed, but by fundamentally undermining the picture of mind that generates the Cartesian divide.

ESSAY 12

Intentionality *De Re*

1. In his characteristically trenchant and forthright book *Intentionality,* John Searle urges an account of how minds are directed at particular objects that he describes as "Fregean in spirit" (p. 197); given how Searle reads Frege, the description is appropriate. In Frege's account, a mind is directed at a particular by virtue of grasping a thought that has as a constituent a sense of the appropriate kind, determining that object as its associated *Bedeutung*. According to Searle's reading of this, a sense of the appropriate kind determines its associated *Bedeutung* by fixing something like a specification or set of conditions that the right object fits.[1]

It seems clear that Searle means formulations on these lines (for which see, e.g., p. 197) to suggest an idea we can usefully put like this: Frege's conception of the relevant sort of sense exploits, in anticipation, something like the leading idea of Russell's Theory of Descriptions. Russell's aim was to isolate a sort of significance that could be attributed to the terms he considered (a partial determinant of the propositions expressed by sentences containing them, and hence—to move to a quasi-Fregean way of putting things—something suitable to be regarded as an element in the contents of possible mental states) whether or not there was anything answering to

1. Searle makes room also for mental states whose Intentional content is less than an entire proposition (p. 7). In Fregean terms, these would involve senses smaller than thoughts, figuring otherwise than as constituents of whole thoughts. I do not know whether Frege himself envisaged this extension of his apparatus. But even if not, this is clearly no problem for Searle's claim to be recommending a position that is Fregean in spirit.

the specifications that figured in making such a significance explicit.[2] Russell's thought was that the very possession of content, on the part of the relevant statements or mental states, ought not to be undermined if the speakers or thinkers were wrong in supposing appropriate objects to exist. So it would be out of line with the point of Russell's construction to allow cases in which the conditions an object must fit, in order to be determined by a significance of the relevant sort, are partly themselves determined by the object itself, so that the conditions could not be stated or entertained in thought if the object did not exist. This would make content vulnerable to non-existence in just the way the construction is meant to prevent. At any rate this object-dependence of the conditions must be disallowed if the threat of loss of content that Russell's construction is designed to avert would be, failing Russell's construction, a live one—that is, if the object in question (if there is one) is of such a kind that subjects can be wrong in supposing one of its members to exist (for instance, if it is an item in the perceived environment). Now in Searle's reading of Frege, the conditions expressed in expressing a singular sense are evidently conceived on the lines of the significance of a Russellian definite description: that is, as something available to be expressed or entertained independently of any object—at any rate, any "external" object—that might fit them. Thus Searle takes it that Fregean object-directed thoughts (at any rate those directed to objects that are not "in the mind" of the subject himself) would still be thinkable even if the objects to which they are directed did not exist. As he graphically puts it, all the Fregean beliefs that his position countenances could be had by a brain in a vat (p. 230; see also pp. 209, 212).[3]

2. Such specificatory (or "descriptive")[4] conceptions of how mental states (and utterances) are directed to particulars have come under attack, especially since the ideas of Saul Kripke's 1969 Princeton lec-

2. See "On Denoting".

3. Russell hardly figures in *Intentionality*, and not in this context. But Searle's gloss on Fregean singular sense, in terms of fit, does not by itself secure the object-independence he insists on; this will emerge below. A tacit Russellian influence (which is plausible in any case) helps to explain why Searle apparently supposes otherwise.

4. This terminology is familiar, and Searle allows himself to use it (e.g., in chap. 9); but it is potentially misleading in suggesting that the specificatory conception is limited to what can be verbally expressed, in purely general terms (see pp. 232–3). I shall not trade on any such assumption.

tures became generally known.[5] The gist of the attack, so far as our present purposes are concerned, is that the materials available in the minds of subjects for constructing the envisaged specifications are insufficient to secure the right particular-directedness for their mental states. ("Right" in the light of what is required to make proper sense of people, which is what the attribution of mental states is for in the first place.) In some cases, according to the objection, the specificatory conception will require us to take a subject's mental state to be directed to a particular other than the right one; in others, although making proper sense of someone will demand crediting him with a particular-directed mental state, the specificatory conception will leave us with materials insufficient to determine any one object as that to which his mental state is directed.

In Searle's view, this kind of objection is based on a failure to take full account of the resources available to the specificatory conception. I shall illustrate the general strategy of his response in connection with what is probably the simplest possible case for it, where a mental state is directed to a particular in a way that exploits the fact that the particular is currently in the subject's field of vision. If we formulate a specification by making explicit, in general terms, how the visual experience represents the object as being, we make ourselves vulnerable to an objection of the relevant kind. The result will often be too unspecific even to seem to stand a chance of individuating something (think of things seen at a distance in poor conditions for vision). And even if the content of the experience is highly specific, a specification constructed by making that content explicit in purely general terms will fit the right object no better than it fits a Twin Earth *Doppelgänger*.[6] (This objection obviously belongs to the second of the two kinds I distinguished in the last paragraph; it cites a case where, allegedly, specificatory content is insufficient to individuate an object at all. It will be clear that the materials of Searle's response would equally apply to an objection of the first kind, where specificatory content is, allegedly, such as to individuate the wrong object.)

5. See *Naming and Necessity*. Another early landmark in the revolt against "descriptive" accounts of reference and singular thought was Keith Donnellan, "Proper Names and Identifying Descriptions".

6. This way of dramatizing objections of this kind is due to Hilary Putnam, "The Meaning of 'Meaning'".

Objections of this sort misfire, Searle argues, because they ignore the possibility of anchoring the particular-directedness of the mental states in question to the particularity of the relevant experiences themselves. Thus, he suggests, the content of a belief that someone who dimly glimpses a man in the distance might express by saying "That man is wearing a red cap" can be expressed (in the right circumstances) in this way: "There is a man there causing this visual experience and that man is wearing a red cap" (p. 212). There is no risk that the specificatory material made explicit here might be satisfied by the wrong man.[7] (Searle builds here on his discussion of the content of visual experience in chap. 2. The very same form of words that I have just cited as giving the content of a belief, according to Searle, might equally be used, according to that discussion, in making partly explicit the content of the visual experience itself; see p. 48.)[8]

3. But what about the particular-directedness signalled here by "this visual experience"? How is this to be made out to conform to the general "Fregean" picture?

This kind of demonstrative expression is enormously important at several points in *Intentionality* (see chaps. 2, 3, 8, and 9); and that

7. It might seem that there is a risk of cases where such a formulation would not select between several candidates (because there are several men in view). I think Searle would respond that "there" functions to select the right aspect of the visual experience, and so secure that the specification selects the right man. See the discussion of Donnellan's case of the two seen patches at pp. 253–4.

8. In sticking to this case, I shall be avoiding some extra complexities introduced by Searle's discussion of indexicality, which imports a reference to the current *utterance* (as "this utterance") in a specification of "conditions of satisfaction"; see pp. 220–8. The simpler case I have rehearsed from Searle contains enough to reveal the shape of his strategy, and to enable me to make the points I want to make. (In passing, I note that it is a curiosity of Searle's discussion that he deals with the first person, for instance, only in the context of his treatment of indexical *expressions,* as if the first-person mode of presentation—to use Fregean terminology—was in play only when one speaks and not also in unexpressed thought. There is no reason to suppose that the general strategy, exemplified in the passage I have focused on, requires this. I note also that the case Searle discusses at p. 212 suggests that the "problem of particularity"—in the content of visual experience—that Searle discusses at pp. 62–71 ought to include more than what he there considers. The explicit discussion of the "problem of particularity" is limited to cases where the particularity relates to a *prior* identification. But one can see something that might be expressed by saying, in suitable circumstances, "That man is wearing a red cap"—that is, the content of one's experience can be particular in a way that the demonstrative indicates—without one's having made any prior identification of the man in question.)

makes it remarkable that the book contains no discussion at all of the questions I have just posed. When he discusses the content of visual experience, Searle insists that a formulation of the sort in question makes explicit what is *shown* by an experience (p. 49; there are similar moves elsewhere, e.g., pp. 213, 223). He seems to be suggesting that these formulations do not actually *give* the content of the mental states in question, but make it available to us by a kind of indirection. But he does not make this manoeuvre with respect to the content of the perceptually based belief (p. 212—the formulation I cited above). And in any case, even where he does exploit the notion of showing, that does not obviously make it legitimate (nor indeed does Searle suggest it does) to duck questions about how expressions like "this visual experience" should be conceived as working in these formulations. Whatever the formulations do, they do it by reminding us of a way in which explicit expression can be given to a certain sort of thinkable content when one is in the right perceptual situation, and even if this content is not itself supposed to *be* the content of the mental state under discussion (the visual experience, say), its particular-directedness ought to conform to the general picture.

Notice that it matters how the visual experience is referred to. Consider the claim that one of Searle's formulations, uttered by me in suitable circumstances, might capture the content of a visual experience or a perceptually based demonstrative belief of mine, whether directly, by being a specification of that content, or indirectly, by making explicit what is shown. This claim would lose whatever plausibility it has if "this visual experience" were replaced by something that designated the visual experience in question as, say, that enjoyed by John McDowell at such-and-such a time. I could have this sort of experience or belief without knowing that I am John McDowell. (For a parallel point, accepted by Searle from John Perry and David Kaplan, see pp. 218–9.)

4. In the absence of help from Searle on this point, then, let me make the following suggestion: the best account of the sort of particular-directedness that is, perfectly intelligibly, signalled by phrases like "this visual experience" in those formulations of his exploits the fact that the experience itself—the very object to which those contents are directed—is a possible focus of the mind's attention, simply by

virtue of being enjoyed.[9] In the right circumstances, namely, that one is having a visual experience, the experience itself can enter into determining a mode of attention or directedness that one might indicate, at least to oneself, by "this visual experience". This is not a specification that is intelligible independently of the object specified; the presence to the mind of the object itself enters into any understanding of these demonstrative modes of presentation.

This notion of the presence of an object to the mind is reminiscent of Russell's notion of acquaintance—a relation that, according to Russell, makes possible a direct targeting on objects of propositions that do not need to be spelled out in terms of the apparatus of the Theory of Descriptions. So one way of expressing the idea that Frege's conception of singular senses is to be understood as a partial anticipation of the Theory of Descriptions (see §1 above) would be to make this suggestion: if one appeals, as I have done, to what looks like a version of Russell's *contrast* or *foil* to the kind of case where he takes propositions to bear on objects by way of descriptions, one is suggesting that in these demonstrative cases the notion of Fregean sense is simply dispensable. What need is there of a Fregean sense to target the mind on the object of its thought, one might ask, if the object is itself present to the mind as a possible focus of its attention?

But this would be a mistake. There is still the standard Fregean reason for saying that *how* the object is presented in a thought makes a difference to which thought it is. As we have seen (§3 above), it matters for my getting hold of the contents I need to get hold of, to make Searle's proposals plausible, that I take the visual experience they concern to be presented as *this visual experience,* and not as, say, the visual experience had by John McDowell at such-and-such a time. There is nothing un-Fregean here—no appeal to the apparatus of "direct reference" and "singular propositions" that Searle is (rightly, to my mind) concerned to avoid (see p. 220). The point is that this recognizably Fregean insistence on discriminating contents more finely than that apparatus does—by modes of presentation, not by objects—is in no way disrupted by our envisaging

9. It is a good question what makes this sort of attention possible, and the best answer may not in the end be congenial to the use to which Searle puts these demonstratives. See n. 11 below.

modes of presentation that exploit the presence to the mind of objects themselves.

Even the idea of fitting or satisfying specifications or conditions can perhaps be made out to apply here. The condition an object must satisfy to be what one of the relevant contents concerns is the condition of being (as only the subject can put it, and only at the time) *this visual experience,* where that form of words is used in a way that essentially exploits the subject's having the very visual experience that is in question. The condition is not one that could be expressed or entertained even if the experience in question did not exist.[10]

5. My suggestion is, then, that "this visual experience" can signal a way in which a visual experience can be presented in a thought, made possible by the fact that the experience itself is present to the mind by virtue of being enjoyed. And now I want to raise the question why it cannot be fully Fregean to parallel this idea for the case of perceived *objects.* The upshot would be to build on a plausible account of Searle's apparatus, in such a way as to yield a different account of the contents that he uses the apparatus to explain. Why should we not suppose that "that man"—when a man is in one's field of vision—expresses a way in which a man can be presented in a Fregean thought, made possible by the fact that the man himself is present to the mind by virtue of being seen? As before, the idea is that such a demonstrative mode of presentation is not capturable in

10. Philosophers who are gripped by the idea that singular sense must be independent of the existence of the relevant object will need to consider, instead of "this visual experience", specifications of the general form "the visual experience that . . .". One candidate that might have some attraction is "the visual experience that I am now having"; with its indexicality, this would not be vulnerable to the objection against "the visual experience that John McDowell is having at . . ." and the like (see §3 above). But this suggestion would at best postpone facing an issue like the one I am addressing in this section, about the modes of presentation expressed (by me, on an occasion) by "I" and "now". In Searle's treatment (which relates exclusively to uses of those indexical *expressions;* see pp. 220–8), the issue would in the end be shifted to one about "this utterance". In a modification of Searle's treatment, preserving its spirit but taking account of the fact that first-person thinking need not be expressed (see n. 8 above), the issue would be shifted to one about something like "this thought". It is natural to suggest that we might as well stay with "this visual experience". ("This utterance" raises extra questions, in view of the fact that utterances are not "in the mind" in the way experiences are: see §5 below. The fact that Searle takes "this utterance" for granted is accordingly perhaps even more remarkable than the fact that he takes "this visual experience" for granted.)

a specification that someone could understand without exploiting the perceived presence of the man himself. In answering the question how the man is presented in such thoughts, there is no substitute for saying "He is presented as *that* man", exploiting his perceived presence to make oneself understood. The condition an object must meet to be what such thoughts bear on—the condition of being *that* man, as one can put it if one is in the right perceptual circumstances—is not one that could be expressed or entertained even if the man in question did not exist. As before, this suggestion does not involve sliding into the apparatus of "direct reference" and "singular propositions", individuated by the objects they are about rather than by modes of presentation. Standardly Fregean arguments still allow us to discriminate a thought expressible in suitable circumstances by "That man is wearing a red cap", understood in this object-dependent way, from thoughts expressible by concatenating the same predication with different designations of the same man.

It is not my aim in this essay to argue positively for this sort of view.[11] For my present purposes, the point is simply that it is a possibility. Apart from one notable difference (which I shall come to in §7 below), it simply parallels a plausible suggestion for filling a gap in Searle's explicit discussion of his own apparatus. So what is there to prevent Searle from accepting it?[12]

11. I do believe it points the way to a general view of object-directed Intentionality that is a great improvement over what Searle suggests. In Searle's picture, "externally" directed particularity in content is secured indirectly, by way of contents targeted on "internal" items, with this latter targeting hardly discussed, as if it can stand unproblematically on its own. In a different view, the targeting of content on "internal" items like experiences is not intelligible independently of the targeting of content on the self. Searle's treatment of indexicality, however acceptable in itself, simply bypasses the deep issues that first-personal content raises (see n. 8 above). The different view of "externally" directed demonstrative content that I have sketched permits us to register a role that it is plausible to suppose the capacity to locate and orient oneself in a perceived environment would play in a full explanation of first-personal content. This inverts the priority that Searle's discussion suggests of "this visual experience" and the like over "that man" ("that rock", "that tree") and the like. (Particularly in the context of this comparison, Searle's priority has a rather Cartesian feel.) For more detail about the sort of different view I have in mind, see Gareth Evans, *The Varieties of Reference,* especially chaps. 6 and 7.

12. I should note that this sort of view of perceptual demonstratives figures here only as one example (though probably the most immediately attractive) of a way of making sense of the phrase I have used for the title of this essay. A fuller discussion would need to look into other possible examples (to say nothing of much more detailed treatment of this sort of case). Compare n. 8 of Essay 11 above; and Evans, *The Varieties of Reference.*

6. Part of the answer is that Searle's reading of Frege precludes a view of this sort. As I remarked in §1, he takes Frege's idea of singular sense, at any rate where the associated *Bedeutung* is "external", to match Russell's idea of the significance of "denoting phrases", at least in that he supposes singular senses are independent of the existence of objects they determine. Searle does not cite chapter and verse in support of this. I believe the basis of this reading of Frege, in which of course Searle is far from alone, is not specific texts so much as a philosophical train of thought that convinces people that Frege's idea *must* have been on these lines. I shall come to Searle's version of this philosophy in §7 below. Meanwhile, although the exegetical issue is less important than the underlying philosophical one, let me briefly try to sow some preliminary doubts about Frege himself.

It is obvious that Frege's guiding aim, in using the concept of singular sense, was to secure a fineness of grain in object-directed contents that could not be achieved if they were individuated simply by the objects they concern.[13] Russell's main point in the Theory of Descriptions, by contrast, was to postulate a kind of significance that is independent of the existence of associated objects; one notable upshot is that Russell could handle existential statements containing the relevant kind of terms in a way that is consistent with the doctrine that existential statements attribute the second-level property of instantiation. Russell's apparatus does secure a fineness of grain, but it is easy to see that as a bonus. The basic motivations diverge.

Now it is not simply given that these two aims—securing fineness of grain and dealing with the issues about existence—*had* to be met by the same apparatus. However neat one finds Russell's use of, in effect, the notion of specification, in order to secure at one stroke *both* significances that are existence-independent *and* fineness of grain, one should be aware that there is a grave risk of anachronism in assuming that a notion of specification used to gloss *Frege*'s way with fineness of grain must similarly involve existence-independence. If it does not, then of course a Fregean needs a different treatment of existential statements involving proper names. But it seems clear in any case that Frege did not suppose attributing sense to names by itself accommodated such statements, in something like the way the

13. See, of course, "On Sense and Reference".

Theory of Descriptions does.[14] It is time philosophers stopped taking it for granted that the notion of singular sense is a half-baked forerunner of the Theory of Descriptions, and started considering the possibility that the fineness of grain that Frege was basically concerned to register can be had with senses that are not independent of the existence of the objects they present.[15]

7. The philosophical train of thought that underpins Searle's reading of Frege starts from the thesis that an *Intentionalist* account of content, such as Frege's notion of thoughts patently is, must be "internalist" (see especially p. 198). In effect Searle glosses "internalist" in terms of the idea that meanings, and more generally contents, are "in the head" (see chap. 8). What this amounts to in his argument is that the contents an "internalist" account can countenance must be capable of being entertained by a brain in a vat (see p. 230, which I cited in §1 above). This would clearly not be the case with contents that could not be entertained or expressed if certain perceived environmental items did not exist. By contrast, if a brain in a vat can have content-involving mental states at all (something Searle evidently sees no difficulty in supposing), the requirement would not preclude contents partly determined by object-involving modes of presentation of those mental states, such as those I envisaged—offering Searle a plausible account of his unexplained appeal to demonstrative phrases like "this visual experience"—in §4 above. This is the difference I alluded to at the end of §5

14. Frege did not even allow that "NN exists" (or "NN does not exist") can be well-formed with the name functioning in its normal way. In *Speech Acts*, p. 165, n. 3, Searle acknowledges this, but makes it an occasion to chide Frege for not seeing that his conceptual equipment permitted a broadly Russellian approach to existentials. Searle's suggestion is that attributing sense to names removes all reason for not allowing such existential statements to be well-formed. But it would have made for better exegesis if Searle had tried to comprehend Frege's notion of singular sense in a way that would warrant his assignment of ill-formedness. The idea of singular senses as object-dependent (but fine-grained) accommodates the texts much better. (Positive support for the idea that Frege envisaged object-dependent singular senses comes from his doctrine of truth-value gaps; see Essay 9 above.) Frege's own treatment of the issues raised by apparent singular terms with no bearer (the existence issues) is sketchy and unsatisfactory, but it does not follow that we do him a favour by equipping him with a conception of singular sense inspired anachronistically by the Theory of Descriptions. For a better (neo-Fregean) treatment on no such basis, see Evans, *The Varieties of Reference*, chap. 10.

15. On object-dependent Fregean singular senses, see further chap. 1 of Evans, *The Varieties of Reference;* and Essay 10 above.

above, between my suggestion about "this visual experience" and the similar suggestion I aired, about demonstrative modes of presentation of perceived "external" objects, in §5. Searle could exploit this difference to claim that modes of presentation that are object-involving (not existence-indifferent) may pass muster—that is, be acceptable to "internalism"—when the objects are "in the mind", but not when they are not.[16]

I think this line of thought begins with an insight, but distorts it into a mistake. The notion of what is "internal" undergoes a shift between what it must amount to in order to make "internalism" clearly incumbent on an Intentionalist and what it amounts to in Searle's requirement about brains in vats.

The insight is best understood in terms of the style of objection against "descriptive" accounts of object-directedness that I mentioned in §2 above. Many philosophers, as Searle notes, have taken such objections to show that Intentionalistic views of content do not have the resources to individuate the objects on which mental states should be taken to be targeted. They have concluded that individuation requires an appeal to extra-Intentional considerations: notably facts about the context and causation of the mental states in question, conceived as investigated "from the third-person or external point of view" (see pp. 62–5—this phrase is from p. 65—and chap. 8).[17] In Searle's view, this "externalist" approach simply shirks facing the right question (see especially pp. 64-5). Directedness to particulars, he insists, is an aspect of the *contents* of some *mental* states; and if giving an account of something requires this sort of stepping outside the subject's point of view, then whatever it is that is being explained, it cannot be the contents of mental states. We can put the point like this: attributing content-involving mental states, including those whose contents are particular,

16. I have no idea whether Searle would accept something like the suggestion I made in §4. The point is only that it supplements his silence about an important part of his own apparatus, and in a way that is not ruled out by his "internalism", so long as we grant his own assumption that brains in vats can have content-involving mental states.

17. The idea of reference as an extra-Intentional relation is made vivid by Richard Rorty, in chap. 6 of *Philosophy and the Mirror of Nature.* Rorty himself does not endorse the idea. He contrives to remain aloof, above the controversy between Intentionalists and "externalists" (to put it in Searle's terms), while leaving unchallenged the "externalist" view about the individuative insufficiency of the Intentionalists' resources, by, in effect, separating the needs of interpretation from any aspiration to delineate the true contours of mental states. For some discussion, see §9 of Essay 11 above.

is delineating the contours of a subjectivity, and it does not make sense to suppose that executing that task could require "external" considerations over and above the whole truth about how the subjectivity in question is arranged.[18]

This line of thought of Searle's strikes me as absolutely right. One could oppose it, on behalf of an "externalist" position, by claiming that there is some strict sense of the notion of mental content according to which mental contents do not have particularity, at any rate if "externally" directed, as a feature. But put baldly like that, this seems merely to deny that there is any such thing as *mental* directedness at "external" objects, and that is hard to swallow. A less bald version of the thought allows for a kind of object-directed content, conceived as having an "internal" and an "external" aspect. But as long as the "external" aspect is taken to come into sight only when we step outside the subject's own point of view (as it usually is, more or less explicitly, in views of this type)[19], this "double aspect" kind of position is vulnerable to a form of Searle's objection: it does not accommodate, but indeed simply flouts, the connection Searle implicitly insists on between content and subjectivity. It is no good protesting that the connection is respected with regard to the supposed "internal" aspect; it is the complete "double aspect" contraption that positions of this kind put to a sort of use—specifically, giving the contents of propositional attitudes—that is genuinely intelligible only if the connection with subjectivity is respected.[20] As Searle suggests, outright "externalism" (a refusal to allow even an "internal" aspect to mental directedness) seems merely to abandon the topic of mental content.

18. I have put it like this in order to allow for a possibility that factors outside a subject's ken might partly determine what I have described (more impressionistically than Searle) as the contours of his subjectivity. What Searle finds intolerable is the idea that *after* noting the whole truth about the contours of a subjectivity (however they are determined), we might *still* need to look outside it in order to establish any particular-directedness of the subject's mental states.

19. For a particularly explicit example, see Colin McGinn, "The Structure of Content" pp. 254–5.

20. I cannot recall anywhere in the now vast literature urging this kind of position where the idea of a general connection between content and subjectivity is so much as considered, let alone attacked. Searle is engagingly selective in his targets; from his discussion alone, one would not realize the baroque proliferation of options now on offer in this very poorly understood area of philosophy. There is a little more elaboration than I have allowed myself here in Essay 11 above.

Searle's "internalism", then, embodies what seems to be a genuine insight. But the right way to understand the insight, as indeed some of Searle's own formulations make clear, is by glossing "internal" with "first-personal"; what is wrong with "externalism" is that it steps outside the delineation of the relevant subjectivity. Searle's "in the head", and his "brain in a vat" requirement, are quite another matter. On Searle's own account, visual experience provides "direct access" to seen objects (pp. 45-6). What is present to the mind, when one sees an object, is not some mental surrogate for it but the object itself. This "direct realism" (see p. 57) yields a perfectly intelligible sense in which the first-personal truth about a subject—the truth about the layout of his subjectivity—is not independent of the external objects that perceptually confront him. One's subjectivity is partly constituted by one's point of view on the objects in one's environment. There is thus no shift to a point of view other than the subject's if we countenance object-dependent contents on the lines I suggested in §5. There is certainly a violation of the "brain in a vat" requirement, but that looks simply irrelevant to Searle's good point against "externalism".[21]

Glossed in terms of "first-personal" and "third-personal", the contrast between "internal" and "external" makes a point about perspective. It takes a slide to get from there to a literally spatial interpretation of the contrast, under which whatever is outside the subject's body is *eo ipso* "external"; and this spatial reading is what Searle's "brain in a vat" requirement involves. Searle contrives to obscure the slide with appeals to a "biological naturalism", which he expresses in remarks like this (p. 230): "The brain is all we have for the purpose of representing the world to ourselves and everything we can use must be inside the brain." On any normal understanding of the words he uses here, this remark is straightforwardly and obviously false. We have all kinds of things other than the brain for the

21. Searle's "brain in a vat" requirement dictates that one's visual experience when one sees, say, a station wagon is something that could have been exactly what it is even if there had not been a station wagon in one's vicinity; this very experience might have been a hallucination. It is hard to see how this is consistent with his admirable "direct realism". How can a mental state that would have been exactly what it is even if there had been no relevant environment constitute, when there *is* a relevant environment, one's being directly presented (see p. 46) with objects and states of affairs in it? (It is beside the point that hallucinations can be indistinguishable, from a subject's point of view, from "veridical" experiences.) This question suggests a doubt about the idea—which Searle evidently does not see as even needing defence—that brains in vats could have dealings with content, so long as it was not dependent on the existence of "external" particulars.

purpose of representing the world to ourselves: sounds, marks on paper, arrangements of models (as in the law-court goings-on that impressed Wittgenstein), in short all kinds of bits of the world outside our brain. (In fact the brain is one thing that we do *not* exploit for any representative purposes that we have.) It is as if Searle has here forgotten, or perhaps never quite took the measure of, the "direct realism" that he resolutely espouses, in an earlier chapter, about perception. When we control our actions by what we see (for instance homing in on an object), the right thing to say, in the spirit of that "direct realism", is that we have no need to represent the relevant bit of the world to ourselves, as if in order to have something by which to guide what we do; we can guide what we do by the relevant bit of the world itself, directly presented as it is to our view. And our other uses of bits of the world, whether in constructing representations or for any other purpose, can be just as direct.

Searle goes on from the passage I have just quoted with this amazing remark: "Each of our beliefs must be possible for a being who is a brain in a vat because each of us is precisely a brain in a vat; the vat is a skull and the 'messages' coming in are coming in by way of impacts on the nervous system." Surely no sane naturalism can possibly compel us to accept the idea that being in the world, for *us,* is being inside our own heads. The idea has a comical ring; and the indirectness it imposes on how we have to picture our dealings with the world (the talk of "messages" coming in) sits ill with Searle's earlier commendable rejection of intermediaries. There is certainly something attractive about his suggestion that mental states need to be understood in the context of a "biological naturalism"; the point of attributing mental states is to make sense of the actions—which are elements in the lives—of creatures such as ourselves. But the natural biological phenomena that we understand in the light of mental states figure in the lives of creatures that engage, as we do, in direct dealings with the objects in their environment; not in something we can call "life" only derivatively, the functioning of organs of behavioural control that relate only mediately to environmental objects.[22]

22. The need to avoid dualism does not justify Searle's readiness to identify us with our brains and so impose the "brain in a vat" requirement. There is nothing to prevent us from saying that a mental state can be "realized in" a brain state (compare p. 265) even though not any case of the type of brain state in question will "realize" a case of the type of mental state in question (specifically, not cases in which the brain is not normally related to the environment, for instance if it is in a vat).

8. The upshot of these considerations is that it may be possible after all, contrary to what Searle claims, to return an affirmative answer to his question (p. 208), "Are there irreducibly *de re* beliefs?" As Searle rightly says, the terminology here has been used in many different ways. In the interpretation I intend, an irreducibly *de re* propositional attitude (belief figures in Searle's question only as an example) is one whose content would not be thinkable if the relevant object did not exist. The twist is that there can be contents that relate in this way to "external" objects but are fully Intentional, contrary to Searle's claim that Intentional content must be thinkable by a brain in a vat.[23] In making room for this rejection of Searle's "brain in a vat" requirement, I have argued that we can respect Searle's insistence that an Intentionalist account of content must be "internalist". I have tried to drive a wedge between two interpretations that he gives of this, one in terms of subjectivity and one in terms of literal interiority. My claim has been that we should applaud the former, but discard the latter, partly on the basis of Searle's own admirable insistence that our access to environmental objects in perception is direct.

23. The confused appeal to "exported" forms that Searle rejects (pp. 216–7) can simply fall away. For more on this, see §7 of Essay 10 above.

ESSAY 13

Putnam on Mind and Meaning

1. To begin with in "The Meaning of 'Meaning'",[1] and in a number of writings since then, Hilary Putnam has argued trenchantly, and I think convincingly, that in the case of at least certain sorts of words, the environment of those who use them enters into determining their extension. We cannot understand what constitutes the fact that a natural-kind word like "water", as used by ordinarily competent speakers of English, has the extension it does without appealing to the actual scientifically discoverable nature of a stuff that figures in their lives in a way that has an appropriate connection to the correct use of the word, and to facts of a broadly sociological kind about relations within the community of English speakers. Now it seems plausible that the extension of a word as a speaker uses it should be a function of its meaning; otherwise we lose some links that seem to be simply common sense—not part of some possibly contentious philosophical theory—between what words mean on speakers' lips, what those speakers say when they utter those words, and how things have to be for what they say to be true.[2] If we keep those links, Putnam's thesis about extension carries over to meaning:

1. Reprinted in *Mind, Language, and Reality*, pp. 215–71.

2. That the extension of a term is determined by its meaning is one of the two assumptions that Putnam plays off against each other in "The Meaning of 'Meaning.'" (The other is that "knowing the meaning of a term is just a matter of being in a certain psychological state" [*Mind, Language, and Reality*, p. 219].) What Putnam argues in the first instance is that the assumptions cannot be true together, and he registers the possibility that one might respond by discarding the assumption that meaning determines extension (e.g., at p. 266). But his own thinking (much more attractively) leaves that assumption in place. So he directs the argument against the other assumption.

that a speaker means what she does by "water" must be constituted at least in part by her physical and social environment. As Putnam memorably puts it: "Cut the pie any way you like, 'meanings' just ain't in the *head!*"[3]

I have rehearsed this basic thesis of Putnam's in a deliberately unspecific way. The question I want to raise in this essay does not require going into possibly disputable details about how the physical and social environments serve to determine extension, or how the roles of the physical and social environments might be related.[4] Nor do I need to go into the question how far similar theses can be made out to apply beyond the original case of words for natural kinds.[5] I am going to take it for granted that, however such details are to be spelled out, Putnam is right in this basic thesis: at least some meanings are at least in part environmentally constituted. My question is at a more abstract level. I want to ask what significance the basic thesis has for how we ought to conceive the nature of the mind.

2. One might take it to be another simply intuitive idea, not a bit of possibly contentious philosophical theory, that command of a word's meaning is a mental capacity, and exercise of such command is a mental act—an act of the intellect and therefore, surely, of the mind. In that case the moral of Putnam's basic thought for the nature of the mental might be, to put it in his terms, that the mind—the locus of our manipulations of meanings—is not in the head either. Meanings are in the mind, but, as the argument establishes, they cannot be in the head; therefore, we ought to conclude, the mind is not in the head. Rather than arguing, as Putnam does, that the assumption that extension is determined by meaning will not cohere with the assumption that knowledge of meanings is wholly a matter of how things are in a subject's mind, we should insist on making the two assumptions cohere, and conceive the mind in whatever way that requires.

I want to pursue this line, and urge a reading of the claim that the mind is not in the head that ought, I believe, to be congenial to Put-

3. *Mind, Language, and Reality,* p. 227.

4. For some discussion of such details, see the Introduction to Philip Pettit and John McDowell, eds., *Subject, Thought, and Context.*

5. Putnam considers this at *Mind, Language, and Reality,* pp. 242–5.

nam, although as far as I can tell it goes missing from the space of possibilities as he considers things, which is organized by the idea that the two assumptions cannot be made out to be compatible.

3. Putnam's argument works against the theory that he sets up as its target, just because the theory is stipulated to include the claim that the mind is in the head. Another way of putting that claim is to say that states of mind, in some strict or proper sense, are what Putnam calls "psychological states in the narrow sense": that is, states whose attribution to a subject entails nothing about her environment.[6] The idea of "psychological states in the narrow sense" contrasts with the idea of "psychological states in the wide sense": these are attributed by intuitively psychological attributions that involve the attributor in commitments about the attributee's environment, as for instance "*x* is jealous of *y*" commits the attributor to the existence of *y*. The conception of meaning that Putnam attacks embodies the claim that knowledge of a meaning is exhausted by a certain psychological state, with "psychological state" stipulated to mean "psychological state in the narrow sense".

Now if we try to preserve the thought that knowledge of a meaning is a psychological state, consistently with Putnam's basic thesis that meanings are environmentally constituted, we have to suppose that knowledge of a meaning (at least of the kind that Putnam's thesis applies to) is a "psychological state in the wide sense". And if we try to make sense of that while maintaining the idea that the mental in a strict or proper sense is characterized by "narrow" psychological attributions, we have to suppose that knowledge of a meaning (of the relevant kind), *qua* mental, is, in itself, a "narrow" psychological state, which, however, can be characterized *as* knowledge of that meaning only by dint of taking into account the subject's placement in a physical and social environment. On this picture, knowledge of a meaning is, in itself, in the head; the moral of Putnam's basic thought is that we need to be looking at relations between what is in the head and what is not, if it is to be available to us that *knowledge*

6. *Mind, Language, and Reality,* p. 220. I have slightly altered Putnam's gloss on "the narrow sense", in line with some remarks of Jerry A. Fodor in "Methodological Solipsism Considered as a Research Strategy in Cognitive Psychology". I think the alteration captures what Putnam intended.

of a meaning (at least if it is a meaning of the relevant kind) is what some state, in itself in the head, is.

According to this picture, then, there is a sense in which the mind is in the head: that is where the relevant states and occurrences are. But this picture does yield a sense in which we might say that the mind is (at least partly) not in the head: the characterizations that display the relevant states and occurrences as ("wide") content-involving states and occurrences are characterizations in terms of meanings of sorts to which Putnam's argument applies, and hence characterizations that get a grip on the states and occurrences only on the basis of relations between the subject and the environment. At least some distinctively mental truths cannot come into view except in an inquiry that takes account of how the mind in question is related to its environment.

The conclusion of this line of thought is that the concept of command of a meaning (at least of the kind that Putnam's argument applies to) is constitutively "duplex", as Colin McGinn puts it: it is the concept of something that is, in itself, in the head, but conceived in terms of its relations to what is outside the head. And this line of thought obviously extends from knowledge of the meaning of "water" (and whatever other meanings Putnam's argument, or something with a similar effect, applies to) to, say, beliefs or occurrent thoughts about water (and similarly for whatever other meanings are relevant). It is widely supposed that Putnam's considerations compel a "duplex" conception of at least large tracts of our thought and talk about the mental. The idea is that part of the complete truth about the mind is the truth about something wholly in the head; another part of the complete truth about the mind is the truth about how the subject matter of the first part is related to things outside the head.[7]

4. This reading of the idea that the mind is not in the head is not what I meant when I suggested that the idea ought to be congenial to Putnam.

7. See McGinn's "The Structure of Content". Other considerations are thought to conspire with Putnam's to necessitate this picture, but in this essay I am restricting myself to the significance of Putnam's basic thesis.

This reading preserves a role for what is in the head, in the constitution of knowledge of meanings, or more generally in the constitution of psychological states and occurrences such as beliefs or thoughts about water, to which Putnam's claim of environmental determination clearly extends. What is the attraction of this? I think the answer is that, on this "duplex" conception, at least one component of the constitutive truth about the psychological in the "wide" sense looks like an unquestionably suitable topic for a straightforwardly natural science, a science that would investigate how states and occurrences in the head are responsive to impacts from the environment, interact with one another, and figure in the generation of behavior. In *Representation and Reality* and elsewhere, Putnam argues that the role played by interpretation, in a proper account of the import of psychological characterizations in terms of ("wide") content, ensures that psychology *in general* cannot be within the scope of natural science. But, however convinced we might be by such arguments, there would still be some comfort for a scientistic orientation to the mental in the idea that, all the same, science can in principle be done, and indeed is already being done, about the intrinsic natures of the states and occurrences—in themselves in the head—that those "wide" characterizations get a grip on, in ways that, according to such arguments, are not amenable to scientific treatment.

On this account, what makes the "duplex" reading of the thesis that the mind is not in the head attractive is that, by leaving part of the truth about the mind wholly in the head, it offers comfort to a possibly residual scientism about how our understanding of the mental works.[8] But at least since his conversion from scientific realism, Putnam's explicit attitude towards scientism has been one of staunch opposition. When I suggested that the thesis could be read in a way that ought to be congenial to Putnam, I had in mind a reading that would not make even this residual concession to scientism. I had in mind a reading that would place our talk about knowledge of mean-

8. I say "possibly residual" because of the attraction that this conception has for someone of a fundamentally scientistic cast of mind who accepts, perhaps on the basis of an argument like Putnam's about interpretation, that ("wide") content is not available to a scientific psychology. Of course there are people who have a less defensive scientism than that, because they are not persuaded by such arguments, or ignore them.

ings, thoughts about water, and so forth entirely out of the reach of a scientistic conception of the role played by our mental lives in our understanding of ourselves and others.

5. It will be helpful to distinguish a second possible reading of the thesis that the mind is not in the head from the one I mean.

This reading is like the one I mean in that it focuses on the literal meaning of "in the head". We might begin on explaining the point of denying that the mind is in the head by saying that the mind is not spatially located at all, except perhaps unspecifically, where its owner is. The mind is not somewhere in particular in the literal, spatial, interior of its owner; it is not to be equated with a materially constituted and space-occupying organ, such as the brain.

But on the conception I am considering now, the mind is still conceived as an organ: it is just that it is not the brain but an immaterial organ. (A well-placed embarrassment might induce one to add "so to speak".) What I mean by saying that the mind is conceived as an organ is that states of affairs and occurrences in a mind are, on this view no less than on the view that the mind is literally in the head, taken to have an intrinsic nature that is independent of how the mind's possessor is placed in the environment. It is just that this intrinsic nature is not conceived as capturable in the terms of any science that deals with matter, for instance neurophysiological terms.

This reading of the thesis that the mind is not in the head clearly cannot serve my purpose, because it is obvious that this conception of the mind, as an immaterial organ of psychological activity, does not open up a possibility of evading Putnam's argument, so that we could after all locate knowledge of meanings wholly in the mind. Characterizations of the mind, as it is in itself, are no less "narrow" on this picture than they are if conceived as characterizations of what is literally in the head. And Putnam's point is obviously not just that what is literally in the head cannot amount to knowledge of meanings, to the extent to which knowledge of meanings is environmentally constituted. *Nothing* "narrow", whether material or (supposing we believed in such things) immaterial, can amount to something that is environmentally constituted. We can put the point by saying that the phrase "in the head", in Putnam's formulation of his basic thesis, is already not restricted to a literal, spatial reading. When Putnam says that meanings are not in the head, that is a vivid way of saying that no "narrow" psychological attribution can amount to knowledge of a meaning of the relevant sort, whether it is a material or an immaterial organ of thought in virtue of whose internal arrangements such attributions are conceived as true.

6. I can now sketch the interpretation I mean for the thesis that the mind is not in the head. On this interpretation, the point of the thesis is not just to reject a more specific spatial location for someone's mind than that it is where its possessor is. It is to reject the whole idea that the mind can appropriately be conceived as an organ: if not a materially constituted organ, then an immaterially constituted organ. As I said, the cash value of this talk of organs is the idea that states and occurrences "in" the mind have an intrinsic nature that is independent of how the mind's possessor is placed in the environment. So the point of the different interpretation is to reject that idea altogether. Talk of minds is talk of subjects of mental life, in so far as they are subjects of mental life; and, on the interpretation I mean, it is only a prejudice, which we should discard, that mental life must be conceived as taking place in an organ, so that its states and occurrences are intrinsically independent of relations to what is outside the organism.

Of course there is an organ, the brain, whose proper functioning is necessary to mental life. But that is not to say that the proper functioning of that organ is what mental life, in itself, is. And if we deny that, we need not be suggesting instead that mental life is, in itself, the functioning of a mysteriously immaterial para-organ (an organ "so to speak"). Mental life is an aspect of *our* lives, and the idea that it takes place in the mind can, and should, be detached from the idea that there is a part of us, whether material or (supposing this made sense) immaterial, in which it takes place. Where mental life takes place need not be pinpointed any more precisely than by saying that it takes place where our lives take place. And then its states and occurrences can be no less intrinsically related to our environment than our lives are.

7. Putnam himself expresses scepticism about whether there is any point in reconstructing the intuitive or pre-theoretical conception of the mental, which counts "wide" states like jealousy as psychological, in the way that is prescribed by "methodological solipsism": that

is, the thesis that psychological states in a strict and proper sense are "narrow".[9] That scepticism seems to recommend pushing his reflections about terms like "water" in the direction that I am suggesting. What is to be learned from those reflections is not, as Putnam himself argues, that it cannot be true both that "knowing the meaning of a term is just a matter of being in a certain psychological state" and that "the meaning of a term determines its extension"; so that if we retain the second of these assumptions, we must renounce the first. This presupposes that anyone who embraces the first assumption must be restricting psychological states to "narrow" states. Rather, the moral of Putnam's considerations is that the idea of a psychological state, as it figures in the first assumption, cannot be the idea of a "narrow" state. That is: we should not leave in place an idea of the mind that is shaped by the tenets of "methodological solipsism", and conclude that meanings are not in the mind, since they are not in the head. Rather, we should read the two assumptions in such a way that they *can* be true together, and exploit such a reading to force us into explicit consideration of a different conception of the mind.

At one point in "The Meaning of 'Meaning'", Putnam concedes that "it may be trivially true that, say, *knowing the meaning of the word 'water'* is a 'psychological state'".[10] The idea that this concession is trivial points to an accommodation of the basic thesis on the lines of the "duplex" conception of the mental. The concession is trivial, on this account, because it does not undermine the view that the two assumptions cannot be true together; given that psychological states in the strict and proper sense are "narrow", knowing a meaning (of the appropriate sort) would not be "*just* a matter of being in a certain psychological state", any more than, on that view, any "wide" psychological state would be. What Putnam never seems to consider is the possibility of a position that holds that command of a meaning is wholly a matter of how it is with someone's mind (the first assumption), and combines that with the determination of extension by meaning so as to force a radically non-solipsistic conception of the mind to come to explicit expression. Instead he assumes that anyone who wants to conceive knowledge of a meaning as wholly a matter of how it is with someone's mind must be already

9. *Mind, Language, and Reality*, pp. 220–1.
10. *Mind, Language, and Reality*, p. 220.

committed to a theoretical conception of the mind—a conception of the mind as in the head—which, in conjunction with Putnam's reflections about meaning, guarantees that the wish cannot be fulfilled.[11]

There may be some temptation to deny that the idea that the mind is in the head is a bit of theory, on the ground of evidently untheoretical usages like "I did the calculation in my head, not on paper". But that idiom does not mesh with the sense that "in the head" bears in Putnam's argument. One might equally take in one's stride, say, "It came into my head that I wanted a drink of water"; here the meaning of "water" is "in the head" in the sense of the idiom, and the possibility of talking like this obviously poses no threat to what Putnam means by saying that meanings are not in the head.[12]

The radically non-solipsistic conception of the mental that I am urging would dictate a way of talking about Twin-Earth cases that contrasts with Putnam's. In one of Putnam's cases, the correct extensions of "beech" and "elm" are reversed on Twin Earth, where Putnam has a *Doppelgänger* who is as unable to tell the two kinds of tree apart as Putnam blushingly confesses he is. The words are nevertheless secured their different extensions, on the lips of Putnam and his *Doppelgänger*, by the fact that each defers to a different set of experts.[13] Putnam says, about himself and his *Doppelgänger* when each is in a psychological state that he would express using one of those terms: "It is absurd to think *his* psychological state is one bit different from mine." On the conception I am urging, this is not absurd at all. Putnam's psychological state involves his mind's being directed towards, say, beeches (if beeches constitute the extension of the word that he is disposed to use in order to give expression to his psychological state); his *Doppelgänger*'s psychological state involves his mind's being directed towards elms. The psychological state of each as it were expands in accordance with the determination of the extensions of their terms, in a way that is compelled if we are to maintain both of the two assumptions.

11. Given a Principle of Charity, this raises a question (which is made all the more pressing by Putnam's own lack of sympathy with "methodological solipsism") whether Putnam may have misinterpreted at least some of the philosophers against whom he directs his basic thesis. I am particularly doubtful about the case of Frege. But I do not want to go into questions about Putnam's reading of his targets here.

12. On the ordinary idiomatic use of "in the head", compare Wittgenstein, *Philosophical Investigations* §427.

13. *Mind, Language, and Reality*, pp. 226–7.

The possibility of talking like this would be merely trivial, in a sense like the one involved in Putnam's concession that we can count knowing a meaning as a psychological state, if the divergent psychological attributions ("thinking of elms" and "thinking of beeches") had to be seen as applying in virtue of some shared underlying psychological state, with the divergence resulting from different ways in which that shared underlying state is embedded in its environment. That is how the "duplex" conception would see things; on this view, Putnam and his *Doppelgänger* do not differ in fundamental psychological properties. But we need not see things this way. It is certainly true that Putnam and his *Doppelgänger,* in the case described, have something psychological in common. (We can make this vivid by noting that if Putnam were transported to Twin Earth without knowing it, he would not be able to tell the difference.) But it is perfectly possible to insist that the psychological common property holds of each in virtue of his "wide" psychological state, rather than that the "wide" state is constituted by the common property, together with facts about how each is embedded in his environment. The common property need not be fundamental.

Compare the psychological feature that is unsurprisingly shared between someone who sees that such-and-such is the case and someone to whom it merely looks as if such-and-such is the case. (Again, if one were switched without knowing it between possible worlds that differ in that way, one would not be able to tell the difference.) It is not compulsory to conceive seeing that such-and-such is the case as constituted by this common feature together with favourable facts about embedding in the environment. We can understand things the other way round: the common feature—its being to all intents as if one sees that such-and-such is the case—intelligibly supervenes on each of the divergent "wide" states. And it is better to understand things this way round. It is very common for philosophers to suppose that Twin-Earth comparisons compel the idea that "wide" attributions bear on states that are in themselves "narrow", with the "wide" attributions coming out differently by virtue of the different ways in which those supposedly fundamental psychological states are embedded in extra-psychological reality. But this idea is closely parallel to the Argument from Illusion, and that by itself should be enough to make us suspicious of it.[14]

14. There is some discussion of issues in this vicinity in Essay 11 above.

8. Putnam does not seem to consider the possibility that his reflections about meaning might be brought to bear against the idea that the mind is the organ of psychological activity. In fact much of his own thinking seems to presuppose just such a conception of the mind.

In *Representation and Reality* (p. 7), he describes Jerry Fodor's "mentalism" as "just the latest form taken by a more general tendency in the history of thought, the tendency to think of concepts as scientifically describable ('psychologically real') entities in the mind or brain". There is an equivalence implied here between "psychologically real" and "scientifically describable", which cries out to be questioned: it looks like simply an expression of scientism about what it might be for something to be psychologically real. (We do not need to surrender the term "psychological" to *scientific* psychology.) But as far as I can see Putnam leaves the equivalence unchallenged, even though a great deal of his point in that book is to attack the effects of scientism on how philosophers conceive the mental. The term "mentalism" has a perfectly good interpretation as a label for the view that the mental is a genuine range of reality. (We do not need to accept that the nature of reality is *scientifically* determined.) But Putnam, without demur, lets "mentalism" be commandeered for the view that the topic of mental discourse can appropriately be specified as "the mind/brain". Talk of the mind/brain embodies the assumption that the mind is appropriately conceived as an organ, together, of course, with the idea—which is in itself perfectly sensible—that *if* the mind is an organ, the brain is the only organ it can sensibly be supposed to be. The assumption that the mind is an organ is one that Putnam does not challenge.[15]

An assumption to the same effect seems to underlie Putnam's argument, in *Reason, Truth, and History,* that one cannot suppose that mental states or occurrences are intrinsically referential—intrinsically directed at the world—without falling into a magical conception of reference. Putnam's governing assumption here is that a mental state or occurrence that is representational, say an occurrence in which one is struck by the thought that one hears the sound of water dripping,

15. It is only in connection with mentalism on this interpretation that Putnam considers Gareth Evans's views in *The Varieties of Reference:* see *Reality and Representation,* p. 129, n. 4. Evans's thinking actually opens up the possibility of a satisfactory understanding of thought (a mental phenomenon, surely) and meaning as environmentally constituted: an understanding that ought to be welcome to Putnam. But Putnam restricts himself to finding it puzzling how Evans could conceive his thinking as a kind of mentalism, since Evans obviously does not equate thoughts with "representations *inside* the mind/brain".

must in itself consist in the presence in the mind of an item with an intrinsic nature characterizable independently of considering what it represents. (Such a state of affairs would be what an internal arrangement in an organ of thought would have to amount to.) It clearly follows, from such a conception of that which is strictly speaking present in the mind, that such items cannot be intrinsically endowed with referential properties; to suppose that they might be would be to appeal to magic, just as Putnam argues. What never comes into view is this possibility: that being, say, struck by a thought is not, in itself, the presence in the mind of an item with a non-representational intrinsic nature. The argument is controlled by the assumption that occurrences in the mind are, in themselves, "narrow".

Am I suggesting that being struck by a thought might not involve mental representation? It seems truistic that a thought that such-and-such is the case is a representation that such-and-such is the case. But this is not the notion of mental representation as it figures in Putnam's argument.

In Putnam's argument, mental representations are representations in the sense in which, say, drawings or sentences are representations. A representation is an item whose intrinsic nature is characterizable independently of its representational properties: a symbol. The nerve of Putnam's argument is that symbols are not intrinsically endowed with their representational properties, and that claim seems beyond question. But from the fact that thinking, say, that one hears the sound of water dripping is *representing* that one hears the sound of water dripping, it does not follow that thinking that one hears the sound of water dripping must in itself consist in the presence in the mind of a symbol: something into which the significance that one hears the sound of water dripping can be read, as it can be read into the sign-design "I hear the sound of water dripping", although in both cases the symbol's bearing that significance is extraneous to its intrinsic nature. Putnam's solid point cannot dislodge the possibility that thinking that one hears the sound of water dripping is a mental representation, in the sense of a mental *representing,* that intrinsically represents what it represents.

What this means is that being struck by that thought, say, would not be the mental occurrence that it is if it were not *that* that one found oneself thinking. What the mental occurrence is in itself already involves that referential directedness at the world. The firm point in Putnam's argument is that this could not be so, except by magic, if the intrinsic nature of the mental occurrence were constituted by the presence in the mind of a representation, in Putnam's sense. So the possibility that goes missing in Putnam's argument could be described as the possibility of mental representing without representations.

Putnam would dispute something I have been suggesting, that it is just an assumption on his part that the contents of the mind when we think are representations in his sense. His claim is that this thesis is established by introspection. "Stop the stream of thought when or where we will, what we catch are words, images, sensations, feelings."[16] (This is meant to be a list of kinds of items that are not intrinsically representational.) But to me it seems wildly inaccurate to suggest that when I am struck by the thought that I hear the sound of water dripping, the fact that my thought is, say, about *water* is not part of what I find in my stream of consciousness, but has to be read into what I find there. Putnam's phenomenological claim is not an unprejudiced introspective report. It is theory-driven; he tells us not what he finds in his stream of consciousness but what *must* be there, given the pre-conceived theory that the contents of representing consciousness are representations in his sense. I think an unprejudiced phenomenology would find it more accurate to say that the contents of consciousness, when we have occurrent thoughts, are thoughts themselves, on something like Frege's usage for "thought" (or "*Gedanke*"): senses potentially expressed by assertoric sentences, not vehicles for such senses. Similarly with imagery: if I close my eyes and visualize, say, my wife's face, it seems wildly wrong to suggest that the fact that what I am visualizing is my wife's face—a fact that relates my mental state to the extra-psychological environment—is extraneous to the contents of my consciousness, extraneous to what I find when I "stop the stream of thought". So far from supporting the apparatus of his argument, Putnam's phenomenological claim here is unconvincing enough to give us reason to raise questions about the theory that underlies the argument.[17]

16. *Reason, Truth, and History*, p. 17; see also p. 27 for a parallel appeal to introspective evidence.

17. For a "cry of disbelief" (p. 69) against similar phenomenological falsifications, forced on philosophers by the theory that "an occurrent conscious thought bears its 'intention' or content in the same way as a bit of language bears its significance" (p. 86), see M. R. Ayers, "Some Thoughts". One of Ayers's targets is Wittgenstein; I suggest a rather different reading of Wittgenstein (although I would not dispute that there are passages that fit Ayers's reading) in "Intentionality and Interiority in Wittgenstein".

9. Putnam has often expressed suspicion of the idea that there is good philosophy to be done by grappling with questions like "How does language hook on to the world?"[18] It ought to be similar with questions like "How does thinking hook on to the world?" Such a question looks like a pressing one if we saddle ourselves with a conception of what thinking is, considered in itself, that deprives thinking of its characteristic bearing on the world—its being about this or that object in the world, and its being to the effect that this or that state of affairs obtains in the world. If we start from a conception of thinking as in itself without referential bearing on the world, we shall seem to be confronted with a genuine and urgent task, that of reinstating into our picture the way thinking is directed at the world. But if we do not accept the assumption that what thinking is, considered in itself, is a mental manipulation of representations in Putnam's sense, no such task confronts us. The need to construct a theoretical "hook" to link thinking to the world does not arise, because if it is thinking that we have in view at all—say being struck by the thought that one hears the sound of water dripping—then what we have in view is *already* hooked on to the world; it is already in view as possessing referential directedness at reality.[19]

It would be a mistake to suppose that what I am doing here is what Putnam describes as "just postulating mysterious powers of mind"; as Putnam says, surely rightly, that "solves nothing".[20] The proper target of that accusation is a way of thinking in which we try to combine conceiving the mind as an organ of thought, so that what an episode of thinking is in itself is a mental manipulation of a representation, with supposing that an episode of thinking has its determinate referential bearing on the world intrinsically. Putnam's cogent point is that this combination pushes us into a magical picture of the reference of the supposed mental symbols, and hence into a magical

18. His suspicions are expressed in several of the essays in his *Realism with a Human Face*.

19. And the world that it is already hooked on to is not The World as contemplated by the metaphysical realism that Putnam has attacked. My thought that I hear the sound of water dripping has its point of contact with reality in the fact that I hear the sound of water dripping, or perhaps in the fact that I do not hear the sound of water dripping. I use my conceptual capacities (I just did) in pinpointing which possible facts these are; the world (which is all the facts, as Wittgenstein said in the *Tractatus*) is not here pictured as beyond the reach of concepts.

20. *Reason, Truth, and History*, p. 2.

picture of the powers of the mind. But the conception I am urging needs no appeal to a magical theory of reference, precisely because it rejects the supposed mental symbols. My aim is not to postulate mysterious powers of mind; rather, my aim is to restore us to a conception of thinking as the exercise of powers possessed, not mysteriously by some part of a thinking being, a part whose internal arrangements are characterizable independently of how the thinking being is placed in its environment, but unmysteriously by a thinking being itself, an animal that lives its life in cognitive and practical relations to the world. "Just postulating mysterious powers of mind" would be an appropriate description for a misguided attempt to respond to a supposed problem that I aim to join Putnam in rejecting.

It would equally be a mistake to suppose that what I have said about the phenomenology of thinking is merely a version of what Putnam calls "the attempt to understand thought by what is called 'phenomenological' investigation".[21] Putnam's objection to this is that any such attempt must miss the point that understanding, or more generally the possession of a concept, is an ability rather than an occurrence. "The attempt to understand thought" is the attempt to respond to a philosophical puzzlement about how thought "hooks on to the world". But my aim is to bring out a way of conceiving thought in which there is no need to try to embark on such a project at all.

It is true that understanding, or more generally the possession of a concept, is an ability rather than an occurrence. But it does not follow that there cannot be occurrences that are intrinsically directed at reality in the way that I have suggested is characteristic of occurrent thought. If the concept of water is an ability that is exercised in thinking about water, we can conceive its exercises as, precisely, occurrences that are intrinsically episodes of thinking about water.[22]

21. *Reason, Truth, and History*, p. 20.

22. These remarks are directed against the close of chap. 1 of *Reason, Truth, and History*, where Putnam suggests that the perfectly correct point that concepts are not mental occurrences, combined with the phenomenological claim about which I have already expressed doubts, demolishes the very idea that there can be mental episodes with an intrinsic referential bearing on the world. By claiming that concepts are "signs used in a certain way" (p. 18), Putnam makes it look as if exercises of concepts would have to be occurrences (tokenings) of signs. He thereby forces on us a "narrow" conception of what exercises of concepts must be in themselves. This obliterates a perfectly workable conception according to which exercises of concepts are, for instance, acts of judgement, intrinsically possessed of referential bearing on the world.

10. What is the attraction for Putnam of the idea that "the stream of thought" is populated by representations in his sense, rather than representings? Any answer must be speculative; an answer that seems to me to have some plausibility is that Putnam is himself swayed by the residual influence of a scientism like the one I mentioned in connection with the "duplex" conception of "wide" psychological attributions. Without the idea of intrinsic structurings in some inner medium, it is hard to see how we could picture a mapping of our psychological talk into a subject matter susceptible of scientific treatment. In particular, mental representings occupy a position in the causal order; and if we want to be able to integrate that fact into a natural-scientific conception of the causal order, it is very tempting to suppose that representings must owe their causal character to the causal character of structures in a medium that is ultimately susceptible of physical description.[23] Putnam's phenomenological claim reflects a plausible conception of the most that could be available to introspection, if we understand introspection as a capacity to scan or monitor such inner structures.[24]

What goes missing here is the thought that mentalistic talk can be intellectually respectable without any such mapping being needed. I do not suggest that this is an easy thought for us to get our minds around, subject as we are to intelligible pressures to scientize our conception of the causal order. But we ought to ensure that we are fully conscious of the effects of such pressures on our thinking, and we ought to be alive to the possibility that it is not compulsory to succumb to them.

The suggestion that Putnam's thinking is partly shaped by a residual scientism will surely provoke from some people the response "So what? What's so bad about scientism?" In another context, I should feel obliged to say something in answer to that. Here, though, I shall not even begin to do so, since I am confident that that response will not be Putnam's own.

Putnam ends "The Meaning of 'Meaning'" with this remark: "Traditional philosophy of language, like much traditional philosophy, leaves out other people and the world; a better philosophy and

23. See John Haugeland's suggestive discussion of "the paradox of mechanical reason", in *Artifical Intelligence: The Very Idea,* pp. 36–41.

24. For an unusually explicit expression of such a view of introspection, see McGinn, "The Structure of Content", pp. 253–4.

a better science of language must encompass both."[25] I am not sure how "traditional" the approach to language that Putnam attacks really is, but I do not want to make anything of that here. My point in this essay is that the "isolationist" conception of language that Putnam objects to is all of a piece with a similarly "isolationist" conception of the mind—at least of the mind as it is in itself. And Putnam's attack on the "isolationist" conception of language leaves the counterpart conception of the mind unquestioned. Taking on the whole package would have yielded a deeper understanding of what underlies the "isolationist" conception of language. I think this broader project would have been better suited than Putnam's partial move is to his admirable aim of showing us what "a better philosophy" would be like. A general attack on "isolationism" promises a satisfyingly cohesive and radical reorientation, very much in the spirit of Putnam's own best thinking, of philosophy's approach to the relations between the individual subject and the world.

25. *Mind, Language, and Reality*, p. 271.

PART III

REALISM AND ANTI-REALISM

ESSAY 14

On "The Reality of the Past"[1]

1. Philosophers have found attractions in the idea that a theory of meaning for a language might include a component capable of specifying, for any indicative sentence of the language, a condition under which it is true.[2] But suppose we are dealing with a language that, like our own, permits formation of sentences with the following property: we have no method that we can bank on to equip us, within a finite time, with knowledge that a given sentence is true, or, failing that, with knowledge that it is not. Thus inability, however protracted, to detect that a sentence is true need not put us in a position to rule out the possibility that it is. It seems, then, that if we credit ourselves with a conception of conditions under which such sentences are true, we have to picture them as conditions that may obtain beyond all possibility of bringing them to our awareness. Now the idea that truth-conditions may thus transcend possible verification is characteristic of a realism that Michael Dummett has urged us to find problematic.[3]

1. The topic of this essay is not the reality of the past, but rather realism and anti-realism as discussed by Michael Dummett in his paper "The Reality of the Past". I was helped, in writing this, by Gareth Evans, Graeme Forbes, Colin McGinn, and Christopher Peacocke. My view of Wittgenstein is close to that independently adopted by Samuel Guttenplan in his *Meaning and Truth*.

2. Donald Davidson has recommended the idea in a series of papers beginning with "Truth and Meaning". For a sketch of the justification as I see it, see §1 of Essay 1 above. Indexicality dictates a modification (not sentences *tout court*, but sentences as uttered on occasions); I have silently introduced this at various subsequent points.

3. As well as "The Reality of the Past", see "Truth"; *Frege: Philosophy of Language;* and "What Is a Theory of Meaning? (II)".

A theory of meaning for a language should be a theoretical representation of the practical capacity that constitutes understanding it.[4] The capacity would be perspicuously described by a theory that related the language, in detail, to the world, in such a way that someone who explicitly knew the theory (and knew enough about the world) would be able to use the language as if he had an ordinary, unreflective competence in it. Alternatively, we might conceive ordinary, unreflective competence as actually consisting in implicit knowledge of such a theory.[5] Now suppose the realistic notion of truth-conditions is employed in a proffered theory, implicit knowledge of which is thus to be thought of as constituting competence in a language. According to the anti-realist position that Dummett describes, it is impossible to make sense of a speaker's possessing that state of knowledge. All that can be imparted, by the training that results in competence with a language, is an ability to suit one's linguistic behaviour to circumstances that impinge on one's consciousness. How can the capacity so acquired involve the idea of states of affairs that may obtain even though they defeat all attempts to bring them to our awareness? How could the training have given one any conception of what it would be for such a state of affairs to obtain?[6]

Some sentences with the problematic property—in particular, sentences in the past tense—are, however, quite intelligible. So the line of argument I have just sketched motivates the aim of constructing theories of meaning in a contrasting, anti-realist style: theories that use—in their expression of the content of the implicit knowledge in which (if we formulate their claims in that way) competence with such sentences is conceived as consisting—not the notion of possibly undetectable conditions under which the sentences are true, but rather the notion of conditions guaranteed detectable when they obtain, to which the language-learner has been trained to respond as making it correct to assert the sentences.

4. See, e.g., Dummett, *Frege: Philosophy of Language,* p. 92.

5. There are dangers here; see §9 below.

6. Couching the anti-realist argument, as I have done here, in terms of theses about the learning of language makes it seem vulnerable, in ways in which it really should not be, to accusations of reliance on armchair learning theory; see Crispin Wright, "Truth Conditions and Criteria". The acquisition version of the argument is, however, the one most prominent in "The Reality of the Past", and it provides a natural context for my discussion of the appeal to truth-value links (§§2 and 4). See, further, §§7 and 8 below.

2. At the very least, then, anti-realism poses a challenge to a realist: to explain how someone can acquire a realistic conception of truth-conditions from training that relates the correct use of sentences only to accessible states of affairs.

Now, according to Dummett, a realist about the past might claim to meet the challenge by an appeal to the "truth-value link": the principle, that is, that a suitably dated past-tensed sentence, uttered, say, now, is true just in case a suitably related present-tensed sentence, uttered at the appropriate past time, would then have been true.[7]

How is the truth-value link supposed to help? In the case of *present*-tensed sentences—so long as we waive anti-realist difficulties other than those that stem from the past's lack of guaranteed accessibility—a description of competence in terms of truth-conditions can be seen, by an anti-realist, as a harmless variant of his style of theory. For whether those truth-conditions obtain is always, in principle, ascertainable—if we waive those other difficulties—by the person whose competence is being described, so that no anti-realist query arises here about how the person can have a conception of what it is for such a condition to obtain. The realist's idea, now, would be that by way of the truth-value link one can transfer to applicability to *past*-tensed utterances the conception whose innocence is thus established for the case of the present tense. Equipped with a conception of what it is for, say, a sentence reporting rain to be true when the rain is falling now, the language-learner uses the truth-value link to project a conception of that very same circumstance—the falling of rain—into the past. What is required is a conception of the sort of state of affairs that would have made an utterance of "It's raining now" true at some past time; and that is the very sort of state of affairs a conception of which we have already found it harmless to ascribe to our subject.

An anti-realist insists that linguistic competence cannot involve a conception of sorts of circumstance other than those that a language-learner had available to his consciousness in learning the language. Dummett's realist is attempting, with the truth-value-link manoeuvre, to respect that principle. His idea is that a circumstance of the relevant sort (say, an instance of the falling of rain) can indeed have been available to the language-learner's consciousness—namely, on occasions when the appropriate *present*-tensed sentence was cor-

7. Dummett, "The Reality of the Past", pp. 362–3, 364.

rectly assertible; and that the truth-value link suffices to entitle a theorist, on the basis of that fact, to represent competence with *past*-tensed sentences as implicit knowledge whose content involves precisely those sorts of circumstance (rainfall or whatever) that would figure in a truth-conditional description of competence with the related present-tensed sentences—the difference being only that in the projected employment they are tagged as having obtained in the past. On these grounds, he disavows an obligation to restrict the materials of his description of competence to circumstances accessible to the consciousness of a competent speaker at the times when the relevant past-tensed sentences are *themselves* correctly assertible. He claims to bypass those circumstances, crediting the speaker with a conception that reaches out beyond them to the past occurrences and states of affairs themselves. We might imagine him expressing his view of the efficacy of the truth-value link like this: "If I suppose that it rained yesterday, then I am simply supposing that there obtained yesterday just the same condition as I have so often observed." Or perhaps, to bring out how he purports to have made superfluous any consideration of present warrants for past-tensed assertions: "Rain is rain—whether it fell yesterday or is falling now; and however I come to know whether it fell yesterday or not."[8]

These echoes emphasize how the debate between realist and anti-realist about the past, as Dummett presents it, runs parallel, in certain structural respects, with a familiar philosophical dialectic about sentience in others. If we think of ourselves as possessing a conception of truth-conditions for sentences suitable for ascribing, say, sensations to others, we have to picture those conditions as not necessarily accessible to our knowledge-acquiring powers, since the truth-value of an utterance of such a sentence need not be ascertainable either way (compare §1). An anti-realist response to that realism would be a form of behaviourism: competence with those sentences relates their correct use only to circumstances guaranteed accessible if they obtain, under which the language-learner has been taught that assertive utterances of the sentences are in order.[9] As be-

8. Compare Wittgenstein, *Philosophical Investigations* §§350, 351.

9. "A form of behaviourism": presumably the relevant accessible circumstances will be broadly behavioural, and "behaviourism" seems an appropriate name for a view that restricts the circumstances mentioned in an account of competence with the utterances in question to such circumstances. But I intend no suggestion that anti-realism must be

fore, this puts the onus on a realist to show how the relevant competence can be anything else. And here too, a certain sort of realist will be inclined to appeal to a truth-value link: a statement ascribing, say, pain to another person is true just in case a self-ascription of pain by him would be true. The point of this is, again, to bypass those behavioural warrants for other-ascriptions of pain that the anti-realist insists are all that can figure in a description of competence with the relevant forms of words, while purporting to respect the anti-realist's principle that linguistic competence can involve a conception only of sorts of circumstance that were available to the language-learner's consciousness in his learning of the language. The relevant sort of circumstance is that of a person's being in pain. According to this realist, circumstances of that sort can indeed have been present to the language-learner's consciousness—namely, on occasions when the person in question was himself. (We know what pain is from our own case.) The truth-value link enables the language-learner to project a conception of that same sort of circumstance—a person's being in pain—past the detectable behavioural conditions at which the anti-realist sticks, and into the inner lives of others. An other-ascription of pain is true—if it is true—in virtue of an instance of the very sort of circumstance of which the language-learner has acquired a conception, harmlessly from the standpoint of anti-realism, by having instances of it present to his awareness in his own case.

3. A realist who thinks he needs to appeal to a truth-value link, in order to meet the anti-realist challenge, shows—unless he is confused—that he pictures the truth-conditions of the problematic sorts of sentence not merely as not being always accessible but rather as being always inaccessible.

The anti-realist principle that he is attempting to respect (see §2) is that a description of linguistic competence may credit its possessor with a conception only of sorts of circumstance that he has had available to his consciousness during his training in the use of the language. He tries to respect it by pointing to the availability of circumstances that according to him belong to the required sorts, only on occasions when they constitute the truth-conditions of *present-*

crudely reductionist; see Dummett, "The Reality of the Past", pp. 359–62, and compare some remarks in §10 below.

tensed utterances, or *self*-ascriptions of sensation. If he thought circumstances of the required sorts were sometimes available to consciousness on occasions when they constitute the truth-conditions of *past*-tensed utterances, or *other*-ascriptions of sensation, he could claim that the allegedly problematic conception was acquired, directly, on those occasions. There would be no need for appeal to a truth-value link, since there would be no need to regard the allegedly problematic conception as acquired by projection from the unproblematic cases of the present, or oneself. This realist, then, turns down a chance to claim that some occasions when circumstances justify assertive utterances of sentences of the problematic kinds are occasions when their *truth*-conditions—which may on other occasions keep hidden from us—make themselves manifest. By appealing, instead, to truth-value links, he indicates that he agrees, rather, with the anti-realist to this extent: he regards the circumstances that actually impinge on the consciousness of a speaker, even on the prime occasions for training in the assertoric use of the sentences, as not themselves constituting cases of the obtaining of truth-conditions, realistically construed—that is, construed as conditions of sorts that may, on other occasions, obtain undetectably. The assertion-warranting circumstances that do manifest themselves, however conclusive the evidential relation between them and the truth-conditions, are distinct from the truth-conditions; and the obtaining of the truth-conditions, since he thinks of it as distinct from what is available to consciousness even when one has the best possible justification for asserting the sentences, is pictured by him as something that, in itself, transcends what is accessible to awareness.

All this fits comfortably into place in that familiar complex of realistic ideas about sentience in others (§2). Another person's pain, in that sort of view, is something essentially concealed from us, behind a screen of facial expression and behaviour. In the case of the past, the analogous thought would be that a past occurrence is dead and gone, necessarily lost to our view.[10]

10. Such realism can perhaps purport to make room for the concession that there is sometimes conclusive justification for other-ascriptions of sensation, or for past-tensed assertions. (This would be the position of the conciliatory realist envisaged at p. 365 of Dummett, "The Reality of the Past".) But there would be an easy slide into scepticism. Not that *that* is the case against this sort of realism. The situation is not that we understand well enough the propositions represented as conclusions from the evidence of behaviour or traces, but find the inferences shaky; rather, the purported conclusions are (pur-

4. Truth-value links are actually impotent to do what realists of this kind want them to do.[11] According to a truth-value-link realist, the state of affairs that consists in another person's being in pain is never itself accessible to consciousness. An anti-realist finds it unintelligible that a conception of such a state of affairs should be involved in linguistic competence. The realist's purported answer is, in effect, this: "You can see how a person can have the idea of what it is for someone to be in pain—when the someone in question is himself. Well, a sentence like 'He is in pain', uttered in a context that fixes a reference for the pronoun, is understood as saying, of some appropriate other person, that he is in that very same state." But, so far from solving the problem, this simply ignores it. If someone cannot see how another person's being in pain—on an interpretation of that circumstance that makes it inaccessible—can possibly enter into the meaning one attaches to some form of words, one does not allay his worry by baldly re-asserting that it does.[12]

Similarly with the past. An anti-realist finds it unintelligible that a conception of the truth-condition of a past-tensed utterance, thought of as something whose obtaining is, in itself, inaccessible, should be involved in linguistic competence. The realist's purported reply is on these lines: "You can see how someone can know what it is for rain to be falling. Well, a sentence like 'It was raining' is understood as saying that that very circumstance obtained at some past time." Again, this does not meet the worry, but simply restates the claim that gave rise to it. The problem was precisely an inability to see how the past obtaining of that circumstance—an instance of a kind of circumstance that the realism we are considering makes inaccessible—can possibly enter into any meaning one could succeed in attaching to a sentence.

Of course I am not advocating rejecting the principles that constitute the truth-value links. In fact room must surely be found for them in any acceptable position. The point is just that they cannot serve to answer the anti-realist challenge.

---

portedly) conceived in such a way as to make it impossible to see how we can so much as understand them.

11. Curiously enough, the temporal truth-value link figures in "The Reality of the Past" only as a weapon against the anti-realist, who is put to some trouble to show he can accommodate it. The realist's use of the link as a response to the anti-realist challenge goes unscrutinized.

12. "The explanation by means of identity does not work here": Wittgenstein, *Philosophical Investigations* §350.

It is instructive to compare the uselessness of appeals to truth-value links, in the two areas I have considered so far, with a role they might play in a third. Consider adverbial modifiers that yield sentences suitable for making assertions about how things are elsewhere. The truth-conditions of such sentences, as uttered on given occasions, would consist in the obtaining of appropriate states of affairs elsewhere; and those circumstances—the obtaining of those states of affairs in places specified as being other than where the speaker is—might be inaccessible to the speaker's awareness. So a form of the anti-realist challenge might seem to be in place. Here, however, appeal to truth-value links yields an effective justification for continuing to use the notion of truth-conditions in a theory of meaning. For the truth-value links appealed to in this case would point to ways in which—by travelling and then checking whether the truth-conditions of the unmodified sentences obtain—a person could, in principle, decide whether the truth-conditions ascribed to the modified sentences, by a theory that incorporates the links, obtained before the travel was undertaken. (Of course this needs qualification—for instance, to cover ruling out the possibility of change during the travel.) In this case, then, as not in the others, appeal to truth-value links might genuinely help a realist, serving to remove an initial appearance that a description of linguistic competence in terms of truth-conditions is inimical to the broadly verificationist principles of the anti-realist.

5. The attraction of truth-value links lies in their seeming to permit a realist to bypass detectable assertion-warranting circumstances. No doubt he would have to allow that such circumstances play a role in the *acquisition* of the problematic competence; but the role would be at best indirect, pointing the language-learner to the place where the required conception of a truth-condition is to be found.[13] The conception itself is to be one to whose content those detectable assertion-warranting circumstances are strictly irrelevant: "Pain is pain—whether *he* has it, or *I* have it; and however I come to know whether he has a pain or not."[14]

When we are tempted towards a realism of this sort about other-ascriptions of sensation, we are inclined to rely on a picture of the inner world as a sort of concealed receptacle. In another person's re-

13. This is how, in the light of §3, we must understand the concession Dummett envisages the realist making: "The Reality of the Past", p. 365.

14. Wittgenstein, *Philosophical Investigations* §351.

ceptacle—so we encourage ourselves by thinking—a given item, say pain, is either present or not; at any rate the receptacle's owner knows which, and so, perhaps, does God. The picture "by itself seems to make the sense of the expressions *unmistakable:* 'Now you know what is in question'—we should like to say".[15] The parallel realism about the past draws comfort, similarly, from picturing a God's-eye view of the course of history—an extra-temporal standpoint from which events in our past can be witnessed in just the same way as events in our present. In the series of occurrences and states of affairs laid out timelessly under God's imagined gaze, a given event, say, is either present or not: God knows which, even if we do not. Here too, while we are under the spell, that seems to justify "Now you know what is in question".

Of course we *do* know what is in question. But these transcendently realistic positions are under attack as making it impossible to see how we could have any such knowledge; and we must not let ourselves be prevented, by our possession of an ordinary, unproblematic understanding of the sorts of sentence at issue, from seeing that insisting on instances of the law of excluded middle, with the associated pictures, constitutes no genuine rebuttal of the attack. The anti-realist's objection was that we cannot have a conception of a sort of state of affairs that is in principle inaccessible to us. To say that God, or another person who is in pain, or a participant in a historical event, knows, or knew, what is in question does nothing towards showing how it is possible that we do, given that what is in question is, as transcendent realism makes it, a state of affairs of a sort beyond our ken.[16]

15. *Philosophical Investigations* §352.

16. Compare Dummett, "What Is a Theory of Meaning? (II)", pp. 98–101. Note that Wittgenstein's point, at *Philosophical Investigations* §352, is not that we are not entitled to claim truth for the relevant instances of the law of excluded middle, but just that insisting on them does nothing to justify "Now you know what is in question". The error is to think of "Either he is in pain or not" as picturing logical space, as it were, like this:

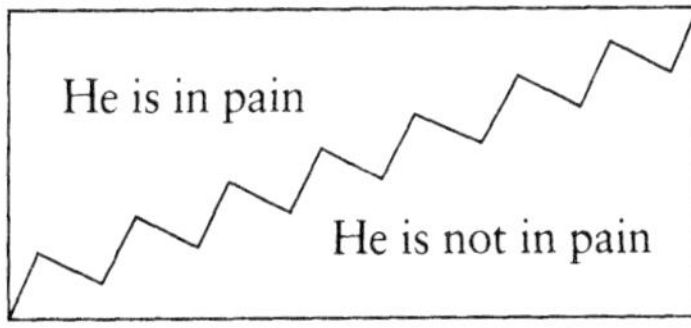

whereas if we are to think of it as a picture, it should be conceived on the pattern of the Bellman's map ("a perfect and absolute blank"). None of this requires doubts about classical logic.

6. The truth-value-link realist wanted to avoid mentioning, in his description of competence with the problematic sorts of sentence, circumstances that, when they manifest themselves to awareness, warrant assertions of the sentences; and it seems that his hopes of doing so were vain (§§4, 5). If truth-value-link realism and anti-realism were the only options, as Dummett's treatment suggests, that conclusion would leave anti-realism in possession of the field. But there is another option: a realism that meets the anti-realist challenge in the way I distinguished, in §3, from appeal to a truth-value link.

That is, there are two distinct ways of allowing, in the description of linguistic competence, mention of circumstances that, when they detectably obtain, justify the making of assertions: anti-realism, and this different variety of realism. We can bring out the difference by contrasting two answers to this question: In what sorts are we to classify the circumstances that justify assertion of the problematic sentences, on the paradigmatic occasions for training in their assertoric use? An anti-realist thinks of the circumstances as belonging to sorts that are available to awareness *whenever* they obtain. That, together with the fact that the truth-values of the problematic sentences need not be ascertainable either way, blocks thinking of the circumstances as actually being truth-conditions of the sentences. The realist whom I distinguished in §3 from the truth-value-link realist thinks of the circumstances, by contrast, as belonging to sorts that are sometimes available to consciousness—as they are on the occasions that constitute opportunities for training—*but sometimes not.* Thus he enables himself to think of them as actually *being* truth-conditions, realistically construed, for the sentences.

According to this position, what warrants the assertion that another person is in pain, on one of the relevant occasions, is the detectable obtaining of the circumstance of that person's being in pain: an instance of a kind of circumstance—another person's being in pain—that is available to awareness, in its own right and not merely through behavioural proxies, on some occasions, including this one, although, on other occasions, the obtaining of other instances can be quite beyond detection. Similarly, what warrants the assertion, on one of the relevant occasions, that, say, some event of a specified kind occurred in the past is the obtaining of a circumstance that consists simply in such an event's having occurred: an instance of a kind of circumstance that is available to awareness, in its own right and not merely through traces going proxy for it, on some occasions, including this one, although, on other occasions, the obtaining of other instances can be quite outside our reach.

A truth-value-link realist represents the truth-condition of an other-ascription of pain as something that is, in itself, inaccessible (§3); that another person is in pain can be known, if at all, only by inference from circumstances that are accessible. A realist of our different kind rejects this relegation of truth-conditions to the far side of something that would in fact—as the anti-realist sees—operate as a barrier, preventing our minds from penetrating to a genuine conception of what it is for the truth-conditions to obtain. In the view of this different realist, then, we should not jib at, or interpret away, the common-sense thought that, on those occasions that are paradigmatically suitable for training in the assertoric use of the relevant part of a language, one can literally perceive, in another person's facial expression or his behaviour, that he is in pain, and not just infer that he is in pain from what one perceives.[17]

The analogue, in the case of the past, would be insistence that knowledge of the past occurrence of an event of a specified kind (say) is sometimes non-inferential. Events make impacts on our senses while they occur;[18] mastery of forms of words suitable for describing contemporary events is acquired by training that begins by instilling propensities to respond to those impacts with appropriate verbal behaviour. The fact that training that imparts mastery of the past tense can get started at all is presumably due to the persistence

17. P. F. Strawson's use, in chap. 3 of *Individuals*, of the notion of "criteria of a logically adequate kind" for other-ascription has been criticized (e.g., by Hilary Putnam, "Brains and Behaviour") as involving the idea of a somehow guaranteed *inference* from purely behavioural descriptions of others to statements about their minds; but I believe Strawson intended something more like the idea that I express here. Note that it is *not* the point of the idea to suggest an *answer* to scepticism about other minds. On Wittgenstein's concept of a criterion, see especially the "Postscript" to Rogers Albritton, "On Wittgenstein's Use of the Term 'Criterion'". (The idea that there must be an inference, to be labelled "tacit" if necessary, stems, I believe, from the same error as the idea that a consistent use of an expression must be informatively definable in terms of necessary and sufficient conditions.) Wittgenstein's best thoughts in this area constitute a subtle and characteristic refusal to take sides in the typically *philosophical* debate between transcendent (truth-value-link) realism and anti-realism; it is sad to find him widely construed as enrolling himself with the anti-realists.

18. This is strictly false (the time-lag argument), but I believe the fact is not germane to my purpose, which is to suggest a way for a kind of realist to meet the anti-realist challenge.

sometimes, presumably in the nervous system, of some trace of the impact of a previous event on the senses, so that suitable training is able to institute a differentiation of verbal dispositions, with respect to forms of words systematically related to those with which present events are apt to be greeted, according to whether or not those presumed traces are present. Times when the persisting effects are likeliest to be present are, on this view, the best occasions for initial training in the assertoric use of the past tense. A person whose nervous system contains one of the persisting effects—a trace of the impact of an event on a knowledge-acquiring capacity—is, potentially at least, in possession of knowledge that an event of the relevant sort has occurred.[19] And the knowledge is, as required by our different kind of realist, immediate. There is nothing for it to be the product of inference from: certainly not the presumed trace, which figures in this sketch not as something available, even potentially, to the consciousness of someone who remembers—it is no such thing—but as an element in a speculative, though plausible, physiological explanation of why the training works. On this view, then, the circumstance of such an event's having occurred is, as our realist requires, sometimes itself available to awareness.

It helps to take care over how we specify the truth-condition of a past-tensed utterance. If we think of the truth-condition of an utterance, today, of "It rained yesterday" as *yesterday's rain,* it is easy to slip into the idea that that is something that could be directly available only to an awareness enjoying the extra-temporal God's-eye view that a truth-value-link realist is likely to draw comfort from picturing (compare §5). If we express the truth-condition, more accurately, as *its having rained yesterday,* it becomes easier to swallow our realist's suggestion that its obtaining can be, in memory, immediately available to consciousness.

19. Depending on our view of knowledge, we may want to say the potentiality is not actual until the past tense has been mastered. The point is general; on a view of knowledge that requires conceptualization, mere confrontation with a state of affairs, however receptive one is, cannot suffice for knowledge, in the absence of an ability to conceptualize the state of affairs one is confronted with. But there is no obvious damage to the effectiveness of a response to the anti-realist challenge on the lines I am suggesting. The suggestion is not, absurdly, that confrontation with instances of the putatively problematic kinds of states of affairs would *suffice* for acquiring the relevant linguistic competence. But truth-value-link realism made any such confrontation impossible; to the extent to which the anti-realist objection is a protest against that, the different kind of realism that I am distinguishing here can be seen to be immune to the objection, without there being any need to go into detail about what more might be necessary to teach someone the past tense.

7. An anti-realist insists that the sorts of circumstance mentioned in a theory of meaning must be such that a language-learner can be trained to respond to them *whenever* they obtain. Our realist is differentiated from an anti-realist by his rejection of that thesis (§6). What is the justification for the thesis?

An answer emerges from a version of the anti-realist case that, rather than exploiting difficulties over the acquisition of linguistic competence, proceeds on the following lines. Linguistic competence ought to be exhaustively manifestable in behaviour; but there cannot be an exhaustive behavioural manifestation of a competence described—as competence with a language is described by a realistic theory of meaning—in terms of sorts of circumstance whose obtaining need not impinge on the consciousness of its possessor.[20] According to this version of the argument, then, realism induces an unacceptable theoretical slack between what linguistic competence essentially is—something exhaustively manifestable in behaviour—and what a realistic theory of meaning would describe it as being. Underlying the argument is the plausible principle that if a dispositional state is exhaustively manifestable in behaviour, the circumstances to which its operations are responses must belong to sorts that are always capable of eliciting those responses; that linguistic competence is such a state is exactly the thesis that distinguishes the anti-realist from our realist.

How convincing is the argument? Certainly it seems reasonable to insist that a practical capacity, such as competence with a language, should be observable in its operations. But our realist can claim that linguistic competence, as he describes it, is indeed observable in linguistic behaviour. Competence with sentences of one of the problematic sorts involves a conception of the sort of circumstance that constitutes their truth-conditions: possession of the conception *sometimes* manifests itself in linguistic behaviour that—on our realist's view (§6)—can be observed as a response to the detectable obtaining of a truth-condition.

A theory of meaning in the style of our realist ascribes to a competent speaker (among other things) dispositions to respond to the obtaining of truth-conditions—circumstances of sorts that need not be detectable—when they *are* detectable. Of course nothing could be observed to be a response to the *undetectable* obtaining of a truth-

20. See n. 6 above.

condition; but that was not the kind of response that a realistic theory credited the speaker with ability to make.

It is crucial to this realist rejection of the anti-realist argument that the conception that the realist claims the right to ascribe is a conception of a *kind* of circumstance. He claims the right to ascribe it on the basis of behaviour construable as a response to *some* instances of the kind, in spite of the admitted fact that *other* instances, on his view, are incapable of eliciting any response from the possessor of the conception. There will be an inclination to protest that the force of the word "exhaustive", in the anti-realist argument, is being ignored. But the realist can reply, with great plausibility, that if the requirement of exhaustive manifestability is construed so as to rule out his position, it is too strong. What we have to deal with, primarily, is *general* competence with other-ascriptions of pain, or with the past tense. Certainly we picture such general competence as embracing sub-competences with specific sentences or utterances; and the realist cannot claim that each such sub-competence, if described as involving a conception of a truth-condition, is directly manifestable in behaviour. But the anti-realist cannot make the parallel claim either. In fact no acceptable principle can require that we be able to observe operations of *each* of the individual sub-competences ascribed, by whatever style of theory, to a competent speaker.

The fundamental articulations, within the practical capacity that constitutes mastery of a language, must relate not to individual utterances but to the repeatable semantic atoms and constructions that figure in them. Ascription of general competence with a construction, say the past tense, carries with it ascription of suitably described sub-competences with all the potential utterances in which the construction figures (conditional, of course, on possession of competence with the other materials of those utterances). Ascription of the general competence is justified if events construable as manifestations of the implied sub-competences actually present themselves to observation in the case of *some* utterances of the relevant sort: the speaker responds, with (say) an assertion, to the detectable obtaining of a truth-condition (as the realist puts it), or to the obtaining of an assertibility condition (as the anti-realist might insist). In the nature of the case we shall be unable to get others of the implied sub-competences—*whichever* way they are conceived—to manifest themselves. Still, their ascription is warranted, since the general competence of which they would be applications can be observed in the operation of others of its applications.[21]

8. It will be revealing to revert now to the version of the anti-realist case that concentrates on the *acquisition* of linguistic competence. That version starts (see §1) from this premise: all that can be imparted, by the training that results in command of a language, is a complex correlation between sensory inputs and behavioural output. The slack between an anti-realist description of the acquired capacity and one in realistic terms is offensive, then, because it implies that the language-learner mysteriously extracts more out of the teaching to which he is subjected than there is in it. The implicit knowledge in which his acquired competence is conceived as consisting includes a gratuitous contribution from himself.[22] But if it is partly a product of free invention, or guesswork, how can it be right to count it a case of knowledge?

Against realism of our different variety, this version of the argument does no better than the other. If the premise is interpreted in the way it must be for the argument to work, the question is already begged. Our realist's claim is that the sorts of circumstances to which one learns to respond linguistically, in the relevant parts of the training, are truth-conditions of sentences; thus the fact that a truth-condition obtains is indeed, on the relevant occasions, an input to the senses, or available to awareness by way of a retained trace of such an input. (Of course the notion of sensory input involved here is quite different from the one that is required if the anti-realist argument is to work.)

What the acquisition version of the anti-realist argument does effectively tell against is realism of the truth-value-link variety. According to a truth-value-link realist, circumstances accessible to the awareness of a person who is learning a language can serve, at best, as pointers in the direction of the sort of state of affairs of which he is to form a conception, in acquiring an understanding of sentences belonging to one of the problematic kinds (§5). The learner has to do the essential thing himself.[23] He has to break out of the confines

21. See §10 of Essay 1 above.

22. See Dummett, "The Reality of the Past", p. 365: "a certain latitude of choice".

23. Compare Wittgenstein, *Philosophical Investigations* §210 and its context, with §§362 and 71.

of his own means of acquiring knowledge, and, in a void where he is not constrained by anything he can have been shown in learning the language, fix on some inaccessible sort of circumstance to be what he is going to express with sentences of a given kind.

Our different realist cannot be saddled with any of that. In his view, formation of the required conception needs no leap beyond the bounds of awareness; it can be drawn from actual confrontation with instances of the sort of circumstance involved.

9. According to our realist's response to the anti-realist challenge, confrontation with particular states of affairs—themselves, of course, detectable—figures in the acquisition of conceptions of *sorts* of states of affairs whose instances need not be detectable. An anti-realist may want to press this question: How can one derive, from confrontation with a detectable circumstance, an idea of what it would be for a circumstance of some kind to which it belongs to obtain undetectably? The puzzlement is about how the person's mind can make contact with the state of affairs in question, given that it cannot be by way of his picturing a confrontation with it.

There is no real difficulty here. Acquiring one of the problematic conceptions is acquiring competence with the relevant part of a language. Exercising the conception, then, is nothing but exercising the relevant linguistic competence, in speech of one's own or in understanding the speech of others. Puzzlement over how the relevant sort of circumstance can figure in a person's thoughts, if not by way of imagery, is misplaced. The possibility of its figuring in his thoughts is secured, without any need for speculation about a vehicle, by the possibility of its figuring *in his speech*. A competent speaker has words to express, if need be, what state of affairs it is about whose perhaps undetectable obtaining he is capable of, for instance, self-consciously speculating, or understanding a fellow-speaker of his language to be speculating.

> "When I imagine that someone who is laughing is really in pain I don't imagine any pain-behaviour, for I see just the opposite. So *what* do I imagine?"—I have already said what.[24]

A source of dissatisfaction with this dissolution of the disquiet might be the idea that, from an account of the state in which under-

24. *Philosophical Investigations* §393.

standing a language consists, we should be able to derive psychological accounts of how a speaker manages to exercise linguistic competence. On this view, to conceive a theory of meaning as specifying the content of implicit knowledge is to conceive it as a recipe for correct speech, the following of which is what keeps the competent speaker on the rails. When we defuse the puzzlement on the lines I suggested above, we imply that if competence with, say, the sentence "He is in pain" is conceived as implicit knowledge, the content of the knowledge can be formulated on these lines: the state of affairs expressed by the sentence, on an occasion of utterance that fixes a reference for the pronoun, is that which consists in the appropriate person's being in pain. But if we want to explain a speaker's ability, in general, to cope with pain-ascribing language, in terms of his following a set of instructions, any such formulation is useless, since understanding it requires an exercise of the very ability for which an explanation is being sought.

Explanatory aspirations can make it seem that any realism must be transcendent. In suitable circumstances, I can understand an utterance of, say, "That person is in pain". We might suppose that what that comes to is this: I can hear the utterer to be, not merely making some sounds, but asserting (say), of some identifiable person, precisely that he is in pain. However, if it is only on such lines as those that an exercise of my linguistic competence can be correctly described, it would seem that if we picture the exercise of the competence as the bringing to bear of implicit knowledge, then the content of the knowledge involved, in so far as it relates in particular to the sentence uttered, will be specifiable only in the sort of explanatorily unsatisfactory terms that I considered in the last paragraph. If, then, we suppose that an account of competence must be explanatory, it will seem that, in a genuine realism, something else must lie behind those insubstantial formulations. Understanding another person's utterance, according to a view into which this makes realism tend to slide, is not, after all, simply hearing what is being said, but rather effecting a connection, in thought, between the words uttered and a state of affairs: one that enters into the thought in some way independent of the linguistic capacity in question, so that the thought can be represented as an application of a piece of knowledge that might explain this and other operations of the capacity. It must now seem urgently necessary to ask, as at the beginning of this section, how the state of affairs makes its appearance in the thought and the knowledge. As before, realism precludes its being in general by way of imagining a confrontation. What might well seem to do the trick is one of those transcendent conceptions that the truth-value-link realist purported to find intelligible.

An anti-realist theory of meaning, for its part, would be tailor-made to satisfy those explanatory aspirations. Indeed, that is arguably the deepest origin of anti-realism's attractiveness.

It is not, however, a good argument in favour of anti-realism. The best course is to deny that a theory of meaning should explain how people contrive to exercise linguistic competence. A speaker is not kept in line by inward consultation of a recipe; that idea is a myth, pernicious in its view of the mind as the locus of hypothesized mechanisms. Constructing a theory of meaning is not part of the postulation of a psychological mechanism; the aim is to say in detail what a competent speaker can do, not to explain how he does it.[25] The insubstantial formulations that I considered above are perfectly suitable, as they stand, to play a part in the execution of that descriptive enterprise.

10. How, finally, does the issue between realism and anti-realism bear on the reality of the past?

There is something right about the inclination to answer like this: only realism presupposes the reality of the past; anti-realism represents the past as unreal in itself, enjoying a sort of vicarious existence in its traces. Certainly we seem to pull in our horns if we limit ourselves, in our account of the meaning of past-tensed utterances, to circumstances guaranteed to be detectable, if they obtain, at the times when the utterances are made; according to anti-realism, we mean rather less by our past-tensed utterances than, with our realistic prejudices, we had thought we did. However, such a characterization of the difference might suggest that an anti-realist ought to disallow assertions that, say, specified past events really happened, in favour of reports of their traces—which would then, with the past dropping out of the picture altogether, cease to be viewed even as traces of it. But if an anti-realist theory of meaning can be constructed at all, it will certainly have to allow that, in approved circumstances, it is correct to assert some past-tensed sentences: that

25. See Dummett, *Frege: Philosophy of Language,* p. 681, and "What Is a Theory of Meaning? (II)", p. 70.

is—by way of such truisms as that someone who asserts "It rained yesterday" thereby asserts that it rained on the day before[26]—that it is correct to assert that certain specific events or states of affairs happened or obtained (really happened or obtained, if you like). So an anti-realist should refuse to be described as denying the reality of the past. He should insist, rather, on an account of the divergence as one over how the reality of the past is to be conceived.

As long as the only realism in the field is truth-value-link realism, the best characterization of the divergence seems to be one that the anti-realist might give, in the spirit of a diagnosis of what he sees as the realist's mistake. The realist's view of what it is, say, for something to have occurred is unintelligible. He conceals that from himself with a confused thought of a being with knowledge-acquiring powers different from ours (compare §5). Thus the realist's view of the reality of the past can be described, with only the mildest caricature, as the idea of another place, in which past events are still occurring, watched, perhaps, by God. The anti-realist's view of the reality of the past is the thought, simply, that certain specific events and states of affairs occurred and obtained: a thought to which he is committed by past-tensed assertions that, according to his theory, present circumstances entitle him to make.

Such an account of the divergence suggests, surprisingly, that realism, whose view about how words (and thoughts) relate to the past seems intuitively obvious and straightforward, can in fact maintain itself only by appealing to a grotesque piece of philosophical mythology; whereas anti-realism, which seemed an affront to common sense, has a monopoly of sanity over what it is for something to have happened.

Once we understand, however, that realism can include not only the transcendent variety that merits that anti-realist diagnosis, but also the different variety that I distinguished in §3 and §6, which does not, we can see the possibility of reintegrating the inclinations of common sense. I do not believe anti-realism has any good positive reasons in its favour; its attractions lie entirely in the thought that it is compulsory if we are to avoid the sort of transcendence that is characteristic of truth-value-link realism.

26. I am actually far from convinced that anti-realism can make out its entitlement to these truisms.

ESSAY 15

Anti-Realism and the Epistemology of Understanding[1]

1. Fellow-speakers of a language normally understand one another's utterances; that is to say, they know what the utterances mean. We cannot, then, be content with a conception of meaning that makes it a mystery how those states can be knowledge, and consequently how there can be such a thing as understanding a language. The point of the slogan "Meaning cannot transcend use" is to suggest a constraint imposed on our conception of meaning by the requirements of a credible epistemology of understanding: that the significance of utterances in a language must, in general, lie open to view, in publicly available facts about linguistic behaviour in its circumstances.

This constraint stands opposed to a conception of understanding that is characteristic of psychologism: a conception according to which the significance of others' utterances is a subject for guesswork or speculation as to how things are in a private sphere concealed behind their behaviour. (That is to put the matter from the viewpoint of acceptance of the constraint; adherents of psychologism would no doubt find the description unjust.)

Now Michael Dummett has suggested, first, that the slogan expresses an insight on which Frege is trying to focus, in at least some of his strictures against psychologism in the philosophy of language;[2] and, second, that the insight thus anticipated by Frege will not cohere with another pillar of his doctrine, namely, realism.[3] For the

1. The argument of this essay was influenced by Marcus Giaquinto.

2. *Frege: Philosophy of Language*, pp. 637–42.

3. "What Is a Theory of Meaning? (II)", pp. 135–6.

purposes of this essay, realism is the thesis that a theory of meaning for a language can give a central role to the notion of conditions under which sentences are true, conceived as conditions that we are not, in general, capable of putting ourselves in a position to recognize whenever they obtain.[4]

The insight is difficult to hold in focus in a Fregean context, because Frege fails to question the acceptability of a psychologistic conception of the psychological. (This means that his opposition to psychologism in the philosophy of language has to take the form of an obsessive, and surely doomed, rooting out of everything psychological from our account of how language works.)[5] Frege himself is prepared to consign psychological facts about other people, in the relevant sense of "psychological", to utter unknowability. But someone concerned to maintain the acceptability of a psychologistic conception of the psychological in its own right—as opposed to simply assuming it, like Frege, as a foil to anti-psychologism in the philosophy of language—would be unlikely to be content with that. If the domain of the mental is marked out by the line between the inner and the outer, as that line is conceived by psychologism, then the epistemological problem that psychologism poses is the traditional problem of knowledge of other minds; and there are traditional (purported) solutions, notably the argument from analogy. Hence as long as psychologism is not opposed—as it is by Wittgenstein—in the philosophy of mind as well, the argument from analogy will seem to cast doubt on our slogan. Frege's insight will be capable of being held in focus, and seen for the insight it is, only in the context of a philosophy of mind that refuses to make sense of the supposed epistemological predicament that the argument from analogy is meant to get us out of. Such a philosophy of mind would supersede the traditional oscillation between behaviourism and psychologism; as long as we are bound to that seesaw, the slogan is liable to look like nothing but a behaviourist dogma.

These remarks are programmatic, and this essay will not directly aim at setting them on a firmer foundation.[6] That means that I can-

4. This is the immediate target of the anti-realist argument as set out, e.g., in Dummett, *Truth and Other Enigmas,* pp. 223–5. See, further, §9 below.

5. Platonism about thoughts does not help to show how the rooting out might be possible. (See Putnam, "The Meaning of 'Meaning'", pp. 218, 222.)

6. I shall, however, aim to make plausible a view of the slogan as something much bet-

not here exclude a defence of realism against Dummett, with which, however, I now record that I have no sympathy; one, namely, that, conceiving psychologism as the only alternative to behaviourism, and supposing that something like the argument from analogy can equip psychologism with a plausible epistemology of understanding, refuses to concede that the slogan expresses any insight at all. What I want to do, rather, is to accept that the slogan expresses an insight, but question whether it undermines the possibility of realism.[7]

2. The claim that a theory that systematically generates specifications of truth-conditions for indicative sentences might constitute part of a theory of meaning for a language—that is, a characterization of what it is to understand the language[8]—would have to be grounded on the claim that its specifications of truth-conditions would serve to determine some aspect of the significance of those sentences, and consequently some aspect of the significance of speech acts effected by utterances of those (and related) sentences.[9] So the slogan ought to bear on this putative component of a theory of meaning; at least on its deliverances about whole sentences (the smallest units of significant discourse).[10] Dummett's argument is that if the truth-conditions would need to be conceived realistically, as in the case of sentences for which there is no effective method for determining their truth-value, then the requirement of the slogan cannot be satisfied.

> When the sentence is one which we have a method for effectively deciding, there is . . . no problem: a grasp of the condition under which the sentence is true may be said to be manifested by a mastery of the decision procedure, for the individual may, by that means, get himself into a position in which he can recognise that the condition for the truth of the sentence obtains or does not obtain, and we may reason-

ter than a behaviourist dogma, and hence indirectly to reinforce the thesis that we do not need to choose between psychologism and behaviourism.

7. The idea of such a defence is prompted by Dummett's remark (*Truth and Other Enigmas,* p. 188) that the slogan allows for disputes about what the relevant characterization of use should be.

8. See Dummett, *Frege: Philosophy of Language,* pp. 92–3.

9. For Frege, specifying truth-conditions serves to determine the senses of sentences (*Grundgesetze der Arithmetik,* vol. 1, §32); and the sense of a sentence determines the content of speech acts (this is clear from "On Sense and Reference").

10. See Dummett, "What Is a Theory of Meaning? (II)", pp. 71–2.

> ably suppose that, in this position, he displays by his linguistic behaviour his recognition that the sentence is, respectively, true or false. But when the sentence is one which is not in this way effectively decidable, . . . the situation is different. Since the sentence is, by hypothesis, effectively undecidable, the condition which must, in general, obtain for it to be true is not one which we are capable of recognising whenever it obtains, or of getting ourselves in a position to do so. Hence any behaviour which displays a capacity for acknowledging the sentence as being true in all cases in which the condition for its truth can be recognised as obtaining will fall short of being a full manifestation of the knowledge of the condition for its truth: it shows only that the condition can be recognised in certain cases, not that we have a grasp of what, in general, it is for that condition to obtain even in those cases when we are incapable of recognising that it does. It is, in fact, plain that the knowledge which is being ascribed to one who is said to understand the sentence is knowledge which transcends the capacity to manifest that knowledge by the way in which the sentence is used. The [realistic] theory of meaning cannot be a theory in which meaning is fully determined by use.[11]

3. This argument turns on the assumption that, when we seek to ground a theory of truth-conditions in linguistic practice, the behaviour to which we may look is restricted to (behaviour construable as) acknowledgements of the truth or falsity of sentences, in response to the recognizable obtaining, or not, of those truth-conditions. With that assumption, the argument seems conclusive. There simply is not enough, in the place where we are instructed to look, to manifest knowledge of what it would be for some sentence to be true even when the subject cannot tell that it is, or that it is not. If we are to find knowledge of truth-conditions that are not necessarily recognizable, then we need to widen our view. But we ought to wonder whether it is right to suggest, as Dummett does, that the widened view must involve a shift of attention from what is overtly available in behaviour to a psychologistically hypothesized inner item.[12]

Dummett's restriction reflects an assumption about the character of the internal articulation in a theory of meaning. Any theory of meaning that admits a distinction on the lines of Frege's distinction

11. *Truth and Other Enigmas*, pp. 224–5.

12. It is worth comparing Dummett's own complaint (*Frege: Philosophy of Language*, pp. 615–6) against W. V. Quine's restriction of the behavioural data to which we are permitted to appeal in radical translation.

between sense and force will fall into, broadly, two parts: a core theory, which determines the conditions for the application, to sentences of the language, of some meaning-relevant property (candidates being, for instance, truth or warranted assertibility); and a supplementary part, the theory of force, which gives an account, in terms of the central notion of the core theory, of what it is to effect each of the various possible types of speech act.[13] Now Dummett's restriction reflects the thesis that this articulation in the theory of meaning must match an articulation in the psychological state—understanding of the language—that the theory aims to characterize, in the following sense: the core theory must correspond to a component psychological state that is in principle isolable—one that could in principle be possessed independently of the component psychological state to which the supplementary theory corresponds. Isolating the core psychological state, given that we are not to conceive it psychologistically, requires us to find a behavioural manifestation for it in particular, separable from what we might go on to count as a behavioural manifestation of the psychological state corresponding to the theory of force. And now it is indeed difficult to see what one could legitimately appeal to, in attempting to certify the non-psychologistic acceptability on its own of a truth-conditional core theory, over and above acknowledgements of the truth or falsity of sentences in response to the obtaining, or not, of the truth-conditions that the theory ascribes to them.[14]

But to force the truth-conditional conception of meaning into this mould—or rather, to try to do so, and then take failure as discrediting it—is actually not even to take note of the best version of the truth-conditional proposal.

That version is on these lines. We may reasonably set ourselves the ideal of constructing, as a component of a complete theory of meaning for a language, a sub-theory that is to serve to specify the contents of (for instance, and surely centrally) assertions that could be made by uttering the language's indicative sentences. Ignoring index-

13. See "What Is a Theory of Meaning? (II)", pp. 72–6.

14. Actually it is questionable whether the underlying principles of Dummett's position would (as he supposes) permit appeal even to these materials. See §8 below. That Dummett thinks of the core theory as corresponding in this way to an isolable psychological state emerges from, e.g., "What Is a Theory of Meaning? (II)", pp. 129–31.

ical expressions for simplicity's sake,[15] a direct assault on that task would be to look for a sub-theory that generates, on the basis of structure in the object-language sentences, a theorem, for every appropriate sentence, of this form: "*s* can be used to assert that *p*." Now there is a truistic connection between the notion of the content of an assertion and a familiar notion of truth (one whose significance we might think of as fully fixed precisely by this connection); the connection guarantees, as the merest platitude, that a correct specification of what can be asserted, by the assertoric utterance of a sentence, cannot but be a specification of a condition under which the sentence is true.[16] A radical proposal at this point would be as follows: as long as the ends of the theorems (think of them as having the form "*s* . . . *p*") are so related that, whatever the theorems actually say, we can use them as if they said something of the form "*s* can be used to assert that *p*", it does not actually matter if we write, between those ends, something else that yields a truth in those same circumstances; our platitude guarantees that "is true if and only if" fills that bill, and this gives a more tractable target than that of the direct assault.[17] But even if we do not make this radical move, but somehow bring off the direct assault, the platitude still ensures that our theorems, if acceptable, must specify what are in fact truth-conditions for the sentences they mention—even though, on this second option, they do not explicitly represent themselves as doing that.

If this is the justification for the idea that a core theory might specify what are in fact truth-conditions (whether or not it explicitly labels them as such), then one simply misses whatever point the proposal has,

15. This cavalier manoeuvre seems legitimate here, since the problem Dummett is posing for the truth-conditional conception of meaning is not some technical difficulty about its ability to handle this or that kind of expression, but a general difficulty of principle.

16. It is a philosophical issue whether there are respectable purposes for which a stronger notion of truth is required. A familiar sort of non-cognitivist about values, for instance, making play with the idea that real truth is correspondence to objective reality, will not be content with the application of my platitude to, say, ethical assertions. (See Wiggins, "What Would be a Substantial Theory of Truth?", n. 21 and the text it relates to.) I am inclined to suppose that this is a matter not so much of an alternative notion of truth as of a characteristically philosophical misconception of the only notion of truth we really have: one that the platitude in fact suffices to determine. (Some will think this shows there is certainly no realism to be had from this notion of truth. I believe they suffer from a variant of the same philosophical misconception. See, further, §§4 and 9 below.)

17. See Donald Davidson, "Truth and Meaning", p. 23.

or at best refuses to see any point in it, if one complains that such a core theory cannot be found a behavioural manifestation of its own, independent of the behavioural warrant for the accuracy of the theory of force. In this proposal, the truth-conditional core does not purport to characterize an isolable prior psychological state: something from which one might progress to a command of what, in general, one is doing when one utters a sentence assertorically, by acquiring a further psychological state characterizable by the supplementary theory. A specification of a truth-condition is not something from which, in conjunction with suitable statements from a substantial theory of force, a specification of the content of assertions that one might effect by uttering the sentence in question is to be *derived.*[18] The specifications of truth-conditions in which we are interested simply *are* specifications of the content of assertions, and that is why we are interested in them. What entitles them to figure in the theory of meaning is whatever entitles us to suppose they correctly determine what people would be asserting in assertoric utterances of the sentences in question.[19] Only those whom we left behind in §1 could think any supposition about what people are asserting in assertoric utterances must be psychologistic speculation. And no one could think the linguistic behaviour in which people manifest knowledge of what sentences can be used to assert—knowledge of their truth-conditions, on the view I am recommending—is restricted to the area where Dummett looks in vain for a manifestation of knowledge of truth-conditions.

When Dummett sets out the picture of a theory of meaning as articulated into a core component and a theory of force, he insists that the core theory must be surrounded—still inside the theory of force, so to speak—with a "shell" that correlates specific propositions of the core theory with specific practical abilities possessed by speakers of the lan-

18. Compare Dummett, "What Is a Theory of Meaning? (II)", p. 104.

19. Dummett's different view of the relation between the core theory and the theory of force generates a deafness to the claims of the truth-conditional conception as I have sketched it. For instance, P. F. Strawson complained ("Scruton and Wright on Anti-Realism etc."), against a candidate version of anti-realism that denies that a sentence such as "Jones is in pain" has a truth-condition at all, that it gives us no account of what one might be doing if one uttered such a sentence. Dummett conjectures (*Truth and Other Enigmas,* p. xxxvi): "I suppose Strawson's idea is that an account of this kind leaves out the important thing, which is that the speaker says what he does because, rightly or wrongly, he believes it to be *true.*" Strawson's complaint is much simpler: that an account that leaves out truth-conditions *eo ipso* leaves out what is certainly important, namely, what the speaker would be saying.

guage.[20] This is to insist on the thesis that I have identified as underpinning the argument I cited in §2: namely, that the core component must be grounded in linguistic practice on its own. Adherence to our slogan requires that we have something like Dummett's "shell" somewhere;[21] but we have not yet seen reason for supposing that we must effect our correlations with practice where Dummett's picture requires them, and not, so to speak, outside the theory of force instead.[22]

4. My main purpose in this essay is not to speak in favour of realism, but to question the cogency of Dummett's argument against it. But the importance of the divergence that I identified in §3 will be clearer if we pause briefly at this point, in order to see how the position I have outlined generates something that conforms to the characterization of realism in §1.

Knowledge of what a sentence can be used to assert is knowledge that can be directly manifested, on appropriate occasions, by using the sentence in such a way as manifestly to assert precisely that. Of course one may never have occasion for the assertoric utterance of some sentence that is within one's syntactic reach; but no one, however anti-realistically inclined, should suppose this suffices to show that one does not know what one would be asserting if one did have occasion to utter the sentence assertorically.[23] Specifications of con-

20. "What Is a Theory of Meaning? (II)", p. 74.

21. But the correlations I have in mind are with capacities described in such terms as these: a capacity to use the sentence "Michael Dummett has toothache", should it suit some conversational purpose one might have, in order to assert that Michael Dummett has toothache. This would certainly not strike Dummett as satisfactory. See §5 below.

22. At p. 82 of "What Is a Theory of Meaning? (II)", having set out a version of the argument that I cited in §2, Dummett remarks that the problem he is posing for truth-conditional views of meaning does not relate to the theory of force. That simply reflects his insistence that the "shell" must be constructed before we embark on the theory of force. Thus, when Dummett goes on to remark that "knowing the condition which has to obtain for a sentence to be true is not . . . something of which anything that [someone] does is the direct manifestation" (pp. 82–3), a proponent of the truth-conditional view I have sketched would have to complain that Dummett has, for no reason we have yet seen, precluded himself from considering, as something a speaker can do that directly manifests knowledge of the truth-condition of a sentence, asserting whatever it is that the sentence can be used to assert. See the beginning of §4 below.

23. The counterfactual element here introduced into our account of the behavioural manifestation of a theory of meaning should be compared with the counterfactual element we would need if we claimed, say, that understanding a mathematical sentence consisted in knowing the conditions under which one would have a proof of it (think of understanding false mathematical sentences).

tents of potential assertions are, by way of our platitude, specifications of conditions under which the sentences used to effect those assertions would be true. Now if a sentence lacks an effective decision procedure, then the condition that any competent speaker knows he would be asserting to obtain if he used the sentence in order to make an assertion—which is in fact a condition under which the sentence would be true, whether or not a theory of meaning explicitly calls it that—is *ex hypothesi* not a condition whose obtaining, if it does obtain, a competent speaker can be sure of being able to put himself in a position to recognize. Thus, without lapsing into psychologism, we seem to have equipped ourselves with a kind of realism: a description of linguistic competence that makes central use of the idea that speakers have a knowledge of conditions that they are not, in general, capable of recognizing whenever they obtain.

Proponents of anti-realism of Dummett's sort will dissociate their intended victim from this unextravagant doctrine. I shall return to the question what realism is at the end of this essay (§9). Meanwhile I want to note some of the ways in which the attempt to force a truth-conditional conception of meaning into Dummett's mould seems to compel it into the sort of extravagance that anti-realists find suspect.

So long as we look where Dummett wants the "shell" located, we cannot find a behavioural anchoring for the distinctive aspects of a truth-conditional core theory. If, now, we persist in thinking of the core theory as corresponding to an isolable psychological state—retaining Dummett's general structure, but despairing of constructing the "shell"—then we must be conceiving the psychological state psychologistically: thus, as something ulterior, lying behind and governing the various performances that, on this view, we conceive as its at best partial manifestations, with its existence at best a hypothesis as far as an observer of the performances is concerned. Once in this avowedly psychologistic position, we have a problem about how a truth-condition figures in the ulterior psychological state that constitutes grasping it. The ordinary words whose truth-condition it is will not serve to bring the grasped condition into the picture; or, if we do think we can use them, at least in telling ourselves what it is that we grasp, it must be because we think that in such a private performance we can inject into the words more meaning than they have by virtue of their use in the public practice of speaking a language. So we are led to think of the truth-condition itself as strictly ineffable, grasped by the mind in some peculiar language-transcendent way. And we are led to conceive the role of truth, in an account of linguistic behaviour, as that of some strictly inexpressible ideal, by which we picture ourselves as piously seeking to guide our assertoric practice. This picture must be mythical, since no genuine project could be governed by an ideal of such shimmering remoteness from our actual abilities to tell (say) how things are.[24]

This extravagantly realist conception of language seems forced on us if we try to fit the truth-conditional proposal into Dummett's mould. The thin position that I described above needs none of it.

5. Why, then, does Dummett insist on trying to force the truth-conditional conception of meaning into his mould, with the consequence—since we fail to correlate the core by itself with linguistic practice—that the core must be conceived psychologistically?

This involves modelling truth-conditional theories of meaning on Dummett's own more favoured candidates. A verificationist theory, for instance, has as its core a sub-theory that determines, in some systematic way, conditions under which sentences count as verified. Since the specified conditions are recognizable whenever they obtain, the core can be straightforwardly correlated with behavioural indications of assent to sentences; that is, there is no problem about the "shell".[25] And evidently a substantial theory of force is needed in order to display the relation between, on the one hand, an isolable competence consisting in an ability to assent to sentences when they are recognizably verified and, on the other, knowledge, for instance, of what one would be saying if one uttered the sentences assertorically (which is not, in general, that some recognizable verification-condition obtains). But it does not answer our question to point out that Dummett's favoured candidates fit the mould; the fact is evi-

24. This is the point of Wright's analogy with "tribe-chess" ("Truth Conditions and Criteria", pp. 231–3). The analogy strikes home against its target, but it does not tell at all against what I would regard as a sensible conception of the role of truth-conditions in an account of a language. If one is to have a feasible assertoric project, one needs to be certain of the ability to recognize, not that one has succeeded in saying something true, but that one has succeeded in saying what one intends to say—thus, uttering a sentence that is true if and only if what one intends to say is the case.

25. No problem, that is, if behavioural indications of assent may legitimately be appealed to by Dummett's principles; see n. 14 above, and §8 below.

dently that he favours them because they fit the mould, rather than that he thinks the mould must be generally acceptable because his favoured candidates fit it.

According to the version of the truth-conditional proposal that I outlined in §3, we are justified in using the notion of truth-conditions in a theory of a language by virtue of the availability in linguistic practice of such facts as this: that someone is saying that Michael Dummett has toothache. I think the answer to our question lies in an objection to stopping here.[26] Of course such facts are overtly available in linguistic behaviour, but the objection is that a proper theory of a language would yield a more illuminating account of what it is for such facts to be available. If we rest content with characterizations of behaviour in the "saying that . . ." idiom, we simply help ourselves to the specifically linguistic notion of a saying with a given content. But Dummett holds that a proper theory of a language "must not, in its completed form, make use of notions specifically related to the use of language (for instance, the notion of assertion or that of communication) which it leaves unexplained".[27]

Obviously this principle of Dummett's has an immediate impact on how we are to conceive the nature of a theory of force.[28]

Dummett establishes the need for a theory of force by means of the following fantasy.[29] Martians have a method of communicating so unlike human language that they cannot recognize human speech as a way of doing the same thing. Observing a human community, some Martians, by an extraordinary chance, hit on the possibility of constructing a systematic theory that determines the conditions for the application, to sentences of their language, of a certain predicate.[30] The predicate is, in fact, coextensive with our "is true". But the Martians have, so far, no idea of any significance it might

26. Dummett's objection to "modest" theories of meaning (see "What Is a Theory of Meaning?") would be underpinned by the considerations I am about to discuss, if they were cogent. Those considerations would consequently undermine my response to the objection, in §10 of Essay 8 above, which rests on the conception of the truth-conditional proposal that I outlined in §3 above.

27. *Frege: Philosophy of Language,* p. 681.

28. See "What Is a Theory of Meaning? (II)", p. 76.

29. *Frege: Philosophy of Language,* pp. 295–8.

30. We may not even be able to divine what the "extraordinary chance" would be like (short of magic or divine revelation), but this is irrelevant to Dummett's point, which—pruned of the restrictive principle I am discussing—seems to me to be unquestionable.

have over and above the fact that it applies to a certain sort of abstract object, abstracted out of human linguistic performances, in the manner determined by the theory. And we mark exactly the same deficiency in their knowledge if we say that the Martians have, so far, no comprehension of what human beings are doing when they speak; they can apply some descriptions to the behaviour, but they cannot make sense of it. To fill this gap, what the Martians need is a characterization of the various types of act that human beings perform by uttering sentences: a characterization that both makes human linguistic practices comprehensible and essentially employs, in doing so, the central notion of the hitherto abstract initial theory, so that the notion acquires a more than merely formal significance from the use to which it is put in the supplementary theory. And whatever the Martians need, we need too, if we want a reflective understanding of our own linguistic practice; so it ought to be possible to construe the fantasy as an innocent expository device. (But compare §6 below.)

Dummett's principle, now, imposes a restriction on the conceptual resources available to the Martians when they construct the supplementary theory: namely, that they are not to draw on their prior mastery of their own method of communicating.[31] They must be able to come to a comprehension of what human beings are doing when they, for instance, make assertions, without needing to rely on such thoughts as (a Martian equivalent of) this: the practice is a human way of purporting to communicate that something or other is the case.[32] The supplementary theory, then, must be formulable in such a way as to yield the required comprehension without drawing on

31. Consider this claim: "Now, just as it is possible to describe to someone what it is to play chess without presupposing that he understands what winning is, and therefore that he already understands some similar activity, so it should be possible to describe the activity of using language without presupposing that it is already known what significance it has to call one class of sentences the class of 'true' sentences and the other the class of 'false' sentences . . ." (*Frege: Philosophy of Language,* p. 297). The "just as . . . so" construction should warrant glossing "without presupposing that it is already known . . . 'false' sentences" with "without presupposing that the audience already understands some similar activity". The Martians must be able to communicate with each other, in order to be able to give each other explanations of human linguistic behaviour. But the implication is that that is the only role their own ability to communicate needs to play, in their coming to understand human linguistic behaviour.

32. Would they have this thought after they had come to comprehend human linguistic behaviour? Nothing Dummett says seems to require this.

the forbidden materials. What is needed is a characterization of linguistic practice that the Martians could use, without appealing to their understanding of their own practice, in order to master linguistic practice: a set of principles of conduct, expressible without the forbidden materials, such that to engage in a practice that consists in conforming one's behaviour to those principles is to speak intelligibly, and with comprehension of what one is doing, in some human language. And once again, whatever is needed by the Martians is needed by us too, in a properly fundamental account of our own linguistic practice. So, although it cannot be denied that it may be overtly available in linguistic behaviour that someone is, for instance, saying that such-and-such is the case, a proper theory of meaning, according to this line of argument, would not leave it at that; it would equip us with a formulation of what it is that is available on such an occasion, expressed without presupposing the "saying that . . ." idiom: something whose availability, it would claim, constitutes the availability of what we express, irreproachably but superficially, in terms of the "saying that . . ." idiom.

This conception of what a properly fundamental theory of force would be like has obvious corollaries about the nature of the core theory. In §3 I suggested a justification for interest in a truth-conditional sub-theory; that justification is manifestly incapable of showing that a truth-conditional sub-theory has any place in a properly fundamental theory of a language, constructed in conformity with Dummett's principle. Indeed, it is clear that a sub-theory conceived in that way can have no such place. For the correctness of its employment of the notion of truth-conditions was to be grounded on the availability, in overt behaviour, of facts expressible in the "saying that . . ." or "asserting that . . ." idiom; so that to insist on giving such a sub-theory a central place in a theory of meaning is, in effect, to insist on stopping at the superficial level.[33]

6. If a theory of a language of the sort that Dummett envisages is possible, though, no doubt, mind-bogglingly difficult to construct, it would be sheer defeatism to plead the difficulty as a pretext for not,

33. I believe this explains why Dummett thinks the only way to benefit from a distinction like Frege's between sense and force (by virtue of the theoretical simplification afforded by distinguishing core and supplementary theory) is by constructing a theory of meaning that fits his mould—locating the "shell" where he does, or else being avowedly psychologistic about the core. (See, e.g., "What Is a Theory of Meaning? (II)", pp. 72–6.)

at least, thinking about the task. But do we actually have any reason to suppose that the task is even in principle possible?

Dummett argues for his claim that the task is possible in tandem with a parallel claim about board games.[34] A formal theory of such a game might specify the starting position, give rules determining which moves are permissible in which positions, and effect a classification of positions on reaching one of which the procedure terminates; this classification would correspond with one that we might effect by characterizations like "The player who moves first (say, White) wins", "White loses", and "Stalemate", although the formal theory by itself cannot confer this significance on the classification it effects. Equipped with no more than a theory of this kind, one would not be in a position to comprehend games of, say, chess; one's knowledge about chess would be analogous to the knowledge about a human language achieved by Dummett's Martians, when they had a theory that sufficed to specify conditions for the possession by sentences of a property that was in fact truth, although they were not yet able to give their predicate that significance. Something analogous to the theory of force is needed in the chess case too. And Dummett imposes a restriction on what the supplementary theory may appeal to, in the chess case, analogous to the restriction he imposes on the theory of force. Just as the theory of force may not appeal to a prior mastery, on the part of the Martians, of an activity similar to language, so the supplementary theory in the chess case may not presuppose "that something is known about the activity of playing games in general"—that its audience "already understands some similar activity".[35]

A general view, of which both these restrictions are applications, emerges from the following passage:

> The theory of meaning . . . cannot be required to provide more than the kind of sense which any account of a pattern of rational behaviour is required to have. Suppose that an anthropologist observes people of an alien culture engaging in some complicated co-operative activity. Its nature eludes him: is it a game? a religious ritual? a decision-making process? Perhaps it is none of these: perhaps it does not fall squarely into any category with which we are familiar. He will strive to make sense of it, to render it intelligible to himself as a rational activity: to discover what exactly would count as engaging in that activity cor-

34. See *Frege: Philosophy of Language*, pp. 295–8.
35. *Frege: Philosophy of Language*, p. 297.

rectly; what subsequent consequences it has, if any; what role it plays in the life of the community. If it is classifiable as an activity of some familiar type, then he will so describe it; but, even if it is not, once he has learned to understand it, he will be able to describe it so as to make it intelligible to us, and hence he does not need to rely upon a term such as "game" or "ritual" already tailored to tell us the kind of point it has.[36]

But it is not obvious that the parallel with games tends in what is, for Dummett, the right direction. Suppose Martians play no competitive games. Are we nevertheless entitled to be confident that, supposing we learned to communicate with them, we could find something to say that would give them a comprehension of the point of those activities? They are activities that we must concede to be, from a cosmic perspective, very strange: competitive activities in which the outcome competed for has (at least in the pure cases) no instrumental value, and no intrinsic value apart from its occurrence as the outcome of these very activities. No doubt we could simply tell them that we see a point in such activities; but if they remained baffled as to what point we can possibly see, they would not succeed in making sense of the activity of (say) playing chess.

Common sense suggests two ways of trying to remove the bafflement. First, we might try to show the Martians the point of competitive games in the way we show it to human children: not discursively, but by training them in such activities. (Of course this might not work with Martians.)[37] Or, second, we might try to find resemblances between competitive games and some activity that already has a place in Martian life, in the hope of exploiting the similarities so as to make comprehension spread out from the familiar to the unfamiliar. But both these procedures violate Dummett's restriction. If we are forbidden these procedures, or find them unavailing, have we any reason to suppose otherwise than that there is an area of our lives that we are unable—absolutely unable, or at least unable with

36. *Frege: Philosophy of Language*, pp. 681–2.

37. I do not mean by this that they may be unable to master what is to be done (though that is possible too). Dummett seems prone to assume that a complete knowledge of what counts as correct behaviour in some practice cannot fall short of comprehension of it. But we can imagine a co-operative Martian becoming an adept at chess, solely in order to please us; but being perfectly sincere in saying "I still don't see what point you see in doing all this". He would not have a proper understanding of his own flawless chess-playing behaviour.

the materials that we have been permitted—to make intelligible to the Martians?

The general view with which Dummett purports to justify his restrictions has the following implication: any intelligible human activity can be described, in such a way as to reveal its point or significance, from the perspective of a cosmic exile—a perspective, that is, that is not to any extent coloured or affected by the occupant's own involvement in a form of life; for the capacity of the description to make the activity comprehensible is not to depend on any such involvement. Now Dummett is no doubt right that not every activity we can understand is one for which we have a ready-made significance-revealing classification (like "game" or "ritual"), available immediately to us by virtue of our own self-conscious involvement in that very activity. But that does not begin to show that, in the case of any activity that it is within our power to understand, there is a way for us to achieve that understanding without either seeing the activity as a way of doing something we already do (perhaps having learned to do it in the course of being brought to the understanding), or else drawing on points of similarity between it and some aspect of our own lives. Nor does such a general thesis have the slightest plausibility. On the contrary: from the perspective of the cosmic exile, there is no reason to suppose that any point or significance, of the sort that human activities have, would be discernible in anything.[38] What seems plausible is, rather, this: if we insist on eliminating dependence upon prior involvement in forms of life, then we eliminate the very possibility of understanding.

The prior involvement to which, according to this counter-thesis, a significance-revealing characterization of an activity necessarily appeals need not be involvement in that very activity.[39] But in the particular case of looking for a reflective understanding of our own linguistic practice, the implausibility of Dummett's general prohibition leaves us with no ground for hostility to the following thought: the possibility of achieving such reflective understanding would essen-

38. Compare David Wiggins, "Truth, Invention, and the Meaning of Life", pp. 118–22.

39. This is why I left open, above, the second possible way of giving non–game-playing Martians an understanding of games. (For my present purposes, I do not need to say anything general about the sorts of similarities that can be exploited, or about how they can be exploited.)

tially depend on a not particularly reflective mastery of the practice itself. The fact is that, in consequence of certain training, we find ourselves equipped with the perspective, on a certain set of linguistic practices, of a comprehending participant. According to Dummett's restriction, it should be possible for us to reconstruct that participant perspective in terms of materials wholly available to the cosmic exile. According to the counter-thesis, the sense that, from our participant perspective, we see in our linguistic behaviour would be invisible from the cosmic exile's perspective.[40] The counter-thesis permits us to see a profound truth in this claim: in theorizing about the relation of our language to the world, we must start in the middle, already equipped with command of a language; we cannot refrain from exploiting that prior equipment, in thinking about the practice, without losing our hold on the sense that the practice makes.

Dummett's Martians are an innocent expository device to this extent: they show the need for a theory of force over and above the core theory. But when he exploits them to justify his restriction on the materials available to a theory of force, that constitutes an insinuation of the cosmic exile's perspective. And that is not innocent at all; nor is it capable of justifying the conception of what a proper theory of meaning would be like that I described in §5. The truth-conditional conception that I described in §3 can be justly stigmatized as superficial only if something deeper is available; and there is a better basis for doubting that than mere timidity in the face of a daunting task.[41]

40. The "saying that . . ." idiom is not reducible to materials available at the cosmic exile's standpoint. This thesis is related to (perhaps a case of) the thesis that "intentional" (content-specifying) discourse is not reducible to "non-intentional" discourse; on which see Davidson, "Mental Events".

41. In a sense I do here propose that in theorizing about a language we "help ourselves" (compare §5 above) to, e.g., the "saying that . . ." idiom—to serve in a sense-making characterization of a practice with which we are familiar by virtue of its role in our ordinary life. Do I, then, turn my face against the idea that there might be philosophical issues about, say, the notions of assertion and content? Not at all. Here are a couple of worthwhile issues (just for the sake of examples). (i) What, if any, metaphysical conclusions can we draw from the differences (or the similarities) between the roles of ethical assertions and, say, scientific assertions in our lives? (Compare n. 16 above.) (ii) How can a mere object have content (be capable of representing the world)? (About (ii), see Essay 2 above.) What I dispute is only this: that the philosophical task that assertion confronts us with is to give an account of our assertoric practice intelligible from the cosmic exile's standpoint.

7. What is the attraction, for Dummett, of the idea of the cosmic exile's perspective? I think the answer is that he thinks epistemological considerations make it compulsory.[42]

When one understands an utterance, one knows what someone is saying (in a sense of "saying" that includes other types of speech act than the assertoric). Now how can this state be knowledge? Dummett's restrictive principle—his insistence on the cosmic exile's perspective—would be mandatory if, and I think only if, an adequate answer to that question were required to take this form: the state's right to the title of knowledge must be demonstrated by displaying that it consists in awareness of some fact whose availability to the knower we can assume without begging the question; that is, without prejudging the status of our attribution of knowledge. But although this idea has some plausibility, I believe it is disastrously wrong.

Of course there are facts about linguistic behaviour, in its circumstances, of whose availability we can be confident without question-begging. Now Dummett's interpretation of our slogan presents us, in effect, with a dilemma: either the acquisition of knowledge in which, on appropriate occasions, the understanding of a language is exercised consists in awareness of such unproblematically detectable facts; or else we must be conceiving it psychologistically, as involving hypotheses about inner states of the speaker lying behind the behaviour. Avoiding psychologism, Dummett opts for the first horn. But if "unproblematically detectable" here means "detectable by anyone whatever, whether or not he understands the language", then we must reject the dilemma. A path between the horns is opened by this thought: there can be facts that are overtly available (so that convic-

42. I used to think it an adequate diagnosis to ascribe to Dummett the idea that a theory of meaning for a language is an object of implicit knowledge possessed by speakers, whereby they guide their linguistic behaviour. (See the partial discussion of Dummett in §10 of Essay 8 above.) But the diagnosis is at best incomplete; for the idea of inward consultation of a recipe for correct speech is profoundly psychologistic, whereas Dummett is hostile to psychologism, and disavows it precisely in those passages in which he offers the conception of a theory of meaning as an object of implicit knowledge. (See "What Is a Theory of Meaning? (II)", p. 70; *Frege: Philosophy of Language*, pp. 679–81.) What I am going to suggest is, in effect, this: Dummett is attracted by that psychologistic idea (and blinded to its psychologistic character) because, ironically, he thinks it is the inexorable outcome of considerations whose point lies in opposition to psychologism.

tion that they obtain need not be a matter of speculation as to something hidden behind what is overtly available), but awareness of which is an exercise of a perceptual capacity that is not necessarily universally shared. Command of a language is partly constituted by just such a perceptual capacity; one whose acquisition makes a new range of facts, not hitherto within one's perceptual ken, available to one's awareness.

I mean the idea of a perceptual capacity to be taken seriously. Some may think it can amount to no more than this: in learning a language, one learns to put a certain theoretical construction on the facts that one "really" perceives to obtain (these being, as before, facts that are detectable by anyone whatever, whether or not he understands the language). But that is not what I mean. Both Dummett's idea (on the present construal of "unproblematically detectable") and this one falsify the phenomenology of understanding speech in a familiar language: Dummett's, in that it cannot capture the thought that we hear more, in speech in a language, after we have learned the language; and this idea, in that it cannot capture the thought that the extra is simply *heard.* It is not clear, moreover, that this suggestion can avoid impaling itself on the second horn of Dummett's dilemma. In any case, I mean to be offering a more radical alternative: one that rejects the assumption, common to both horns of the dilemma, that our genuine perceptual intake can be exhaustively described in terms that do not beg the question of the status, as knowledge, of what we ascribe to people when we say they understand utterances.[43]

43. If we do not sharply distinguish understanding a language one speaks from interpreting a foreign language, it seems impossible to mount a genuine resistance to the idea that understanding utterances is putting a construction on what one hears. Since I am unconvinced that this idea can separate itself from psychologism, I cannot see that Colin McGinn's response to Dummett ("Truth and Use"), which makes play with the idea that fellow-speakers of a language interpret one another (in a sense of "interpret" discussed by Davidson and others in connection with the interpretation of radically foreign languages), is clearly distinguishable from the sort of response I have declared myself against (§1 above). (This is not at all to suggest that the discussions of radical interpretation by Davidson and others are irrelevant to the topic of understanding. On the contrary, there is a clear connection: a good interpretation of a foreign language would equip its possessor to put a construction on what he hears when people speak it, in such a way as to arrive at a position that cognitively matches that of those who simply understand utterances in the language. But the difference is essential.) I have other objections to McGinn's response to anti-realism. McGinn takes the less fundamental acquisition challenge first (rather than the more fundamental manifestation challenge, which is what he addresses with the talk of

How are we to make room for the phenomenological insight that one hears more, in speech in a language, when one has learned the language? How can drilling in a behavioural repertoire stretch one's perceptual capacities—cause one to be directly aware of facts of which one would otherwise not have been aware? In this essay I can only sketch, not so much the lines on which I think this question should be answered, as the reason why I think it is so difficult to answer.

The natural metaphor for the learning of a first language is "Light dawns". For light to dawn is for one's dealings with language to cease to be blind responses to stimuli: one comes to hear utterances as expressive of thoughts, and to make one's own utterances as expressive of thoughts. This seems indistinguishable from coming to have something to say, and to conceive others are having something to say; as opposed to merely making and reacting to sounds in a way one has been drilled to feel comfortable with. And light does not dawn piecemeal over particular sentences: "Light dawns gradually over the whole"[44]—a more or less coherent totality, that is, of sentences that one has been drilled into simply accepting. A difficulty in saying anything satisfying about the phenomenology of understanding is thus that working one's way into language—or better, being cajoled into it—is, simultaneously, working one's way into a conception of the world, including a conception of oneself as a person among others.[45] This idea would be enormously hard to elaborate further; but we cannot even recognize the difficulty—a real problem of description with which we are presented by the phenomenology of understanding—if we accept the assumption that learning a language leaves the content of our perceptions unaltered.

The new facts that I want to say understanding of a language makes available to our senses are of course, facts about what people are saying—the sort of thing whose overt availability, according

---

interpretation), and he is (naturally enough) unable to see more in it than an uncompelling empiricist dogma. Hence the best he can uncover, in the way of an underpinning for anti-realism, is a shallow empiricist reductionism; the deep epistemological roots of anti-realism do not emerge. Further, if the acquisition challenge is seen in its proper place, it will no longer seem, as it does to McGinn, to be no business of the philosophy of language to meet it. (See below, on the relation between working one's way into language and working one's way into a conception of the world.)

44. Wittgenstein, *On Certainty* §141.

45. See John Wallace, "A Query on Radical Translation".

to the position I outlined in §3, justifies putting a theory of truth-conditions in a central place in a theory of meaning for a language.[46] What I am claiming now is that the objection I attributed to Dummett in §5—that it is superficial to stop at that level—involves a view of understanding that leads to a phenomenological falsification.

In Dummett's defence, however, it might seem possible to occupy a position that concedes that a language sounds different when one has learned it, but stops short of allowing the irreducibility of the "superficial" level of description. According to this position, new facts do become available to one when one learns a language. Indeed, the new facts may correctly be expressed in, for instance, the "saying that . . ." idiom. But, as before, such formulations are superficial. The new facts would be more revealingly expressed by describing patterns into which understanding of the language enables one to organize sequences of individual pieces of behaviour, with the individual pieces of behaviour still characterized in terms that would be accessible to people who do not understand the language. So the way in which, say, an assertion sounds different to someone who understands the language, which is superficially captured by a formulation in terms of the "saying that . . ." idiom, would, according to this position, be more illuminatingly expressed by saying that the utterance is heard as conforming to such a pattern. This position preserves the conception of a theory of meaning that I described in §5: all the facts about a language are accessible from the cosmic exile's perspective, without presupposing mastery of notions like that of saying. But, since the facts are not all available to casual or unschooled observation, it is, according to this position, unfair to suggest, as I did above, that Dummett is unable to capture the phenomenological truth that we hear more, in speech in a language, when we understand it.

I think it is only to a prejudiced view that there could seem to be enough here to make intelligible the magnitude of the phenomenological leap involved in learning a language; for instance, to account

46. This is why, although there is certainly a mysterious transition in my view of language acquisition ("Light dawns"), it is not the gratuitous leap involved in realism in the mould into which Dummett forces it, where we have "a certain latitude of choice" (*Truth and Other Enigmas*, p. 365) as to what to mean by our words. The transition in my picture is a transition to this: meaning by one's words just what those words mean in the public language (e.g., that Michael Dummett has toothache).

for the intuition that in acquiring one's first language one acquires a conception of the world. (Not an intuition with which Dummett is out of sympathy.)[47] But it would be inconclusive to wrangle over this at the phenomenological level. It will be better to go straight to the epistemological prejudice that makes it seem that things must be like this: the idea that only so can we demonstrate that exercises of understanding are entitled to count as cases of knowledge. I shall make two points.

First, if that idea is an application of a general epistemological principle, it must be one on these lines: the title of a state to count as knowledge depends on there being facts, unproblematically available to its possessor, that constitute a *guarantee* that the content of the putative knowledge is true.[48] But as a general requirement for knowledge, this is worthless. Consider, for instance, the acquisition of knowledge by hearsay. Generally speaking, if one's informant knows what he tells one, and one understands what he says, one acquires his knowledge at second hand; whereas if he does not know, what one acquires cannot be knowledge. It does not undermine the possibility of acquiring knowledge by testimony that no informant is absolutely reliable;[49] the difference between the cases cannot consist in one's having available to one in the first, but not in the second, a guarantee of the truth of what one is told.[50] What makes it knowl-

47. See *Truth and Other Enigmas,* p. 311.

48. Dummett uses the word "guarantee" at *Truth and Other Enigmas,* p. 218.

49. President Nixon was not entitled to say "I didn't know" simply on the basis of the fact that his informants were not always tellers of the truth. (The epistemological importance of this example has been pointed out by Saul Kripke.)

50. A move that might tempt some philosophers at this point is the following. Requiring a guarantee was too strong; correlatively, it was too strong to insist that the fact that someone is saying some specified thing consists in the fact that he is behaving in some way characterizable from the cosmic exile's standpoint. However, we can preserve what is essentially the position discussed in §5, by holding that facts characterized in the latter terms are "criteria", in what is alleged to be Wittgenstein's sense, for statements made in the former terms. (See, e.g., Gordon Baker, "Criteria: A New Foundation for Semantics", pp. 163–4, 178.) I cannot discuss this suggestion fully here. But it seems, in fact, quite implausible that the suggestion could successfully handle the difference between acquiring knowledge by testimony and acquiring, say, a true belief from the say-so of a highly veracious person who does not actually know what he tells one. Generally, "criterial epistemology" seems insufficiently radical, in that it retains this assumption, which is characteristic of traditional epistemology: the right of some state to count as knowledge turns on the strength of a ground that the knower has for the truth of what he knows. Cartesian epistemology insists on a relation of something like entailment; the "criterial" proposal allows an evidential relation that is both conclusive and defeasible. However, the "criterial"

edge that is acquired in the first case is not the knower's warrant for believing what he knows, in the sense of something from which he could cogently argue to its truth, but rather something on these lines: that what he has acquired is a belief that is true, and does not merely chance to be so.[51] Obviously a similar idea will apply to the understanding of utterances, conceived in the way that Dummett's position labels "superficial"; it is no accident that our beliefs that people are saying what it sounds as if they are saying—our beliefs that their utterances can be taken at face value—are true, when they are.

Second, in Dummett's picture the status, as knowledge, of our takings of one another at face value is founded on our ability to discern patterns in one another's behaviour, as described in terms that function below the "superficial" level of the face-value descriptions. But these materials could not yield the firm epistemological foundation that Dummett is looking for. If we suspend our propensity to take one another at face value, and look for a foundation for it where we are told to look, we are confronted with such questions as this: supposing our awareness of someone's linguistic behaviour to date has run smoothly and without puzzlement, so that the behaviour has seemed to conform to a familiar pattern, how do we know this was not a short stretch of a pattern that equally fits the behaviour so far, but that, over a longer stretch, we would find unintelligible? There is nothing, where we are looking for our foundations, to allay the doubt that—if we conceive our epistemological predicament in Dummett's way—this question should raise.

---

proposal does not establish the coherence of the combination, but leaves it looking as if the claim is this: one can know that *p* when for all one knows it may be that it is not the case that *p*. My finding that incoherent is not, I think, a mere expression of weddedness to what Baker calls "Classical Semantics". (If "criterial" semantics can make it a coherent thing to say, so much the worse for "criterial" semantics.) The underlying point is that the following Cartesian principle is perfectly all right: if the title of some state to count as knowledge depends on the strength of a ground that the knower has, then the foundation constituted by the ground must be absolutely solid. (Otherwise we are picturing something we cannot conceive as knowledge.) This principle need not push epistemology in a Cartesian direction, if we are willing, as we should be, to deny its antecedent in the cases in which it is exploited for Cartesian purposes. (I do not regard these remarks as a programme for an attack on anything in Wittgenstein.)

51. Of course a proper account of knowledge by testimony would need to say more. But I do not see how any account could be satisfying without making room for the thought that in communication knowledge rubs off on others like a contagious disease. (At p. 98 of *Meaning and the Moral Sciences,* Hilary Putnam ascribes this "happy phrase" to me, but I actually acquired it from Gareth Evans.)

We ought not to conclude that, for all we know, other people's behaviour may suddenly cease to conform to patterns we can comprehend, in such a way that their previous apparent intelligibility would come to seem an allusion. We do know that that will not happen. But our right to the conviction that it will not happen is anchored upward, so to speak, in our right to take one another at face value; it is not something we have independently, on which our right to take one another at face value can be founded.

Suppose Martians look exactly like human beings, and every sentence of their language sounds exactly like an English sentence, but, in general, means something quite different. A short burst of Martian speech might chance to occur in such circumstances that it seemed to be intelligible as English; but sooner or later, no doubt, something would happen that would make it clear that we had not understood even the utterances that we had thought we understood. (It would not have been understanding even if, by coincidence, the Martian sentences had meant exactly the same as their English homophones.) Now if Dummett's picture of the epistemology of understanding were correct, it ought to be a serious question how it can be that, say in a brief conversation with a total stranger, one really understands his utterances. For one would need to be able to exclude, purely in terms of what is available to one at the putatively foundational level, the possibility that he is just such a Martian; and has one enough, at that level, to exclude that possibility? Once one has this worry, extending to any finite length the periods during which things seem to go smoothly cannot make any difference of principle. So it comes to seem that any claim to understand someone's utterances goes beyond what we have any genuine epistemic right to. On the picture I am setting against Dummett's, the position is as follows: if the total stranger is (as we say) one of us, then—since it is no accident that we are correct to take him at face value—we do understand his utterances; and if we do understand them, then we know they are part of a pattern whose earlier and later parts we would find familiar (hence, not as with the envisaged Martians). Someone might say at this point, "But aren't you shutting your eyes to a possible doubt?" To answer "They are shut"[52] would be, on Dummett's view, indistinguishable from confessing that we do not really know.

52. Compare Wittgenstein, *Philosophical Investigations*, p. 224.

On the picture that inverts Dummett's, the answer is something to which we have a right.

8. The epistemological root of anti-realism, then, is a demand for solid foundations for the knowledge involved in understanding utterances; but the demand is inadequately justified in general epistemology, and anyway incapable of satisfaction. To reinforce this last conclusion, I should like now to consider Dummett's unquestioning acceptance that acknowledgements of the truth of sentences are straightforwardly available in the behavioural foundations for a theory of meaning.[53]

The issues here recapitulate issues that arise in W. V. Quine's work on radical translation. Identification of assent behaviour is, in Quine's phrase, an analytical hypothesis.[54] That is to say: that such-and-such behaviour manifests assent to a sentence is not something definitively ascertainable in advance of making sense of the language under study. Prior to one's being satisfied that one has a workable scheme of interpretation for the language, an identification of assent behaviour has the status, however well motivated, of a guess. If one finds oneself incapable of constructing a scheme that works well enough across the board, on the basis of such a guess, one must discard the guess; and if one does succeed in constructing a workable scheme, the guess is retrospectively confirmed to exactly the same extent as the whole scheme is—that is, as part of a scheme for superimposing sense-making characterizations on the hard behavioural data, whose relation to those data is essentially holistic. One does not learn one's first language by constructing such a scheme of superimposition, but the point still holds that the scheme into which one works one's way—including knowledge of what it is to assent to a sentence—relates holistically to the hard behavioural facts. Thus: that certain behaviour manifests assent is not one of the hard behavioural facts, but already part of the holistically superimposed scheme.[55]

Quine concedes something like the above quite casually, but in fact the point has a catastrophic impact on the strategy of his at-

53. See, e.g., "What Is a Theory of Meaning? (II)", pp. 80–1. This underlies Dummett's concession that a truth-conditional theory would be unobjectionable if all sentences were effectively decidable. The idea would be essential for a verificationist theory.

54. This is implicit at p. 30 of *Word and Object,* and explicit at p. 312 of Davidson and Hintikka, eds., *Words and Objections.*

55. See, further, Christopher Peacocke, *Holistic Explanation.*

tempt to discredit the "intuitive" notion of meaning. The strategy is to construct a scientifically respectable concept of meaning, explained in terms of assent and dissent in response to stimuli, and then to point out how short a distance that concept carries us towards the full-fledged intuitive notion.[56] If this is to have the capacity to shock us that it is meant to have, it is important that we should be convinced that the scientifically respectable concept really is a concept of meaning; then we can worry ourselves with the thought that there is a scientific alternative to the conceptual slough in which we usually wallow. Scientific respectability, however, is supposed to involve not dirtying one's hands with the holistically superimposed scheme of sense-making discourse;[57] and what we have just seen is that to appeal to the notion of assent is inevitably to dirty one's hands. (And that an identification of assent behaviour will be confirmed only as a result of total immersion.) But appeal to the notion of assent seems essential if Quine's "stimulus meaning" is to look like a kind of meaning. So either Quine's *Ersatz* is not scientifically respectable (in his sense), or it is not recognizable as a notion of meaning at all.[58] This largely wrecks the strategy. Such notoriously disturbing doctrines as that no sentence has an empirical meaning of its own lose a great deal of their bite when we realize that, in the relevant sense, there is no such thing as empirical meaning.[59]

Dummett's motivation is not Quine's, but the upshot is curiously similar. Dummett's search for solid foundations for understanding, like Quine's respect for the concepts and methods of the natural sci-

56. See especially chap. 2 of *Word and Object.*

57. See, e.g., §45 of *Word and Object.*

58. The crunch comes, with marvellous predictability, in "Mind and Verbal Dispositions". Quine opts, in effect, for scientific respectability; but he still thinks he can have it both ways, retaining the applicability to bits of language of the notion of truth—to which, with the move from assent to "surface assent", he is no longer entitled.

59. I cannot deal properly with Dummett's many discussions of holism in this essay. Briefly: he finds holism disturbing because his idea of a respectable notion of meaning is close to Quine's notion of empirical meaning; hence he cannot make holism cohere with such indispensable ideas as "that each sentence may be represented as having a content of its own depending only upon its internal structure, and independent of the language in which it is embedded" (*Truth and Other Enigmas,* p. 304). Dummett always forgets that a sentence itself is as accurate a vehicle for its own molecular content as one could wish for. This will seem a trivial cavil if one thinks there must be a more substantial notion of content. But that thought is grounded only in the conception of the epistemology of understanding that I have attacked. (In terms of the nearest we can come to the desired notion, Quine's thesis is right: no sentence has a "content", of that sort, of its own.)

ences, leads him to try to build a theory of meaning on facts ascertainable from linguistic behaviour without presupposing the truth of what we claim to know when we claim to understand utterances. A respectable notion of meaning, for Dummett, is one according to which knowledge of meaning would be firmly grounded on a presupposition-free base, and his thesis is that a realist conception of meaning is not respectable by that standard. But the standard is one that nothing meets. Once we appreciate the status of identifications of assent behaviour, we see that Dummett's chosen base is not presupposition-free; and that if he purifies the base, what is grounded on it will no longer look like knowledge of meaning.[60]

9. I have argued that Dummett has no adequate ground for insisting that something deeper must be available than the kind of truth-conditional theory of meaning that I described in §3. We saw in §4 that, for languages whose sentences are not all effectively decidable, that kind of truth-conditional theory of meaning conforms to my characterization of realism in §1. I should like now to return to the question that I shelved in §4; is this really realism?

Dummett might not recognize the target of his attacks, because I have not mentioned the principle that every (non-vague, non-indexical) sentence is determinately either true or false (which I shall call, not quite accurately, "the principle of bivalence");[61] and acceptance of that principle is, according to Dummett, definitive of realism. The fact is, however, that, if we call realism, as I have formulated it, "R", Dummett's anti-realist attacks on the principle of bivalence take the following form: commitment to the principle of bivalence, in the presence of sentences that are not effectively decidable, entails R; but if R, then meaning transcends use; and meaning cannot transcend use; so not R; so we must not undertake commitment to the principle of bivalence.[62] The nerve of this argument is the rejection of R, on the basis of considerations in the epistemology of understanding; and in this essay I have severed that nerve without needing to take a

60. The relation between Dummett and Quine would repay more protracted treatment. For some suggestions, see §11 of Essay 1 above, and McGinn, "Truth and Use".

61. See Dummett, "What Is a Theory of Meaning? (II)", p. 93.

62. A "therefore", at p. 105 of "What Is a Theory of Meaning? (II)", is highly misleading, in suggesting that we are to conclude that R is unacceptable from the abandonment of the principle of bivalence. The preceding pages make it clear that the claim is, rather, that abandoning the principle of bivalence is necessitated by the unacceptability of R.

stand on the principle of bivalence. The principle is thereby saved from Dummett's attack; but I leave its status open, because I think there could be a reasoned abandonment of it on quite other grounds, compatibly with the retention of R.[63] Dummett conflates R and the principle of bivalence, apparently because he can see no reason why anyone might saddle himself with R other than that he takes himself to be committed to the principle of bivalence.[64] But §4 shows that the simple realization that not all sentences are effectively decidable is enough to yield R, without one's needing so much as to raise the question whether the principle of bivalence is acceptable.[65]

Crispin Wright might distinguish my position from the target of anti-realist attacks by saying that the acceptability of my position is a mere reflection of "grammar", in one of Wittgenstein's senses.[66] There is a truth here, but it needs to be handled carefully.

In effect Wright refuses to count anything as realism except the heady brew of ulterior conceptions that I distinguished from my position in §4. Of course he has a right to use the term as he chooses. But what made anti-realism of the sort that Dummett and Wright expound so fascinating was precisely its attack on R. On compelling grounds, we were to be dislodged from what seemed sheer common sense: the barely metaphysical conception of the world as possibly transcending our abilities to find out about it. If we now find that conception entrenched in "grammar", it cuts no ice to say "But that's just 'grammar'". So much the better for the conception. If what anti-realism attacks is only some other position—one that may well strike common sense as not nearly so obviously what it wanted—then anti-realism, as a negative thesis, is not as interesting as we had been led to believe.

Anti-realism of Dummett's and Wright's sort is not a purely negative thesis. It makes positive claims about what a proper theory of meaning would be like. To call my position "a mere reflection of

63. See Essay 1 above.

64. See, e.g., "What Is a Theory of Meaning? (II)", p. 90.

65. To place these remarks on a firmer footing, I would need to tackle head-on Dummett's assumption that a theory of meaning (understanding) for a language must be built on (employ the same concepts as) a "semantics" for it, in the sense of something that yields a validation for a logic. (See "The Justification of Deduction", and, now, *The Logical Basis of Metaphysics*.) There are some remarks about this in Essay 5 above.

66. See, e.g., the remarks about Strawson's "rocks of truth" in Wright, "Strawson on Anti-Realism".

'grammar'" is of a piece with the accusation of superficiality that I discussed in §5; the word "mere" is appropriate only if something deeper is available. So the idea must be this: the conception of a possibly verification-transcendent world appears, as it were on the surface, in an account of how things strike someone who is uncritically immersed in a language with the right sort of "grammar"; but a more critical perspective on that linguistic practice is attainable, from which the world, as realistically conceived, drops out of the picture.[67] But the only reason for believing in this more critical perspective—the cosmic exile's perspective—is the argument from the epistemology of understanding that I have undercut.

What is at issue here is the status of a position that is analogous to a kind of idealism, but with linguistic practice in place of "ideas". Wright is evidently impressed by this thought: if R is a matter of "grammar", then the possibly verification-transcendent world that R countenances is in some sense a reflection of our ways of talking about it. But if it is true that we cannot think about the relation between language and reality except from the midst of language as a going concern, then we must insist on this: if the "reflection" thesis is a truth, then it is a transcendental truth, the sort of thing that shows but cannot be said. For there is no standpoint from which we can give a sense-making characterization of linguistic practice other than that of immersion in the practice; and from that standpoint our possibly verification-transcendent world is certainly in the picture. If the "reflection" thesis licenses an anti-realism, then it is a transcendental anti-realism, one that need not clash with a conviction of the ineradicable necessity of R in our making sense of ourselves.

The *volte-face* between the earlier and the later work of Wittgenstein is in part a replacement of realism with anti-realism at this transcendental level.[68] When Dummett and his followers, purporting to be fighting under Wittgenstein's banner, put forward such positive theses as that linguistic competence must consist in dispositions to respond to circumstances that are detectable whenever they obtain, they are offering a much less interesting doctrine: a meaning-theoretical anti-realism, which stands to the misperceived deep doctrine as a shallow empirical idealism would stand to an analogous

67. Note especially the position called "(D)" in Wright, "Strawson on Anti-Realism".

68. This now (1997) strikes me as not sufficiently distanced from the Dummettian conception of how Wittgenstein's early and late work are related.

transcendental idealism. The transcendental realist claims that from the cosmic exile's perspective one would be able to discern relations between our language and a realistically conceived world. Anti-realists justifiably recoil, but in different ways. The meaning-theoretical anti-realist recoils into giving a different picture of how things would look from that perspective; but the right course is to set our faces against the idea of the cosmic exile.

ESSAY 16

Mathematical Platonism and Dummettian Anti-Realism

1. Goldbach conjectured that every even number greater than two is the sum of two primes. It might be claimed that if this conjecture is false, we could sooner or later ascertain that it is, by checking even numbers one by one until a counter-example appears.[1] But we have no procedure that would be guaranteed to equip us, in due course, with either a proof or a refutation.

Now suppose someone insists that the conjecture nevertheless conforms to the principle of bivalence: that is, that it is determinately either true or false.[2]

It may be that he conceives this insistence as obedience to a convention with, as it were, no semantic depth to it: it is simply, he thinks, that in the linguistic practice that we have learned, it is the done thing to apply the principle of bivalence to any utterance of the appropriate syntactic form—any potential affirmation. There are no obvious grounds for a substantial objection to this, although no doubt there is room for argument about whether any such convention exists.[3]

1. Some philosophers may think that this claim would abuse the notion of ascertainability, since with very large numbers the computation involved would be unsurveyable. I need not discuss this issue; if the suggestion is correct, that would simply reinforce the objection to platonism that I am about to set out.

2. For an explanation of the role of "determinately" in this formulation, see Michael Dummett, *The Interpretation of Frege's Philosophy*, pp. 435–6.

3. See Crispin Wright, "Dummett and Revisionism". Dummett would surely find such a position unattractive, in view of his idea that logic must have deep foundations in semantics (rather than reflecting "mere" conventions). But, although I cannot argue the point here, I think this contrast is suspect; and, as will emerge, we can endorse Dummett's rejection of platonism without espousing his view of the foundations of logic.

Alternatively, however, the idea may be that the principle of bivalence is justified by a deep connection between meaning and truth. We can summarize this supposed justification, for the case at hand, on the following lines: the meaning of the conjecture is such as to associate it with a specific possible configuration in arithmetical reality (the state of affairs that would obtain if the conjecture were true); and that configuration must determinately either obtain or not obtain, regardless of our lack of an effective procedure for deciding which of these alternatives is the case.[4] Here we have an expression of mathematical platonism; and this does raise substantial questions.

A platonist will not equate what it would be for the conjecture to be true with what it would be for us to be able to find a proof. Taken with the parallel thesis about what it would be for the conjecture to be false, that would make his picture of the justification for the principle of bivalence commit him to certainty that we could—at least in principle—find either a proof or a refutation. The metaphysical picture by itself does not seem capable of licensing such certainty. It needs independent warrant, and what could that be? An effective method for finding one or the other would do the trick; but that is the very thing we do not have.

So the platonist credits himself with a conception of what it would be for Goldbach's conjecture to be true that can be detached from any possibility—even in principle—that we might discover a proof.[5] As long as no one comes up with a counter-example, the platonist is willing to suppose that the conjecture may be true even in the absence of the sort of circumstance that would permit us to construct a proof—even in the absence of a uniform reason why each even number must be the sum of two primes, or a finite partitioning of the even numbers with a uniform such reason for each subset. It seems fair to say this: the platonist proceeds as if it makes sense to suppose that it may just *happen* to be the case that *every* even number is the sum of two primes (although of course if that is the case, it will

4. The justification rests on an assumed connection between "not true" and "false". On this, see *The Interpretation of Frege's Philosophy,* pp. 434–5.

5. Notice how insistence that the principle of bivalence may justifiably be applied even where we have no *effective* method for deciding truth value has generated a disconnection between truth and ascertainability even *in principle.* (See Crispin Wright, "Realism, Truth-Value Links, Other Minds, and the Past", at pp. 118–9.)

be true of *each* even number that *it* is necessarily the sum of two primes).[6]

2. This idea seems profoundly suspect. But if the position is wrong, what exactly is the mistake?

The immediate temptation is to begin a diagnosis as follows. The natural world is definitely independent of us, but there is some sense in which mathematics is nothing over and above the practices of proof and refutation that we learn in learning the subject. Since that is so, mathematical reality (if we allow ourselves to use such a term) is not to be expected to outrun our capacities to find out about it. That is what we might expect with the natural world; the platonist's mistake is to model his conception of truth and meaning in mathematics on a conception that would be appropriate about ordinary empirical reality.[7]

According to Dummett, however, any diagnosis that began like that would be misguided; the platonist's basic mistake does not lie in a special misconception of mathematical discourse in particular.[8]

So what is the platonist's mistake? He begins by taking someone's grasp of the meaning of a sentence to consist in his knowing what it would be for it to be true.[9] Now consider the platonist's picture of what it would be for an arithmetical sentence to be true (or false): namely, it would be a matter of the obtaining of a state of affairs that need not amount to the availability of a proof (or a refutation). *Provided that we reject that picture,* we can understand knowledge of what it would be for such sentences to be true as something that its possessor can (in principle) fully display in his linguistic behaviour: specifically, by assenting to them or dissenting from them on being presented with proofs or refutations. Bad luck or lack of ingenuity may defeat all efforts to devise a proof or a refutation, and may thus prevent a specific display of knowledge, in the case of some

6. See Dummett, *Truth and Other Enigmas,* p. 154.

7. See P. F. Strawson, "Scruton and Wright on Anti-Realism etc.", pp. 17–18.

8. See *Truth and Other Enigmas,* pp. xxiv–xxix. On this view of Dummett's, the use I made in §1 of natural-world imagery—the picture of configurations in mathematical reality—can at best serve to give the flavour of platonism; it cannot capture platonism's fundamental character.

9. "Knowing", in this formulation, makes for vividness, but it is not essential to the argument. Dummett's views on the connection between understanding and knowledge are complex and partly unresolved: see *The Interpretation of Frege's Philosophy,* p. xiii.

such sentences. But the appropriate specific display is not ruled out in principle for any, and will be actually forthcoming in the case of some; we cannot reasonably put a stronger interpretation on any requirement to the effect that understanding of sentences must be fully displayable in linguistic behaviour.[10] (Notice that this reveals the original equation between grasp of meaning and knowledge of truth-conditions to be innocent as far as it goes; if truth-conditions are conceived in this way, the equation does not represent understanding as not fully displayable.)[11]

The platonist, by contrast, has it that our understanding of the relevant sentences consists in a conception of what it would be for them to be true that might outrun what we could display in sensitivity to proofs and refutations—even including all those that could in principle be devised. But what other aspect of our use of arithmetical sentences could be cited as potentially manifesting the supposed residue of understanding? There seems to be no acceptable answer to this question. Affirmation of the principle of bivalence without restriction, or conformity with classical methods of inference, will not serve; the platonist wanted these practices to be *justified* by an *independently* acceptable account of the relation between meaning and truth. So platonism apparently makes no concession to the thought that someone's understanding of a sentence must be able to be made fully overt in his use of it. The trouble is that this leaves it a mystery how one person can know another person's meaning.[12]

Dummett's account of the platonist's mistake, then, is that he purports to conceive the understanding of the relevant sentences in such a way that it is not guaranteed to be fully displayable in the use that is made of them. And that is a mistake that it is open to us to fall into outside the area of mathematical discourse.

3. If we take Dummett's point, it seems that we must refuse to let the platonist distinguish what it would be for an arithmetical sentence to be true from what it would be for a proof of it to be in principle feasible. To put the point from the perspective of understanding: we must explain understanding of arithmetical sentences (which

10. See Wright, "Realism, Truth-Value Links, Other Minds, and the Past", pp. 127–8.

11. See *Truth and Other Enigmas*, p. xxii for this point, which corrects some of Dummett's earlier expositions of anti-realism.

12. For this line of thought, see especially "The Philosophical Basis of Intuitionistic Logic".

we can continue, if we like, to equate with knowledge of their truth-conditions) in terms of a propensity to respond appropriately to proofs.

Now being confronted with a proof of a sentence is a kind of circumstance that is, in an obvious sense, *decidable;* whenever a circumstance of that kind obtains, it can be ascertained to obtain. This notion figures crucially in the moral that Dummett draws from the unacceptability of platonism. Dummett's conclusion is that, on pain of representing meaning as transcending use, accounts of meaning in general, outside mathematics as well as within it, must characterize understanding in terms of propensities to respond appropriately to kinds of circumstance that can be ascertained to obtain whenever they obtain.

When the attack on platonism is thus generalized outside mathematics, there are two different sorts of case to be distinguished.

In the first sort of case, there is an analogue to proof: that is, there is such a thing as conclusively establishing that a sentence is true.[13] Here the generalization is straightforward; we must not allow a separation between knowledge of what it would be for a truth-condition to obtain and knowledge of what it would be like to be confronted with a conclusive verification.

In the second sort of case, there is no such thing as conclusive verification. Here the generalization requires us to explain understanding a sentence in terms of a capacity to respond appropriately to the less than conclusive evidential bearing on it of kinds of circumstance that still possess the crucial property: that is, they are capable of impinging on the responsive capacity whenever they obtain.[14] This has the same aim as in the correction of platonism: namely, to ensure that we conceive understanding in a way that makes it fully displayable.[15] (Notice, incidentally, that if we retain the equation of un-

13. When we move to considering empirical discourse, it can no longer be quite right to speak without qualification of the truth of *sentences,* in view of context-sensitivity. But nothing turns on this, and I shall ignore the point.

14. See, e.g., *Truth and Other Enigmas,* pp. xxxiv–v, xxxviii. I have avoided a formulation in terms of circumstances that are *detectable* whenever they obtain, in order to leave room for the sort of position envisaged at pp. 241–8 of Wright, "Anti-Realist Semantics: The Role of *Criteria*". But see n. 41 below.

15. Can there be accounts of meaning with elements from both sorts of case? Not obviously: if the first pattern fits, then it is not clear that there is any work left to be done by the apparatus of the second. (Compare Wright, "Realism, Truth-Value Links, Other Minds, and the Past", pp. 119–20.) There is a link here with the idea that if conclusive verification is possible for any sentences of a given kind, then it is (in principle) possible

derstanding with knowledge of truth-conditions for this kind of case, it will need different treatment; we can no longer plausibly identify what it would be for a sentence to be true with what it would be for one of the relevant decidable circumstances to obtain.)[16]

In either case, the result of generalizing the rejection of platonism in accordance with Dummett's conclusion is that understanding makes contact with the world, so to speak, only at circumstances that are decidable in the relevant sense. It becomes impossible to suppose that our understanding of our language impinges on a reality that is determinate beyond our possible access to it. This is what makes the label "anti-realism" appropriate; although "verificationism", understood in a broad sense, would be a more immediate fit.

Now suppose someone recoils from this upshot in connection with some extra-mathematical area of discourse: suppose, that is, that he endorses realism in some field of discourse, in a sense that simply registers dissent from anti-realism on that use of the label. Anti-realism results from a generalization of the response to platonism; and Dummett standardly takes the recoil from anti-realism to signal adherence to an analogue of platonism. I shall single out now, for comment later, two aspects of this treatment of the recoil.

First, Dummett takes it to be *constitutive* of being a realist, in the relevant sense, that one refuse to be dislodged from the principle of bivalence, as applied to sentences of a given kind, by the lack of any assurance that one would be able to establish, in the case of any such sentence, either that it is true or that it is false.[17]

Second, he takes it that any resistance to anti-realism about (say) ascriptions of sensations to others must make play with a purported conception of what it would be for them to be true to which our ways of deciding whether they are true are simply irrelevant. (This is an analogue of the platonist's proof-independent conception—or purported conception—of what it would be for a number-theoretic

---

for all. The denial of this, in the mathematical case, is platonism; perhaps this explains why Dummett does not find it necessary to argue for the generalization of the idea to observation, which is in fact quite unobvious (see p. 95 of "What Is a Theory of Meaning? (II)").

16. We shall need to equate knowledge of truth-conditions with a propensity to respond to the relevant circumstances, without supposing that there is any formula saying what it is for a truth-condition to obtain in terms of the obtaining of the relevant circumstances. See the description of position (D) in Wright, "Strawson on Anti-Realism", and Dummett, *Truth and Other Enigmas*, pp. xxxiv–v.

17. See *The Interpretation of Frege's Philosophy*, p. 437.

sentence to be true.) As an interlocutor voice puts it in Wittgenstein's *Philosophical Investigations* (§351):

> Pain is pain—whether *he* has it or *I* have it: and however I come to know whether he has a pain or not.

This is an expression of a familiar philosophical syndrome (devastatingly attacked by Wittgenstein) in which one supposes that one knows what pain is from one's own case, and that one projects oneself, without any need to advert to the accepted ways of finding out about others, into a conception of what it is for them to be in pain that is quasi-platonistic (at least from one's own point of view—of course the relevant others are supposed to be quite differently related to the same states of affairs).[18] Dummett's conviction that the issue between verificationism and a recoil from it is simply a generalization of the issue between anti-platonism and platonism comes out in the fact that if one does no more than express suspicion about anti-realism—the thesis that an account of meaning must make play only with decidable sorts of circumstances—in this area, he feels entitled straight away to saddle one with this whole disreputable collection of ideas.[19]

4. I think Dummett's diagnosis of platonism's basic flaw—as consisting in its refusal to tailor the meaning of mathematical sentences to the use that we learn to make of them—is very plausible. It is true that the capacity to respond appropriately to proofs and refutations is a central element in that use. And it is true that being confronted with a proof is a kind of circumstance that is decidable—that can make itself apparent to one whenever it obtains. However, it does not follow that an account of meaning for any sort of sentence whatever must accordingly restrict itself to decidable kinds of circum-

18. The position is actually even more objectionable, in one way, than platonism. Platonism can admit the idea that proof gives us access to truth-conferring states of affairs, so that grasp of truth-conditions, for the relevant kind of sentence, is at least partly displayable in responses to proofs. According to this quasi-platonistic view of ascriptions of sensations to others, by contrast, one "could in principle have no access to that which renders such ascriptions correct or incorrect" (*Truth and Other Enigmas,* p. xxxii).

19. See the amazing remarks about Strawson at *Truth and Other Enigmas,* pp. xxxii–vii.

stance, on pain of falling into an analogue of the fundamental error of platonism and making meaning transcend use. On a different view—one that permits us to endorse Dummett's rejection of platonism, including his diagnosis, but dissents from his view of how these considerations generalize—the reason why the notion of responsiveness to decidable circumstances figures centrally in a plausible argument against platonism is not that absolutely any fully displayable understanding must be explicable in terms of such responsiveness, but rather that that is a characteristic feature of competence in the use of mathematical sentences in particular.

Before I expand a little on this (§5 below), let me mention an epistemological thought that may seem to justify Dummett's generalization, by independently conferring a special role on decidable circumstances. The appearance is, I believe, illusory. Clearing it away should help us to recognize how special the role of responsiveness to decidable circumstances is, as a feature of linguistic competence in the discourse of pure mathematics.

The thought I have in mind is on the following lines. Suppose we do take it that the paradigm display of understanding—whatever kind of discourse is in question—is assent to, or dissent from, a sentence in response to a kind of circumstance that is decidable. The attraction of this is that it might seem to equip us with a satisfying epistemology for knowledge of someone else's meaning. For on that assumption we can claim that what constitutes the other person's meaning what he does can in principle be made fully overt, in such a way that it is cognitively accessible to just anyone. Whereas if a purported account of someone's meaning makes ineliminable play with circumstances that may obtain without being capable of eliciting a response from him, then, so the thought goes, any amount of linguistic response to circumstances on his part will leave his full meaning irredeemably occult. His linguistic behaviour, described without prejudice, will not constrain an outsider into attributing the right meaning to him. And if we are forced to suppose that someone can make his understanding of an expression cognitively available only to a non-outsider, someone who knows the language being spoken, that will preclude our extracting the promised epistemological advantage from the idea that understanding can be overt. The advantage was going to be that, given a particular case of putatively knowing someone else's meaning, we would be able to establish its epistemic credentials without merely begging the question; that is the accusation that threatens us if we are forced to appeal to an audience's familiarity with the language being spoken.

However, it seems to be an illusion to suppose that this kind of avoidance of question-begging is possible.

For one thing, assent to or dissent from sentences—the essential ingredient in the supposedly paradigmatic manifestations of understanding—cannot be definitively recognized from outside competence in the language in question. Assent or dissent can be knowledgeably identified only by someone who understands the language; or, parasitically, by someone who relies for his criterion on the testimony of someone who understands.[20]

And even if we waive that familiar point, this one remains: any display of assent to a sentence would leave undetermined, for the outsider to whom these displays are conceived as made available, exactly which sort of circumstance it is to which the assent constitutes a response. Any number of descriptions of the subject's environment (to look no further afield) might be candidates for being specifications of the kind of circumstance in question. Hence, if meaning something in particular by a sentence is conceived as constitutively involving an appropriate sensitivity to a specific sort of circumstance, the envisaged paradigmatic manifestations would after all fail to reveal a speaker's meaning. Further assent or dissent behaviour would no doubt rule out some hypotheses left open by the first display that one witnessed. But when we find it plausible that meaning can be wholly overt, what we are finding plausible is that the meaning that someone attaches to a particular utterance can be all out in the open at the time, not that it may gradually emerge in the future. And in any case, no sequence of assents, however protracted, could enable an outsider to eliminate all but one hypothesis as to what was eliciting them.[21]

The upshot is that, since we cannot do better, there cannot be good reason to be disappointed with a less ambitious construal of the thesis that meaning can be fully overt in linguistic behaviour: a construal according to which whenever someone who is competent

20. See Essay 15 above, §8.

21. I elaborate this point in "Wittgenstein on Following a Rule" and Essay 4 above.

in a language speaks, so long as he speaks correctly, audibly, and so forth, he makes knowledge of his meaning available—to an audience who understands the language he is speaking.[22] Of course it is a good question how it can be that what he makes available is knowledge. But without the idea that epistemology requires this, it need no longer seem that the answer *must* appeal to the notion of responses to sorts of circumstances that are capable of impinging on us whenever they obtain. In saying this, I am not suggesting that the answer will appeal instead to the incoherent idea of responses to circumstances that are incapable of eliciting any response. Rather, it is unobvious that the answer must focus especially on the idea of *responses to circumstances* at all. According to the position I want to advocate, the appropriateness of such a focus is a special feature of the mathematical case.

5. There are, after all, some striking differences between competence in the discourse of pure mathematics and competence in discourse about the natural world. In particular, consider the way in which acquiring the capacity to talk about the world of nature involves acquiring the idea that one inhabits a world, shared with one's fellows, that has more to it than one has any prospect of finding out. This idea is part of something one is initiated into accepting, when one masters this kind of discourse: something it is natural to call "a shared world-view". This label would scarcely fit in a parallel remark about competence with mathematical language. Certainly there are some analogies: for instance, questions of verification are not allowed to arise about fundamental aspects of the "shared world-view", and there is some parallel here with the axioms of mathematical theories. But the analogy is limited: where questions of verification are allowed to arise, the role of the "world-view" is not to provide premises for justifications, as mathematical axioms do, but rather to constitute the unquestioned background of anything we can recognize as a justification at all. There is no real parallel here to

22. If he is saying something, he makes available knowledge of what he saying: that is, knowledge of what has to be the case if his utterance is true. Contrast "What Is a Theory of Meaning? (II)", p. 75, where Dummett denies that a sentence's truth-condition is a feature of its use. This reflects a tendentious conception of use, and a relatedly tendentious conception of what it comes to for something to be true.

the central position that is occupied by self-contained demonstration in the practice of pure mathematics. Conversely, the nearest analogue in pure mathematics to the idea that mutual intelligibility involves shared occupancy of a world is the bare fact that mathematicians tell one another their results.

If we pay attention to this sort of difference (which could obviously do with a great deal of elaboration), it should come to seem quite implausible that, just because that is how it is with mathematical discourse, it ought to be possible to characterize the competent use of language in general in terms of sensitivity to decidable circumstances, such as would be constituted by verifications, conclusive or inconclusive. (Note that the point I am making here would not be met by moving to an account of meaning in terms of falsification,[23] or the "criterial" position envisaged sometimes by Wright.)[24] No doubt meaning must not be represented as transcending use, and in the mathematical case that recommends a "verificationist" (or falsificationist) approach to meaning; but that is because of the quite special role of verifications (proofs and refutations) *in the competent use of mathematical sentences in particular*. It should become quite unsurprising that no realist position, in the appropriate sense, is a live option in the case of mathematics, as soon as we advert to the fact that mathematical practice does not embody any full-blown version of the idea that mutual intelligibility is inextricably connected with shared occupancy of a world conceived as determinate beyond its impinging on us. There is nothing for linguistic competence to show itself in, in mathematics, apart from responses to proofs and refutations. But any analogous claim about extra-mathematical linguistic practice would be simply false. Linguistic competence outside mathematics actually embodies the idea of a realistically conceived reality; this shows (of course) in aspects of the use of language other than responses to decidable kinds of circumstances, and the status of the idea is bound to be distorted if we are required to restrict ourselves to such responses in our account of how understanding is manifested.[25]

23. See "What Is a Theory of Meaning? (II)", p. 126.

24. See n. 14 above.

25. At p. 131 of "Realism, Truth-Value Links, Other Minds, and the Past", Wright tries to neutralize a thought of this sort with the suggestion that those aspects of linguistic practice that most distinctively appear to embody something like the idea in question are

6. If we reject the way Dummett generalizes his argument against platonism, we allow realism outside mathematics to refuse to model itself on platonism. I shall mention two aspects of this liberation, corresponding to the two aspects of Dummett's view that I singled out before (§3 above).

First: what defines realism, we can say, is the claim that in understanding our language, we can contemplate in thought a reality that is determinate *beyond our access to it.* On the face of it, this falls short of the claim that every well-formed assertoric utterance is determinately true or false—the claim, that is, that reality is *fully* determinate. So, for all its importance in platonism, the principle of bivalence need not be essential, as Dummett claims, to the rejection of anti-realism. The important point about this is that, contrary to what Dummett suggests, realism can be separated from the idea that there is a deep semantical justification for classical logic.[26]

Second: a realist (in the relevant sense) need not go beyond rejecting the distinctive thesis of anti-realism—the thesis that an account of how understanding connects with the world must restrict itself to

---

merely "grammatical" (in a late-Wittgensteinian sense). But it would not follow that those aspects of linguistic practice can be correctly pictured as mere ornaments, so to speak, tacked on to a linguistic practice that can otherwise be completely described in anti-realist terms (like acceptance of the law of excluded middle by a non-platonist classical logician). It is simply not true that "our training (in the problematic parts of language) is necessarily restricted to confrontation with experienceable situations" (Wright, p. 112). We also learn, for instance, to accept standing sentences (such as "People can conceal their pain"), and it seems bizarre to suppose that they have no effect on our understanding of things we do sometimes say in response to experience (so that language is all ostensive, apart from an isolable "grammatical" remainder). Notice that there is no analogue here to the "bootstrapping" objection that tells against using a merely "conventional" ("grammatical") acceptance of classical logic in order to construct a purported semantic justification of it. There is no question of *justifying* the conception of shared occupancy of a world; this is part of what is correct about Wright's suggestion that such things are "grammatical".

26. Of course a realist will endorse the principle of bivalence wherever there is good reason to do so. Perhaps that means everywhere (apart from irrelevancies like vagueness). In that case there may seem to be no issue here. However, in the first place, it remains important that realism can be detached from the claim that logic—classical logic in particular—flows from a correct account of meaning. And second, it is worth considering a possible position about other minds in particular: one that, while resisting anti-realism (not restricting itself to decidable circumstances), refuses to apply the principle of bivalence to, say, ascriptions of sensations to others, on the ground that there is nothing to recommend this except a suspect picture of the mind as a receptacle. There may be hints of such a position in Wittgenstein, although—*pace* an insinuation at *Truth and Other Enigmas,* p. xxxvii—he does not, in passages like *Philosophical Investigations* §352, suggest that the principle of bivalence should be abandoned.

decidable circumstances. (Anti-realism—verificationism, in a suitably broad sense—is the positive thesis here. If this is hard to remember, it may help to conceive the position I am talking about as anti-anti-realism rather than realism.) There is no need for an opponent of generalized anti-realism to volunteer a quasi-platonistic positive view, to the effect that we can know what it would be for some utterance to be true even though verification, or less than conclusive evidence, is not even in principle available. (Far better to leave to anti-realists the unattractive task of trying to make such uses of "in principle" clear.) More specifically, about the case of ascriptions of sensations to others: there is no need to choose between confining ourselves (anti-realistically) to decidable circumstances, on the one hand, and, on the other, purporting (quasi-platonistically) to command a conception of what it would be for them to be true to which our ways of deciding whether to make them are simply irrelevant.[27]

A third liberation results from discarding the idea—which naturally takes a "verificationist" shape—that an account of how language relates to the world must centre on a conception of ways in which circumstances impinge or might impinge on cognitive subjects. Dummett standardly represents realism as retaining that idea; Dummett's realist standardly aims to credit himself with a conception of what it would be for something to be true in a way that transcends his own capacities to tell whether it is, by exploiting the notion of a being whose cognitive capacities are not thus limited—a being capable of a direct insight into the whole of some pictured region of reality. As a response to the anti-realist's manifestation challenge, this is at best self-deceptive, as Dummett has no difficulty in arguing: even if there were no problems about how the pictured being might manifest his supposed recognitional capacity (to whom?), the capacity is

27. Anti-realists tend to hold that if conclusive verification is ever possible for sentences of a given kind, then it is always (at least in principle) possible for such sentences (see n. 15 above). It goes against the grain to suggest that ascriptions of sensation to others are always conclusively verifiable, if true. So according to that epistemological view they never are. (But one can know that another person is in pain, say; so knowledge has to be separated—awkwardly—from any possibility of conclusively verifying what one knows.) This reflects the influence of the mathematical model. Dropping it frees us from that awkward separation, and permits us to reject both anti-realism and an analogue to platonism about others' sensations. Wright claims ("Realism, Truth-Value Links, Other Minds, and the Past", pp. 121, 129) that any realism (anti-anti-realism) about others' "inner" states must appeal to the idea of a projection from one's own case; but this derives from forcing anti-anti-realism into a quasi-platonist mould.

precisely not possessed by the merely human beings to whom the supposedly associated grasp of truth-conditions was to be attributed.[28] But realism, properly understood, simply does not need this forlorn attempt to conform itself to a verificationist shape.[29]

7. If we accept Dummett's thesis that platonism is intolerable because it represents meaning as transcending use, we still need to ask why the platonist falls into his error. After all, it is scarcely plausible that he finds the idea that meaning can transcend use compelling in its own right, and then devises a philosophy of mathematics to accommodate it.

Now one advantage of rejecting Dummett's generalization of the argument against platonism is that we can reinstate the intuitive answer to this question (see §2 above): the platonist pictures the relations between meaning, truth, and knowledge in mathematics on the inappropriate model of the natural world. The suspicion arises, indeed, that generalized anti-realism—anti-realism about the natural world—perpetrates a converse error: it pictures the relations between meaning, truth, and knowledge outside mathematics on the inappropriate model of mathematics. This has a debilitating effect, which we can, I suggest, begin to appreciate by considering the difference between primary and secondary qualities.

A conception of what it is for something to have a given secondary quality is not separable from a conception of what it would be like to establish that that is so in the most direct way: that is, by a suitable sensory experience in suitable circumstances (say, having the thing look red to one in appropriate lighting conditions). That is what it means to say that secondary qualities are essentially phenomenal qualities. Contrast primary qualities. A sound epistemology should accept that an object's possession of at least some primary qualities (the perceptible ones) can be established in the same direct way: by experiencing things to be so. Now on anti-realist principles, that should imply that there is no content to a conception of what it is for things to be so, over and above a conception of what it would be like to have such an experience. (This would be a case of the first

28. See, e.g., "What Is a Theory of Meaning? (II)", pp. 98–101.

29. On the difference between realism and "ideal verificationism", see Gareth Evans, *The Varieties of Reference,* pp. 94–100. The distinction undermines pp. 120–1 of Wright, "Realism, Truth-Value Links, Other Minds, and the Past".

of the two sorts that I distinguished in §3 above: separating a conception of what it would be for things to be so from a conception of what it would be like to have the experience would be analogous to platonism.) That is, it should imply that primary qualities are phenomenal qualities too. But primary qualities are not phenomenal qualities in the relevant sense. A conception of a specific primary quality is what it is, not simply by virtue of embodying a thought of the sensory experiences to which instances of the quality would give rise, as with a secondary quality, but crucially by virtue of the place occupied by the quality in our general understanding of the ways in which objects occupy space.[30] Anti-realist epistemology seems incapable of countenancing this distinction without undermining the thesis that some primary qualities are directly perceptible. And the upshot is an unattractive flattening—literally and figuratively—of the reality that is accessible to experience.

There is clearly not a whiff of platonism in the idea that primary qualities are both non-phenomenal and, in some cases, directly available to experience.[31] Rejecting the principles that would make primary qualities phenomenal if their presence can be established by experience does not require us to withhold assent from the following thesis: to conceive a primary quality's being instantiated is to conceive its being possible, in principle, for that circumstance to become available to experience. The crucial point is just that a conception of the circumstance has a content that is not exhausted by a conception of suitable experiences. And these considerations admit of a sort of generalization. Anti-realism restricts the points at which our understanding of our language makes contact with reality to what is phenomenal in an extended sense—a sense explicable in terms of appearance in general rather than sensory appearance in particular.

30. See pp. 94–100 of Evans, "Things without the Mind".

31. Insistence on direct accessibility makes this position a case of "naive realism" in the sense of *The Interpretation of Frege's Philosophy,* p. 449. Dummett takes it (p. 450) that the point of "direct", in formulations of such positions, is to exclude Cartesian doubt; and by excluding Cartesian doubt, he appears to mean (see p. 451) something like refusing to accept the fact of fallibility. This is a common misconception of "direct realism". It results from an incomplete view of the epistemological possibilities (see §§9 and 10 below). (See the similar remarks, betraying a similar misconception, of J. L. Mackie, *Problems from Locke,* pp. 43–4.) In fact the point of "direct" is to reject the falsification that would make primary qualities, by virtue of being non-phenomenal, merely hypothetical (behind a veil of appearance).

We can protest that this results in a flattening of our world that makes it unrecognizable, without forfeiting the right to deny the quasi-platonistic thesis that a conception of what it is for things to be thus and so is something to which whatever capacities we have to find out how things stand are simply irrelevant.[32]

8. To bring home how the anti-realist modelling of epistemology at large on the epistemology of mathematics induces a flattening of empirical reality, consider the following proposal of Crispin Wright's for a general account of verification, based on an account of why computation counts as verification:[33]

> Let S be any statement for which there is an investigative procedure, *I;* and let the *I-class* of statements for S contain [all] and only statements R satisfying the following conditions: *(a)* any rational agent who considers that the upshot of performing *I* is a justified belief in S commits himself to believing R; *(b)* one admissible explanation of the agent's coming falsely to believe S on the basis of *I* would be the falsity of R; and *(c)* S does not entail R nor vice versa . . . We can now make the following proposal: S is capable of *actual verification* if and only if there is some investigative procedure, *I,* such that (i) we can actually implement *I* and, on that basis, achieve, if we are rational, what we will consider to be a grounded belief in S; but (ii) subsequent grounds sufficient to call S into question would, if we are rational, have to be allowed to call into question simultaneously the truth of at least one member of the original *I*-class.

Wright suggests that this will capture the idea that by looking and counting one could verify something expressible, in a suitable context, by "There are nine cigarettes left in this packet".

32. This denial need not in all cases take the special form it can take in the case of primary qualities, where we can say a conception of a truth-condition is a conception of its being possible in principle to establish that things are thus and so. In the case of other minds it should not take that form (see *Philosophical Investigations* §393): the fact (if it is one) that one can always get someone to confess his "inner" states by torture or enormous incentives is not analogous to the fact that one can always in principle put oneself in a position to see what shape something is. However, as with primary qualities, there should be no question of a veil of appearance in the case of other minds (although "direct" is perhaps not quite right here). See Essay 17 below.

33. "Strict Finitism", pp. 216–7. It would be more appropriate if there were material from Dummett to discuss at this point, but Wright is, so far as I know, the only philosopher of anti-realist sympathies who has devoted serious attention to the epistemological questions that the programme raises. Wright's epistemological reflections deserve much more detailed attention than I can give them here.

For reasons that are familiar from long-standing epistemological discussions, however, it seems false that what Wright intends here will allow ordinary observational procedures to verify the obtaining of states of affairs that are substantial rather than "flat". To shift to a more familiar example, the ordinary procedure of looking and seeing cannot, by these standards, verify something expressible by "That is a tomato". A belief to that effect, arrived at by that procedure, may be wrong *simply* because what looks like a tomato is in fact a cunningly hollowed façade; and the statement that that is so fails the third condition for membership in the relevant *I*-class. (Statements suitable to be in the *I*-class—for instance "These are ideal circumstances for telling by looking whether that is a tomato"—will all be *true* on the most natural reading; they will be false only if understood in the light of how things turn out, that is, in such a way as to violate the third condition.)[34] And something similar could be said about the seeming cigarettes in Wright's example. When one models verification on computation, as Wright does here, the upshot—and this is very familiar—is to make it look as though one could verify the obtaining of a substantial state of affairs only by a procedure that would strike anyone uncorrupted by philosophy as neurotic.

What has gone wrong here? Considering mathematics on the model of our dealings with empirical reality, the platonist seemed to weaken the connection of mathematical truth with necessity (see §1). What he failed to accommodate is the thought that mathematical reality—if we allow ourselves to talk like this—has no properties be-

34. Howard Stein raised a question about statements such as "That thing is what it looks to be". This does not violate the conditions as formulated: it neither entails nor is entailed by "That is a tomato". But I am inclined to think this merely brings out that Wright has not quite succeeded in formulating his intuition; properly formulated, the intended idea still has the unintended consequence I complain of in the text. The intuitive idea is that if the members of the *I*-class are true, that secures, *independently of the results in the case at hand,* the excellence of the investigative procedure being followed (including the relevant capacities of the investigator)—the idea being that flawlessness in the procedure eliminates all possible sources of error. (See §9 for a forerunner of this formulation of Wright's, which makes this idea clearer.) In the present case, the procedure is: seeing how things look (from here), and saying that they are that way. Stein's candidate statement says that this procedure will not lead one astray in the case at hand, but it does not do so independently of the results in the case at hand; not that it is not logically independent of the actual specific result obtained (that the thing is a tomato), but it is not logically independent of the thesis that whatever the specific result turns out to be, that is how things are.

yond those it can be proved to have. A flattening of the empirical world looks like the natural result of the converse modelling, with that thought now given due weight. What makes both directions unsuitable—what both platonist and anti-realist fail to accommodate—is that mathematical objects, so to speak, are unlike empirical objects in having no solidity; no backs, as we might say.

9. Wright's proposal supersedes a different suggestion, which it will be helpful to consider: namely, that an account of verification should generalize the following feature of computation:

> . . . *if* someone (i) comprehendingly carries out the computation correctly; and (ii) correctly apprehends the outcome; and (iii) possesses a correct understanding of the statement in question, the opinion he forms concerning the truth-value of the statement is bound to be correct; there is no *further* scope for error.[35]

Wright's reason for superseding this proposal is as follows. In the case of computation, the "outcome" would need to be that one has actually produced a certain numeral, and not that one seems to have produced it; otherwise "satisfaction of (i)–(iii) would not preclude an error resulting from a divergence between what seemed to have resulted and what actually had". In a generalization to make this cover observational verification, the analogous "outcome", Wright thinks, would be that one "*observes* certain circumstances and goings-on". But that would render the proposal trivial.

This ground for superseding the proposal is not obviously cogent. A numeral *represents* (rather than being) the sum or product or whatever that a computation determines; an "outcome" analogous to the actual production of a numeral might be that one has experience *as of* "certain circumstances and goings-on", and this would leave the generalization non-trivial. In any case, I think the character of the epistemology is clearer in the superseded proposal, and for the moment I shall stick to it.

35. "Strict Finitism", p. 213; compare "Realism, Truth-Value Links, Other Minds, and the Past", p. 124. It is not clear to me that Wright's purposes require a generalization of computation, which is an effective method of deciding certain questions, as opposed to a generalization of assessing whether something—which may be at one's disposal only through luck or ingenuity—is a proof of some statement. See "Realism, Truth-Value Links, Other Minds, and the Past", pp. 118–9. But this query will not affect my point.

Knowledge confers a right to certainty, and we naturally want to be able to understand that in terms of something like the idea of having a fact within one's cognitive grasp. It can seem unintelligible that a cognitive position that deserves such a description might be constituted, even in part, by a state of affairs that is blankly external to one's subjective situation. Now mathematical knowledge conforms satisfyingly to this intuitive desideratum. We have to admit that computation (say) is fallible, but its fallibility can be wholly accounted for by our propensity to overlook matters that are nevertheless fully available to us—not outside the reach of our subjectivity. Wright's superseded proposal looks like a clear case of succumbing to a familiar temptation, that of supposing that empirical knowledge can be made to conform to the intuitive desideratum only in a completely parallel way: that is, by contriving to deny that the substantiality—the non-flatness—of some empirically accessible states of affairs carries with it a *quite additional* fallibility in our cognitive access to them, something with no counterpart in mathematics.

As the case of the tomato façade brings out, the motivation for this thought is not satisfiable without flattening the states of affairs to which we may take ourselves to have empirical access.[36] The alternative, keeping the intuitive desideratum in place, would be to see our way to taking seriously the idea that experience is an essentially fallible, but unmediated, openness on our part to a reality that includes substantial (non-flat) states of affairs; on this conception the solidity of a state of affairs should not seem to put it at least partly outside our subjective reach. But this idea is perennially blocked by a familiar philosophy that sets up, in a familiar place, a boundary or interface between the "inner" and the "outer".[37]

It may seem strange to associate Wright—at least in his superseded proposal—with this familiar epistemological and metaphysical tradition. After all, the tradition typically involves a search for absolute epistemic security, whereas Wright is concerned to affirm the perva-

36. This may suggest abandoning the intuitive desideratum; abandoning it yields some form of the epistemological position known as "externalism". (See Robert Nozick, *Philosophical Explanations,* pp. 280–3.) But it is a mistake to suppose that this is the only alternative to the mathematical model.

37. In these terms, anti-realism appears as an attempt to avoid the untoward effects of the barrier between "inner" and "outer", by thinning down our conception of what lies outside the barrier. It would be better not to allow the barrier to be set up in the first place.

sive defeasibility of our claims to knowledge. But I believe this difference is superficial. One might say, to minimize the difference: as always, the aspiration is for such epistemic security as mathematics affords; it is just that Wright is unusual (although—remember Descartes—not unique) in not forgetting that even computation is fallible.[38] And it seems clear that the attraction of the superseded proposal lies in the aspiration to disarm an apparent epistemological threat posed by fallibility in the general case, in just the way that fallibility can be made out to be epistemologically unthreatening in the case of computation in particular.

Wright's subsequent proposal brings out something that might be obscured by the suggestion that it supersedes. The leading idea is that we can disarm the threat that a particular source of fallibility might seem to pose to the possibility of knowledge, by showing that one could in principle *ensure* that in putting the relevant investigative procedure into practice one did not run the associated risk of error. Now it might look as if this would be simply a matter of care in the execution of the investigative procedure. But the subsequent proposal registers that this would not suffice, even in the case of computation (consider a very long computation, inscribed in some highly labile material). One would need to step outside the procedure itself and check various statements about how it is operating. It remains the case, however, that the sources of error that this picture will allow to cohere with the possibility of verification cannot include *sheer misleadingness in the objects* on which an investigative procedure is exercised, as in the case of the tomato façade.[39] What the subsequent proposal does is at best to enrich our conception of what lies within our subjective reach. There is still a flattening of the reality that this approach can count as accessible to experience. In order to avoid this, we should altogether reject the picture of a barrier between "inner" and "outer". (I have suggested the substitute picture of openness.) It amounts to the same thing to say that if we are to make room for knowing, just by looking, that one is in the presence of a substantial (solid) state of affairs, we must recognize

38. Defeasibility (of particular claims) is actually quite distinct from fallibility in the procedure that produces them, and we can concede the latter without admitting defeasibility to be all-pervasive; see Essay 17 below. Wright's insistence on defeasibility, and not just fallibility, is one symptom of his embracing the epistemology that I am deploring.

39. See n. 34 above.

that knowledge[40] is achievable by exercising capacities with the sort of ineliminable fallibility that, in view of the possibility of tomato façades, we have to attribute to any capacity to see that there is a tomato before one. What stands in the way of recognizing this is the traditional metaphysical and epistemological framework that I have mentioned.[41]

10. The epistemology that I have been discussing, with its familiar panicky response to the fact of fallibility, seems tailor-made to underwrite the supposed requirement that it be possible to demonstrate the epistemic status of cases of knowing others' meaning without question-begging. The feasibility of satisfying this supposed requirement seemed to be an illusion; and I suggested that the illusion blocks recognizing the significance of differences in linguistic practice inside and outside pure mathematics. (See §4.) It is unlikely that this is a mere coincidence. Dummettian anti-realism is supposed to

40. A state that there is now no reason to distinguish from possessing a conclusive verification.

41. Wright does contemplate the possibility that nothing may count as verifiable by the standards he sets, and he moots an alternative:

> . . . it needs investigation whether the crucial ideas for the anti-realist, of a recognitional ability and an ostensively definable state of affairs, might be elucidated not in terms which presuppose the notion of verification but in terms of something akin to the later Wittgenstein's concept of art, *criterion*. Here it would be essential to understand the first term of the criterial relation as lying on the worldly side of the language/reality distinction. Criteria would not themselves be statements but recognisable and ostensible aspects of reality. But for no statement would they constitute a sufficient condition of *truth;* the ground which they provided for accepting any statement would always be defeasible. On this view, the way in which language engaged with the world would not be truth-conditional at all but through-and-through criterial.

("Strict Finitism", p. 221; compare pp. 241–8 of "Anti-Realist Semantics: The Role of *Criteria*".) This proposal inherits the difficulties of the supposed Wittgensteinian "concept of art"—something that I believe commentators would not read into Wittgenstein if they were not locked into the sort of epistemology that I am deploring. (See Essay 17 below.) In addition, the proposal involves a conception of states of affairs ("aspects of reality") that is characteristic of an extreme and contentious realism (here I use this label to mark a contrast other than opposition to Dummettian anti-realism). These language-independent "aspects of reality" are just the sort of thing in virtue of which, according to this different sort of realist (we might call him "a Realist"), true statements are true. It is the idea that we have to think of langage engaging with a world made up of this sort of thing that is philosophically confused, not specifically the thought that it is truth that such items confer on statements; the confusion is not cured by substituting something else, warranted assertibility in Wright's version, for truth in this role.

challenge realism on the basis of general considerations in the philosophy of language, conceived as a branch of philosophy prior to epistemology and metaphysics. I believe this is quite misleading. The agreed starting-point—that platonism makes meaning unacceptably occult—yields no general presumption against realism (see §§4, 5); that this goes unnoticed, and that it seems so much as a starter to model the relation between truth, meaning, and knowledge in the case of empirical reality on the relation between truth, meaning, and knowledge in mathematics, can be explained by the presence of an independent and quite traditional epistemological framework. This suggests that, so far from exemplifying a new order of priorities within philosophy, the new anti-realism is no more than a novel way of bringing old, and suspect, conceptual pressures to bear.

PART IV

ISSUES IN EPISTEMOLOGY

ESSAY 17

Criteria, Defeasibility, and Knowledge[1]

It is widely believed that in his later work Wittgenstein introduced a special use of the notion of a criterion. In this proprietary use, "criteria" are supposed to be a kind of evidence.[2] Their status as evidence, unlike that of symptoms, is a matter of "convention" or "grammar" rather than empirical theory; but the support that a "criterion" yields for a claim is defeasible: that is, a state of information in which one is in possession of a "criterial" warrant for a claim can always be expanded into a state of information in which the claim would not be warranted at all.[3] This special notion is thought to afford—among much else[4]—a novel response to the traditional problem of other minds.

What follows falls into three parts. In the first, I shall express, in a preliminary way, a doubt whether the supposed novel response can work. In the second, I shall question the interpretation of Wittgen-

1. I profited from comments on an earlier draft of this essay by Gilbert Harman, Richard Jeffrey, David Lewis, Colin McGinn, Christopher Peacocke, Philip Pettit, Nathan Salmon, and Charles Travis.

2. I shall put "criterion" or "criteria" in quotation marks to signal the supposed Wittgensteinian use that I am about to describe. (Similarly with "criterial" and "criterially".)

3. A view of Wittgenstein on these lines is unquestioned in W. G. Lycan's survey article, "Non-Inductive Evidence: Recent Work on Wittgenstein's 'Criteria'". Its outlines seem to date from Sydney Shoemaker's *Self-Knowledge and Self-Identity;* see P. M. S. Hacker, *Insight and Illusion,* p. 293. My aim is to capture the common spirit of several readings that diverge in detail; so I shall try to preserve neutrality on nice questions about, e.g., what exactly the terms of the criterial relation are. (See Hacker, pp. 285–8, and Gordon Baker, "Criteria: A New Foundation for Semantics", p. 160; and, for a contrasting view, Crispin Wright, "Anti-Realist Semantics: The Role of *Criteria*", pp. 233–8.)

4. See Baker, "Criteria: A New Foundation for Semantics".

stein that yields it. I believe it issues from reading Wittgenstein in the light of tacit epistemological assumptions whose strikingly traditional character casts suspicion on their attribution to Wittgenstein himself. My concern, however, is less with exegesis than with those epistemological assumptions, and in the third part I shall begin on the project of undermining an idea that seems central to them.

1. It will help me to articulate my epistemological distrust if I let the "criterial" position define its stance towards our knowledge of other minds in explicit contrast with a possible alternative: namely, a position according to which, on a suitable occasion, the circumstance that someone else is in some "inner" state can itself be an object of one's experience.[5]

In Essay 14, I tried to capture this idea by suggesting that such a circumstance could be "available to awareness, in its own right and not merely through behavioural proxies"; and similarly by suggesting that

> we should not jib at, or interpret away, the common-sense thought that, on those occasions that are paradigmatically suitable for training in the assertoric use of the relevant part of a language, one can literally perceive, in another person's facial expression or his behaviour, that he is [for instance] in pain, and not just infer that he is in pain from what one perceives.

In the interest of a "criterial" position, Crispin Wright has protested against this attempt to describe an alternative (which he labels "M-realism"); he writes as follows:

> But that no inference, via "proxies" or whatever, should be involved is quite consistent with what is actually perceived being not that someone is in pain, *tout court,* but that criteria—in what I take to be the *Philosophical Investigations* sense—that he is in pain are satisfied. Criteria are not proxies, and they do not form the bases of inferences, correctly so described. But, in contrast with truth-conditions, a claim made on the basis of satisfaction of its criteria can subsequently be jettisoned, consistently with retention of the belief that criteria were indeed satisfied. So the M-realist about a particular kind of statement has to hold not just that inference via proxies is not invariably involved when the

5. I introduce this position here not in order to defend it (see §3 below for some difficulties in it), but just to exploit the contrast in order to clarify the "criterial" view.

> assertoric use of those statements is justified, but more: that the occasions which are "paradigmatically suitable" for training in their assertoric use involve not just satisfaction of criteria—otherwise experience of them will be experience of a situation whose obtaining is consistent with the falsity of the relevant statements—but realisation of truth-conditions, properly so regarded.[6]

For my present purposes, what is important about this passage is not the issue it raises about the formulation of M-realism, but rather its account of the "criterial" alternative. Wright's remarks bring out clearly how the "criterial" view is committed to the thesis that, even on the occasions that seem most favourable for a claim to be able to see that someone else is in some "inner" state, the reach of one's experience falls short of that circumstance itself—not just in the sense that the person's being in the "inner" state is not itself embraced within the scope of one's consciousness, but in the sense that what is available to one's experience is something compatible with the person's not being in the "inner" state at all.

Now is this position epistemologically satisfactory?

M-realism offers a conception of what constitutes knowing that someone else is in an "inner" state, at least on certain favourable occasions: namely, experiencing that circumstance itself. Wright asks us to consider whether what is experienced on those occasions may not be something less: namely, the satisfaction of "criteria". One might incautiously assume that experiencing the satisfaction of "criteria" is meant to take over the role played in M-realism by experiencing the circumstance itself: that is, to be what, on those favourable occasions, constitutes knowing that the circumstance obtains. But since "criteria" are defeasible, it is tempting to suppose that to experience the satisfaction of "criteria" for a claim is to be in a position in which, for all one knows, the claim may not be true. That yields this thesis: knowing that someone else is in some "inner" state can be constituted by being in a position in which, for all one knows, the person may not be in that "inner" state. And that seems straightforwardly incoherent.

This line of thought is partly vitiated by the incautious assumption. A "criterial" theorist can say: experiencing the satisfaction of

6. "Realism, Truth-Value Links, Other Minds, and the Past", p. 123. (Clearly the last sentence should read ". . . involve the availability to perception not just of the satisfaction of criteria . . . but of the realisation of truth-conditions . . .".)

"criteria" is meant to be, not what constitutes knowing that things are thus and so, but rather a "criterion" for the claim to know it. Its "criterial" support for the claim to know that things are thus and so would be defeated by anything that would defeat the original "criterial" support for the claim that that is how things are. So the "criterial" view is not required to acknowledge that someone may be correctly said to know something when what he supposedly knows cannot itself be correctly affirmed.[7]

Nevertheless, the "criterial" view does envisage ascribing knowledge on the strength of something compatible with the falsity of what is supposedly known. And it is a serious question whether we can understand how it can be knowledge that is properly so ascribed. Rejecting the incautious assumption leaves unchallenged the tempting thought that, since "criteria" are defeasible, someone who experiences the satisfaction of "criteria" for the ascription of an "inner" state to another person is thereby in a position in which, for all he knows, the person may not be in that "inner" state. And the question is: if that is the best one can achieve, how is there room for anything recognizable as knowledge that the person is in the "inner" state? It does not help with this difficulty to insist that being in that supposed best position is not meant to be constitutive of having the knowledge. The trouble is that if that is the best position achievable, then however being in it is supposed to relate to the claim to know that the person is in the "inner" state, it looks as if the claim can never be acceptable.

Of course my characterization of the supposed best position is tendentious. If experiencing the satisfaction of "criteria" does legitimize ("criterially") a claim to know that things are thus and so, it cannot also be legitimate to admit that the position is one in which, for all one knows, things may be otherwise. But the difficulty is to see how the fact that "criteria" are defeasible can be prevented from compelling that admission; in which case we can conclude, by contraposition, that experiencing the satisfaction of "criteria" cannot legitimize a claim of knowledge. How can an appeal to "convention" somehow drive a wedge between accepting that everything that one has is compatible with things not being so, on the one hand, and ad-

7. This partly undermines n. 50 of Essay 15 above. But, as will emerge, I stand by the spirit of what I wrote there.

mitting that one does not know that things are so, on the other? As far as its bearing on epistemological issues is concerned, the "criterial" view looks no more impressive than any other instance of a genre of responses to scepticism to which it seems to belong: a genre in which it is conceded that the sceptic's complaints are substantially correct, but we are supposedly saved from having to draw the sceptic's conclusions by the fact that it is *not done*—in violation of a "convention"—to talk that way.[8]

This line of thought may seem to be an indiscriminate attack on the idea that knowledge can be based on an experiential intake that falls short of the fact known (in the sense I explained: namely, being compatible with there being no such fact). That would put the line of thought in doubt; but the objection fails. We can countenance cases of knowledge in which the knower's epistemic standing is owed not just to an experiential intake that falls short of the fact known, in that sense, but partly to his possession of theoretical knowledge: something we can picture as extending his cognitive reach beyond the restricted range of mere experience, so that the hostile line of thought does not get started. But that cannot be how it is in the "criterial" cases. To hold that theory contributes to the epistemic standing, with respect to a claim, of someone who experiences the satisfaction of "criteria" for it would conflict with the insistence that "criteria" and claim are related by "grammar"; it would obliterate the distinction between "criteria" and symptoms.

I have granted that experiencing the satisfaction of "criteria" had better not be conceived as constituting the associated knowledge. It is tempting to ask: when the ground for attributing knowledge is experience of the satisfaction of "criteria", what *would* constitute possessing the knowledge? Someone who admits the question might be inclined to try this reply: the knowledge is constituted by experiencing the satisfaction of "criteria"—given that things are indeed as the person is said to know that they are. But does that specify something we can intelligibly count as knowledge? Consider a pair of cases, in both of which someone competent in the use of some claim experi-

8. Such responses to scepticism are quite unsatisfying. Without showing that the "conventions" are well founded, we have no ground for denying that the concession to the sceptic is an admission that we have reason to change the way we talk. And it is hard to see how we could show that the "conventions" are well founded without finding a way to withdraw the concession.

ences the satisfaction of (undefeated) "criteria" for it, but in only one of which the claim is true. According to the suggestion we are considering, the subject in the latter case knows that things are as the claim would represent them as being; the subject in the former case does not. (In both cases it would be "criterially" legitimate to attribute the knowledge, but that is not to the present purpose.) However, the story is that the scope of experience is the same in each case; the fact itself is outside the reach of experience. And experience is the only mode of cognition—the only mode of acquisition of epistemic standing—that is operative; appeal to theory is excluded, as we have just seen. So why should we not conclude that the cognitive achievements of the two subjects match? How can a difference in respect of something conceived as cognitively inaccessible to both subjects, so far as the relevant mode of cognition goes, make it the case that one of them knows how things are in that inaccessible region while the other does not—rather than leaving them both, strictly speaking, ignorant on the matter?

Proponents of the "criterial" view will have been impatient with my broaching a query about the notion's epistemological status outside any semantical context. Things would look different, they will suggest, if we took note of the notion's primary role: namely, as an element in a novel, "anti-realist" conception of meaning, adumbrated in Wittgenstein's later work to replace the "realist", truth-conditional conception of Frege and the *Tractatus*.[9] In particular, it may be suggested that the question with which I have just been trying to embarrass the "criterial" view—"What would constitute possession of 'criterially' based knowledge?"—seems to need asking only in the superseded "realist" way of thinking. In the new framework, questions of the form "What would constitute its being the case that P?" lapse, to be replaced by questions of the form "What are the 'criteria' for the acceptability of the assertion that P?"

I believe that this account of the relation between the truth-conditional conception of meaning and the conception implicit in Wittgenstein's later work is quite misguided. Of course that is not a

9. See Hacker, *Insight and Illusion,* chap. 10; Baker, "Criteria: A New Foundation for Semantics"; Wright, "Anti-Realist Semantics: The Role of *Criteria*". The general outlines of this conception of Wittgenstein's development, and of the issue between realism and anti-realism in the philosophy of language, are due to Michael Dummett; see *Truth and Other Enigmas,* especially essay 11.

belief I can try to justify in this essay.[10] But it is worth remarking that the "criterial" view seemed already to be problematic, epistemologically speaking, before I raised the contentious question what would constitute "criterially" based knowledge. If the supposed semantical context is to reveal that "criterial" epistemology is satisfactory, two conditions must be satisfied: first, it must be shown that the epistemological qualms I have aired—supposing we bracket the contentious question—arise exclusively out of adherence to the supposedly discarded "realist" framework; and, second, it must be made clear how the supposedly substituted "anti-realist" framework puts the qualms to rest. It is not obvious that either of these conditions can be met. As for the first: my account of the epistemological qualms certainly made implicit play with a notion of truth-conditions, in my talk of "circumstance" and "fact". But the notion involved nothing more contentious than this: an ascription of an "inner" state to someone is true just in case that person is in that "inner" state. That is hardly a distinctively "realist" thought, or one that the later Wittgenstein could credibly be held to have rejected.[11] As for the second condition: we are told to model our conception of "anti-realist" semantics on the mathematical intuitionists' explanations of logical constants in terms of proof-conditions. But proof is precisely not defeasible, so there is nothing in the model to show us how to make ourselves comfortable with the defeasibility of "criteria".[12]

10. I think what I shall say will contribute indirectly to justifying it, by casting doubt on a conception of our knowledge of others that is implicit in the standard arguments for anti-realism, and casting doubt on whether that conception should be attributed to Wittgenstein. There is more in this vein in Essay 15 above and "Wittgenstein on Following a Rule".

11. See, e.g., Dummett, *Truth and Other Enigmas,* pp. xxxiv–v. Baker, "Criteria: A New Foundation for Semantics", pp. 177–8, finds, behind the thought that "criteria" are epistemologically insufficient, a baroque argumentative structure involving the notion (supposedly characteristic of "Classical Semantics") of maximally consistent sets of possible states of affairs; but I cannot find that notion implicit in what I have said. (I believe the idea that truth-conditions are a matter of "language-independent possible states of affairs"—Baker, p. 178, compare p. 171—is a fundamental misconception of the intuition about meaning that Wittgenstein adopted from Frege in the *Tractatus;* and that this is in large part responsible for a distortion in the Dummettian conception of the issue between realism and anti-realism, and of the relation between Wittgenstein's earlier and later philosophies. There is more in this vein in Essay 4 above.)

12. In "Strict Finitism", Wright formulates a position in which defeasibility extends even to proof-based knowledge; see also "Anti-Realist Semantics: The Role of *Criteria*",

2. Understood in the way I have been considering, the notion of a criterion would be a technical notion; so commentators who attribute it to Wittgenstein ought to be embarrassed by his lack of self-consciousness on the matter. Mostly he uses "criterion" or "Kriterium" without ceremony, as if an ordinary mastery of English or German would suffice for taking his point. The striking exception (*The Blue Book*, pp. 24–5: the well-known passage about angina) should itself be an embarrassment, since it introduces the word, with some ceremony, in the phrase "defining criterion"; there seems to be no question of a defeasible kind of evidence here.[13] The idea that criteria are defeasible evidence has to be read into other texts, and the readings seem to me to be vitiated by reliance on non-compulsory epistemological presuppositions. I shall consider three characteristic lines of argument.[14]

The first is one that Gordon Baker formulates as follows:

> . . . *C*-support [criterial support] depends on circumstances. It might be thought that dependence on circumstances might be reduced or even altogether avoided by conditionalization; e.g. if *p* *C*-supports *q* under the proviso *r*, then one could claim that the conjunction of *p* and *r* *C*-supports *q* independently of the circumstance *r*, and successive steps of conditionalization would remove any dependence on circumstances, or at least any that can be explicitly stated. Wittgenstein, however, seems to dismiss this possibility with contempt. This rejection, unless groundless, must be based on the principle that C-support may *always*

---

p. 244. I do not believe that this yields an adequate epistemology of proof, on the model of which we might construct an acceptable account of defeasible "criterial" knowledge; rather, it saddles the epistemology of proof with problems parallel to those I have been urging against "criterial" epistemology. (Wittgenstein, *On Certainty* §651—cited by Wright at p. 244 of "Anti-Realist Semantics: The Role of *Criteria*"—makes a point about *fallibility*. Reliance on a *defeasible basis* is quite another matter. See §3 below.)

13. Baker, pp. 184–5, seems to deny this, but I cannot see how he would explain the presence of the word "defining". Most commentators in the tradition I am concerned with deplore the passage as uncharacteristic; see, e.g., Hacker, *Insight and Illusion,* p. 288; Wright, "Anti-Realist Semantics: The Role of *Criteria*", p. 227. There is a satisfying explanation of its point at pp. 133–6 of John W. Cook, "Human Beings".

14. There may be others; but I think the ones I shall consider illustrate the characteristic assumptions of the reading of Wittgenstein I want to question. (Baker, pp. 159–60, 162, mentions also the ancestry of the criterial relation in Wittgenstein's thought. But he would presumably not suggest that its descent from a relation of *a priori* probabilification carries much independent weight.)

be undermined by supposing the evidence-statements embedded in a suitably enlarged context.[15]

The idea that criterial knowledge depends on circumstances is obviously faithful to Wittgenstein; but this argument rests on an interpretation of that idea that is not obviously correct. Baker's assumption is evidently this: if a condition[16] is ever a criterion for a claim, by virtue of belonging to some type of condition that can be ascertained to obtain independently of establishing the claim, then any condition of that type constitutes a criterion for that claim, or one suitably related to it. Given that such a condition obtains, further circumstances determine whether the support it affords the claim is solid; if the further circumstances are unfavourable, we still have, according to this view, a case of a criterion's being satisfied, but the support it affords the claim is defeated. But when Wittgenstein speaks of dependence on circumstances, what he says seems to permit a different reading: not that some condition, specified in terms that are applicable independently of establishing a claim, is a criterion for the claim anyway, though whether it warrants the claim depends on further circumstances, but that whether such a condition is a criterion or not depends on the circumstances.

At *PI* §164,[17] for instance, Wittgenstein says that "in different circumstances, we apply different criteria for a person's reading". Here the point need not be that each of a range of types of condition is anyway a criterion for a person's reading, though an argument from any to that conclusion may always be undermined by embedding the condition in the wrong circumstances. The point may be, rather, that what is a criterion for a person's reading in one set of circumstances is not a criterion for a person's reading in another set of circumstances.

At *PI* §154 Wittgenstein writes:

> If there has to be anything "behind the utterance of the formula" it is *particular circumstances*, which justify me in saying I can go on—when the formula occurs to me.

15. "Criteria: A New Foundation for Semantics", pp. 161–2.
16. Or whatever is the right kind of item to be a criterion: see n. 3 above.
17. I shall cite *Philosophical Investigations* in this way.

I think we can take this to concern the idea that the formula's occurring to one is a criterion for the correctness of "Now I can go on", as opposed to a mere symptom, "behind" which we have to penetrate in order to find the essence of what it is to understand a series.[18] And there is no suggestion that the formula's occurring to one is a criterion anyway, independently of the circumstances. It is a criterion, rather, only in the "particular circumstances" that Wittgenstein alludes to: namely, as *PI* §179 explains, "such circumstances as that [the person in question] had learnt algebra, had used such formulae before".

In a schematic picture of a face, it may be the curve of the mouth that makes it right to say the face is cheerful. In another picture the mouth may be represented by a perfect replica of the line that represents the mouth in the first picture, although the face is not cheerful. Do we need a relation of defeasible support in order to accommodate this possibility? Surely not. What is in question is the relation of "making it right to say"; it holds in the first case and not in the second. Since the relation does not hold in the second case, it cannot be understood in terms of entailment. But why suppose the only alternative is defeasible support? That would require assuming that the warranting status we are concerned with must be shared by all members of a type to which the warranting circumstance can be ascertained to belong independently of the claim it warrants. (In this case, it would be the type of circumstance: being a picture of a face in which the mouth is represented by such-and-such a line.) That assumption looks in this case like groundless prejudice; perhaps the generalized version of it, which yields the conception of criteria that I am questioning, is similarly baseless. (I shall come shortly to the reason why commentators tend to think otherwise.)[19]

The second line of argument I want to mention starts from the fact that criteria for a type of claim are typically multiple, and concludes that criteria may conflict. If that is so, the criterial support afforded

18. The word "criterion" does not figure in the passage, but the subject is the tendency to think that in reviewing the phenomena we find nothing but symptoms, which we have to peel away (like leaves from an artichoke: *PI* §164) in order to find the thing itself. On the connection with §354 ("the fluctuation in grammar between criteria and symptoms") see Cook, "Human Beings", pp. 135–6.

19. This paragraph was suggested by pp. 138–40 of Norman Malcolm, "Wittgenstein on the Nature of Mind".

by at least one of the conflicting criteria must be defeated.[20] This argument clearly rests on the same assumption about the generality of criterial status: that if some condition (specified in a non-question-begging way) is a criterion for a claim in some circumstances, then it is a criterion in any. Without that assumption, we are not forced to accept that the pairs of considerations that stand in some sort of confrontation, in the kind of case the commentators envisage, are both criterial. A condition that fails to warrant a claim in some circumstances—trumped, as it were, by a criterion for an incompatible claim—may not be a criterion for the claim in those circumstances, even though in other circumstances it would have been one. And its failure when it is not criterial is no ground for saying that criterial warrants are defeasible.

The third line of argument, which is the most revealing, consists in a reading of Wittgenstein's treatment of psychological concepts in the *Philosophical Investigations.* In Wittgenstein's view, clearly, there are criteria in behaviour for the ascription of "inner" states and goings-on (see *PI* §§269, 344, 580). Commentators often take it to be obvious that he must mean a defeasible kind of evidence; if it is not obvious straight off, the possibility of pretence is thought to make it so.[21] But really it is not obvious at all.

Consider a representative passage in which Wittgenstein uses the notion of a criterion for something "internal". *PI* §377 contains this:

> . . . What is the criterion for the redness of an image? For me, when it is someone else's image: what he says and does.

I think that amounts to this: when one knows that someone else has a red image, one can—sometimes at least—correctly answer the question "How do you know?", or "How can you tell?", by saying "By what he says and does". In order to accommodate the distinction between criteria and symptoms, we should add that inability or refusal to accept the adequacy of the answer would betray, not ignorance of a theory, but non-participation in a "convention"; but with

20. See Anthony Kenny, "Criterion", p. 260; and Baker, "Criteria: A New Foundation for Semantics", p. 162.

21. For versions of this line of interpretation, see Kenny, p. 260; Hacker, *Insight and Illusion,* pp. 289–90; John T. E. Richardson, *The Grammar of Justification,* pp. 114, 116–7. Baker, p. 162, goes so far as to claim: "This principle, that C-support is defeasible, is explicitly advanced in the particular case of psychological concepts."

that proviso, my paraphrase seems accurate and complete. It is an extra—something dictated, I believe, by an epistemological presupposition not expressed in the text—to suppose that "what he says and does" must advert to a condition that one might ascertain to be satisfied by someone independently of knowing that he has a red image: a condition someone might satisfy even though he has no red image, so that it constitutes at best defeasible evidence that he has one.

Commentators often take it that the possibility of pretence shows that criteria are defeasible.[22] This requires the assumption that in a successful deception one brings it about that criteria for something "internal" are satisfied, although the ascription for which they are criteria would be false. But is the assumption obligatory? Here is a possible alternative; in pretending, one causes it to *appear* that criteria for something "internal" are satisfied (that is, one causes it to appear that someone else could know, by what one says and does, that one is in, say, some "inner" state); but the criteria are not really satisfied (that is, the knowledge is not really available). The satisfaction of a criterion, we might say, constitutes a fully adequate answer to "How do you know?"—in a sense in which an answer cannot be fully adequate if it can be really available to someone who lacks the knowledge in question. (Of course we cannot rule out its *seeming* to be available.)

In the traditional approach to the epistemology of other minds, the concept of pretence plays a role analogous to the role of the concept of illusion in the traditional approach to the epistemology of the "external" world. So it is not surprising to find that, just as the possibility of pretence is often thought to show the defeasibility of criteria for "inner" states of affairs, so the possibility of illusion is often thought to show the defeasibility of criteria for "external" states of affairs. At *PI* §354 Wittgenstein writes:

22. The supposed obviousness of this connection allows commentators to cite, as evidence that criteria are defeasible, passages that show at most that Wittgenstein is not unaware that pretence occurs. Note, e.g., Hacker's citation (p. 289) of *PI* §§249–50, as showing that criteria for pain may be satisfied in the absence of pain. In fact the point of those passages is not the vulnerability to pretence, in general, of our judgements that others are in pain, but the *invulnerability* to pretence, in particular, of judgements "connected with the primitive, the natural, expressions of the sensation" and made about someone who has not yet learned "the names of sensations" (PI §244).

> The fluctuation in grammar between criteria and symptoms makes it look as if there were nothing at all but symptoms. We say, for example: "Experience teaches that there is rain when the barometer falls, but it also teaches that there is rain when we have certain sensations of wet and cold, or such-and-such visual impressions." In defence of this one says that these sense-impressions can deceive us. But here one fails to reflect that the fact that the false appearance is precisely one of rain is founded on a definition.

Commentators often take this to imply that when our senses deceive us, criteria for rain are satisfied, although no rain is falling.[23] But what the passage says is surely just this: for things, say, to look a certain way to us is, as a matter of "definition" (or "convention", *PI* §355), for it to look to us as though it is raining; it would be a mistake to suppose that the "sense-impressions" yield the judgement that it is raining merely symptomatically—that arriving at the judgement is mediated by an empirical theory. That is quite compatible with this thought, which would be parallel to what I suggested about pretence: when our "sense-impressions" deceive us, the fact is not that criteria for rain are satisfied but that they *appear* to be satisfied.

An inclination to protest should have been mounting for some time. The temptation is to say: "There must be something in common between the cases you are proposing to describe as involving the *actual* satisfaction of criteria and the cases you are proposing to describe as involving the *apparent* satisfaction of criteria. That is why it is possible to mistake the latter for the former. And it must surely be this common something on which we base the judgements we make in both sorts of case. The distinction between your cases of actual satisfaction of criteria (so called) and your cases of only apparent satisfaction of criteria (so called) is not a distinction we can draw independently of the correctness or otherwise of the problematic claims themselves. So it is not a distinction by which we could guide ourselves in the practice of making or withholding such claims. What we need for that purpose is a basis for the claims that we can assure ourselves of possessing before we go on to evaluate the credentials of the claims themselves. That restricts us to what is definitely ascertainable anyway, whether the case in question is one of (in your terms) actual satisfaction of criteria or

23. So Hacker, pp. 289–9; Kenny, p. 260; Wright, "Anti-Realist Semantics: The Role of *Criteria*", p. 227; James Bogen, "Wittgenstein and Skepticism", p. 370.

merely apparent satisfaction of criteria. In the case of judgements about the "inner" states and goings-on of others, what conforms to the restriction is psychologically neutral information about their behaviour and bodily states.[24] So that must surely be what Wittgenstein meant by 'criteria'."

It is difficult not to sympathize with this protest, although I believe it is essential to see one's way to resisting the epistemological outlook that it expresses. I shall return to that in the last section of this essay; the important point now is how the protest exposes a background against which the reading of Wittgenstein that I am questioning seems inescapable. The protest is, in effect, an application of what has been called "the Argument from Illusion", and its upshot is to locate us in the predicament envisaged by a traditional scepticism about other minds, and by the traditional ways of trying to meet that scepticism. The predicament is as follows. Judgements about other minds are, as a class, epistemologically problematic. Judgements about "behaviour" and "bodily" characteristics are, as a class, not epistemologically problematic; or at any rate, if they are, it is because of a different epistemological problem, which can be taken for these purposes to have been separately dealt with. The challenge is to explain how our unproblematic intake of "behavioural" and "bodily" information can adequately warrant our problematic judgements about other minds.

The first two interpretative arguments that I mentioned depended on this assumption: if a state of affairs ever constitutes a criterion for some claim, by virtue of its conforming to a specification that can be ascertained to apply to it independently of establishing the claim, then any state of affairs that conforms to that specification must con-

24. Psychologically neutral information: once the appeal to pretence has done its work—that of introducing the idea of cases that are experientially indistinguishable from cases in which one can tell by what someone says and does that he is in some specified "inner" state, though in these cases he is not—it is quietly dropped. We are not meant to arrive at the idea of behavioural and bodily evidence that would *indefeasibly* warrant the judgement that someone is, so to speak, at least feigning the "inner" state. It is a nice question, on which I shall not pause, how the epistemological motivation for passing over this position should best be characterized. In the case of the "criterial" view, there is a semantical motivation as well; it is plausible that such evidence could not be specified except in terms of the concept of the "inner" state itself, and this conflicts with the idea that criteria should figure in the explanation of the associated concepts. See Wright, "Anti-Realist Semantics: The Role of *Criteria*", p. 231.

stitute a criterion for that claim, or one suitably related to it. What sustains that assumption is presumably the idea to which the protest gives expression: the idea that the question whether a criterion for a claim is satisfied or not must be capable of being settled with a certainty that is independent of whatever certainty can be credited to the claim itself.

With this epistemological framework in place, it is undeniable that the warrants for our judgements about other minds yield, at best, defeasible support for them. We could not establish anything more robust than that, if what we need is a certainty immune to what supposedly makes psychological judgements about others, in general, epistemologically problematic. So if we take Wittgenstein to be operating within this framework, we are compelled into the interpretation of him that I am questioning. According to this view, the sceptic is right to insist that our best warrant for a psychological judgement about another person is defeasible evidence constituted by his "behaviour" and "bodily" circumstances. The sceptic complains that the adequacy of the warrant must depend on a correlation whose obtaining could only be a matter of contingent fact, although we are in no position to confirm it empirically; and Wittgenstein's distinctive contribution, on this reading, is to maintain that at least in some cases the relevant correlations are a matter of "convention", and hence stand in no need of empirical support.

To an unprejudiced view, I think it should seem quite implausible that there is anything but contingency in the correlations of whose contingency the sceptic complains.[25] And I argued in the first section of this essay that it is quite unclear, anyway, how the appeal to "convention" could yield a response to scepticism, in the face of the avowed defeasibility of the supposedly "conventional" evidence. In fact I believe this reading profoundly misrepresents Wittgenstein's response to scepticism about other minds. What Wittgenstein does is not to propose an alteration of detail within the sceptic's position, but to reject the assumption that generates the sceptic's problem.[26]

25. See the splendid recanting "Postscript" to Rogers Albritton, "On Wittgenstein's Use of the Term 'Criterion'". (Such regularities are not "conventions" but the "very general facts of nature" on which "conventions" rest: *PI* II.xi, compare §142.)

26. Without going into even as much detail as I shall about the case of other minds in particular, there is already ground for suspicion of this reading in the way it attracts the label "foundationalist"—something that is surely quite uncharacteristic of Wittgenstein's approach to epistemological questions.

The sceptic's picture involves a corpus of "bodily" and "behavioural" information, unproblematically available to us in a pictured cognitive predicament in which we are holding in suspense all attributions of psychological properties to others. One way of approaching Wittgenstein's response is to remark that such a picture is attainable only by displacing the concept of a *human being* from its focal position in an account of our experience of our fellows, and replacing it with a philosophically generated concept of a *human body*.[27] Human bodies, conceived as merely material objects, form the subject matter of the supposed unproblematically available information. The idea is that they may subsequently turn out to be, in some more or less mysterious way, points of occupancy for psychological properties as well; this would be represented as a regaining of the concept of a human being. In these terms, Wittgenstein's response to the sceptic is to restore the concept of a human being to its proper place, not as something laboriously reconstituted, out of the fragments to which the sceptic reduces it, by a subtle epistemological and metaphysical construction, but as a seamless whole of whose unity we ought not to have allowed ourselves to lose sight in the first place.[28]

Such a response might appropriately be described as urging a different view of the "conventions" or "grammar" of our thought and speech about others. But it is a misconception to suppose the appeal to "convention" is meant to cement our concept of a human being together along the fault-line that the sceptic takes himself to detect. It is not a matter of postulating a non-contingent relation between some of what the sceptic takes to be given in our experience of others, on the one hand, and our psychological judgements about them,

27. This is the key thought of Cook's admirable "Human Beings", to which I am heavily indebted in this section. (One tempting route to the substituted notion is the idea that we can cleanly abstract, from the pre-philosophical conception of a human being, the mental aspect, conceived as something each of us can focus his thoughts on for himself in introspection, independently of locating it in the context of our embodied life. This putatively self-standing conception of the mental is the target of the complex Wittgensteinian polemic known as the Private Language Argument. If this were the only route to the sceptic's conception of what is given in our experience of others, the wrongness of attributing that conception to Wittgenstein would be very straightforwardly obvious; see Cook. But I think the situation is more complex; see §3 below.)

28. I intend this to echo P. F. Strawson's thesis (*Individuals,* chap. 3) that the concept of a person is primitive. Strawson's use of the notion of "logically adequate criteria" for ascriptions of psychological properties to others has often been subjected to what I believe to be a misunderstanding, analogous to the misunderstanding (as I believe it is) of Wittgenstein that I am considering.

on the other. Rather, what Wittgenstein does is to reject the sceptic's conception of what is given.[29]

I have suggested that to say a criterion is satisfied would be simply to say the associated knowledge is available in the relevant way: by adverting to what someone says or does, or to how things look, without having one's epistemic standing reinforced, beyond what that yields, by possession of an empirical theory. That implies an indefeasible connection between the actual, as opposed to apparent, satisfaction of a criterion and the associated knowledge. But it would be a confusion to take it that I am postulating a special, indefeasible kind of evidence, if evidence for a claim is understood—naturally enough—as something one's possession of which one can assure oneself of independently of the claim itself. It is precisely the insistence on something of this sort that dictates the idea that criteria are defeasible. Rather, I think we should understand criteria to be, in the first instance, ways of telling how things are, of the sort specified by "On the basis of what he says and does" or "By how things look"; and we should take it that knowledge that a criterion for a claim is actually satisfied—if we allow ourselves to speak in those terms as well—would be an exercise of the very capacity we speak of when we say that one can tell, on the basis of such-and-such criteria, whether things are as the claim would represent them as being. This flouts an idea we are prone to find natural, that a basis for a judgement must be something on which we have a firmer cognitive purchase than we do on the judgement itself; but although the idea can seem natural, it is an illusion to suppose it is compulsory.

3. The possibility of such a position is liable to be obscured from us by a certain tempting line of argument. On any question about the world independent of oneself to which one can ascertain the answer by, say, looking, the way things look can be deceptive; it can look to one exactly as if things were a certain way when they are not. (This can be so even if, for whatever reason, one is not inclined to believe that things are that way.[30] I shall speak of cases as decep-

29. Note that seeing behaviour as a possibly feigned expression of an "inner" state, or as a human act or response that one does not understand, is not seeing it in the way the sceptic requires. See *PI* §420; and compare n. 24 above.

30. On the "belief-independence" of the content of perception, see Gareth Evans, *The Varieties of Reference*, p. 123.

tive when, if one were to believe that things are as they appear, one would be misled, without implying that one is actually misled.) It follows that any capacity to tell by looking how things are in the world independent of oneself can at best be fallible. According to the tempting argument, something else follows as well; the argument is that since there can be deceptive cases experientially indistinguishable from non-deceptive cases, one's experiential intake—what one embraces within the scope of one's consciousness—must be the same in both kinds of case. In a deceptive case, one's experiential intake must *ex hypothesi* fall short of the fact itself, in the sense of being consistent with there being no such fact. So that must be true, according to the argument, in a non-deceptive case too. One's capacity is a capacity to tell by looking: that is, on the basis of experiential intake. And even when this capacity does yield knowledge, we have to conceive the basis as a *highest common factor* of what is available to experience in the deceptive and the non-deceptive cases alike, and hence as something that is at best a defeasible ground for the knowledge, though available with a certainty independent of whatever might put the knowledge in doubt.

This is the line of thought that I described as an application of the Argument from Illusion. I want now to describe and comment on a way of resisting it.

We might formulate the temptation that is to be resisted as follows. Let the fallible capacity in question be a capacity to tell by experience whether such-and-such is the case. In a deceptive case, what is embraced within the scope of experience is an appearance that such-and-such is the case, falling short of the fact: a *mere* appearance. So what is experienced in a non-deceptive case is a mere appearance too. The upshot is that even in the non-deceptive cases we have to picture something that falls short of the fact ascertained, at best defeasibly connected with it, as interposing itself between the experiencing subject and the fact itself.[31]

But suppose we say—not at all unnaturally—that an appearance that such-and-such is the case can be *either* a mere appearance *or* the fact that such-and-such is the case making itself perceptually mani-

31. The argument effects a transition from sheer fallibility (which might be registered in a "Pyrrhonian" scepticism) to a "veil of ideas" scepticism. For the distinction, see Richard Rorty, *Philosophy and the Mirror of Nature,* p. 94, n. 8, and pp. 139 and ff.

fest to someone.[32] As before, the object of experience in the deceptive cases is a mere appearance. But we are not to accept that in the non-deceptive cases too the object of experience is a mere appearance, and hence something that falls short of the fact itself. On the contrary, the appearance that is presented to one in those cases is a matter of the fact itself being disclosed to the experiencer. So appearances are no longer conceived as in general intervening between the experiencing subject and the world.[33]

This may sound like an affirmation of M-realism, but I intend something more general. The idea of a fact being disclosed to experience is in itself purely negative; it rejects the thesis that what is accessible to experience falls short of the fact in the sense I explained, namely, that of being consistent with there being no such fact. In the most straightforward application of the idea, the thought would indeed be—as in M-realism—that the fact itself is directly presented to view, so that it is true in a stronger sense that the object of experience does not fall short of the fact. But a less straightforward application of the idea is possible also, and seems appropriate in at least some cases of knowledge that someone else is in an "inner" state, on the basis of experience of what he says and does. Here we might think of what is directly available to experience in some such terms as "his giving expression to his being in that 'inner' state"; this is something that, while not itself actually being the "inner" state of affairs in question, nevertheless does not fall short of it in the sense I explained.[34]

32. In classical Greek, ". . . *phainetai sophos ōn* [word for word: he appears wise being] means *he is manifestly wise,* and *phainetai sophos einai* [word for word: he appears wise to be], *he seems to be wise* . . .": William W. Goodwin, *A Greek Grammar,* p. 342.

33. See the discussion of a "disjunctive" account of "looks" statements in Paul Snowdon, "Perception, Vision, and Causation"; and, more generally, J. M. Hinton, *Experiences*—a work that I regret I did not know until this essay was virtually completed, although I expect this section grew out of an unconscious recollection of Hinton's articles "Experiences" and "Visual Experiences".

34. M-realism might be accused of proposing a general assimilation of the second sort of case to the first. How plausible the assimilation is in a particular case depends on the extent to which it is plausible to think of the particular mode of expression as, so to speak, transparent. (This is quite plausible for facial expressions of emotional states: see Wittgenstein, *Zettel* §§220–5. But it is not very plausible for "avowals", except perhaps in the special case of the verbal expression of thoughts.) The motivation for M-realism was the wish to deny that our experiential intake, when we know one another's "inner" states by experience, must fall short of the fact ascertained in the sense I have introduced; it was a mistake to think this required an appeal, across the board, to a model of direct observation.

In *PI* §344—which I quoted earlier—Wittgenstein seems concerned to insist that the appearances he draws attention to, in order to discourage the thought that there is "nothing at all but symptoms" for rain, are appearances that it is raining. If there is a general thesis about criteria applied here, it will be on these lines: one acquires criterial knowledge by confrontation with appearances whose content is, or includes, the content of the knowledge acquired. (This would fit both the sorts of case I have just distinguished: obviously so in the straightforward sort, and in the less straightforward sort we can say that an appearance that someone is giving expression to an "inner" state is an appearance that he is in that "inner" state.)

This thesis about match in content might promise a neat justification for denying that criterial knowledge is inferential. The content of inferential knowledge, one might suggest, is generated by a transformation of the content of some data, whereas here the content of the knowledge is simply presented in the data.[35] But this does not establish the coherence of a position in which criteria are conceived as objects of experience on the "highest common factor" model, but the accusation that criteria function as *proxies* can be rejected. If the object of experience is in general a mere appearance, as the "highest common factor" model makes it, then it is not clear how, by appealing to the idea that it has the content of the knowledge one acquires by confrontation with it, we could save ourselves from having to picture it as getting in the way between the subject and the world. Indeed, it is arguable that the "highest common factor" model undermines the very idea of an appearance having as its content that things are thus and so in the world "beyond" appearances (as we would have to put it).

This has a bearing on my query, in §1, as to whether the blankly external obtaining of a fact can make sense of the idea that someone experiencing a "criterion" might know that things were thus and so. Suppose someone is presented with an appearance that it is raining. It seems unproblematic that if his experience is in a suitable way the upshot of the fact that it is raining, then the fact itself can make it the case that he knows that it is raining. But that seems unproblematic precisely because the content of the appearance is the content of

35. However, this idea is not available to Wright, in view of his insistence that grasp of criteria should not presuppose possession of the associated concepts; see "Anti-Realist Semantics: The Role of *Criteria*", p. 231.

the knowledge. And it is arguable that we find that match in content intelligible only because we do *not* conceive the objects of such experiences as in general falling short of the meteorological facts. That is: such experiences can present us with the appearance that it is raining only because when we have them as the upshot (in a suitable way) of the fact that it is raining, the fact itself is their object; so that its obtaining is not, after all, blankly external.[36] If that is right, the "highest common factor" conception of experience is not entitled to the idea that makes the case unproblematic. It would be wrong to suppose that the "highest common factor" conception can capture, in its own terms, the intuition I express when I say that the fact itself can be manifest to experience—doing so by saying that that is how it is when, for instance, experiences as of its raining are in a suitable way the upshot of the fact that it is raining. That captures the intuition all right; but—with "experiences as of its raining"—not in terms available to someone who starts by insisting that the object of experience is the highest common factor, and so falls short of the fact itself.

The "highest common factor" conception has attractions for us that cannot be undone just by describing an alternative, even with the recommendation that the alternative can cause a sea of philosophy to subside. The most obvious attraction is the phenomenological argument: the occurrence of deceptive cases experientially indistinguishable from non-deceptive cases. But this is easily accommodated by the essentially disjunctive conception of appearances that constitutes the alternative. The alternative conception can allow what is given to experience in the two sorts of case to be the same *in so far as* it is an appearance that things are thus and so; that leaves it open that whereas in one kind of case what is given to experience is a mere appearance, in the other it is the fact itself made manifest. So the phenomenological argument is inconclusive.

A more deep-seated temptation towards the "highest common factor" conception might find expression like this: "*Ex hypothesi* a mere appearance can be indistinguishable from what you describe as a fact made manifest. So in a given case one cannot tell for certain whether what confronts one is one or the other of those. How, then, can there be a difference in what is given to experience, in any sense

36. This fits the first of the two sorts of case that I distinguished above; something similar, though more complex, could be said about a case of the second sort.

that could matter to epistemology?" One could hardly countenance the idea of having a fact made manifest within the reach of one's experience, without supposing that that would make knowledge of the fact available to one.[37] This protest might reflect the conviction that such epistemic entitlement ought to be something one could display for oneself, as it were from within; the idea being that that would require a non-question-begging demonstration from a neutrally available starting-point, such as would be constituted by the highest common factor.[38]

There is something gripping about the "internalism" that is expressed here. The root idea is that one's epistemic standing on some question cannot intelligibly be constituted, even in part, by matters blankly external to how it is with one subjectively. For how could such matters be other than beyond one's ken? And how could matters beyond one's ken make any difference to one's epistemic standing?[39] (This is obviously a form of the thought that is at work in the argument from §1 that I have recently reconsidered.) But the disjunctive conception of appearances shows a way to detach this "internalist" intuition from the requirement of non-question-begging demonstration. When someone has a fact made manifest to him, the obtaining of the fact contributes to his epistemic standing on the

37. This is to be distinguished from actually conferring the knowledge on one. Suppose someone has been misled into thinking his senses are out of order; we might then hesitate to say he possesses the knowledge that his senses (in fact functioning perfectly) make available to him. But for some purposes the notion of being in a position to know something is more interesting than the notion of actually knowing it. (It is a different matter if one's senses are actually out of order, though their operations are sometimes unaffected; in such a case, an experience subjectively indistinguishable from that of being confronted with a tomato, even if it results from confrontation with a tomato, need not count as experiencing the presence of a tomato. Another case in which it may not count as that is one in which there are a lot of tomato façades about, indistinguishable from tomatoes when viewed from the front: compare Alvin Goldman, "Discrimination and Perceptual Knowledge". One counts as experiencing the fact making itself manifest only in the exercise of a capacity—which is of course fallible—to *tell* how things are.)

38. The hankering for independently ascertainable foundations is familiar in epistemology. Its implications converge with those of a Dummett-inspired thesis in the philosophy of language: namely, that the states of affairs at which linguistic competence primarily engages with extra-linguistic reality, so to speak, must be effectively decidable (or fall under some suitable generalization of that concept). See Baker, "Defeasibility and Meaning", pp. 50–1. For criteria as decidable, see Wright, "Anti-Realist Semantics: The Role of *Criteria*", p. 230.

39. See, e.g., Laurence Bonjour, "Externalist Theories of Empirical Knowledge".

question. But the obtaining of the fact is precisely not blankly external to his subjectivity, as it would be if the truth about that were exhausted by the highest common factor.[40]

However, if that reflection disarms one epistemological foundation for the "highest common factor" conception, there are other forces that tend to hold it in place.[41]

Suppose we assume that one can come to know that someone else is in some "inner" state by adverting to what he says and does. Empirical investigation of the cues that impinge on one's sense-organs on such an occasion would yield a specification of the information received by them; the same information could be available in a deceptive case as well. That limited informational intake must be processed, in the nervous system, into the information about the person's "inner" state that comes to be at one's disposal; and a description of the information-processing would look like a description of an inference from a highest common factor. Now there is a familiar temptation, here and at the analogous point in reflection about perceptual knowledge of the environment in general, to suppose that one's epistemic standing with respect to the upshot of the process is constituted by the availability to one's senses of the highest common factor, together with the cogency of the supposed inference.

When one succumbs to this temptation, one's first thought is typically to ground the cogency of the inference on a theory. But the conception of theory as extending one's cognitive reach beyond the confines of experience requires that the theory in question be attainable on the basis of the experience in question. It is not enough that the experience would confirm the theory; the theory must involve no concept the formation of which could not intelligibly be attributed to a creature whose experiential intake was limited in the way envisaged. And when we try to conceive knowledge of the "inner" states of others on the basis of what they do and say, or perceptual knowl-

40. The disjunctive conception of appearances makes room for a conception of experiential knowledge that conforms to Robert Nozick's account of "internalism", at p. 281 of *Philosophical Explanations;* but without requiring, as he implies any "internalist" position must, a reduction of "external" facts to mental facts.

41. Nozick must be a case in point. The way he draws the boundary between "internal" and "external" must reflect something like the "highest common factor" conception; and in his case that conception cannot be sustained by the "internalist" intuition that I have just tried to disarm.

edge of the environment in general, on this model, that condition seems not to be met.[42]

Keeping the highest common factor in the picture, we might try to register that thought by grounding the cogency of the inferences on "grammar" rather than theory; this would yield something like the conception of criteria that I have questioned. But we have been given no idea of how to arrive at specifications of the content of the supposed "grammatically" certified warrants, apart from straightforward empirical investigation of what impinges on someone's senses on occasions when we are independently prepared to believe he has the knowledge in question. The truth is that, for all their similarity to inferences, those processings of information are not transitions within what Wilfrid Sellars has called "the logical space of reasons",[43] as they would need to be in order to be capable of being constitutive of one's title to knowledge. Acquiring mastery of the relevant tracts of language is not, as acquiring a theory can be, learning to extend one's cognitive reach beyond some previous limits by traversing pathways in a newly mastered region of the "space of reasons". It is better conceived as part of being initiated into the "space of reasons" itself.[44]

I want to end by mentioning a source for the attraction of the "highest common factor" conception that lies, I think, as deep as any. If we adopt the disjunctive conception of appearances, we have to take seriously the idea of an unmediated openness of the experiencing subject to "external" reality, whereas the "highest common factor" conception allows us to picture an interface between them. Taking the epistemology of other minds on its own, we can locate the highest common factor at the facing surfaces of other human

42. To the point here is Wittgenstein's polemic against the idea that "from one's own case" one can so much as form the idea of someone else having, say, feelings. On the case of perception in general, see P. F. Strawson, "Perception and its Objects".

43. "Empiricism and the Philosophy of Mind", p. 299.

44. These remarks are extremely sketchy. Here are two supplementations. First: when we allow a theory to extend someone's cognitive reach, we do not need to find him infallible in the region of logical space that the theory opens up to him; so we do not need to commit ourselves to the idea that the theory, together with the content of experience, must *entail* the content of the putative knowledge. Second: the rejection of the inferential model that I am urging does not turn on mere phenomenology (the absence of conscious inferences). Theory can partly ground a claim to knowledge even in cases in which it is not consciously brought to bear; as with a scientist who (as we naturally say) learns to see the movements of imperceptible particles in some apparatus.

bodies. But when we come to consider perceptual knowledge about bodies in general, the "highest common factor" conception drives what is given to experience inward, until it can be aligned with goings-on at our own sensory surfaces. This promises to permit us a satisfying conception of an interface at which the "inner" and the "outer" make contact. The idea that there is an interface can seem compulsory; and the disjunctive conception of appearances flouts that intuition—twice over, in its view of knowledge of others' "inner" states.[45]

No doubt there are many influences that conspire to give this picture of the "inner" and the "outer" its hold on us. The one I want to mention is that we are prone to try to extend an *objectifying* mode of conceiving reality to human beings. In an objectifying view of reality, behaviour considered in itself cannot be expressive or significant; human behaviour no more than, say, the behaviour of the planets.[46] If human behaviour is expressive, that fact resides not in the nature of the behaviour, as it were on the surface, but in its being the outwardly observable effect of mental states and goings-on. So the mind retreats behind the surface, and the idea that the mental is "internal" acquires a quasi-literal construal, as in Descartes, or even a literal one, as in the idea that mental states are "in the head".[47]

Modern adherents of this picture do not usually take themselves to be enmeshed in the problems of traditional epistemology. But objectifying human behaviour leads inexorably to the traditional problem of other minds. And it is hard to see how the pictured interface can fail to be epistemologically problematic in the outward direction too; the inward retreat of the mind undermines the idea of a direct openness to the world, and thereby poses the traditional problems of knowledge about "external" reality in general. Without the "highest

45. Am I suggesting that the disjunctive conception of appearances precludes the idea that experience mediates between subject and world? It depends on what you mean by "mediate". If experience is conceived in terms of openness to the world, it will not be appropriate to picture it as an interface. (I am sceptical whether a conception of experience as anything but an interface is available within the dominant contemporary philosophy of mind.)

46. See Charles Taylor, *Hegel*, pp. 3–11.

47. This movement of thought can find support in the idea that the mental is conceptually captured by introspective ostensive definition. (That idea is perhaps naturally understood as a response to the obliteration of the notion of intrinsically expressive behaviour.) But some versions of the position are not notably introspectionist. (See n. 27 above.)

common factor" conception of experience, we can leave the interface out of the picture, and the traditional problems lapse. Traditional epistemology is widely felt to be unsatisfying; I think this is a symptom of the error in the "highest common factor" conception, and, more generally, of the misguidedness of an objectifying conception of the human.

Knowledge and the Internal[1]

1. I am going to work with an idea from Wilfrid Sellars, that knowledge—at least as enjoyed by rational animals—is a certain sort of standing in the space of reasons.[2] My concern is a familiar philosophical dialectic, which I shall approach in terms of what happens to the Sellarsian idea when the image of standings in the space of reasons undergoes a certain deformation. That it is a deformation is something we can learn from how unsatisfactory the familiar dialectic is.

2. The deformation is an interiorization of the space of reasons, a withdrawal of it from the external world. This happens when we suppose we ought to be able to achieve flawless standings in the

1. I first delivered this essay in the 1989/90 lecture series of the Center for the Philosophy of Science at the University of Pittsburgh. I presented an ancestor to a conference on Belief and Knowledge in Albi, France, in July 1981. Charles Travis commented helpfully on the ancestor, and Simon Blackburn on a revised version of it. A less distant descendant of some of that material forms part of Essay 17 above. More recently, I have benefited from conversations with Jonathan Dancy; from comments on a more recent draft by Robert Brandom; and from the responses of audiences at Ohio State University, Haverford College, and the Chapel Hill Colloquium, especially Robert Kraut, L. Aryeh Kosman, and Jay Rosenberg. Robert Brandom's response at the Chapel Hill Colloquium has been published as "Knowledge and the Social Articulation of the Space of Reasons".

2. "In characterizing an episode or a state as that [better: one] of *knowing*, we are not giving an empirical description of that episode or state; we are placing it in the logical space of reasons, of justifying and being able to justify what one says" ("Empiricism and the Philosophy of Mind", p. 298–9). I put in the parenthetical qualification so as to allow that a concept of knowledge might be applied to non-rational animals too; but nothing in this essay will depend on that.

space of reasons by our own unaided resources, without needing the world to do us any favours.

Consider the Argument from Illusion. Seeing, or perhaps having seen, that things are thus and so would be an epistemically satisfactory standing in the space of reasons. But when I see that things are thus and so, I take it that things are thus and so on the basis of having it look to me as if things are thus and so. And it can look to me as if things are thus and so when they are not; appearances do not give me the resources to ensure that I take things to be thus and so, on the basis of appearances, only when things are indeed thus and so. If things are indeed thus and so when they seem to be, the world is doing me a favour. So if I want to restrict myself to standings in the space of reasons whose flawlessness I can ensure without external help, I must go no further than taking it that it *looks* to me as if things are thus and so.

One might hope that this inward retreat is only temporary. Take a particular case in which it looks to me as if things are a certain way. If things are indeed that way, that is—so far—a favour the world is doing me. The hope is that I might start from the fact that things look that way to me; add in anything else that the ground rules allow me to avail myself of, if it helps; and move from there, by my own unaided resources, without needing the world to do me any favours, to a satisfactory standing in the space of reasons with respect to the fact that the world is arranged the way it looks. And now that would no longer be a favour the world is doing me, a kindness I must simply hope for. Now I would have a derivatively satisfactory standing in the space of reasons, with respect to the fact that things are as they look, that I achieved by myself without needing to be indebted to the world.

Anyone who knows the dreary history of epistemology knows that this hope is rather faint. That will matter in due course, but it does not matter for what I am doing now, which is simply reminding you, in perhaps slightly unfamiliar terms, of a familiar epistemologists' syndrome.

Of course perception could not yield us standings in the space of reasons at all without some indebtedness to the world. The position I am describing does not involve the fantasy that pure unaided reason could give us knowledge of the external world, without our needing the world to oblige us by affording appearances. The thought is that we need no outside help in avoiding being led astray by whatever appearances the world is kind enough to afford us.

The Argument from Illusion is of course familiar in the epistemology of perception. But an argument with the same structure is tempting whenever it can seem right to say that we need a favour from the world if there is to be application for a locution of the relevant kind: a locution that belongs with "see that . . ." in that it is epistemic and thereby factive. This will be so whenever appearances can be misleading, in such a way that one cannot blame their potential for deception on defects in how one has conducted oneself in the space of reasons. What is at fault must then be the unkindness of the world. And when an appearance is not misleading, that is, correspondingly, a favour from the world. Whenever we have that structure, it will seem that the epistemic position signalled by the original locution can be at best derivative; the true starting-point in the space of reasons must be something common to the favourable and the potentially misleading cases (like having it look to one as if things are thus and so).[3]

Factive locutions that are vulnerable to this treatment include "remember that . . ." (with "seem to remember that . . ." as the upshot of the retreat), and "learn from so-and-so that . . ." (with "hear so-and-so say that . . ." as the upshot of the retreat).[4] A negative instance may help to make the point clear: consider "prove that . . .". Suppose one is subject to a misleading appearance that one has a proof of something. In that case, surely, one must have miscon-

3. I am deliberately leaving the idea of blameworthiness, in one's moves in the space of reasons, unspecific. If someone arrives at a false belief from which she would have been deterred by some investigation she chose not to engage in because of its high cost and low probability of overturning the other evidence, is she blameworthy? Different answers are possible. But no reasonable interpretation of the idea of doxastic obligations could make falsehood in an empirical belief show, all by itself, that an obligation has not been met. That is the central insight (a genuine insight, even though it is typically mishandled) of the familiar genre of philosophy according to which empirical knowledge is problematic. I want to focus on this gap, nearly universally acknowledged, between doxastic blamelessness in a sense that connects with doxastic obligation, on the one hand, and empirical knowledge, on the other, without being distracted by details about how doxastic blamelessness should be understood. (The epistemological outlook I shall recommend should make such questions seem less urgent.)

4. In the case of testimony, one is literally done a favour by an informant. But there will have to be, figuratively, a favour from the world at some point in the epistemic ancestry of a piece of knowledge by testimony. (At least outside the area of, for instance, being told of something that has been proved; see the text below.)

ducted oneself in the space of reasons; it cannot be that the world is the only thing one can blame for what has gone wrong.[5]

3. I spoke of hoping that the inward retreat is only temporary, and I suggested that the hope is faint. I think this is true in all the applications, but I shall stick to perception to bring out what this implies.

One need not restrict oneself to the particular perceptual appearance whose credentials are in question. I allowed that one could add in anything else that might help, if it is available according to the ground rules. Here we might think of surrounding appearances and background knowledge. (It will emerge that it is open to doubt whether the ground rules make any background knowledge available, but we can let that pass at this stage.)

Clearly one is not stuck with simply believing, come what may, that things are as they appear. One can refine one's policies or habits of basing beliefs on appearance, taking more and more circumstances into account, with a view to improving the proportion of truths to falsehoods in their output. And it is not just that one *can* engage in this refining procedure. Surely reason positively requires one to do so. If it turns out to be an effect of interiorizing the space of reasons that we become unable to make sense of this critical function of reason, we ought to conclude that the very idea of the space of reasons has become unrecognizable. I think that is what turns out; I want to bring that out by giving the idea of something that is both

5. This is essentially the feature of proof (or computation) that Crispin Wright aims to generalize, in his account of what it is to have verified a statement ("Strict Finitism", pp. 210–18). Wright strangely combines an understanding of this feature of proof (or computation) with applying the Argument from Illusion even here. He writes (p. 210): "If arithmetical computation is to be a paradigm of verification, then to be entitled to claim to have verified a statement cannot be to be entitled to claim a conclusive, *indefeasible* warrant for its assertion; for the most painstaking and careful execution of a computation confers no guarantee that is correct." This is in effect a form of the familiar retreat (in respect of what warrants one's assertion), from "I have proved that it is so" (which, if true, surely equips one with a conclusive, indefeasible warrant) to "I have before me what, on painstaking and careful inspection, appears to be a proof that it is so". To suppose that this retreat is required is to miss the significance of the fact that if I am misled in such a case, the fault is in my moves in the space of reasons, not in the world. I suppose it is because Wright thinks mathematical proof and empirical verification are on a par in respect of vulnerability to the Argument from Illusion (and so in respect of the defeasibility of available warrants) that he thinks he can model empirical verification on mathematical verification without risking an undue concession to scepticism. (In effect Wright is committed to withholding, in respect of empirical verification, the acknowledgement that in n. 3 above I described as nearly universal.) I think the epistemology of empirical knowledge that results is disastrous; I try to bring this out in Essay 16 above.

interiorized and still recognizably the space of reasons a run for its money.

So we are to try to reconstruct the epistemic satisfactoriness implicit in the idea of seeing that things are thus and so, using the following materials: first, the fact that it looks to a subject as if things are that way; second, whatever further circumstances are relevant (this depends on the third item); third, the fact that the policy or habit of accepting appearances in such circumstances is endorsed by reason, in its critical function, as reliable. And now the trouble is this: unless reason can come up with policies or habits that will *never* lead us astray, there is not enough here to add up to what we were trying to reconstruct. Seeing that things are thus and so is a position that one *cannot* be in if things are not thus and so. Given that one is in that position, it follows that things are thus and so. And if reason cannot find policies or habits that are utterly risk-free, the reconstructing materials cannot duplicate that. However careful one is in basing belief on appearances, if one's method falls short of total freedom from risk of error, the appearance plus the appropriate circumstances for activating the method cannot ensure that things are as one takes them to be.

There are various possible responses to this point. The one I recommend is that we should jettison the whole approach to knowledge that structures epistemology around the Argument from Illusion. I shall mention three others.

Obviously one response is scepticism. In my Sellarsian framework, I can put the sceptical response like this. An epistemically satisfactory position would have to be a standing in the space of reasons—Sellars is right about that. But the argument I have just sketched shows that we cannot reconstruct a standing in the space of reasons, suitable to amount to knowledge, with respect to the fact that things are as they perceptually appear. So it must be a mistake to think we can achieve knowledge through perception. This thought clearly generalizes, in a way that matches the generalization of the Argument from Illusion.

A second response would be to claim that there must be policies or habits of basing belief on appearance that *are* utterly risk-free. It is obvious how this response might be attractive, in the context of the threat of scepticism; but I do not think it has any plausibility in its own right. It would express a rather touching *a priori* faith in the power of human reason to devise fully effective protections against the deceptive capacities of appearance. No doubt it would suit our vanity, or at least help us feel safe, if we could suppose our reason had such power, but obviously that is no ground to believe it is so; in fact it is a ground to be suspicious of the idea. (I shall return to a point of this sort later.)[6]

A third response is to keep the Sellarsian idea I began with, in its interiorized form, but only as one element in a composite conception of knowledge; we are to add an external element in order to cope with the problem I am considering. The upshot is a position that looks like this. At least for rational animals, a satisfactory standing in the space of reasons is a necessary condition for knowledge. But since the positions one can reach by blameless moves in the space of reasons are not factive, as epistemically satisfactory positions are, a satisfactory standing in the space of reasons cannot be what knowledge is.[7] Rather, knowledge is a status one possesses by virtue of an appropriate standing in the space of reasons when—this is an extra condition, not ensured by one's standing in the space of reasons—the world does one the favour of being so arranged that what one takes to be so is so.

It calls for comment that the external addition I am envisaging is the familiar truth requirement for knowledge, that what one takes to be so is indeed so. This figures, in the position I am considering, as a necessary extra condition for knowledge, over and above the best one can have in the way of reliability in a policy or habit of basing belief on appearance. Such reliability figures in the hybrid position I am considering as part of its internal apparatus: as something to be taken into account when one determines, within the space of reasons conceived in the interiorized way, whether a standing in that space is acceptable.

6. It is important not to assume that, in rejecting this response, I am making unavailable the common-sense thought that we sometimes know how things are by seeing how they are. That would be so only if the epistemic status of such knowledge had to consist in the excellence of a policy or habit of basing belief on appearance, focused as it were on the particular case at hand. But that assumption is simply a form of what is under attack. (The status consists, rather, in the fact that one sees that things are so.)

7. On "blameless", see n. 3 above. However precisely it is spelled out, the idea of blameworthiness that we need must belong with an idea of obligations as within one's power to discharge, on pain of losing contact with the point of interiorizing the space of reasons. So it is not to the point here to suggest that one can be blamed for a false belief based on appearance just because of its falsehood, on the analogy of the idea that one can be blamed for unintended consequences of one's intentional acts.

This internal placement of reliability may seem surprising, in view of the fact that reliability is part of the stock in trade of full-blown externalist approaches to knowledge. But the point of full-blown externalist approaches is to reject the Sellarsian idea I began with, not to incorporate it as part of an account of knowledge, as in the hybrid approach I am considering. According to a full-blown externalist approach, knowledge has nothing to do with positions in the space of reasons; knowledge is a state of the knower, linked to the state of affairs known in such a way that the knower's being in that state is a reliable indicator that the state of affairs obtains. In the purest form of this approach, it is at most a matter of superficial idiom that we do not attribute knowledge to properly functioning thermometers.[8] Now from the fact that the concept of reliability plays this external role in an approach that simply rejects questions about the knower's position in the space of reasons, it clearly does not follow that when we move to an approach that does not reject such questions (although, being hybrid, it insists that they do not exhaust the issues that need to be addressed), the concept must still be conceived as operating outside the space of reasons. And the point I made earlier stands: if a purported picture of the space of reasons makes no room for the critical function of reason in raising questions about the reliability of this or that policy or habit of belief-formation, the picture cannot be what it purports to be. So it would be a mistake to suppose that reliability must be external in a hybrid approach, just because it figures in full-blown externalist approaches. Reliability must operate in the internal reaches of a hybrid approach, on pain of the internal element's becoming unrecognizable as what it was supposed to be.[9] The problem with the resources that are available in an interiorized conception of the space of reasons is that, even including the best that can be had in the way of reliability, they cannot duplicate the factiveness of epistemically satisfactory positions. So it is pre-

8. If a full-blown externalist approach preserves epistemological relevance for a concept of justification, it is certainly not one that functions as in the quotation from Sellars in n. 2 above.

9. For an example of the kind of hybrid account of knowledge that I am rejecting here, see Christopher Peacocke, *Thoughts: An Essay on Content,* chaps. 9 and 10, especially pp. 153–5. Peacocke has reliability as an external ingredient in a hybrid account of knowledge, one that also imposes an internal condition involving rationality. There is something similar in Simon Blackburn, "Knowledge, Truth, and Reliability", pp. 178–9 (although on pp. 179–80 Blackburn comes close to acknowledging the internal importance of considerations of reliability).

cisely the truth requirement that these considerations motivate conceiving as an external condition that needs to be added to internal requirements for knowledge.[10]

4. This hybrid conception of knowledge has an evident instability, in the way it separates truth, which figures as an external element, from reliability in policies or habits of belief-formation, which figures as an internal element. The truth requirement has to be an added external element, because the interiorization of the space of reasons means that there cannot be standings in that space that simply consist in a cognitive purchase on an objective fact, for instance something that one perceives to be so, or remembers to have been so. But if there cannot be such standings in the space of reasons, how

10. Blackburn, "Knowledge, Truth, and Reliability", supposes that there is some deep error in insisting that a knower must be in an informational state that excludes all possibility that things are not as he takes them to be (a "guaranteeing" informational state). In reaction to that, he claims that titles to knowledge must be defensible "in the face of an open, acknowledged, possibility that the world might not be as we have come to take it to be" (p. 179). This may account for the fact that he seems not even to consider the truth requirement as an external condition on knowledge. But rejecting the idea that a knower's informational state is "guaranteeing" looks to me like rejecting a piece of plain common sense, that our locutions marking epistemically satisfactory positions ("see that . . .", "remember that . . .", and the like) are factive. That this is disastrous shows up in Blackburn's positive proposal, that one knows when no real possibility ("chance") that things are not as one takes them to be is left open by one's informational state, conceived as the upshot of the retreat supposedly forced by the Argument from Illusion—an "indicative" state, as opposed to a "guaranteeing" state. Blackburn applies this account of knowledge to the general hypotheses on which skeptical arguments trade (such as that one is a brain in a vat); the result is that whether one counts as knowing that such hypotheses do not obtain depends on who has the onus of proof in a dispute with a sceptic. But given how things look to someone on any particular occasion (and any other circumstances that might be relevant to reason's decision as to whether believing that things are that way is exercising a reliable policy or habit), there is surely a real possibility that things are not that way. That is just the point that (to put it in my terms) blamelessness in the space of reasons does not ensure factiveness in the position that results. In Blackburn's terms, misleading perceptual appearances, without surrounding clues to their misleadingness, are among "the kinds of things that happen" (p. 185). This point generalizes to other "indicative" states. So even if Blackburn achieves an onus-swapping standoff with the kind of sceptic who attempts to wield general sceptical hypotheses to undermine whole regions of knowledge all at once, his picture will deprive us of pretty much the same knowledge, only piece by piece. If we deny ourselves a "guaranteeing" conception of a putative knower's informational state, there will always be perfectly real possibilities (not the sceptic's arguably unreal possibilities) that he is wrong, given the lesser informational state we are committed to limiting him to. Blackburn simply misses this point; he concentrates on the general sceptical hypotheses, as if there could be no threat to ordinary knowledge claims except from them.

can reason have the resources it would need in order to evaluate the reliability of belief-forming policies or habits? If we press this question, the idea that something can be both interiorized in the way I am considering and recognizably a conception of the space of reasons starts to unravel, as I have already hinted that it would.

I shall return to that point; meanwhile I want to urge another problem about the hybrid conception of knowledge. In the hybrid conception, a satisfactory standing in the space of reasons is only part of what knowledge is; truth is an extra requirement. So two subjects can be alike in respect of the satisfactoriness of their standing in the space of reasons, although only one of them is a knower, because only in her case is what she takes to be so actually so. But if its being so is external to her operations in the space of reasons, how can it not be outside the reach of her rational powers? And if it is outside the reach of her rational powers, how can its being so be the crucial element in an intelligible conception of her knowing that it is so—what makes the relevant difference between her and the other subject? Its being so is conceived as external to the only thing that is supposed to be epistemologically significant about the knower herself, her satisfactory standing in the space of reasons. That standing is not itself a cognitive purchase on its being so; it cannot be that if the space of reasons is interiorized. But then how can the unconnected obtaining of the fact have any intelligible bearing on an epistemic position that the person's standing in the space of reasons is supposed to help constitute? How can it coalesce with that standing to yield a composite story that somehow adds up to the person's being a knower?

One way to appreciate what I am driving at here is to consider the familiar point that true belief need not amount to knowledge. Why not? A good simple answer is that mere truth in a belief leaves it open that the believer has hold of the truth by accident, and knowledge excludes that. Now in the hybrid conception of knowledge, it is admittedly not a complete accident, relative to someone's standing in the space of reasons, if things are as she takes them to be; the position of her belief in the space of reasons makes it likely to be true. But the reason why the extra stipulation that the belief *is* true—what is distinctive of the hybrid approach—is needed is that likelihood of truth is the best that the space of reasons yields, on the interiorized conception of it: the closest we can come to factiveness. The extra that we need for knowledge—the fact that the case in question is not one of those in which a largely reliable habit or policy of belief-formation leads the subject astray—is, relative to the knower's moves in the space of reasons, a stroke of good fortune, a favour the world does her. So if we try to picture epistemic status as constituted in the way the hybrid conception has it, we are vulnerable to a version of the familiar point that distinguishes knowledge from mere true belief.

I think the moral of this is that if we cannot see our way to accepting the Sellarsian idea in full, we should reject it, as in full-blown externalist accounts. It is not a good idea to suppose a satisfactory standing in the space of reasons might be part but not the whole of what knowledge is.

5. A hybrid conception of knowledge is often taken to be obvious.[11] But in the light of what I have just argued, I think this depends on not thinking directly about the conception's epistemological credentials. What makes the hybrid conception seem obvious is that, leaving aside the full-blown externalism according to which standings in the space of reasons are irrelevant to knowledge, this view of knowledge seems to be the only alternative to scepticism. But this is one of those set-ups that are familiar in philosophy, in which a supposedly exhaustive choice confers a spurious plausibility on a philosophical position. The apparent plausibility is not intrinsic to the position, but reflects an assumed framework; when one looks at the position on its own, the plausibility crumbles away, or so I have tried to suggest. In such a situation, the thing to do is to query the assumption that seems to force the choice. And in this case, the culprit is the interiorized conception of the space of reasons.

I have described that conception in a way that equips it with an intelligible motivation. The aim is to picture reason as having a proper

11. When double-aspect views of content-involving mental states were a novelty, it used to be routine to cite the supposedly obvious compositeness of knowledge as an already familiar parallel. See, e.g., Daniel C. Dennett, "Beyond Belief", pp. 11–12; and Colin McGinn, "The Structure of Content", p. 215. In querying the credentials of a hybrid conception of knowledge, I mean to do more than remove an expository prop from under those double-aspect views; I believe that direct extensions of the considerations in this essay show that those views miss the point of the conceptual apparatus they aim to explain. I shall not be able to elaborate this here, though it will be close to the surface in §6.

province in which it can be immune to the effects of luck; not in the sense of sheer chance, but in the sense of factors that reason cannot control, or control for. The idea is that reason can ensure that we have only acceptable standings in the space of reasons, without being indebted to the world for favours received; if we exercise reason properly, we cannot arrive at defective standings in the space of reasons, in a way that could only be explained in terms of the world's unkindness.[12] The upshot of this interiorization is that knowledge of the external world cannot be completely constituted by standings in the space of reasons. The hybrid view concedes that such knowledge is partly a matter of luck in the relevant sense, something outside the control of reason. The hope is that this admission of luck is tolerable, because it comes only after we have credited reason with full control over whether one's standings in the space of reasons are satisfactory.[13]

It seems clear where our suspicions should attach themselves. Although the motivation I have suggested for interiorizing the space of reasons is intelligible, it is surely something we ought to find suspect. The hybrid view's concession to luck, tagged on to a picture of reason as self-sufficient within its own proper province, comes too late. The very idea of reason as having a sphere of operation within which it is capable of ensuring, without being beholden to the world, that one's postures are all right—like the obvious analogues of this idea in thought about practical reason—has the look of a fantasy, something we spin to console ourselves for the palpable limits on our powers.[14]

To avoid fantasy, we would need to see our way to accepting that we cannot eliminate what the interiorized conception of reason conceives as a quite alien factor, the kindness of the world, as a contributor to our coming to occupy epistemically satisfactory positions in the space of reasons. This points to a different conception of factive

12. As I noted in §2, we owe the world thanks for presenting us with appearances at all. But that point is accommodated by the formulation in the text. (If the world withheld appearances from us, reason would achieve its goal by deterring us from unsupported guesses as to how things are.)

13. Of course one can make mistakes; but the idea is that proper exercise of reason would eliminate them.

14. On the parallels in the sphere of practical reason, see Bernard Williams, "Moral Luck".

positions such as seeing that things are a certain way. When someone enjoys such a position, that involves, if you like, a stroke of good fortune, a kindness from the world; even so, the position is, in its own right, a satisfactory standing in the space of reasons, not a composite in which such a standing is combined with a condition external to the space of reasons.[15] Whether we like it or not, we have to rely on favours from the world: not just that it presents us with appearances—which, as I remarked, the fantasy view can already accept as a favour the world does us—but that on occasion it actually is the way it appears to be. But that the world does someone the necessary favour, on a given occasion, of being the way it appears to be is not extra to the person's standing in the space of reasons. Her coming to have an epistemically satisfactory standing in the space of reasons is not what the interiorized conception would require for it to count as her own unaided achievement. But once she has achieved such a standing, she needs no extra help from the world to count as knowing.[16] If we rescue the idea of the space of reasons from the distortions of fantasy, we can say that the particular facts that the world does us the favour of vouchsafing to us, in the various relevant modes of cognition, actually shape the space of reasons as we find it.

15. This formulation should make it clear how wildly off-target Blackburn is ("Knowledge, Truth, and Reliability", p. 176) in supposing that my appeal to "guaranteeing" informational states belongs within the general framework of the attempt "to ensure that there is no element of luck, or even contingency, in the true believer's title to knowledge". The traditional effect of this attempt to transcend luck is that the area of known fact shrinks "potentially down to an entirely subjective realm". Blackburn takes me to offer a different option within the same general framework, in which, instead of that shrinkage in what can be known, the mind (the seat of these supposed luck-free "guaranteeing" states) expands to "embrace" all sorts of worldly states of affairs. This idea, which Blackburn rightly finds bizarre, has nothing to do with what I am proposing here, and was proposing in the work Blackburn is discussing (Essay 17 above). Blackburn is so locked in to the framework thought that epistemology must centre on a luck-free zone (a role played in his favoured epistemology by the "indicative" states to which we are pushed back by the generalized Argument from Illusion) that he cannot comprehend how I can have been questioning the framework; so he has saddled me with the insane position that is the only interpretation my words will bear within the framework.

16. Exorcizing the fantasy should weaken the inclination to say that such a standing is not one's own unaided achievement. Compare one of the practical analogues. The concept of what one does, understood as applying to one's interventions in the objective world, cannot mark out a sphere within which one has total control, immune to luck. It is only if we recoil from this into a fantasy of a sphere within which one's control is total that it can seem to follow that what one genuinely achieves is less than one's interventions in the objective world. (This is one of many places at which much more discussion is needed.)

The effect is a sort of coalescence between the idea of the space of reasons as we find it and the idea of the world as we encounter it.[17]

Of course we are fallible in our judgements as to the shape of the space of reasons as we find it, or—what comes to the same thing—as to the shape of the world as we find it. That is to say that we are vulnerable to the world's playing us false; and when the world does not play us false we are indebted to it.[18] But that is something we must

17. Seeing (or more generally perceiving) that things are a certain way is just one of the "factive" (or, in Blackburn's term, "guaranteeing") states that is restored to its proper status when the generalized Argument from Illusion is undermined; others include remembering how things were and learning from someone else how things are (see §2 above). In resisting the damaging effect of letting the Argument from Illusion structure epistemology (as in Essay 17 above), I do not commit myself to assimilating all these "factive" positions to perception. Compare Crispin Wright, "Facts and Certainty". Commenting on that essay of mine, he writes, at pp. 443–4: "Just as 'lifting' the veil of perception is to put us, on occasion anyway, in direct perceptual touch with material states of affairs, so a story has to be told explaining how we are similarly, on occasion, in direct perceptual touch with others' mental states and with past states of affairs—or at least, in direct perceptual touch with states of affairs which do better than provide inconclusive basis for claims about other minds and the past." I do think we are sometimes in direct perceptual touch with others' mental states, and certainly with states of affairs that do better than provide inconclusive basis for claims about them; but why should I accept the crazy idea that we are in direct *perceptual* touch with past states of affairs, when remembering them will plainly do instead? Similarly, when one learns something from someone else, the cognitive transaction is of course not a sort of perception of the state of affairs one is told about; resistance to letting the Argument from Illusion structure the epistemology of testimony need not involve denying that obvious fact (compare Elizabeth Fricker, "The Epistemology of Testimony", pp. 74–5). I discuss the epistemology of testimony in Essay 19 below.

18. When it turns out that the world has played us false, we conclude that it has presented us with a mere appearance rather than a manifest fact. Moreover, when the world does present us with a manifest fact, it does so by presenting us with an appearance. It is essential not to confuse these two pieces of common sense with the conclusion of the Argument from Illusion. Of course the content of the appearances that the world presents us with ("appearances" is here neutral as between "mere appearance" and "manifest fact") is not irrelevant to our possession of factive standings in the space of reasons. Our being able to count as, say, seeing that things are thus and so depends on our being properly sensitive (where "properly" expresses a rational assessment) to how things look to us. But it is a mistake to think this dependence is a matter of the appearance's functioning as a starting-point in the space of reasons, with the status of seeing how things are supposedly reconstructed in terms of a sufficiently cogent argument with the appearance as a premise. If the additional premises we can appeal to are restricted to what is available to reason on the interiorized conception of it, no such argument will be sufficiently cogent; that is a way of putting the reason why, once epistemology has started along the path marked out by the Argument from Illusion, the external supplementation is needed (§3 above). This is how we get into the position in which we have to choose between scepticism and the hybrid view. But the common-sense point that appearance bears on the rational status of belief is detachable from a commitment to that choice. (There is more discussion of this in Essay 19 below.)

simply learn to live with, rather than recoiling into the fantasy of a sphere in which our control is total.[19]

6. The space of reasons is the space within which thought moves, and its topography is that of the rational interconnections between conceptual contents; we might equally speak of the space of concepts.[20] So we can see the interiorization of the space of reasons as a form of a familiar tendency in philosophy: the tendency to picture the objective world as set over against a "conceptual scheme" that has withdrawn into a kind of self-sufficiency. The fantasy of a sphere within which reason is in full autonomous control is one element in the complex aetiology of this dualism.[21] The dualism yields a picture in which the realm of matter, which is, in so far as it impinges on us, the Given, confronts the realm of forms, which is the realm of thought, the realm in which subjectivity has its being. It is of course

19. Wright mentions two further reservations (besides the one I dealt with in n. 17 above) about my way with scepticism ("Facts and Certainty", p. 444). The first is this: "McDowell's proposal has . . . to be worked up into a demonstration that the sceptic actually has the epistemology of the various kinds of propositions *wrong*. The mere depiction of more comforting alternatives is not enough." I hope the present formulation of what I was trying to get at makes it clearer that this criticism misses the mark. My idea is that scepticism looks urgent only in the context of a visibly dubious assumption, which imposes a certain shape on the space of epistemological possibilities; so that the sceptic does indeed have the epistemology of the various kinds of propositions wrong. (But let me remark that my move is not well cast as an *answer* to sceptical challenges; it is more like a justification of a refusal to bother with them.) Wright's other reservation is that "'lifting' the veil of perception" has no obvious bearing on a style of sceptical argument exemplified by the attempt to undermine perceptual knowledge, or even perceptually grounded reasonable belief, on the basis that at any time at which one takes oneself to have it, one lacks sufficient reason to believe that one is not dreaming. But I should have thought the bearing was quite obvious. Only if the veil is supposed to be in place can it seem that one would need to establish, or equip oneself with good reason to suppose, that one is not dreaming *before* one can be entitled to take one's apparent perceptions at face value. Once the veil is lifted, things can be the other way round; one's good reason to believe one is not dreaming, on the relevant occasions, can reside in all the knowledge of the environment that one's senses are yielding one—something that does not happen when one is dreaming. (See Essay 11 above, §5).

20. I am quite unapologetic about the imagery here. Blackburn's *de haut en bas* remarks about my spatial imagery for the mental ("Knowledge, Truth, and Reliability", pp. 177–8) depend on a gross missing of its point; see n. 15 above.

21. Another element is the temptation to push all facts worthy of the name into an objective mould; the dualism results if we try to conceive subjectivity in an objectivistic way. I say more about this in Essay 11 above, and in "Functionalism and Anomalous Monism". A third element will emerge at the end of this essay (§8).

a second Sellarsian idea that this picture is hopeless; it is the source of the basic misconception of modern philosophy, the idea that the task of philosophy is to bridge an ontological and epistemological gulf across which the subjective and the objective are supposed to face one another.[22]

This full-fledged dualism of subjective and objective—or inner and outer—is a good context in which to think about something I promised to come back to: the instability of an epistemology in which truth is external and reliability is internal.

When the dualism becomes full-fledged, it defeats itself. If we conceive what we want to think of as the space of concepts, the realm of thought, in a way that alienates it so radically from the merely material that we seem to be faced with those familiar modern problems of reconciling the subjective with the objective, we undermine our right to think of it as the realm of thought at all. When we set it off so radically from the objective world, we lose our right to think of moves within the space we are picturing as content-involving. So we stop being able to picture it as the space of concepts. Everything goes dark in the interior as we picture it.[23]

Now in the epistemological syndrome I have been discussing, the aim is to set off the inner from the outer, but in a way that stops short of that disastrous extinguishing of content. The idea is that the outer injects content into the inner; the world affords us appearances, and we thereby have dealings with content (it seems to us that things are, or were, thus and so). Appearances are starting-points from which we can move about in the interior space, the space of reasons, drawing inferences from them in ways reason can endorse, for instance on the ground that a particular inference exemplifies a mode of arriving at beliefs that is reliable. But the instability I pointed to, the separation of truth as external from reliability as internal, reveals that this attempt to stop short of disaster is hopeless. If moves in the space of reasons are not allowed to start from facts, riskily accepted as such on the basis of such direct modes of cognitive contact with them as perception and memory, then it becomes unintelligible how our picture can be a picture of a space whose po-

22. For an elaboration of this Sellarsian theme, see Richard Rorty, *Philosophy and the Mirror of Nature.*

23. I talk about this in Essay 11 above.

sitions are connected by relations reason can exploit, such as that one of them is a reliable ground for moving by inference to another. If the space of reasons as we find it is withdrawn from the objective world as it makes itself manifest to us, then it becomes unintelligible how it can contain appearances, content-involving as they must be, either. We are here in the vicinity of a third Sellarsian idea, that reality is prior, in the order of understanding, to appearance; I am drawing the moral that it makes no sense to suppose a space sufficiently interiorized to be insulated from specific manifest fact might nevertheless contain appearances.[24]

7. The considerations I have offered suggest a way to respond to scepticism about, for instance, perceptual knowledge; the thing to do is not to answer the sceptic's challenges, but to diagnose their seeming urgency as deriving from a misguided interiorization of reason. But at least one familiar form of scepticism is not obviously within reach of this move. At first appearance, at any rate, scepticism about induction does not turn on interiorizing the space of reasons. In connection with inductive knowledge, we seem not to need an Argument from Illusion to achieve the effect that the Argument from Illusion achieves in the cases where sceptics do appeal to it: the effect of focusing our attention on a basis—a starting-point in the space of reasons—that falls short of the facts supposedly known.

24. Having invoked Sellarsian ideas (knowledge as a standing in the space of reasons; the rejection of the Given, or, what comes to the same thing, the rejection of a view of our conceptual scheme as what is set over against the Given; and the priority of reality over appearance), I ought to confess that I do not find in Sellars himself the direct figuring of manifest fact in the space of reasons that I am recommending. "Empiricism and the Philosophy of Mind", which is my source for all three of the ideas I have invoked, contains (in §35 and ff.) an account of the authority of observational reports that expresses a good thought—that the capacity to make observational reports requires general knowledge of the world, even in cases as conceptually undemanding as saying what colour something is—in what seems to me a suspect way, in terms of the subject's ability to infer a judgement about the world from her own tokening (or propensity towards a tokening) of an observational form of words. I am suspicious of this avoidance of the straightforward idea that the authority of the report consists in the fact that things are manifestly so. (That idea is perfectly consistent with the good thought, not a relapse into a form of the Myth of the Given.) Sellars's account reflects some such idea as this: the content an expression has by virtue of its role in language-entry proprieties is non-conceptual content; conceptual content comes into play exclusively on the basis of inferential proprieties. I think this view of language-entry proprieties is a vestige of a bad way of thinking, which the main themes of Sellarsian philosophy show us how to undermine. But this essay is not meant as commentary on Sellars, and I shall not take these issues further here.

Without trying a full treatment, I shall mention a fourth Sellarsian idea, whose effect is to bring inductive scepticism into the same framework. Consider a characteristic Humean formulation of the predicament that is supposed to invite inductive scepticism:

> It may, therefore, be a subject worthy of curiosity, to enquire what is the nature of that evidence, which assures us of any . . . matter of fact, beyond the present testimony of our senses . . .[25]

If we are to take it seriously that what is in question is *testimony* of our senses, we must think in terms of something content-involving—something in which, say, colours figure as apparent properties of objects. A mere wash of chromatic sensation, not referred to a supposedly perceived environment, could not count as testimony of our senses. Now my fourth Sellarsian idea can be put like this: there cannot be a predicament in which one is receiving testimony from one's senses but one has not yet taken any inductive steps. To stay with the experience of colour, whose simplicity presumably makes it maximally favourable to the contrary view: colour experience's being testimony of the senses depends on the subject's already knowing a great deal about, for instance, the effect of different sorts of illumination on colour appearances; and a subject could not know that without knowing a great deal, outside the immediate deliverances of the senses, about the objective world and our cognitive access to it.

This makes for an easy extension to inductive scepticism of the epistemological move I have been recommending. The key thought so far has been that if we refuse to make sense of the idea of direct openness to the manifest world, we undermine the idea of being in the space of reasons at all, and hence the idea of being in a position to have things appear to one a certain way. There is no making sense of perceptual appearances—the testimony of one's senses—without making sense of the possibility that the objective world can be immediately present to the senses. Now Sellars's point about colour experience is a specific case of that point; there is no making sense of that possibility unless one's conceptual space already embraces a world with more to it than is immediately present to the senses. Nothing could be immediately present to one's senses unless one already had knowledge that goes beyond what is immediately present to the

25. *An Enquiry Concerning Human Understanding* §4.

senses. So the supposed predicament of the inductive sceptic is a fiction. And the mistake is really the same as the one I have already discussed: that we can make the inward withdrawal that the Argument from Illusion is supposed to compel, but stop short of extinguishing content. It is superficial to object that an Argument from Illusion does not typically figure in recommendations of inductive scepticism. Hume's formulation can seem to describe a predicament only if one does not think through the idea that its subject already has the testimony of the senses, and this means that scepticism about induction can seem gripping only in combination with a straightforwardly interiorizing epistemology for perception.

8. There may be a temptation to object that the interiorization I have been discussing cannot be a fantasy, as I have been suggesting it is; it is simply a version of a perfectly intuitive thought, a piece of common sense, to the effect that the mental is internal. If this intuitive thought is taken anything like literally, it can seem to compel the conclusion that minds make contact with the external world at an interface, and then cognitive states, with their factive nature, surely cannot but be composites of interior and exterior circumstances.[26] And a literal construal can be very tempting; after all, it is unquestionable that human beings do literally have insides, and that they are partly occupied by complex mechanisms about whose operations we can in principle, and to some extent in practice, do natural science, in such a way as to account in some sense for behaviour—the very thing that appealing to the mental was supposed to do.

I cannot deal with this properly now; but I shall end by mentioning two reasons for doubt about this line of objection.

First, there is a familiar and impressive tradition of reflection about common-sense psychology, according to which the point of its concepts lies in their providing a kind of understanding of persons and their doings that is radically unlike the understanding that the natural sciences can yield. This tradition's insights are never taken sufficiently seriously by people who suggest "folk psychology" is a proto-theory of the operations of those internal mechanisms, to be refined and perhaps wholly superseded as we learn more about what

26. This is the basis of the denial, common in philosophy, that knowledge is a mental state: see, e.g., A. J. Ayer, *The Problem of Knowledge*, pp. 14–26. (Compare also n. 11 above.)

goes on inside our heads. For instance, natural-scientific investigation of how what is literally internal controls behaviour would seek theories whose power to explain would be proportional to their power to predict. But folk-psychological concepts can express a kind of understanding of a person that seems to have little or no relation to predictive power. And we do not find this kind of understanding any the worse for that, at least until methodologically inclined people try to put us on the defensive. If the understanding that commonsense psychology yields is *sui generis,* there is no reason to regard it as a primitive version of the understanding promised by a theory of inner mechanisms. The two sorts of understanding need not compete for room to occupy.

Second, about the intuitive idea that the mental is internal. I suppose this idea makes it natural, when we learn about advances in the scientific understanding of how our behaviour is controlled by literally internal mechanisms, to suppose that that is what we must have had some dim conception of all along. But I think this is a confusion. At its most abstract, the content of the pre-theoretical notion of the mental as inner lies in such facts as that at least some mental states and occurrences, unlike perceptible states of affairs, are "internal accusatives" to the consciousness of their subjects.[27] But the character of the notion comes out more concretely in the idea that one can sometimes see what someone's mental state is by (as we say) looking into her eyes. And this idea carries its nature on its face: it is a picture, a piece of imagery.[28] (This is not something to be embarrassed about.) It has nothing to do with the idiotic thought that one can look through the eyes into the interior of a person's skull. There is no comfort to be derived here, by way of a literal construal of a piece of common sense, for the idea that the mental is withdrawn from direct engagement with the world—the idea expressed by the differently figurative interiorization that has been my main target.

27. This is how it is with the mental states and occurrences that are most congenial to the notion of the mental as inner. The idea of the mental is complex, and it can easily spread to cover states and occurrences of which this claim is not true. But these outliers do not trigger the philosophical moves that focus on the idea of interiority.

28. At *Philosophical Investigations* §423, the idea of things that go on in someone figures as a picture that Wittgenstein does not reject, though he suggests there are difficulties in understanding its application. See also §427, on wanting to know what is going on in someone's head: "The picture should be taken seriously." (By "seriously" here he clearly does not mean "literally".)

ESSAY 19

Knowledge by Hearsay[1]

1. Language matters to epistemology for two separable reasons (although they are no doubt connected).

The first is the fact that if someone hears a remark and understands it, or reads and understands a sentence in a book or a newspaper, he can thereby acquire knowledge. I do not mean—what is already implicit in crediting him with understanding—that he knows what it is that is being said. I mean that he can acquire knowledge (at second hand) about the topic of the remark or sentence.

The second reason comes into view when we reflect that much of the knowledge we have through language was surely not acquired by understanding a linguistic production. Part of the point here is that we were not yet capable of understanding the elements of what we know through language when we started to acquire them. The body of sentences we accepted from our elders needs to have become quite comprehensive before any of them were comprehended. "Light dawns gradually over the whole".[2] But the image of dawning light does not apply only to coming to understand the members of a stock of sentences accepted from one's elders. The image also fits a general sense in which growing into language is growing into being in pos-

1. My interest in testimony derives from Gareth Evans, as does my conviction that it cannot be accommodated by the sort of account of knowledge that I attack in this essay. I believe I also owe to him my interest in the sorts of case I discuss in §4 below, where knowledge is retained under the risk that what would have been knowledge if the relevant fact had still obtained is not knowledge because the fact no longer obtains. This essay has also benefited from comments by Robert Brandom and Jonathan Dancy.

2. Wittgenstein, *On Certainty* §141.

session of the world, as opposed to having a mere animal ability to cope with a habitat.[3] And much of the knowledge that enters into our possession of the world, even though we have it through language, is not something we have been told. It need never have been enunciated in our hearing; rather, we find it implicit in the cognitive-practical ways of proceeding into which we were initiated when we learned our language.[4]

I have mentioned this second way language matters to epistemology only to make sure it is not forgotten. The topic of this essay is the first: acquiring knowledge by way of understanding what one is told.

2. I shall start with an idea of Wilfrid Sellars, that knowledge, at least on the part of rational animals, is a standing in the space of reasons.[5] This idea is what underlies the aspiration to analyse knowledge in terms of justification. Properly understood, I think the idea is correct; but I want to suggest that reflecting on knowledge by testimony is a good way to start undermining a misconception of it.

The conception I want to question can be put like this. If an epistemically satisfactory standing in the space of reasons, with respect to a proposition, is mediated rather than immediate, that means the standing is constituted by the cogency of an *argument* that is at its occupant's disposal, with the proposition in question as conclusion. After all, we might think in recommending such a conception to ourselves, it is precisely by laying out arguments that we delineate the shape of the space of reasons; surely there is nothing else that a mediated standing in that space could be.

3. "Language is not just one of man's possessions in the world, but on it depends the fact that man has a *world* at all": Hans-Georg Gadamer, *Truth and Method,* p. 443.

4. Much of *On Certainty* is about the status of this sort of knowledge. Wittgenstein himself is dubious about counting it as knowledge; but I think that is inessential to his main point, which is to warn against assimilating the sort of thing in question—propositions that function as pivots on which our practices of looking for grounds for belief can hinge, by not being on the agenda for testing and confirmation—to cases where it makes sense to look for the grounds of a belief. (Wittgenstein's doubt about counting these propositions as known may reflect the influence of the kind of conception of knowledge I am going to attack.)

5. "In characterizing an episode or a state as that [better: one] of *knowing,* we are not giving an empirical description of that episode or state; we are placing it in the logical space of reasons, of justifying and being able to justify what one says": "Empiricism and the Philosophy of Mind", pp. 298–9.

Once we accept this conception of mediated standings, we are under strong pressure to suppose that there are immediate standings in the space of reasons, since the justificatory arguments we are envisaging must start somewhere. There is a heroic position that tries to combine this conception of mediated standings with supposing all epistemically satisfactory standings are mediated. I sympathize with the motivation for this, and I shall come back to it (§5), but we need not consider it now. Apart from the heroic position, different epistemologies in this overall vein differ in respect of the immediate standings they allow; again, I do not think we need to go into the details at this stage.

What I want to suggest is that whatever plausible candidates we pick as the available starting-points in the space of reasons, and whatever we think about whether they are, as it were, absolute starting-points or themselves mediated, to be given parallel treatment at a different point in one's overall epistemology, the basic conception of mediated standings is epistemologically disastrous, in a way that reflecting on knowledge by testimony brings out.

I need first to clarify the conception of mediated standings that I have in mind. There is a completely cogent argument from the fact that someone, say, *sees* that things are thus and so to the conclusion that things *are* thus and so. But that argumentative transition cannot serve to explain how it is that the person's standing with respect to the fact that things are thus and so is epistemically satisfactory. The concept of seeing that things are thus and so is itself already the concept of an epistemically satisfactory standing with respect to the fact that things are thus and so. It makes no sense to suppose someone might understand what it is to see that something is the case, although he does not yet conceive seeing as a way of getting to know how things are. So there is no point in using the notion of a mediated epistemically satisfactory standing so as to count as having application on the basis of that kind of argumentative transition. The cogency of the argument from the fact that someone sees that things are thus and so to the fact that things are thus and so directly reflects the epistemic acceptability of the standing we characterize as seeing that things are thus and so. It does not reveal that standing as mediated. Genuinely mediated epistemic standing, on the conception I have in mind, would have to consist in the cogency of an argument whose premises do not beg the relevant question of epistemic standing.

It is a truism that one cannot see that things are thus and so unless things are indeed thus and so. And a truism should be neutral between different epistemological positions. In particular, the considerations I have just given do not rule out the possibility of an epistemology in which the epistemic standing constituted by seeing that things are thus and so is mediated. The point is that if we want to represent it as mediated, we must not suppose the truistic transition is the only transition in the space of reasons that is relevant to the standing's being an epistemically satisfactory one. What we must suppose, if we stick to the governing conception of mediation, is that the standing we characterize as seeing that things are thus and so is constituted by the availability to the subject of an argument from *different* premises (perhaps involving how things look) to the conclusion that things are thus and so.

Now if a standing in the space of reasons with respect to a fact is acquired in hearing and understanding a remark, the standing is surely a mediated one. It is not as if the fact directly forces itself on the hearer; his rational standing with respect to it surely depends on (at least) his hearing and understanding what his informant says, and this dependence is rational, not merely causal. The question is, then, whether the conception of mediated standings that I have described can make room for testimony knowledge.

Consider a tourist in a strange city, looking for the cathedral. He asks a passer-by, who is in fact a resident and knows where the cathedral is, for directions, hears and understands what the passer-by says, and finds the cathedral just where his informant said he would. Intuitively, this counts as a case of acquiring knowledge by being told; what makes it so is that the informant knows where the cathedral is, and passes on his knowledge in the linguistic exchange. In fact that remark encapsulates what promises to be the core of a good general account of testimony knowledge: if a knowledgeable speaker gives intelligible expression to his knowledge, it may become available at second hand to those who understand what he says.[6]

6. A principle on these lines was stated by Ernest Sosa in "The Analysis of 'Knowledge that P'", p. 8. It matters that I say "may become available to" and not "is acquired by". For one thing, the opportunity for knowledge may not be there for a hearer even if the speaker is giving expression to his knowledge; see §6 below. For another, one cannot be forced to avail oneself of knowledge that one is in a position to acquire; excessive caution, for instance, may lead one to pass up an opportunity.

If we accept the conception of mediated standings that I have described, can we match the intuitive verdict? That would require the tourist to have at his disposal an argument to a conclusion about the whereabouts of the cathedral, with the cogency of the argument sufficient to make it plausible that the fact that this justification of the proposition is available to him amounts to his being in an epistemically satisfactory position with respect to it.[7] I believe this is hopeless; any lifelike attempt to apply the basic thought to this case will fail to equip the tourist with an argument sufficiently compelling for him to seem to count as knowing where the cathedral is, if that is what his title to knowledge is to consist in. For our purposes, we can think of the argument as starting from what the tourist understands his interlocutor to say (we do not need to settle whether that is an absolute starting-point).[8] There is no hope of getting from there to the cathedral's being where the interlocutor said it is without ancillary premises. If we make the ancillary premises seem strong enough to do the trick, it merely becomes dubious that the tourist has them at his disposal; whereas if we weaken the premises, the doubt attaches to their capacity to transmit, across the argument, the right sort of rational acceptability for believing its conclusion to amount to knowledge.

Suppose we take the first option. This involves appealing to ancillary premises on these lines: the informant is competent (at least on the present topic) and trustworthy (at least on the present occasion).[9] But can we really say the tourist knows those things, in such a way that they are available to him as starting-points in an argument that could certify, without question-begging, his standing with respect to the whereabouts of the cathedral? Does he really know, in the kind of way that that would require, that (for instance) the supposed in-

7. See Elizabeth Fricker, "The Epistemology of Testimony", especially pp. 60–2, for some discussion of the different possibilities here; in particular, what might be meant by requiring the knower to possess the justification. I agree with her that we lose the point of invoking the space of reasons if we allow someone to possess a justification even if it is outside his reflective reach.

8. This is a point at issue between Fricker and David Cooper's contribution to the same symposium, "Assertion, Phenomenology, and Essence". I think Fricker is quite right that this knowledge is perceptual. (That is not to say that it constitutes an absolute starting-point; see §5 below.) Cooper suggests that this phenomenological and epistemological position must miss the insights of Romanticism, but that strikes me as the reverse of the truth. However, the point is not central to my concerns here.

9. See Fricker, "The Epistemology of Testimony", pp. 72–3.

formant is not another tourist, equally ignorant of the city's layout, who thinks it might be fun to pretend to be a resident?[10]

In the face of this, we might be tempted to take the other option, and retreat to premises on which we might claim that our candidate knower has a firmer grip: for instance, that the apparent informant is moving about in the city without apparent hesitation, that he displays no signs of being engaged in a practical joke (such as suppressed giggles), and so forth. But if the candidate knower's grip on the premises we retreat to is supposed to be firmer by virtue of their being weaker, so that they leave it open that the apparent informant is an ignorant practical joker, as opposed to someone who is putting his own knowledge into words (although no doubt they reveal it as improbable), it should be an urgent question how the argument can be good enough for possessing it to constitute an epistemic position that can count as knowledge. If the tourist's title to know depends on the best argument he can muster for the proposition he believes, and the premises of the argument leave it open that his supposed informant is not giving expression to knowledge, then surely the verdict ought to be that for all the tourist knows the cathedral is somewhere else.

There may be a temptation to say I have simply chosen an unfortunate example. The tourist does not know where the cathedral is, but if one is more careful to equip oneself with the needed premises about competence and trustworthiness, one *can* acquire knowledge by being told things.[11] I think this verdict on the case of the trusting

10. Willingness to say "No" may seem to preclude claiming that the tourist does get to know where the cathedral is. But what is threatened is only that he *knows that he knows* where the cathedral is (on one reading of that claim). And it is quite dubious that someone who knows must know that he knows, in the relevant sense. (See David Wiggins, "On Knowing, Knowing That One Knows, and Consciousness".) There may be another reading of the principle that a knower knows that he knows; I have phrased my sceptical queries so as to leave it open that, if we stop looking for non-question-begging certifications of epistemic standing, we may be able to retrieve a possibility of crediting the tourist with knowledge that his informant is competent and trustworthy, as something on a level with the knowledge he acquires in the transaction, not prior to it in the space of reasons. (Compare the idea that knowledge that one is not dreaming is on a level with the knowledge of the environment that one's senses are yielding one, not something one would need to be able to credit oneself with first, in order to be able to take it that one's senses are indeed yielding one knowledge of the environment. See Essay 11 above, §5.)

11. Some such suggestion is implicit in Fricker's argument ("The Epistemology of Testimony", p. 75) against the idea that one can be entitled to a presumption of sincerity and competence in the absence of special evidence to the contrary. She responds "I would not

tourist is counter-intuitive, but that is not by itself conclusive against it; we can allow a good general account of what knowledge is to alter our intuitions about particular cases. However, the difficulty is more general than such a move acknowledges. Consider a different case of putatively acquiring knowledge by testimony. Let it be the most favourable case we can imagine. Let the hearer have all kinds of positive evidence that the speaker is speaking his mind: a steady honest-looking gaze, a firm dry handclasp, perhaps years of mutual reliance. Surely it is always possible for a human being to act capriciously, out of character? And even if the speaker is speaking his mind, how firm a hold can the hearer possibly have on the premise, needed on this view, that the speaker is not somehow misinformed about the subject matter of the conversation? However favourable the case, can the hearer really be said to know that his informant can be relied on now, in such a way that this verdict can be used in a non-question-begging certification that what he has acquired is an epistemically satisfactory standing? The supposition that the informant is, perhaps uncharacteristically, misleading the hearer or, perhaps surprisingly, misinformed about the topic is not like the typical suppositions of general sceptical arguments (e.g., "Maybe you are a brain in a vat"), where it is at least arguable that no real possibility is expressed. In Simon Blackburn's phrase, mistakes and deceptions by putative informants are "kinds of thing that happen".[12] It is not clear that the approach I am considering can make out the title to count as knowledge of *any* beliefs acquired from someone else's say-so. And too much overturning of intuitions must surely make it questionable whether the general account of knowledge is a good one.

---

like to be obliged to form beliefs in response to others' utterances in accordance with this presumption!" But I do not want to defend the idea that Fricker is attacking here, that there is a general presumption of sincerity and competence (as if gullibility were an epistemic right, or even an obligation). In the case I am considering, I think the tourist is entitled to his belief about where the cathedral is, without taking care to rule out the possibility of a practical joke; but I do not think that is because he is exercising a general presumption of sincerity and competence. That is the sort of thing it is natural to appeal to in a version of the conception I am attacking, one that keeps the idea that mediated standings consist in the cogency of arguments, but is less optimistic than Fricker about how cogent the available arguments are, unless they are beefed up with general presumptions of this sort. I want a more radical departure from the governing conception. This should become clearer in due course.

12. "Knowledge, Truth, and Reliability", p. 185.

3. I have been exploiting a principle to this effect: if we want to be able to suppose the title of a belief to count as knowledge is constituted by the believer's possession of an argument to its truth, it had better not be the case that the best argument he has at his disposal leaves it open that things are not as he believes them to be. If it does, what we are picturing is an epistemic position in which, for all the subject knows, things are not as he takes them to be; and that is not a picture of something that might intelligibly amount to knowing that they are that way. The argument would need to be conclusive. If you know something, you cannot be wrong about it.

That conditional principle strikes me as obviously correct. But many philosophers would reject it out of hand. This attitude reflects an assumption that encapsulates the approach to knowledge I am considering. The assumption is that when epistemic standing is mediated, the antecedent of the conditional is satisfied. In that case the effect of the principle is an intolerable scepticism in respect of mediated epistemic standings, since the arguments we can find are almost never that good. (Some form of the principle is indeed the nerve of standard arguments for scepticism.) Accordingly, if we do not contemplate querying the antecedent, it seems that, on pain of scepticism, it must be possible for a title to knowledge to consist in possession of a less than conclusive argument for what is known—that an argument that does no better than display its conclusion as highly probable can be good enough to certify a standing with respect to the conclusion as knowledge. In fact that is a quite mysterious thought, given what I think is spurious plausibility by the idea that the only alternative is scepticism. And we can keep the conditional principle without risking undue concessions to scepticism, if we are willing to contemplate denying that in respect of mediated epistemic standings the antecedent must hold.[13]

4. Consider a device about which one knows (unproblematically, let us suppose) that it will produce outcome A in, on average, ninety-nine cases out of a hundred, and otherwise outcome B. Think of a roulette wheel with ninety-nine red slots and one white one. Given the task of predicting the outcome of a given spin, one will of course

13. Induction can have a confusing effect here: it can seem to be a counter-example to the principle. But demanding that an argument be conclusive is not the same as demanding that it be *deductive*.

predict red (even if white is "overdue", since that does not make the probability of white on any one spin any greater). Suppose one makes one's prediction, the wheel is spun, and the result is red. Did one's prediction then amount to knowledge? Surely not; for all one knew, the result was going to be white. The fact that one had an argument that established a high probability for the outcome one predicted—so that one had excellent reasons for one's prediction—makes no difference at all to that. We can change the example to make the probability higher, but I cannot see how changing the figures can make any difference of principle. If there is one white slot out of thousands or millions, one does not know that the result will not be white.[14] I think the moral is that being known cannot be intelligibly seen as some region at the high end of a scale of probabilification by considerations at the knower's disposal, perhaps with room for argument about how high the standards need to be set. Of course that is an application of the conditional principle that I discussed in the last section.

It is instructive to contrast the roulette-wheel case with the following one. Consider someone who keeps himself reasonably well up-to-date on events of note; suppose he listens to a reliable radio news broadcast at six o'clock every evening. Can we credit such a person, at three o'clock in the afternoon on some day late in the life of, say, Winston Churchill, with knowledge that Churchill is alive? (I do not mean to consider a period when the news is full of bulletins of Churchill's failing health. Churchill has simply not been in the news lately.) Intuitively, the answer is "Yes". Something like that is the position we are all in with respect to masses of what we take ourselves to know, concerning reasonably durable but impermanent states of affairs to whose continued obtaining we have only intermittent epistemic access. If challenged, we might say something like "If it were no longer so, I would have heard about it"; and we are quite undisturbed, at least until philosophy breaks out, by the time-lag between changes in such states of affairs and our hearing about them.

14. Perhaps some will be tempted to maintain that even so, one does know the result will be red; they will think they can protect that claim from being undermined by the fact that one does not know the result will not be white, on the ground that knowledge is not closed under known implication. (See Robert Nozick, *Philosophical Explanations*, pp. 206–11.) Whatever the merits of that thesis, such an application of it strikes me as desperate.

Of course it matters that the time-lag is quite short; we would not claim to know this kind of thing after months out of touch with the news.[15]

We can think of the subject in such a case as, in effect, following a policy of claiming to know (if the question arises) that things are still the way he formerly knew they were, if a change would have been reported and has not yet been.[16] A subject who follows that policy can be sure that there will be a period, between Churchill's death and the next news bulletin, when following it will produce claims to knowledge that are definitely false. That may not by itself deter him from following the policy. No doubt if Churchill is known to be in failing health, a reasonably cautious subject will not go on taking Churchill to be still alive. Asked whether Churchill is still alive, a doxastically responsible subject in such circumstances will answer that he does not know. But suppose Churchill dies unexpectedly, so that there is not that sort of specific reason for suspending the policy. And suppose our subject follows the policy to the end, so that he is committed to false knowledge claims, since what he claims to know is not so, for the period between Churchill's death and his next access to the news. According to my intuition, the falsity of these late products of the policy does not undermine the truth of its earlier products. As long as Churchill was still alive, the subject knew it.

This intuition does not seem unreasonable. It would be difficult to overstate how much of what ordinarily passes for knowledge would be lost to us, if our epistemology of retained knowledge did not allow that sort of knowably risky policy to issue in acceptable knowledge claims when the risks do not materialize. I think I know, as I write, that Bill Clinton is President of the United States.[17] Can I rule out the possibility that, since my last confirmatory experience,

15. It is a familiar experience to find, some time after one has, say, missed the newspapers for a week, that things one thought one knew have for some time been no longer true. It is striking that the experience has no tendency to dislodge one's belief that one knows a great deal else in the sort of way in which one thought one knew what one has just been disabused of.

16. We can take the former knowledge as unproblematic, for the purposes of the example. Perhaps it was derived from broadcast coverage of Churchill's latest birthday. (The point I am making with this example is about the retaining of knowledge; it is not meant to turn especially on the fact that the knowledge retained was originally acquired by testimony.)

17. Lightly revising this essay in 1997, I have updated the example.

he has been assassinated, and even at this moment the Chief Justice is swearing in his successor? No. But even so, when I have my next confirmatory experience, I shall not take it that I then know *again* that Clinton is President, having not known it in the interim. I shall take the experience to confirm that I *still* know it—to confirm the continued existence of a piece of knowledge I shall take myself to have had all along, including now as I write. All my supposed knowledge of impermanent circumstances in the realm of current affairs is, most of the time, between confirmations. If we reject the intuition I have expressed, we shall be committed to supposing we know a great deal less than we ordinarily think.[18]

I have been using examples involving retaining knowledge that was first acquired by testimony, in the broad sense in which one acquires knowledge by testimony in listening to a news broadcast or reading a newspaper. But the point is obviously not restricted to such cases. Consider a child at school. Does she know the arrangement of the furniture in the living room of her house? We are inclined to answer that she probably does; most people know that sort of thing. But what if, after she left home, her parents acted on the whim of trying a different arrangement? Well, in that case she does not know. But if the furniture is still in the familiar places when she gets home at the end of the school day, then, according to my intuition, that confirms that she *still* has the knowledge she had when she left the house in the morning. She does not need to acquire anew a piece of knowledge that has gone out of existence in the interim.[19] (Rather as with the occurrence of bulletins on Churchill's failing health, the case is altered if the parents have lately been, say, talking about improving the layout—in such circumstances, taking it that the furniture is where it has always been might be doxastically irresponsible.)

Suppose that in the case of the roulette wheel one were to follow the policy of claiming to *know,* at each spin, that the outcome will

18. There may be a temptation to say that the same goes for the roulette-wheel case, on the basis that if we disallow it, we disallow all knowledge by induction. But it is simply not true that in the roulette-wheel case one knows that the outcome will be red. If induction is a way of coming to know things, that is not an example of it. (Knowing that the outcome will *probably* be red is of course quite another matter.)

19. A case like this one, involving retaining knowledge not originally acquired by testimony, is briefly discussed by David Braine, "The Nature of Knowledge", p. 42.

be red. That would be a policy about which one would be in a position to know that, on some occasions (on average one in a hundred, in the case as first introduced), it would issue in one's making a knowledge claim that is certainly false, since what one claims to know is not so. Now when one claims to know, between confirming episodes, such things as that Bill Clinton is President, one in effect follows a knowledge-claiming policy that is, in a certain formal respect, parallel to that one. (It would be silly to try to give definite numbers, but why should that matter?) But the intuition I am expressing discerns a substantive difference alongside the structural parallel. In the roulette-wheel case, *none* of the knowledge claims would be true (in fact no sane person would seriously adopt such a policy), whereas in the case of claims to retained knowledge, those that are not falsified by the falsity of what one claims to know can be true, even though the policy of issuing them in the relevant sort of circumstances will certainly yield some that are so falsified.

That intuitive difference does not seem to be one that we can make intelligible in terms of the idea that the subject possesses a better argument, of the sort the governing conception would need to cite for purposes of non-question-begging certification of his epistemic standing, in the favourable case. It may be that on the basis of material available for constructing such arguments, it is a better bet that Clinton is President, between confirming episodes, than it is that the roulette wheel will come up red. But that does not seem to be the right kind of point. If we change the roulette-wheel case to give white one chance in millions, we may make the comparison of bets at least less clear; but it still does not seem right to say that I know that the wheel will come up red, and it does seem right to say that if it turns out when I next tune into the news that Clinton was still President as I wrote this, it will have turned out that I do now know that he is.[20]

20. Blackburn, in "Knowledge, Truth, and Reliability", proposes that one knows when one's informational state, conceived otherwise than as having the fact known in one's cognitive grasp, leaves no real possibility ("chance") that things are not as one takes them to be. (Having the fact known in one's cognitive grasp would leave no chance at all of being wrong, but Blackburn contemptuously dismisses conceptions of knowledge on these lines.) He applies that account of knowledge to the general hypotheses on which sceptical arguments trade (that one is a brain in a vat, and so forth). The upshot is that whether one counts as knowing that such hypotheses do not obtain depends on who has the onus of proof in a dispute with a sceptic. But if my informational state, between intakes of news,

What the intuition suggests is that we conceive knowledge of the right kind of truth as a sort of continuant. With fully eternal truths, such a conception is unproblematic. But the intuition indicates that we extend the conception, more interestingly, to knowledge of changeable, though reasonably durable, states of affairs. Like a living thing, such knowledge needs something analogous to nutrition from time to time, in the shape of intermittent confirmation that the state of affairs known to obtain does still obtain. But the persistence of knowledge does not need the constant operation of a sustaining cause; between the intermittent confirmations, we allow a kind of inertia to operate in the dynamics of epistemic life. If someone counts, at some time, as having a state of affairs of the right kind within his cognitive grasp, say by seeing that things are thus and so, we allow that that epistemic status can outlast the original mode of access to the known fact. We can capture the credentials of his epistemic position, at a later time at which he no longer has the state of affairs in view, by saying that he retains a piece of knowledge originally acquired by perception. Of course that cannot be so if the state of affairs no longer obtains. But if the state of affairs does still obtain, he can continue to count, at least for a while, as having it within his cognitive grasp.

It is very hard to see how the governing conception of mediated standings in the space of reasons can make room for such an idea. Perhaps the governing conception can make some sort of stab at a lifelike account of my epistemic credentials with respect to the proposition that Clinton is President while I am, say, watching a White House press conference broadcast live on television. But it does not seem to be able to make sense of the idea that those very credentials (reinforcing an accumulation of credentials from the re-

---

with respect to who is President is not allowed to embrace the fact that Clinton is still President, it surely leaves a real possibility that Clinton is no longer President. Assassinations, or other sudden deaths, of Presidents are "kinds of things that happen". So are misleading perceptual appearances (and so on; different kinds of real possibility are relevant to the different sorts of knowledge). So even if Blackburn achieves an onus-swapping standoff with the kind of sceptic who attempts to wield general sceptical hypotheses to undermine whole regions of knowledge all at once, it looks as if his picture will deprive us of pretty much the same knowledge, only piece by piece. If we deny ourselves a "guaranteeing" conception of a putative knower's informational state, the less rich informational state we thereby restrict ourselves to will always leave open perfectly real possibilities (not the sceptic's arguably unreal possibilities) that he is wrong. (Blackburn simply misses this point; he concentrates entirely on the general sceptical hypotheses, as if there could be no threat to ordinary knowledge claims except from them.)

moter past) can persist after the set is switched off. How can a justification I no longer have (the screen is dark) be parlayed into a justification I somehow still have? Perhaps I can add material about the reliability of my memory. But that does not address the possibility, which is left open if my present information is not allowed to include the fact itself, that since my latest confirmation the state of affairs itself has changed. It would not be a fault in my memory if that had happened. That is why it makes such a difference to shift from retained knowledge of standing states of affairs to retained knowledge of states of affairs that may stop obtaining between confirmations. The shift undermines all hope of constructing an argument from what I have between confirmations that is sufficiently cogent to serve the purposes of the governing conception, if what I have between confirmations is not allowed to include my still being on to the fact in question.[21]

If I am allowed, contrary to the governing conception, to say that my continuing knowledge that Clinton is President is itself the relevant standing in the state of reasons, these difficulties go away. The justification I still have, for saying that Clinton is President, is that I still know he is. I achieved, in whatever way, an epistemically satisfactory position with respect to the fact that he is President, a position of a sort that can persist between injections of nourishment, and now the darkness of the television screen does not imply that anything relevant to that position has changed.

5. If knowledge is a standing in the space of reasons, someone whose taking things to be thus and so is a case of knowledge must have a reason (a justification) for taking things to be that way. But that is allowed for if remembering that Clinton is President is itself the relevant standing in the space of reasons. Someone who remembers that things are a certain way, like someone who sees that things

21. Christopher Peacocke discusses retained knowledge in chap. 10 of *Thoughts: An Essay on Content.* He defends a "Model of Virtual Inference", according to which such knowledge requires the knower to have at his disposal a sound abductive argument to the truth of what he is said to know. Peacocke considers only knowledge of standing states, such as that Hume died in 1776. Perhaps someone who finds himself seeming to remember that fact can have a sound abductive argument from his present informational state, considered as not embracing the information that Hume died in 1776, to the conclusion that that is so. But that does not carry over to retained knowledge of changeable states. From my willingness to vouch for Clinton's being President, I cannot get by abduction to his being President now, as opposed to his having been President when I last checked.

are a certain way, has an excellent reason for taking it that things are that way; the excellence comes out in the fact that from the premise that one remembers that things are thus and so, as from the premise that one sees that things are thus and so, it follows that things *are* thus and so.[22] The epistemic positions themselves put their occupants in possession of reasons for their beliefs; those reasons do not need to be supplemented with less cogent arguments from non-question-beggingly available premises.

As I noted in §2, the availability of an inference from an epistemic position to a fact does nothing towards representing the epistemic position as a mediated standing in the space of reasons. It seems clear that knowing that Clinton is President cannot be a rationally immediate matter. So if we stick to the governing conception of what a mediated standing in the space of reasons is, we have to suppose that the standing constituted by remembering that Clinton is President can be reconstructed as possession of an argument that starts from the content of informational states that we can credit to the subject without presupposing that he has that standing. The point of §4 is that at the relevant times no available argument will be good enough. The best it can yield is high probability, but we wanted to reconstruct knowledge that Clinton is President, not knowledge that he probably is.

It should be starting to seem that the governing conception misconstrues the idea that knowledge is a standing in the space of reasons. I do not want to suggest the inferential transitions that the governing conception aims to exploit in its reconstructive task are epistemologically irrelevant. But I do want to suggest that their relevance needs to be differently understood.

22. In Blackburn's terms, seeing that . . ., remembering that . . ., and so forth are "guaranteeing" epistemic positions. Blackburn suggests ("Knowledge, Truth, and Reliability", pp. 176–8) that if one traffics in the idea of "guaranteeing" states, in the usual stamping-grounds of sceptics (knowledge of the external world and so forth), one lapses into bizarre imagery (see his remarks about "the glassy blob of the mind", p. 177). But the relevant concepts belong to sheer common sense. What would be bizarre is to suggest that we do not achieve such "guaranteeing" positions as seeing that things are thus and so. Blackburn's moves are skewed, I think, by an aspiration (which he tends to read into others) to *answer* sceptical challenges. I think the epistemological outlook I am recommending makes sceptical challenges seem less urgent, but obviously not by answering them. (If someone is exploiting a general sceptical hypothesis in order to attack a knowledge claim, he will not be impressed if one attributes to oneself a "guaranteeing" informational state with respect to the proposition one claims to know; if the sceptical hypothesis holds, the attribution cannot be true.)

Suppose one has become informed of some impermanent but durable state of affairs, and goes on taking it to obtain after one's original epistemic access to it has lapsed. I do not claim that if the state of affairs still obtains then, come what may, one's continued taking it to be so amounts to knowledge. On the contrary: one's status as a knower is undermined, even if things still are as one takes them to be, if one's taking things to be that way is, as I put it, doxastically irresponsible. We have seen some examples of how the notion of doxastic responsibility (which is surely perfectly intuitive) works. It is doxastically irresponsible to go on taking it that some state of affairs of the right kind still obtains if the interval since one's last confirmation is too long, or more generally if the intervals between confirmations are too long, say if one has missed the news for an excessive period.[23] It is doxastically irresponsible to take it, between confirmations, that some state of affairs still obtains, even one of the right general kind, if one is in a position to know that its persistence is hanging by a thread, as in the case of the bulletins about Churchill's failing health.[24]

If one's takings of things to be thus and so are to be cases of knowledge, they must be sensitive to the requirements of doxastic responsibility. Since following the dictates of doxastic responsibility is obviously an exercise of rationality, this can be a partial interpretation of the thought that knowledge in general, and the specific epistemic positions like remembering and seeing, are standings in the space of reasons. We could not conceive remembering that things are thus and so, say, as a standing in the space of reasons if a subject could count as being in that position even if he were not responsive to the rational force of independently available considerations—the material to which the governing conception appeals. But we can se-

23. What counts as excessive depends on the proposition known. If one missed the British news media for a fairly long period, and when one tuned in again there were no lingering traces of national mourning, it might not be doxastically irresponsible to take it that a greatly loved national figure like Churchill was still alive; it would be different with someone else.

24. The topic of doxastic responsibility is clearly complex. Note that the standards can depend on what is at stake. Consider again the case of the child at school. If nothing turns on it, we might casually credit her with knowledge of the arrangement of the furniture in the living room of her house. But if we tell the story so that something that matters a great deal to her depends on whether she is right, it may become doxastically irresponsible for her to vouch for the layout's being as she recalls it to be. In such circumstances, it starts to be significant for her epistemic status that her parents may have moved the furniture, and she is in a position to know that that kind of thing does happen.

parate that point from the idea that one can reconstruct the epistemic satisfactoriness of the standing in terms of the rational force of those considerations.

What I am proposing is a different conception of what it is for a standing in the space of reasons to be mediated. A standing in the space of reasons can be mediated by the rational force of surrounding considerations, in that the concept of that standing cannot be applied to a subject who is not responsive to that rational force. But that is not to say that the epistemic satisfactoriness of the standing *consists in* that rational force. I think we should apply this distinction to all the specific epistemic standings with respect to the empirical world—not just remembering, but also the various modes of perceiving (and testimony too, to anticipate). We could not conceive seeing (say) that things are thus and so as a standing in the space of reasons at all, if a subject could count as being in that position even if he were not rationally responsive to the bearing of how things look on the question how things are. Here too there are requirements of doxastic responsibility.[25] Acknowledging those requirements can be kept distinct from the idea that we can reconstruct the epistemic satisfactoriness of seeing in terms of the cogency of an argument from how things look to how they are—an idea that the history of epistemology surely reveals as hopeless.

On this account, seeing that things are thus and so is a standing in the space of reasons no less mediated than any other. What makes a standing mediated is not that its epistemic satisfactoriness consists in the compellingness of an argument from the mediating considerations, but that it could not be a position in the space of reasons at all if a subject could occupy it without being rationally responsive to the mediating considerations. This brings us to the heroic position that I mentioned with sympathy in §2, according to which there are no immediate standings in the space of reasons—no absolute starting-points. An absolute starting-point would be a position in the space of reasons that one could occupy without needing a suitable rational sensitivity to its surroundings. Seeing is not such a position. Indeed,

25. One does not count as seeing something to be the case (even if the fact that that is how things look to one results, in the way that is characteristic of seeing, from the fact that that is how things are), if one's taking it that that is how things are is doxastically irresponsible. Consider, for instance, a case in which one has excellent reasons for distrusting one's vision, although as a matter of fact it is functioning perfectly.

it should now be apparent that nothing is. It does not help to retreat from *seeing that things are thus and so* to *having it look to one as if things are thus and so*. That is not a position one could occupy all on its own, without a rational responsiveness to surrounding considerations.[26]

In the context of the governing conception of what it would be for a standing to be mediated, the thought that there are no absolute starting-points seemed heroic. It amounted to the idea that a rational standing with respect to one proposition is *always* inferentially derivative from rational standings with respect to others, so that when we set out to establish such standing by retracing the inferential steps we would go round in circles—large circles, no doubt, but it is quite unclear why that should seem to help. But now that we have it in the proper context, with inferential transitions in the required background but not conceived as constituting the satisfactoriness of rational standings, the thought emerges as acceptable.[27]

Of course I am not suggesting that doxastic responsibility ensures that what one has is knowledge. Exactly not: that would preclude making room for knowledge in cases where a maximally careful exercise of doxastic responsibility still leaves it open that the world may be playing one false, as in the examples of §4—cases in which the state of affairs improbably ceases to obtain. What one takes to be the case without doxastic irresponsibility may even so—through no fault of one's doxastic conduct—not be the case, and then one certainly does not know that it is the case.

This may suggest that doxastic responsibility suffices for knowledge, given that the world co-operates—given that what one takes to be so is so. But that seems wrong too. Consider a case in which there is no doxastic irresponsibility in, say, taking an apparent perception at face value, and things are indeed as they appear, but the apparent

26. The idea that perceptual appearances can be absolute starting-points is one form of the Myth of the Given, which Sellars demolishes in "Empiricism and the Philosophy of Mind".

27. The thesis that there are absolute starting-points is a way to formulate epistemological foundationalism. The traditional competitor of foundationalism is coherentism, and that label fits the position I am endorsing here. But we need to get straight how inferences (other than those involving the factiveness of the epistemic concepts) are relevant before we embrace coherentism as an alternative to foundationalism. Otherwise the coherentist alternative is the heroic position, and it is not clear that it yields any real improvement over foundationalism. (See Crispin Wright, "Facts and Certainty", p. 469.)

perception is not a genuine perception for lack of the appropriate relation between the fact and the experience. In such a case, taking the apparent perception at face value ought not to constitute knowledge. It seems over-optimistic about the efficacy of doxastic responsibility to suppose that a believer who was really doxastically responsible would not miss the fact that the required relation did not obtain. Similarly in a case in which there is no doxastic irresponsibility in taking another person's word on some question, and what he says is true, but his saying it is not an expression of knowledge on his part. (I shall return to the idea that knowledge is to be understood as a cooperative product, involving our exercising doxastic responsibility and the world doing its part, in §7 below.)

In the framework I am proposing, we can have a satisfying view of how probabilities are epistemologically significant. As long as we are trying to reconstruct epistemic standing in terms of an argument that moves to the proposition supposedly known from non-question-beggingly available starting-points, it is an embarrassment if the best we can achieve is an argument that represents the proposition supposedly known as merely probable. But there is no such embarrassment if the point is that one cannot count as occupying an epistemic standing with respect to a proposition unless, in taking things to be so, one is responsive to what is probable given one's informational position apart from the putative epistemic standing. Flying in the face of those probabilities is one way to be doxastically irresponsible, and would undermine one's title to the position in the space of reasons that the epistemic standing is.

What captures the epistemic satisfactoriness of the standings in the space of reasons constituted by positions like seeing that things are thus and so, or remembering that things are thus and so, is not the relation to rational surroundings that is required for them to be standings in the space of reasons at all, but the cogency of the inference from someone's being in such a position to the fact that things are thus and so. If the positions designated in such terms—"seeing that . . .", "remembering that . . .", and the like—are really to be standings in the space of reasons, we must insist on a strict reading of the "that"-clauses, as crediting the positions with conceptually structured contents. That is what the requirement of rational sensitivity to mediating considerations makes room for. But creatures that are not in the space of reasons—the space of concepts—can perceive and remember (and indeed learn through words; as I noted in §1, one starts doing that before one understands the words). It goes with being restrictive about conceptually structured content that we cannot employ the very same notion of factiveness in connection with the states that result from such non-rational or pre-rational capacities. That is part of the point of the idea that language, in initiating subjects into the space of reasons, puts them in possession of the world, which needs to be distinguished from a mere ability to live competently in a habitat. But the capacities are at least, as it were, *pre-factive;* that the states that result from them, once they are taken into the space of reasons, are going to be factive is in the nature of the capacities, even as pre-rationally exercised. Now the epistemological role of the rational sensitivities that I have summed up under the head of doxastic responsibility is to cash out this idea of taking cognitive capacities into the space of reasons—to supply a background that must be in place if we are to take the "that"-clauses strictly. Factiveness takes care of itself. Or at any rate, if more needs to be said, it is not about the space of reasons; it is about the capacities, whether exercised in the space of reasons or not. The style of epistemology that I am attacking goes wrong in trying to make the inferential linkages to which doxastic responsibility requires us to be responsive serve, not just as the necessary background for talking of positions in the space of reasons at all, but also in a task they cannot perform, and need not have been expected to perform: the task of ensuring factiveness, ensuring the excellence of the argument from someone's being in one of the relevant positions to the world's being as he takes it to be.

6. We can now return to the epistemology of testimony.[28] I make no apology for spending so long elsewhere; the upshot is that we now have, on a reasonably independent basis, a general epistemological framework into which we can see how to fit such knowledge.

The epistemic standing one can acquire in conversation is that of having heard from one's interlocutor that things are thus and so.[29]

28. Testimony figured only incidentally, presupposed as a source of knowledge, in the examples I considered in §4.

29. Different descriptions of standings are appropriate for different ways of acquiring knowledge by testimony. One with more general application is "having learned (from such and such a source) that . . .". Consider also the expression "I gather that . . .", which claims knowledge from testimony without identifying the source. (Compare "I heard it through the grapevine".)

One cannot count as having heard from someone that things are thus and so, in the relevant sense, unless, by virtue of understanding what the person says, one is in a position to know that things are indeed thus and so. If it turns out that things are not thus and so, or that although things are thus and so, the person from whom one took oneself to have heard it did not know it, one cannot persist in the claim that one heard from him that things are thus and so. One must retreat to the claim that one heard him say that things are thus and so. Just as one can capture a knower's justification for believing what he does by saying that he sees that things are thus and so, or that he remembers that things are thus and so, so one can capture a knower's justification—his knowledge-constituting standing in the space of reasons—by saying he has heard from so-and-so that things are thus and so.[30]

Acquiring knowledge by testimony is not a mindless reception of something that has nothing to do with rationality; it yields a standing in the space of reasons. We can protect that idea by insisting that the knowledge is available to be picked up only by someone whose taking the speaker's word for it is not doxastically irresponsible. This works in much the same way as the parallel insistence in the case of retained knowledge and perception. A person sufficiently responsible to count as having achieved epistemic standing from some-

30. The point is that hearing from someone that things are thus and so is like seeing that things are thus and so in being a "guaranteeing" informational state. Of course that is compatible with all kinds of differences. In particular, I am not suggesting that in acquiring knowledge by testimony one *experiences* things to be the way one comes to know they are (an obvious phenomenological falsehood that Fricker, "The Epistemology of Testimony", pp. 74–5, spends some time denying). The crucial notion is that of a "guaranteeing" informational state whose being a "guaranteeing" state is not to be understood in terms of how strong a reason for believing the proposition in question is afforded by an underlying non-"guaranteeing" informational state. There is no need to assimilate this to the idea of a direct perceptual or quasi-perceptual mode of access to the state of affairs known. (Compare Crispin Wright, "Facts and Certainty", pp. 443–4.) On the contrary: the epistemic standing constituted by having heard from someone that things are thus and so is clearly mediated by having heard the person say that things are that way; and this mediation (unlike the mediation of seeing that things are thus and so by having it look to one as if things are thus and so) clearly precludes the idea of a direct perceptual access to what one comes to know. What I am objecting to is the prejudice that what this mediation amounts to must be that the non-"guaranteeing" informational state, having heard one's interlocutor say that things are thus and so, yields the subject something on the lines of a premise from which (with other premises if necessary) he can infer the proposition he is said to know, in such a way that his epistemic standing can be made out to consist in the cogency of the argument.

one else's words needs to be aware of how knowledge can be had from others, and rationally responsive to considerations whose relevance that awareness embodies. That requires his forming beliefs on the say-so of others to be rationally shaped by an understanding of, among other things, the risks one subjects oneself to in accepting what people say.[31] There are plenty of ways in which it can be doxastically irresponsible to believe someone, so that even if the other person is giving expression to his knowledge on the subject, knowledge is not to be had by believing him.[32] But although it is obviously doxastically irresponsible to believe someone about whom one has positive reason to believe he is not trustworthy, or not likely to be informed about the subject matter of the conversation, doxastic responsibility need not require positive reasons to believe that an apparent informant is informed and speaking his mind. Here as elsewhere, it need not be doxastically irresponsible to run known risks in taking things to be thus and so. That makes room for knowledge in cases like that of the trusting tourist (§2).

As before, the inferential relations in which what one comes to believe stands to the content of informational states with which one can be credited without presupposing that what one acquires is knowledge do not serve to reconstruct one's standing with respect to that proposition in terms of the cogency of an argument for it that one has at one's disposal. Rather, they constitute a rational structure to which one must be sufficiently responsive, largely in the negative way that one must not fly in the face of its revelations about belief-worthiness, if one is to be capable of being credited with that standing.[33]

31. Here it is important that the topic of this essay is the first of the two sorts of knowledge through language that I distinguished in §1, and not the second. The remark in the text would be quite wrong about the second; as Wittgenstein says (*On Certainty* §143): "A child learns there are reliable and unreliable informants much later than it learns facts which are told it."

32. Peacocke, at pp. 149–50 of *Thoughts: An Essay on Content,* gives an example. Mary forms beliefs about whether it is raining sometimes by looking and sometimes by deduction from astrological principles. Her friend cannot acquire knowledge that it is raining from her say-so, even on the occasions on which what she is giving expression to is knowledge.

33. Fricker, "The Epistemology of Testimony", structures her discussion around a choice between Justificationism and Reliabilism. In the case of Reliabilism as she explains it, it is not clear that it requires that someone who acquires knowledge by testimony even has the concept of another person speaking his mind. If there is such a requirement, it is only fortuitous.

There is scope for some subtlety about the way considerations of doxastic responsibility restrict the occasions on which one can pick up knowledge from testimony. Consider the story of the boy who cried "Wolf". After a long succession of frivolous cries, those who knew the boy were rendered unable to derive knowledge that a wolf was present from him, even on an occasion when his cry really was an expression of knowledge. It would have been doxastically irresponsible for them to take his word for it. But what if a stranger happened to be the only audience on the one occasion on which the boy's cry of "Wolf" did express knowledge? (The point of making him the only audience is to exclude his having indirect evidence of unreliability, in the form of sighs of "There he goes again" and so forth.) The apparatus I am recommending allows us to entertain the idea that the stranger might acquire knowledge from the boy; the stranger's epistemic position is quite like that of the trusting tourist. I do not find such a possibility obviously offensive to intuition.[34] The case would be one in which something that might otherwise be an opportunity for the acquisition of knowledge is closed to those who know too much.[35]

The idea is, then, that one's epistemic standing with respect to what one comes to know by testimony consists in one's, say, having heard from one's informant that that is how things are; not in the compellingness of an argument to the conclusion that that is how things are from the content of a lesser informational state. Not that the subject does not enjoy a lesser informational state. It cannot be true that he heard from so-and-so that things are thus and so unless it is true that he heard so-and-so say that things are that way—a

---

In effect, Reliabilism, in Fricker's contrast, abandons the idea that knowledge is a standing in the space of reasons. I agree with her rejection of this position, but I am taking issue with her implicit suggestion that the only way to keep the space of reasons relevant to the epistemology of testimony is by adopting the sort of view I considered in §2.

34. It is noteworthy that Peacocke's example has Mary talking to her *friend* (who presumably knows her peculiar ways of coming to believe that it is raining). Peacocke does not consider how, if at all, the case is altered if we consider someone who does not know Mary, hearing her say that it is raining on one of the occasions on which her utterance is an expression of knowledge.

35. There seems to be a general possibility of such cases; something can be irresponsible for one person and not for another because the first knows something that the second does not know. (Such cases would be counter-examples to something one might mean by saying that knowledge is seamless. But note that they do not threaten the principle suggested by Gareth Evans at p. 331 of *The Varieties of Reference*.)

truth that leaves it entirely open whether things are that way. Moreover, that lesser state is relevant to the standing in the space of reasons that we ascribe by attributing the more demanding state. But it is not true that the only way the lesser state can be relevant is that its content figures in an argument at the knower's disposal for the proposition he is said to believe.[36]

Compare the fact that one cannot see that things are thus and so unless it looks to one as if things are that way. Here again, the lesser informational state is relevant (rationally, not just causally) to the standing in the space of reasons that we ascribe by attributing the more demanding state. And in this case, we are familiar with the thought (I mentioned it in §5 above) that it is epistemologically hopeless to capture that relevance by trying to reconstruct the epistemic standing constituted by seeing that things are thus and so out of a supposedly strong enough argument for their being that way, at the subject's disposal by virtue of its looking to him as if things are that way.

If we are not to explain the fact that having heard from someone that things are thus and so is an epistemic standing by appealing to the strength of an argument that things are that way, available to the hearer by virtue of his having heard his interlocutor say that they

36. Someone who acquires knowledge by testimony has *some* reason, independently of our crediting him with that knowledge, for believing the proposition in question. That seems guaranteed by his meeting the condition that I have suggested is necessary for doxastic responsibility: that his belief-acquisition be rationally responsive to considerations whose relevance is ensured by an understanding of how the knowledge-acquisition that he takes himself to be engaged in works. Peacocke, *Thoughts: An Essay on Content,* p. 166, writes: "There is a strong intuition that a belief is not knowledge if it is acquired by testimony for which there is no inductive or abductive argument available to the believer to the truth of the testimony." Peacocke goes on to suggest that that intuitive requirement is not met in a case he describes, involving an isolated archaeological relic with a single intelligible sentence inscribed on it. I think that is wrong: the requirement is very weak (simply that one must not be totally without reason for belief), and surely in Peacocke's case there is some inductive argument (from what civilizations generally do with inscriptions) for believing what is written on the relic. The important point is that the requirement is far too weak for meeting it to be intelligible as what makes a case constitute one of knowledge. (The point here is close to one that Peacocke makes himself, at p. 167, n. 9, in arguing cogently against the idea that "Necessarily, most assertions are true" can play a central role in the epistemology of testimony.) The intuition is no recommendation for an inferential model of knowledge by testimony, as Peacocke suggests. (I suspect that the presence of such a model in the context distorts Peacocke's sense of whether the intuition is met in his archaeological case; meeting the intuitive requirement is only a necessary condition for knowledge by testimony, but Peacocke responds to the case as though it were sufficient.)

are, do we need some other account of it? I would be tempted to maintain that we do not. The idea of knowledge by testimony is that if a knower gives intelligible expression to his knowledge, he puts it into the public domain, where it can be picked up by those who can understand the expression, as long as the opportunity is not closed to them because it would be doxastically irresponsible to believe the speaker. That idea seems obvious enough to stand on its own epistemological feet; the formulation makes as much sense of the idea that knowledge can be transmitted from one subject to another as any purported explanation could hope to confer on it.[37]

Supposing I were to grant that we do need more, I would maintain that what we need is an elaboration of points like this: in speaking in such a way as to commit oneself to the truth of what one says, one entitles one's audience to repeat what one says with an authority derivative from one's own, so that if the audience repeats it and is challenged, he has the right to refer the challenge to the original speaker.[38] Claims of that sort make it fully intelligible (if explanation is needed) how, if the authority of the original speaker was that of a knower, that same status can be inherited by a comprehending audience.

Notice that this sketch of an explanation of how it can be that knowledge is transmitted in linguistic exchange simply uses the idea of epistemic authority. It does not aim to explain how it can be that knowledge is transmitted by showing that some reductive account of epistemic authority applies alike both to the original speaker (who may derive his authority from, for instance, perception) and to the audience who learns from him.

7. Two subjects who are candidates for being credited with a given mode of epistemic standing can be alike in respect of informational states that are attributable to them without begging that question, while one of them enjoys the epistemic standing and the other does not. For instance, it can be true of each that he has heard someone whose word he has no reason to doubt say that something is the case; we could tell a detailed story in which the arguments they could construct for the propositions that they are candidates for being said to know, with the contents of the informational states

37. Compare Peacocke's remarks about the need to explain such formulations; *Thoughts: An Essay on Content,* p. 149.

38. See Robert Brandom, "Asserting".

that are non-question-beggingly attributable to them as premises, are equally strong. But my point has been that such arguments always leave open a possibility that their conclusion is false. (That is one way of putting a perennial complaint of sceptics; my aim has been to describe a style of epistemological thinking that deprives the point of sceptical implications.) The inconclusiveness of the arguments guarantees that there can be paired cases in which such a detailed story can be told and only one of the subjects knows; the other does not, because things are not the way he takes them to be, or because, although things are that way, his informant did not know it.

I claim that these differences, outside the respect in which the subjects match, can make it the case that one of them knows and the other does not. It may seem that this marks out the style of epistemology that I am recommending as belonging to a familiar genre, involving a mix of "internalist" and "externalist" elements.[39] But that would miss my point.

A mixed or hybrid epistemology takes it that the non-question-beggingly attributable informational states, and whatever can be reached by inference from their content, are *part* of what constitutes a subject's epistemic standing—in fact, the whole of what is contributed to his epistemic standing by his moves and positions in the space of reasons. That material does not seem to suffice for knowledge. The hybrid epistemology is an alternative to brazening out the claim that it does suffice—that a less than conclusive argument can be good enough for possession of it to constitute a mediated epistemically satisfactory standing (compare §3). Instead, the hybrid epistemology appeals to facts in the world, outside the subject's moves and positions in the space of reasons, in order to finish the job of constituting his epistemic standing.

But the epistemological outlook that I am recommending does not accept this restricted conception of the subject's moves and positions in the space of reasons. Standings in the space of reasons are not limited to the non-question-beggingly attributable informational states, plus good standing with respect to whatever a doxastically responsible subject can infer from the contents of those states. Rather, the

39. For these labels, see, e.g., Nozick, *Philosophical Explanations*, pp. 280–3. For the idea of a mixed or hybrid epistemology, see Peacocke, *Thoughts: An Essay on Content*. In chap. 9 Peacocke sets out an externalist reliability condition for knowledge (see pp. 155, 157); then in chap. 10 he argues that this must be supplemented with a condition requiring "internal rationality" (p. 156).

subject's standing in the space of reasons, in the favourable case in one of those pairs that I mentioned at the beginning of this section, is *his having heard from his informant that things are thus and so.* That leaves no extra constitutive work to be done by an external condition. The epistemic position, having heard from someone that things are thus and so, is a standing in the space of reasons in its own right, not a position that one can be in by virtue of a standing in the space of reasons when (an extra condition) things are indeed thus and so. (Similarly with the other epistemic positions: seeing that things are thus and so, remembering that they are, or were, thus and so, and so forth.)

Why does it seem that we need a mix of internalist and externalist elements in the theory of knowledge? The context is the thought that knowledge has something to do with satisfactory positions in the space of reasons. The externalist admixture is dictated by the supposed perception that knowledge cannot simply *be* a satisfactory position in the space of reasons. (We must distinguish externalism as an element in a hybrid conception of knowledge from the outright externalism that simply abandons the idea of positions in the space of reasons.) In many areas where we are inclined to claim and attribute knowledge, no policy or method of having one's belief-formation determined by the reasons available to one is free from the risk of serving up false beliefs. (I leave aside the super-cautious policy of forming no beliefs at all; this policy is too dubiously feasible for its freedom from risk of falsehood to be much comfort.) That ineliminable riskiness is hard to combine with the thought that reason ought to be self-sufficient, that whether one is in a satisfactory position in the space of reasons ought to be immune to luck—not in the sense of sheer chance, but in the sense of factors that reason cannot control, or control for. One familiar upshot of this thought is a "Cartesian" or sceptical shrinking of what can be known. The hybrid conception of knowledge can seem to be the only alternative.

The attraction of focusing on the restricted informational states is that, together with what a doxastically responsible subject can infer from their contents, they seem to constitute a province within which reason's control over a subject's rational status is not threatened by luck. The idea is that as long as a subject believes only what his restricted informational states give him reason to believe, with the degree of credence he gives to each proposition determined by the strength of the argument that his restricted informational states put at his disposal, he will be rationally blameless.[40] If a proposition to which he gives the degree of credence that is warranted by his restricted informational state turns out to be false, that is the world's fault, not a defect in his rational position.[41] But given the ineliminable riskiness we began with, a subject's position in the supposed luck-free zone cannot suffice for knowledge of a state of affairs of one of the problematic kinds. So it seems compulsory to inject an externalist element into the theory of knowledge. Once the idea of a standing in the space of reasons is cashed out in terms of the supposed luck-free zone, an external extra is a necessity if the total picture is so much as to look as if it might be a picture of knowledge.

The externalist admixture involves conceding that whether what one has is knowledge is to some extent a matter of luck, outside the control of reason. The concession is supposed to be tolerable because a proper position in the space of reasons is only a necessary condi-

40. We could complicate this to allow for cases where the subject is blameworthy because his restricted informational states fail to include something they should have included; he should have checked something but did not. This is an analogue to negligence in the field of practical blameworthiness. The complication makes no difference to my point. Even if one exercises maximal care at achieving the right restricted informational states, one will still be at the world's mercy in believing what they give one reason to believe.

41. The point is peculiar to empirical knowledge. If someone takes himself to have proved a conclusion or computed a result when he has not, there must have been a defect in his moves in the space of reasons; it cannot be that the only thing he can blame for what has gone wrong is the world. That is essentially the feature of proof (or computation) that Crispin Wright aims to generalize, in his account of what it is to have verified a statement ("Strict Finitism", pp. 210–18). In a way that is very strange by my lights, Wright combines understanding that feature of proof (or computation) with endorsing, even in that case, the retreat to a lesser informational state, the move I am trying to explain as motivated by the desire to find a region where thought is immune to the world's unkindness. He writes (p. 210): "If arithmetical computation is to be a paradigm of verification, then to be entitled to claim to have verified a statement cannot be to be entitled to claim a conclusive, *indefeasible* warrant for its assertion; for the most painstaking and careful execution of a computation confers no guarantee that it is correct." That is to retreat (in respect of what warrants one's assertion) from "I have proved that it is so" (whose truth surely *would* constitute a conclusive, indefeasible warrant) to "I have before me what, on painstaking and careful inspection, appears to be a proof that it is so" (which leaves it open that the appearance is illusory). But the retreat seems unmotivated, given the fact that if I am misled in such a case, the fault is in my moves in the space of reasons, not in the world. I suppose it is because Wright thinks mathematical proof and empirical verification are on a par in respect of the necessity of that retreat (and so in respect of the defeasibility of available warrants)—in effect, on a par in respect of vulnerability to the Argument from Illusion—that he thinks he can generalize that feature of mathematical verification without risking an undue concession to scepticism. I think the resulting epistemology is disastrous. See Essay 16 above.

tion of knowledge. So reason can still be credited with full control over whether one's positions in the space of reasons are as they should be.

In fact the upshot makes no sense of how it can be knowledge that someone has in a favourable case. If two believers are on a par in respect of the excellence of their exercises of reason, how can we make sense of the idea that only one of them is a knower, on the basis of the thought that, in a region we are invited to conceive as outside the reach of his reason, things are as he takes them to be, whereas the other is not so fortunate?[42] Are we really giving any weight to the idea that knowledge has something to do with standings in the space of reasons? Would it not be more honest to embrace the outright externalism that abandons that idea? I doubt that anyone would take the hybrid conception seriously if it did not seem to be the only hope of keeping the space of reasons relevant while making room for knowledge in the problematic areas.

But there is an alternative position that really does combine those desiderata. The hybrid conception makes its concession to luck too late. The real trouble is with the thought it does not question, the thought that reason must be credited with a province within which it has absolute control over the acceptability of positions achievable by its exercise, without laying itself open to risk from an unkind world. That thought, like its obvious analogues in the sphere of practical reason, has all the look of a philosophers' fantasy.[43] If we avoid the fantasy, we have no reason not to allow that positions like seeing, or hearing from someone, that things are thus and so are standings in the space of reasons in their own right, even though there is an irreducible element of luck, of kindness from the world, in whether one occupies them.

One reason, then, why the epistemology of testimony is perhaps an especially useful topic for reflection, along with the sort of case I considered in §4 above, is that the propensity of human beings to be erratic and capricious, like the propensity of durable but impermanent states of affairs to lapse, brings out vividly how powers of acquiring and retaining knowledge that common sense has no hesitation in ascribing to us are at the mercy of factors that cannot be

42. I press this question in Essay 17 above.

43. On the analogous temptations in philosophical thinking about practical rationality, see Bernard Williams, "Moral Luck".

made subject to our rational control. That fact has induced epistemologists to suppose that if the space of reasons is relevant to knowledge at all, we have to choose between scepticism and the hybrid conception of knowledge. But in trying to avoid the threat of scepticism, the hybrid conception makes it hard to see how what it depicts as knowledge can deserve the title. The supposedly forced choice reflects a typically unnoticed assumption about how to place epistemic luck: that it must be excluded from the space of reasons. My aim has been to suggest the liberating potential of discarding that assumption.

Bibliography

Ackrill, J. L., "Plato on False Belief: *Theaetetus* 187–200", *The Monist* 50 (1966).

Albritton, Rogers, "On Wittgenstein's Use of the Term 'Criterion'", in George Pitcher, ed., *Wittgenstein: The Philosophical Investigations* (Macmillan, London, 1968).

Austin, J. L., *Philosophical Papers* (Clarendon Press, Oxford, 1961).

Ayer, A. J., *The Problem of Knowledge* (Penguin, Harmondsworth, 1956).

Ayers, M. R., "Some Thoughts", *Proceedings of the Aristotelian Society* 73 (1972–3).

Baker, Gordon, "Criteria: A New Foundation for Semantics", *Ratio* 16 (1974).

——— "Defeasibility and Meaning", in P. M. S. Hacker and J. Raz, eds., *Law, Morality, and Society* (Clarendon Press, Oxford, 1973).

Blackburn, Simon, "The Identity of Propositions", in Blackburn, ed., *Meaning, Reference, and Necessity* (Cambridge University Press, Cambridge, 1975).

——— "Knowledge, Truth, and Reliability", *Proceedings of the British Academy* 70 (1984).

——— *Spreading the Word* (Clarendon Press, Oxford, 1983).

Bogen, James, "Wittgenstein and Skepticism", *Philosophical Review* 83 (1974).

Bonjour, Laurence, "Externalist Theories of Empirical Knowledge", *Midwest Studies in Philosophy* 5 (1980).

Bráine, David, "The Nature of Knowledge", *Proceedings of the Aristotelian Society* 72 (1971–2).

Brandom, Robert, "Asserting", *Nous* 17 (1983).

——— "Knowledge and the Social Articulation of the Space of Reasons", *Philosophy and Phenomenological Research* 55 (1995).

Burge, Tyler, "Belief *De Re*", *Journal of Philosophy* 74 (1977).
——— "Other Bodies", in Andrew Woodfield, ed., *Thought and Object* (Clarendon Press, Oxford, 1982).
——— "Reference and Proper Names", *Journal of Philosophy* 70 (1973).
——— "Sinning against Frege", *Philosophical Review* 88 (1979).
Burnyeat, M. F., "Idealism and Greek Philosophy: What Descartes Saw and Berkeley Missed", in Godfrey Vesey, ed., *Idealism Past and Present* (Cambridge University Press, Cambridge, 1982).
Chisholm, Roderick M., *Perceiving: A Philosophical Study* (Cornell University Press, Ithaca, 1957).
Chomsky, Noam, "Quine's Empirical Assumptions", in Donald Davidson and Jaakko Hintikka, eds., *Words and Objections: Essays on the Work of W. V. Quine* (Reidel, Dordrecht, 1969).
Church, Alonzo, "On Carnap's Analysis of Statements of Assertion and Belief", *Analysis* 10 (1950).
Cook, John W., "Human Beings", in Peter Winch, ed., *Studies in the Philosophy of Wittgenstein* (Routledge and Kegan Paul, London, 1969).
Cooper, David, "Assertion, Phenomenology, and Essence", *Proceedings of the Aristotelian Society,* supp. vol. 61 (1987).
Cornford, F. M., *Plato's Theory of Knowledge* (Routledge and Kegan Paul, London, 1935).
Davidson, Donald, "Eternal vs. Ephemeral Events", in Davidson, *Essays on Actions and Events* (Clarendon Press, Oxford, 1980).
——— "In Defence of Convention T", in Davidson, *Inquiries into Truth and Interpretation* (Clarendon Press, Oxford, 1983).
——— "Mental Events", in Davidson, *Essays on Actions and Events* (Clarendon Press, Oxford, 1980).
——— "On Saying That", in Davidson, *Inquiries into Truth and Interpretation* (Clarendon Press, Oxford, 1983).
——— "Radical Interpretation", in Davidson, *Inquiries into Truth and Interpretation* (Clarendon Press, Oxford, 1983).
——— "Reply to Foster", in Davidson, *Inquiries into Truth and Interpretation* (Clarendon Press, Oxford, 1983).
——— "Theories of Meaning and Learnable Languages", in Davidson, *Inquiries into Truth and Interpretation* (Clarendon Press, Oxford, 1983).
——— "True to the Facts", in Davidson, *Inquiries into Truth and Interpretation* (Clarendon Press, Oxford, 1983).
——— "Truth and Meaning", in Davidson, *Inquiries into Truth and Interpretation* (Clarendon Press, Oxford, 1983).
Davidson, Donald, and Jaakko Hintikka, eds., *Words and Objections: Essays on the Work of W. V. Quine* (Reidel, Dordrecht, 1969).

Dennett, Daniel C., "Beyond Belief", in Andrew Woodfield, ed., *Thought and Object* (Clarendon Press, Oxford, 1982).

Donnellan, Keith S., "Proper Names and Identifying Descriptions", in Donald Davidson and Gilbert Harman, eds., *Semantics of Natural Languages* (Reidel, Dordrecht, 1972).

——— "Speaking of Nothing", *Philosophical Review* 83 (1974).

Dummett, Michael, "Frege and Wittgenstein", in Irving Block, ed., *Perspectives on the Philosophy of Wittgenstein* (Blackwell, Oxford, 1981).

——— *Frege: Philosophy of Language* (Harvard University Press, Cambridge, Mass., 1973).

——— *The Interpretation of Frege's Philosophy* (Harvard University Press, Cambridge, Mass., 1981).

——— "The Justification of Deduction", in Dummett, *Truth and Other Enigmas* (Harvard University Press, Cambridge, Mass., 1978).

——— "Language and Communication", in Alexander George, ed., *Reflections on Chomsky* (Blackwell, Oxford, 1989).

——— *The Logical Basis of Metaphysics* (Harvard University Press, Cambridge, Mass., 1991).

——— "The Philosophical Basis of Intuitionistic Logic", in Dummett, *Truth and Other Enigmas* (Harvard University Press, Cambridge, Mass., 1978).

——— "Presupposition", in Dummett, *Truth and Other Enigmas* (Harvard University Press, Cambridge, Mass., 1978).

——— "The Reality of the Past", in Dummett, *Truth and Other Enigmas* (Harvard University Press, Cambridge, Mass., 1978).

——— "Reply to John McDowell", in Barry Taylor, ed., *Michael Dummett: Contributions to Philosophy* (Martinus Nijhoff, Dordrecht, 1987).

——— "Truth", in Dummett, *Truth and Other Enigmas* (Harvard University Press, Cambridge, Mass., 1978).

——— "What Do I Know When I Know a Language?", in Dummett, *The Seas of Language* (Clarendon Press, Oxford, 1993).

——— "What Is a Theory of Meaning?", in Samuel Guttenplan, ed., *Mind and Language* (Clarendon Press, Oxford, 1975).

——— "What Is a Theory of Meaning? (II)", in Gareth Evans and John McDowell, eds., *Truth and Meaning* (Clarendon Press, Oxford, 1976).

Evans, Gareth, "The Causal Theory of Names", *Proceedings of the Aristotelian Society,* supp. vol. 47 (1973).

——— "Reference and Contingency", *The Monist* 62 (1979).

——— "Semantic Structure and Logical Form", in Gareth Evans and John McDowell, eds., *Truth and Meaning* (Clarendon Press, Oxford, 1976).

——— "Things without the Mind", in Zak van Straaten, ed., *Philosophical*

Subjects: Essays Presented to P. F. Strawson (Clarendon Press, Oxford, 1980).

—— "Understanding Demonstratives", in Herman Parret and Jacques Bouveresse, eds., *Meaning and Understanding* (De Gruyter, Berlin and New York, 1981).

—— *The Varieties of Reference* (Clarendon Press, Oxford, 1982).

Field, Hartry, "Tarski's Theory of Truth", *Journal of Philosophy* 59 (1972).

Fodor, Jerry A., *The Language of Thought* (Harvester Press, Hassocks, 1975).

—— "Methodological Solipsism Considered as a Research Strategy in Cognitive Psychology", in Fodor, *Representations* (Harvester Press, Hassocks, 1981).

Foster, J. A., "Meaning and Truth Theory", in Gareth Evans and John McDowell, eds., *Truth and Meaning* (Clarendon Press, Oxford, 1976).

Frege, Gottlob, *The Foundations of Arithmetic,* trans. J. L. Austin (Blackwell, Oxford, 1959).

—— *Grundgesetze der Arithmetik* (Olms, Hildesheim, 1962).

—— "On Sense and Reference", in Peter Geach and Max Black, *Translations from the Philosophical Writings of Gottlob Frege* (Blackwell, Oxford, 1960).

—— *Philosophical and Mathematical Correspondence,* Gottfried Gabriel and others, eds. (Blackwell, Oxford, 1980).

—— *Posthumous Writings,* trans. P. Long and R. White (Blackwell, Oxford, 1979).

—— "Thoughts", in Frege, *Logical Investigations,* trans. P. T. Geach and R. H. Stoothoff (Blackwell, Oxford, 1977).

Fricker, Elizabeth, "The Epistemology of Testimony", *Proceedings of the Aristotelian Society,* supp. vol. 61 (1987).

Friedman, Michael, "Physicalism and the Indeterminacy of Translation", *Nous* 9 (1975).

Gadamer, Hans-Georg, *Truth and Method* (Crossroad, New York, 1992).

Geach, P. T., "Assertion", *Philosophical Review* 74 (1965).

—— "Critical Notice of Dummett, *Frege: Philosophy of Language*", *Mind* 85 (1973).

—— *Mental Acts* (Routledge and Kegan Paul, London, 1957).

Goldman, Alvin, "Discrimination and Perceptual Knowledge", *Journal of Philosophy* 73 (1976).

Goodwin, William W., *A Greek Grammar* (Macmillan, London, 1894).

Graves, Christina, and others, "Tacit Knowledge", *Journal of Philosophy* 70 (1973).

Grice, H. P., "Meaning", *Philosophical Review* 67 (1957).

—— "Utterer's Meaning and Intentions", *Philosophical Review* 78 (1969).

Guttenplan, Samuel, *Meaning and Truth* (The Open University Press, Milton Keynes, 1976).
Haack, R. J., "On Davidson's Paratactic Theory of Oblique Contexts", *Nous* 5 (1971).
Hacker, P. M. S., *Insight and Illusion* (Clarendon Press, Oxford, 1972).
Haugeland, John, *Artificial Intelligence: The Very Idea* (MIT Press, Cambridge, Mass., and London, 1985).
Hinton, J. M., "Experiences", *Philosophical Quarterly* 17 (1967).
——— *Experiences* (Clarendon Press, Oxford, 1973).
——— "Visual Experiences", *Mind* 76 (1967).
Hornsby, Jennifer, "Saying Of", *Analysis* 37 (1976–7).
Hume, David, *Enquiries,* ed. L. A. Selby-Bigge and P. H. Nidditch (Clarendon Press, Oxford, 1975).
Kaplan, David, "Demonstratives", in Joseph Almog, John Perry, and Howard Wettstein, eds., *Themes from Kaplan* (Oxford University Press, New York, 1989).
——— "On the Logic of Demonstratives", in Peter A. French, Theodore E. Uehling, Jr., and Howard K. Wettstein, eds., *Contemporary Perspectives in the Philosophy of Language* (University of Minnesota Press, Minneapolis, 1979).
——— "Quantifying In", in Donald Davidson and Jaakko Hintikka, eds., *Words and Objections: Essays on the Work of W. V. Quine* (Reidel, Dordrecht, 1969).
Kenny, Anthony, "Criterion", in Paul Edwards, ed., *The Encyclopaedia of Philosophy,* vol. 2 (Macmillan and Free Press, New York, 1967).
Kripke, Saul, *Naming and Necessity* (Blackwell, Oxford, 1980).
Lear, Jonathan, "Leaving the World Alone", *Journal of Philosophy* 79 (1982).
Loar, Brian, *Mind and Meaning* (Cambridge University Press, Cambridge, 1981).
——— "Two Theories of Meaning", in Gareth Evans and John McDowell, eds., *Truth and Meaning* (Clarendon Press, Oxford, 1976).
Lovibond, Sabina, *Realism and Imagination in Ethics* (Blackwell, Oxford, 1983).
Lycan, William G., "Davidson on Saying That", *Analysis* 33 (1972–3).
——— "Non-Inductive Evidence: Recent Work on Wittgenstein's 'Criteria'", *American Philosophical Quarterly* 8 (1971).
Mackie, J. L., *Problems from Locke* (Clarendon Press, Oxford, 1976).
Malcolm, Norman, "Wittgenstein on the Nature of Mind", in Malcolm, *Thought and Knowledge* (Cornell University Press, Ithaca, 1977).
McDowell, John, "Functionalism and Anomalous Monism", in McDowell, *Mind, Value, and Reality* (Harvard University Press, Cambridge, Mass., 1998).

——— "Intentionality and Interiority in Wittgenstein", in *Mind, Value, and Reality* (Harvard University Press, Cambridge, Mass., 1998).

——— "Wittgenstein on Following a Rule", in *Mind, Value, and Reality* (Harvard University Press, Cambridge, Mass., 1998).

McFetridge, Ian, "Propositions and Davidson's Account of Indirect Discourse", *Proceedings of the Aristotelian Society* 76 (1975–6).

McGinn, Colin, "The Structure of Content", in Andrew Woodfield, ed., *Thought and Object* (Clarendon Press, Oxford, 1982).

——— *The Subjective View* (Clarendon Press, Oxford, 1983).

——— "Truth and Use", in Mark Platts, ed., *Reference, Truth, and Reality* (Routledge and Kegan Paul, London, 1980).

McGuinness, Brian, "The So-Called Realism of Wittgenstein's Tractatus", in Irving Block, ed., *Perspectives on the Philosophy of Wittgenstein* (Blackwell, Oxford, 1981).

Morton, Adam, "Denying the Doctrine and Changing the Subject", *Journal of Philosophy* 70 (1973).

Nagel, Thomas, "The Boundaries of Inner Space", *Journal of Philosophy* 66 (1969).

Nozick, Robert, *Philosophical Explanations* (Harvard University Press, Cambridge, Mass., 1981).

Peacocke, Christopher, "Demonstrative Thought and Psychological Explanation", *Synthese* 49 (1981).

——— *Holistic Explanation* (Clarendon Press, Oxford, 1979).

——— *Sense and Content* (Clarendon Press, Oxford, 1983).

——— *A Study of Concepts* (MIT Press, Cambridge, Mass. and London, 1992).

——— *Thoughts: An Essay on Content* (Blackwell, Oxford, 1986).

——— "Truth Definitions and Actual Languages", in Gareth Evans and John McDowell, eds., *Truth and Meaning* (Clarendon Press, Oxford, 1976).

Perry, John, "Frege on Demonstratives", *Philosophical Review* 86 (1977).

Pettit, Philip, and John McDowell, eds., *Subject, Thought, and Context* (Clarendon Press, Oxford, 1986).

Putnam, Hilary, "Brains and Behaviour", in R. J. Butler, ed., *Analytical Philosophy*, second series (Blackwell, Oxford, 1965).

——— *Meaning and the Moral Sciences* (Routledge and Kegan Paul, London, 1978).

——— "The Meaning of 'Meaning'", in Putnam, *Mind, Language, and Reality* (Cambridge University Press, Cambridge, 1975).

——— *Realism with a Human Face* (Harvard University Press, Cambridge, Mass., 1990).

——— *Reason, Truth, and History* (Cambridge University Press, Cambridge, 1981).

——— *Representation and Reality* (MIT Press, Cambridge, Mass., and London, 1988).

W. V. Quine, "Mind and Verbal Dispositions", in Samuel Guttenplan, ed., *Mind and Language* (Clarendon Press, Oxford, 1975).

——— "On the Reasons for the Indeterminacy of Translation", *Journal of Philosophy* 67 (1970).

——— *Ontological Relativity and Other Essays* (Columbia University Press, New York, 1969).

——— "On What There Is", in Quine, *From a Logical Point of View* (Harvard University Press, Cambridge, Mass., 1953).

——— *Philosophy of Logic* (Prentice-Hall, Englewood Cliffs, 1970).

——— "Quantifiers and Propositional Attitudes", *Journal of Philosophy* 53 (1956).

——— "Reply to Davidson", in Donald Davidson and Jaakko Hintikka, eds., *Words and Objections: Essays on the Work of W. V. Quine* (Reidel, Dordrecht, 1969).

——— *Word and Object* (MIT Press, Cambridge, Mass., and London, 1960).

Richardson, John T. E., *The Grammar of Justification* (Brighton, Sussex University Press, 1976).

Rorty, Richard, *Philosophy and the Mirror of Nature* (Princeton University Press, Princeton, 1979).

Russell, Bertrand, *Introduction to Mathematical Philosophy* (George Allen and Unwin, London, 1919).

——— "Knowledge by Acquaintance and Knowledge by Description", in Russell, *Mysticism and Logic* (George Allen and Unwin, London, 1917).

——— *My Philosophical Development* (George Allen and Unwin, London, 1959).

——— "On Denoting", in Russell, *Logic and Knowledge,* ed. R. C. Marsh (George Allen and Unwin, London, 1956).

——— "On the Nature of Truth and Falsehood", in Russell, *Philosophical Essays* (George Allen and Unwin, London, 1910).

——— "The Philosophy of Logical Atomism", in Russell, *Logic and Knowledge,* ed. R. C. Marsh (George Allen and Unwin, London, 1956).

——— *The Problems of Philosophy* (Oxford University Press, Oxford, 1912).

Schiffer, Stephen, "The Basis of Reference", *Erkenntnis* 13 (1978).

Searle, John R., *Intentionality* (Cambridge University Press, Cambridge, 1983).

——— "Russell's Objections to Frege's Theory of Sense and Reference", *Analysis* 18 (1958).

——— *Speech Acts* (Cambridge, Cambridge University Press, 1969).

Sellars, Wilfrid, "Empiricism and the Philosophy of Mind", in Herbert Feigl and Michael Scriven, eds., *Minnesota Studies in the Philosophy of Science,* vol. 1 (University of Minnesota Press, Minneapolis, 1956).

Shoemaker, Sydney, *Self-Knowledge and Self-Identity* (Cornell University Press, Ithaca, 1963).

Smith, Peter, "Blackburn on Saying That", *Philosophical Studies* 30 (1976).

Snowdon, Paul, "Perception, Vision, and Causation", *Proceedings of the Aristotelian Society* 81 (1980–81).

Sosa, Ernest, "The Analysis of 'Knowledge that P'", *Analysis* 25 (1964–5).

Sprute, Jürgen, "Über den Erkenntnisbegriff in Platons Theaitet", *Phronesis* 13 (1968).

Stampe, Dennis W., "Towards a Grammar of Meaning", *Philosophical Review* 77 (1968).

Stich, Stephen P., "What Every Speaker Knows", *Philosophical Review* 80 (1971).

Strawson, P. F., "Identifying Reference and Truth-Values", in Strawson, *Logico-Linguistic Papers* (Methuen, London, 1971).

——— *Individuals* (Methuen, London, 1959).

——— "Intention and Convention in Speech Acts", in Strawson, *Logico-Linguistic Papers* (Methuen, London, 1971).

——— *Introduction to Logical Theory* (Methuen, London, 1952).

——— "Meaning and Truth", in Strawson, *Logico-Linguistic Papers* (Methuen, London, 1971).

——— "On Referring", in Strawson, *Logico-Linguistic Papers* (Methuen, London, 1971).

——— "Perception and Its Objects", in G. F. Macdonald, ed., *Perception and Identity* (Macmillan, London, 1979).

——— "Scruton and Wright on Anti-Realism etc.", *Proceedings of the Aristotelian Society* 77 (1976–7).

——— "Truth", in Strawson, *Logico-Linguistic Papers* (Methuen, London, 1971).

Stroud, Barry, *The Significance of Philosophical Scepticism* (Clarendon Press, Oxford, 1984).

Tarski, Alfred, "The Concept of Truth in Formalized Languages", in Tarski, *Logic, Semantics, Metamathematics* (Clarendon Press, Oxford, 1956).

——— "The Establishment of Scientific Semantics", in Tarski, *Logic, Semantics, Metamathematics* (Clarendon Press, Oxford, 1956).

Taylor, Charles, *Hegel* (Cambridge University Press, Cambridge, 1975).

——— "Theories of Meaning", in Taylor, *Human Agency and Language: Philosophical Papers 1* (Cambridge University Press, Cambridge, 1985).

Unger, Peter, "Propositional Verbs and Knowledge", *Journal of Philosophy* 69 (1972).

Vlastos, Gregory, "The Third Man Argument in the *Parmenides*", *Philosophical Review* 63 (1954).

Wallace, John, "A Query on Radical Translation", *Journal of Philosophy* 68 (1971).

Wiggins, David, "On Knowing, Knowing That One Knows, and Consciousness", in E. Saarinen, R. Hilpinen, I. Niiniluoto, and M. Provence Hintikka, eds., *Essays in Honour of Jaakko Hintikka* (Reidel, Dordrecht, 1979).

——— "Truth, Invention, and the Meaning of Life", in Wiggins, *Needs, Values, Truth* (Blackwell, Oxford, 1987).

——— "What Would Be a Substantial Theory of Truth?", in Zak van Straaten, ed., *Philosophical Subjects: Essays Presented to P. F. Strawson* (Clarendon Press, Oxford, 1980).

Williams, Bernard, "Deciding to Believe", in Williams, *Problems of the Self* (Cambridge University Press, Cambridge, 1973).

——— "Moral Luck", in Williams, *Moral Luck* (Cambridge University Press, Cambridge, 1981).

Wittgenstein, Ludwig, *Notebooks, 1914–16* (Blackwell, Oxford, 1961).

——— *On Certainty,* trans. D. Paul and G. E. M. Anscombe (Blackwell, Oxford, 1969).

——— *Philosophical Investigations,* trans. G. E. M. Anscombe (Blackwell, Oxford, 1953).

——— *Tractatus Logico-Philosophicus,* trans. D. F. Pears and Brian McGuinness (Routledge and Kegan Paul, London, 1961).

——— *Zettel,* trans. G. E. M. Anscombe (Blackwell, Oxford, 1967).

Wright, Crispin, "Anti-Realist Semantics: The Role of *Criteria*", in Godfrey Vesey, ed., *Idealism Past and Present* (Cambridge University Press, Cambridge, 1982).

——— "Dummett and Revisionism", *Philosophical Quarterly* 31 (1981).

——— "Facts and Certainty", *Proceedings of the British Academy* 71 (1985).

——— "Realism, Truth-Value Links, Other Minds, and the Past", *Ratio* 22 (1980).

——— "Strawson on Anti-Realism", *Synthese* 40 (1979).

——— "Strict Finitism", *Synthese* 51 (1982).

——— "Truth Conditions and Criteria", *Proceedings of the Aristotelian Society,* supp. vol. 50 (1976).

Credits

Essay 1

Originally published in *Truth and Meaning,* ed. Gareth Evans and John McDowell (Clarendon Press, Oxford, 1976), pp. 42–66. Reprinted by permission of Oxford University Press.

Essay 2

Originally published in *Philosophical Subjects: Essays Presented to P. F. Strawson,* ed. Zak van Straaten (Clarendon Press, Oxford, 1980), pp. 117–39. Reprinted by permission of Oxford University Press.

Essay 3

Originally published in *Reference, Truth, and Reality,* ed. Mark Platts (Routledge and Kegan Paul, London, 1980), pp. 206–37. Reprinted by permission of Routledge.

Essay 4

Originally published in *Michael Dummett: Contributions to Philosophy,* ed. Barry Taylor (Martinus Nijhoff, Dordrecht, 1987), pp. 59–80. Reprinted by permission of Kluwer Academic Publishers; © copyright 1987 by Martinus Nijhoff Publishers, Dordrecht.

Essay 5

Originally published in *Language, Thought, and Logic: Essays in Honour of Michael Dummett,* ed. Richard G. Heck, Jr. (Oxford University Press, Oxford, 1997), pp. 105–29. Reprinted by permission of Oxford University Press.

Essay 6

Originally published in *Erkenntnis* 13 (1978), 131–52. Reprinted by permission of Kluwer Academic Publishers; © copyright 1978 by D. Reidel Publishing Company, Dordrecht, Holland.

Essay 7

Originally published in *Proceedings of the Aristotelian Society* 70 (1969–70), 181–95. Reprinted by courtesy of the Editor of the Aristotelian Society; © copyright 1970 by the Aristotelian Society.

Essay 8

Originally published in *Mind* 86 (1977), 159–85. Reprinted by permission of Oxford University Press.

Essay 9

Originally published in *Logic, Methodology, and Philosophy of Science VI: Proceedings of the Sixth International Congress of Logic, Methodology, and Philosophy of Science, Hannover, 1979,* ed. L. Jonathan Cohen et al. (North-Holland Publishing Co., New York, 1982), pp. 299–313. Reprinted by permission of Kluwer Academic Publishers, Elsevier Science, and Polish Scientific Publishers; © copyright 1982 North-Holland Publishing Co.

Essay 10

Originally published in *Philosophical Quarterly* 34 (1984), 283–94. Reprinted by permission of Blackwell Publishers.

Essay 11

Originally published in *Subject, Thought, and Context,* ed. Philip Pettit and John McDowell (Clarendon Press, Oxford, 1986), pp. 137–68. Reprinted by permission of Oxford University Press.

Essay 12

Originally published in *John Searle and His Critics,* ed. Ernest LePore and Robert van Gulick (Blackwell, Oxford, 1991), pp. 215–25. Reprinted by permission of Blackwell Publishers.

Essay 13

Originally published in *Philosophical Topics,* 20 (1992), 35–48.

Essay 14

Originally published in *Action and Interpretation: Studies in the Philosophy of the Social Sciences,* ed. Christopher Hookway and Philip Pettit (Cambridge University Press, Cambridge, 1978), pp. 127–44. Reprinted by permission of Cambridge University Press; © copyright 1978 by Cambridge University Press.

Essay 15

Originally published in *Meaning and Understanding,* ed. Herman Parret and Jacques Bouveresse (Walter de Gruyter, Berlin, 1981), pp. 225–48. Reprinted by permission of the publisher.

Essay 16

Originally published in *Dialectica* 43 (1989), 173–92. Reprinted by permission of the publisher.

Essay 17

Originally published in *Proceedings of the British Academy* 68 (1982), 455–79. Reprinted by permission of the British Academy; © copyright 1983 by the British Academy.

Essay 18

Originally published in *Philosophy and Phenomenological Research* 55 (1995), 877–93. Reprinted by permission of the publisher.

Essay 19

Originally published in *Knowing from Words: Western and Indian Philosophical Analysis of Understanding and Testimony,* ed. B. K. Matilal and A. Chakrabarti (Kluwer, Dordrecht, 1993), pp. 195–224. Reprinted by permission of Kluwer Academic Publishers; © copyright 1994 by Kluwer Academic Publishers.

Index